King Trends and the Future
of Public Policy

Also by Hugh Compston

THE NEW POLITICS OF UNEMPLOYMENT (*edited*)

SOCIAL PARTNERSHIP IN THE EUROPEAN UNION (*edited with Justin Greenwood*)

POLICY CONCERTATION AND SOCIAL PARTNERSHIP IN WESTERN EUROPE (*edited with Stefan Berger*)

HANDBOOK OF PUBLIC POLICY IN EUROPE: BRITAIN, FRANCE AND GERMANY (*edited*)

King Trends and the Future of Public Policy

Hugh Compston

Senior Lecturer in Public Policy
Cardiff University

First published 2006 by
PALGRAVE MACMILLAN
Houndmills, Basingstoke, Hampshire RG21 6XS and
175 Fifth Avenue, New York, N.Y. 10010
Companies and representatives throughout the world

PALGRAVE MACMILLAN is the global academic imprint of the Palgrave
Macmillan division of St. Martin's Press, LLC and of Palgrave Macmillan Ltd.
Macmillan® is a registered trademark in the United States, United Kingdom
and other countries. Palgrave is a registered trademark in the European
Union and other countries.

ISBN-13: 978-1-4039-8770-9   hardback
ISBN-10: 1-4039-8770-X   hardback

This book is printed on paper suitable for recycling and made from fully
managed and sustained forest sources.

A catalogue record for this book is available from the British Library.

Library of Congress Cataloging-in-Publication Data

Compston, Hugh, 1955–
    King trends and the future of public policy / Hugh Compston.
        p. cm.
    Includes bibliographical references and index.
    ISBN 1-4039-8770-X (cloth)
    1. Policy sciences. I. Title.

H97.C654 2006
320.6—dc22   2006043211

10   9   8   7   6   5   4   3   2   1
15   14   13   12   11   10   09   08   07   06

Printed and bound in Great Britain by
Antony Rowe Ltd, Chippenham and Eastbourne

Contents

List of Tables

List of Abbreviations

ACF	Advocacy Coalition Framework
BCBS	Basel Committee on Banking Supervision
BIS	Bank for International Settlements
C^{4}I	Command, control, communications, computing and intelligence
CHIPS	Clearing-House Inter-Bank Payments System
CFC	Chlorofluorocarbon
CRBN	Chemical, biological, radiological and nuclear
DNS	Domain Name Server
DTI	Department of Trade and Industry
EPC	Economic Policy Committee (EU)
EU	European Union
EU-15	European Union of 15 Member States as it was prior to the 2004 enlargement
EU-25	European Union of 25 Member States as it has been since the 2004 enlargement
Eurojust	The European Union's Judicial Cooperation Unit
Europol	European Police Office
FATF	Financial Action Task Force on Money Laundering
FDI	Foreign Direct Investment
FLG	Financial Leaders' Group
FTF	Financial Stability Forum
G7	Group of 7: Canada, France, Germany, Italy, Japan, the UK and the US
G8	G7 plus Russia
G10	Group of 10, consisting of eleven industrial countries: Belgium, Canada, France, Germany, Italy, Japan, the Netherlands, Sweden, Switzerland, the UK and the US
G30	The Group of Thirty (Consultative Group on International Economic and Monetary Affairs, Inc.)
GATS	General Agreement on Trade and Services
GDP	Gross Domestic Product
GM	Genetically modified
GMO	Genetically modified organism
IASB	International Accounting Standards Board
ICT	Information and communications technology
IEA	International Energy Agency
IIF	Institute of International Finance
ILO	International Labour Organization
IMF	International Monetary Fund

Interpol	International Criminal Police Organization
IOSCO	International Organization of Securities Commissions
IPCC	Intergovernmental Panel on Climate Change (UN)
IT	Information technology
kT	kilotonnes (1,000 tonnes)
MOX	Mixed-oxide (plutonium oxide and uranium oxide)
MP	Member of Parliament
Mtoe	Million tonnes of oil equivalent
NATO	North Atlantic Treaty Organization
NGO	Non-government organization
OECD	Organization for Economic Cooperation and Development
OPEC	Organization of the Petroleum Exporting Countries
OSCE	Organization for Security and Cooperation in Europe
OTC	Over-the-counter
START	Strategic Arms Reduction Treaty
TNC	Transnational corporation
TRIMS	Trade-Related Aspects of Investment Measures
TRIPS	Trade-Related Aspects of International Property Rights
UN	United Nations
UNICE	Union of Industrial and Employers' Confederations of Europe
VAT	Value added tax
WMD	Weapon of mass destruction
WTO	World Trade Organization

Acknowledgements

First I would like to thank the Leverhulme Trust for enabling me to research and write this book by awarding me a Research Fellowship. I would also like to thank Stephen Aldridge (Acting Director of the Prime Minister's Strategy Unit in the Cabinet Office), Tom Bentley (Director of Demos), Claire Craig (Director of the DTI Foresight Programme) and Geoff Mulgan (Director of the Young Foundation) for agreeing to talk to me about this project and for the insights that they have shared with me. Finally, I would like to thank the following people for their valuable advice at different stages of the project: Ian Bartle, Alistair Cole, Kenneth Dyson, Martin Ferguson, Chris Flockton, Dirk Lehmkuhl, Majella Kilkey, John Madeley and Martin Rhisiart. Responsibility for errors, of course, remains mine alone.

Definitions

Billion   One thousand million
Trillion   One thousand billion

Introduction: Policy Networks and Advocacy Coalitions in Action

Where is public policy headed? Will we get tax cuts or better public services? How will pensioners fare? Will public policy become more and more attuned to the needs of business rather than other groups? Will public policy become more Europeanized and globalized?

Ultimately we cannot tell for sure because there are too many unknowables, but we can get an idea of the matrix of long-term pressures exerted on public policy by major long-term technological, economic, environmental and social trends. This book is about the role of the biggest and most important of these trends, which I call 'king trends' to mark them out from other trends and to stress their significance. King trends are trends that are firmly established in that their existence can be convincingly empirically verified, significant in that they affect the lives of large numbers of people, and persistent in that they are expected by relevant experts to continue for at least the next 20 years or so. Examples of king trends in this sense include the continuing development of information and communication technology, the internationalization of production, and climate change.

The basic idea is simple. Contemporary theories of policy-making such as policy network theory state that major policy changes are caused mainly by external events affecting the views and/or political resources of individuals and groups involved in policy-making. Most such events cannot be predicted, but there is one type of event that can be predicted: events that constitute trends. We can reasonably sure, for example, that if there is a trend towards the internationalization of business, more and more businesses will open production facilities in foreign countries because this is what the internationalization of business consists of.

What this means is that if we can identify major long-term trends and how they affect the views and/or resources of policy actors, we should be able to deduce at least some of the major policy changes we should expect and in this way get an idea of the future direction of public policy. The internationalization of production, for example, strengthens the political leverage of business by making it easier for them to leave the country if governments displease them.

This increases the pressure on governments to make policy concessions to business, which in turn implies, other things being equal, that we should expect public policy to become more business-friendly as time goes on.

This does not mean that we can predict public policy with any certainty, as other causal influences such as short-term trends, one-off events and personalities are also at work. What it does mean is that we can get an idea of the matrix of long-term pressures on public policy within which these other causal factors operate. In other words, within the limits of a focus on Western Europe, which is necessary to keep the analysis manageable, the account in this book provides for the first time a synoptic view of the directions in which major long-term technological, economic, environmental and social trends are pushing public policy.

In this introduction I present the theory that informs my analysis and explain my approach to identifying the pressures exerted by king trends on public policy. The following empirical chapters on 19 king trends and their implications for public policy can be read individually if you are primarily interested in just one or two trends, but taken together they cover the entire range of identifiable major long-term trends. In the final chapter the findings of the empirical chapters are integrated into a synoptic overview of the directions in which these trends are pushing public policy.

Trends, policy networks and advocacy coalitions

My approach is based on two of the most prominent contemporary theories of policy-making: policy network theory and Sabatier's Advocacy Coalition Framework. Other theories, such as political institutionalism and punctuated equilibrium theory as well as Kingdon's policy streams approach, also provide insight into the nature of policy-making, but my object here is to put policy network theory and the Advocacy Coalition Framework in particular to work by using them to generate implications for the future of public policy.

The main defining characteristic of policy network theory is its focus on the patterns of formal and informal contacts and relationships between government and non-government decision makers as influences on policy-making (Parsons 1995: 185). Perhaps the most prominent version, and the one on which I shall concentrate, is that put forward by Rod Rhodes. This follows earlier American work in defining a policy network as 'a complex of organizations connected to each other by resource dependencies' (Benson 1982: 148) and views policy-making as consisting largely of a process of exchanges of resources using specific political strategies within understood 'rules of the game' (Rhodes 1985: 4–5).

As the factors that determine policy outcomes in what is effectively a model of bargaining, namely policy views, bargaining strategies, power resources and coalition possibilities, also determine the membership of the policy network

(Dowding 1995), it follows that if these characteristics of policy actors don't change, policy shifts will remain fairly small, since network membership and the balance of power among network members will remain much the same. This means that for major policy change to occur there must first be pre-existing changes in the views, bargaining strategies, power resources or coalition possibilities of network members, and these can only be brought about by factors external to the model. Business groups, for example, may gain bargaining power as the progressive internationalization of production renders more plausible corporate threats to shift investment elsewhere if their policy demands are not met, which in turn implies greater pressure on governments to shift public policy in a pro-business direction, but the driver for this change, the internationalization of production, is a factor external to the network and to network theory.

The logic is the same for theories that stress the role of modes of interaction between policy actors as an independent factor affecting policy outcomes in addition to the current views, resources and strategies of relevant policy actors (see, for example, Scharpf 1997): if in a given policy area the mode of interaction remains the same then policy output will remain much the same, other things being equal. For the mode of interaction to change there must be a cause, and this can only be changes in the views, resources or strategies of policy actors caused by the impact of events external to the policy network concerned. In Scharpf's theory, for example, if the mode of interaction changes from negotiated agreement to hierarchical direction we must look for external causes such as a change of government.

This limitation also applies to the Advocacy Coalition Framework (ACF) developed by Paul Sabatier as a way of bringing into focus the role of ideas within a holistic theory of policy-making. The ACF portrays public policy as the outcome of interactions between contending advocacy coalitions each of which is bound together by common beliefs about what policy should be, such as free traders and protectionists in relation to trade, or hawks and doves in relation to defence. The central role given to ideas makes the ACF attractive as an alternative – or adjunct – to other current theories, such as public choice theory, policy network theory and the new institutionalism, which often relegate ideas to the role of being the medium through which interests are pursued.

The 1999 version of the ACF starts from the premise that the most useful unit of analysis for understanding policy-making is the policy subsystem, defined as actors from a variety of public and private organizations who are actively concerned with a policy problem or issue. Policy subsystems in this sense include not only officials, legislators and interest group representatives from all levels of government but also journalists, researchers and policy analysts. They are therefore similar to policy networks in the Rhodes sense, and in this book the terms 'policy network' and 'policy subsystem' are used interchangeably. The ACF further posits that actors within a subsystem can generally be grouped into between one and four contending advocacy coalitions that (a) share a set of normative and causal beliefs, or 'policy core', and (b) cooperate in trying to alter the behaviour of government authorities (Sabatier and Jenkins-Smith 1999).

Sabatier sees policy change as resulting from two main sources. The first of these is policy-oriented learning within and between advocacy coalitions. Secondary aspects of coalition belief systems – beliefs about the appropriate instruments with which to implement their policy core – are most affected by this, with policy cores themselves being less affected and deep cores – the fundamental beliefs and axioms on which the policy core is based – rarely affected at all (Sabatier and Jenkins-Smith 1999).

However Sabatier considers that only relatively minor policy changes can be attributed to policy-oriented learning: major changes are seen as the result of external perturbations – changes in government, turnover of personnel in key positions and changes in relevant socio-economic conditions – that alter the composition and/or resources of the contending advocacy coalitions (Sabatier and Jenkins-Smith 1999: 123). The problem here, as with network theory, is that the external origin of these shocks to the policy subsystem means that the ACF by itself cannot be used to predict major policy change because the theory does not include accounts of the origins or timing of these external events.

The important thing is that this limitation can be overcome, at least to some extent. To show how this can be done I take Sabatier's ACF as my point of departure, but the logic applies equally to network theory.

The key insight is the observation that while it is often impossible to predict the ways in which external events can influence public policy, because many if not most of these events are impossible to predict, there is at least one class of events that can be predicted, namely the events that constitute major long-term technological, economic, environmental and social trends.

More specifically, it is possible to predict the events that constitute those trends that are well-established, significant for people's lives and expected by experts to continue for the next 20 years or so: king trends as I define them. We can predict with confidence, for example, that, barring major disruptions such as an energy crisis, Gross Domestic Product (GDP) and incomes will continue to rise. We can predict that international trade and capital movements will expand. We can predict that people aged 65 or over will become a greater proportion of the population as time goes on. We can predict that global warming will continue. Many such trends can be identified.

Given that we can identify these trends, in principle we can then go on to predict how they are likely to alter the composition and/or resources of contending advocacy coalitions (Sabatier and Jenkins-Smith 1999: 123).

For the *composition* of an advocacy coalition to change there must be (a) a change in the membership of the policy subsystem as a whole, for example due to powerful multinational firms entering or leaving the country, or (b) a change in the views of one or more policy actors leading them to switch coalitions, such as a political party (or its leadership) becoming convinced that global warming is real and consequently joining environmentalist coalitions in areas such as transport policy.

For the *resources* of an advocacy coalition to change, logically there must either be a change in its composition, as discussed above, or a change in the resources of one or more of its members. Internationalization of production, for example, would be expected to add to the resources of pro-business coalitions by enabling their business members more plausibly to threaten to redirect investment to other countries if their policy demands are not met.

In short, we can establish how king trends affect the composition and/or resources of contending advocacy coalitions if we can establish how these trends affect policy subsystem composition and/or the views and/or resources of individual policy actors. This means identifying how king trends (a) cause new policy actors to enter policy networks and/or existing policy actors to leave, (b) alter the views of one or more policy actors, or (c) alter the resources of one or more policy actors.

The final step is to identify the implications of this for the direction of public policy. Once we can identify changes in policy subsystem composition and/or the views and/or resources of policy actors, we can use the provisions of the ACF (or network theory) to deduce the direction in which these changes would be expected to push public policy, other things being equal. More specifically, if we accept the view common to the ACF and the Rhodes version of policy network theory that public policy is largely the result of political exchange among policy actors (or advocacy coalitions), then altering network/subsystem composition and/or the views and/or resources of individual policy actors would be expected to lead to different policy outcomes than would have occurred without these changes. If the bargaining resources of business *vis a vis* national governments increase, for example, we can predict that pressure on public policy to become more pro-business will grow as time goes on, other things being equal. Similar predictions can be made in relation to the implications for public policy of changes in policy subsystem/network composition and in the policy views of policy actors.

Note here that the ultimate dependent variable is not a prediction about the specific content of public policy itself but about the direction(s) in which public policy content is being pressured to move by king trends. This is because the pressures exerted by these trends may not necessarily result in a corresponding shift in the content of public policy because their direction and magnitude may be inflected or overridden by other causal factors such as short-term trends, individual events and personalities.

This approach can be made clearer by conceptualizing the direction of policy change as the resultant of a parallelogram of pressures brought to bear by the views, resources and political strategies of relevant policy actors. If these views, resources and strategies remain the same, the main lines of public policy remain the same. When they alter, the balance of pressures alters and public policy changes accordingly. If we can identify how king trends alter the views, resources and strategies of policy actors – or at least the resources – we should be able to deduce changes to one or more lines of pressure operating on public policy and therefore specify not the net resultant policy change, because the parallelogram of pressures is being inflected by short-term trends and fluctuations as well as by individual events and personalities, but the directions in which the underlying king trends are pushing public policy before being inflected by shorter-term pressures.

The theoretical significance of obtaining a synoptic picture of king trends and the direction of the long-term pressures that they are likely to exert on public policy is that this extends the explanatory power of policy network theory and the ACF to cover major policy change. Not all external drivers of policy change would be explained, to be sure, but one very important category, namely major long-term technological, economic, environmental and social trends, would be brought within the purview of these theories. Although there has already been a great deal of research relevant to major trends and their effects on policy-making, this almost invariably focuses on specific trends such as the role of ageing, or globalization. My account provides a more balanced view by including all identifiable king trends.

Identifying king trends and their implications for public policy

Putting my approach into practice involves four main steps: (1) identification of king trends, (2) identification of policy actors and their resources, (3) evaluation of the effects of these trends on policy actors, and (4) evaluation of the direction of consequent pressures exerted on public policy.

1 Identification of king trends

To be predictable, a trend must be believed to be likely to continue well into the future. To be of interest, it must be significant in some way. To be included in the analysis as a king trend, therefore, a trend must meet three conditions:

(a) Its existence as a major current trend in European democracies such as Britain, France and Germany must be convincingly verified;
(b) There must be strong evidence that it directly affects the lives of a large number of people in a significant way;
(c) It must be expected by relevant experts to be likely to continue operating for at least the next 20 years, for example because it has been operating for a very long time already, the factors sustaining it are themselves expected to continue to operate, or there are no obvious countervailing factors on the horizon.

Population ageing is an example of a trend that meets all three criteria and is therefore classified as a king trend: its existence is convincingly verified by sources such as Eurostat and the UN as well as by national statistical services, very few things are more significant for people's lives than the gift of a longer life, and well-established statistical forecasting techniques enable us to predict with some reliability that population ageing will continue.

To identify as many king trends as possible I first scanned a cross-section of relevant technological, economic, environmental and sociological literature to identify possible candidates, then tested these against the three criteria for being a king trend using information gathered by international organizations such as the European Union (EU), Organization for Economic Cooperation and Development (OECD) and the United Nations (UN), especially statistics and projections, as well as relevant findings in the expert literature of disciplines such as futures studies, sociology, technology, business studies and political economy. The emphasis was very much on specific, empirically verifiable trends rather than general trends that are difficult to verify, such as rationalization or differentiation. Political trends and trends in public policy were excluded from consideration because the focus is on the impact of external trends on politics and policy-making.

Table I.1 lists the 19 trends that meet all three criteria and can therefore be classified as king trends. Each of these trends is given a separate chapter, and

Table I.1 Identifiable king trends

Type	Trend
Development and spread of technological innovation	1 Information and communications technology 2 Biotechnology 3 Healthcare technology 4 Military technology
Economic trends	5 Growth and diversification of production and consumption 6 Greater energy use 7 Increasing mobility 8 The shift to services 9 The growth of women's employment 10 The expansion of trade 11 The internationalization of production 12 The internationalization of finance 13 The expansion of mass media
Environmental trends	14 Climate change
Social trends	15 Population ageing 16 Rising levels of education 17 Smaller households 18 Secularization 19 Sexual liberalization

each of these chapters begins by setting out the evidence as to why the trend concerned can be considered to be a king trend, before going on to draw out its implications for policy actors and public policy.

To arrive at this list of king trends I have examined many other trends only to reject them on the grounds that either they are not firmly established as current trends, or that they are not very significant, or that they are not considered by relevant experts to be likely to continue operating for the next 20 years. Where it was unclear whether a given trend met all three criteria, my rule has been: when in doubt, leave it out.

For reasons of space I generally simply omit all mention of apparent trends that did not measure up, but it is worth making a few comments here to give you an idea of some of the reasons for rejection. Some apparent trends are not clear trends at all, at least in Western Europe, such as the supposed increases in income inequality (Förster with Pellizzari 2000, Förster and Pearson 2002, Eurostat 2003, LIS 2003), immigration (European Commission 2002a: 18), urbanization (Brockerhoff 2000) and drug use (UNODC 2000, EMCDDA 2002) as well as the supposed decline in union membership (EIRO 2004). Others were definite trends in the past but now appear to be flattening out, such as the long-term decline in fertility (Pearce *et al.* 1999), most forms of environmental degradation (EEA 2003, EEA 2004a), and the trends towards earlier retirement and shorter working hours (GGDC 2003). Other trends are excluded because they are not major in the sense of directly affecting the lives of a large number of people. Loss of biodiversity is a case in point here: we think it is a shame, but it doesn't really directly affect the lives of very many of us.

Apparent trends in crime cannot be classified as king trends because the clandestine nature of crime means that available information is unreliable and because UN and Interpol figures indicating a steady increase in recorded crime (Entorf and Spengler 2002: 10–16, UN 2002), are contradicted by survey findings: the 2000 International Crime Victims Survey covering 17 industrialized countries found that crime peaked in 1995 and then fell (Van Kesteren *et al.* 2000: 49, Appendix 4). Evidence is inadequate in relation to organized crime as well: although Europol reports that the impact of organized crime within the EU has been growing over the past 15 years, the figures on which this evaluation is based are obviously crude estimates (Europol 2003: 8). As some king trends have implications for crime, however, crime is discussed in that context in the relevant chapters.

Other apparent trends cannot be classified as king trends because the evidence is insufficient or not clear enough, as in the cases of ethnic diversity and attitudes towards women, often because these phenomena have not been measured extensively across several European countries over a long period of time. This is especially the case with cultural and attitudinal trends that can only be measured using several sequential waves of cross-country surveys asking the same questions in different countries and over time.

I cannot be sure that I have identified all king trends, but if a trend significantly affects a lot of people over an extended period of time it would seem likely to be noticed. For this reason I believe that I have identified the great majority of king trends in operation today.

2 Identification of policy actors and resources

The next step is to identify the relevant policy actors, by which is meant those individuals and groups that take an interest in the policy issues raised by the trend under consideration or that are affected by the trend or its consequences.

The indicative policy network model summarized in Table I.2 is intended to introduce the conceptual apparatus used to describe the nature and dynamics of the trend-specific policy networks considered in the chapters on individual king trends. It focuses mainly on policy actors and resources because policy views tend to be specific to the policy area being analysed and are therefore not suited to inclusion in a generic model.

The model adapts Sabatier's model of policy subsystems to the European context and includes eight different types of policy actor: the political executive at national level, other politicians, civil servants, judges, business, other non-governmental organizations (NGOs) such as interest groups and social movements, the media, and non-government experts such as academics. Each of these possesses characteristic types of policy resources that can be used in political exchange over public policy. The model also includes the electorate as a sort of quasi-policy actor on the grounds that political executives often alter public policy in direct response to signals from the electorate via public opinion polls, focus groups, direct action such as demonstrations, and election results. For ease of exposition it is focused mainly on the level of the nation state, but this should not obscure the fact that other levels of governance are also important: in many areas the EU level is dominant, while in other areas subnational levels of government take the lead.

It is generally agreed that in countries such as Britain, France and Germany the critical decisions on major policy issues are normally taken in meetings between the prime minister and relevant minister(s), in the sense that this is generally the last stage at which significant changes are made. In countries such as France the president may also be involved. Cabinet and parliament set broad constraints on what the prime minister, president and ministers may do, but in general cabinet merely ratifies decisions agreed elsewhere beforehand (Burch 1997, Müller-Rommel 1997, Thiebault 1997) and a secure majority in the lower house of parliament will generally guarantee safe passage for legislation, although in countries such as Germany the upper house can veto at least some legislation (Fenney 2000: 47, Roberts 2000: ch. 8, Bell 2002: ch. 11). Although Sabatier specifies that policy subsystem members must be specialists (Sabatier and Jenkins-Smith 1999: 119), the regular involvement of the prime minister in major policy decisions in Western

Table I.2 Generic policy network

Policy actor	Resources
Political executive: head of government (and possibly head of state) plus relevant minister(s), and their parties: • Lead minister • Finance minister • Other affected ministers	Legal authority Command of civil service expertise Support within their party Support within cabinet Support within the legislature Electoral support
Other politicians: • Opposition parties • Faction leaders/rebels • European level, sub-national, foreign	Relevant expertise Legal authority Capacity to deliver legislative support Perceived capacity to deliver popular support Capacity to take legal action Capacity to apply diplomatic, economic or military pressure
Civil servants: • Lead ministry/agency • Finance ministry • Other affected ministries and agencies • European, subnational and international level	Access to the political executive Relevant expertise The role of drafting policy proposals The capacity to facilitate or obstruct policy implementation Independent legal authority
Judges and regulators	Legal authority
Business, especially corporations	Access to the political executive and civil servants Relevant expertise Money The capacity to facilitate or obstruct policy implementation The capacity to take legal action The capacity to take direct action, such as redirection of investment
Non-government organizations: • Employers and unions • Other interest groups • Social movements such as greens, women's movement • National, sectoral, European, sub-national	Access to the political executive and civil servants Relevant expertise Money The capacity to facilitate or obstruct policy implementation Perceived capacity to deliver popular support The capacity to take legal action The capacity to take direct action, such as strike action
Media (television, press)	Perceived capacity to deliver popular support
Non-government experts such as academics and think tanks	Relevant expertise

(Continued)

Table I.2   (*Continued*)

Policy actor	Resources
Electorate	Votes
	The capacity to facilitate or obstruct policy implementation
	The capacity to take direct action, such as mass demonstrations

Europe means that he or she must also be considered a member of many if not most policy subsystems despite not being an expert on all the relevant policy areas. Relevant ministers typically include the minister within whose portfolio the issue is mainly located (lead minister), the finance minister, and ministers from affected departments, especially departments that are competing with the lead department for money or for influence over the specific public policy under consideration.

It is worth looking in more detail at each of the main types of policy actor, as according to our theoretical framework it is through their influence on policy actors that king trends exert pressure on public policy.

The prime minister, relevant minister(s) and, in some countries, the president possess a number of key resources that enable them to have the last word: legal authority, command of civil service expertise, support within the party, support within cabinet, support within the legislature, and electoral support.

In most West European countries it is cabinet that has the constitutional authority to decide on draft legislation and other major issues, while ministers have the authority to make decisions that do not affect any other departments, which mostly means minor decisions only. The prime minister or president is generally given the authority to appoint and dismiss ministers and to decide disputes between ministers and impose his or her view where the ministers disagree. This is generally subject to ratification by cabinet which, as mentioned earlier, rarely uses its powers to overrule the decision.

Command of civil service expertise derives from the legal authority of the political executive but is listed separately to highlight the fact that members of the political executive are generally very well-informed about the policy issue at hand, which helps with detailed argumentation with other policy actors on factual issues and in some cases means that they do not need information from anywhere else to gain an adequate picture of the likely effects of different policy options. The expertise effectively on tap varies according to the information available to civil servants, which varies over time and according to department/agency and policy issue, and the degree to which this is actually made available by civil servants to the political executive, which is limited by the capacity of prime ministers, presidents and ministers to absorb it, given other commitments, and may be skewed by the policy preferences of the civil servants concerned.

The practical autonomy in decision-making of the political executive varies according to the level of its political support. When party support is high, the pressure to make policy concessions to party opinion to protect one's position is less than when party support is low. Wide support within cabinet makes it less likely that the decisions of prime ministers and ministers will be overruled when they go to cabinet. Given that the prime minister or president generally selects the members of cabinet, albeit not with a completely free hand, in general one would expect cabinet to be prepared to go along with what he or she wants, although cabinet support for the prime minister and/or president would be expected to be lower where two or more parties form a coalition government. Prime ministers and presidents need to command a reliable and disciplined majority in the legislature if they are to get legislation through essentially unchanged and maintain their pre-eminent position in policy-making. Dimensions of variation here include whether the government has a majority at all or is a minority government, whether the government is composed of a single party or a coalition, the nature of relations between coalition partners where there is a coalition, and the extent to which government members of parliament typically comply with the wishes of their leaders. Finally, governments always have an eye to re-election, so the decision-making autonomy of the political executive is greater when opinion polls show strong voter support, especially as the next election approaches, because this means it is under less pressure to make policy concessions to public opinion.

While the political executive is generally able to take decisions without regard for the views of others, in practice they often let other actors into the decision-making process and make policy concessions because they see advantages in doing so: information, cooperation in getting legislation approved, cooperation in implementing public policy, and political support.

For public policy to be formulated with as realistic a view as possible of the likely effects of various options, the political executive needs reliable information about what is going on in the policy area, the technical feasibility of policy options and the likely responses of relevant groups to possible policy measures. They turn first to civil servants in their departments, private offices and relevant agencies, who thereby get a chance to influence public policy through technical argumentation, but it may also be considered desirable to supplement in-house information with information from other sources. Possession of relevant and accurate information therefore helps non-state actors to gain access to the prime minister, ministers and, where relevant, the president, as well as to civil servants, which gives them the chance to use technical argumentation to persuade them to make policy concessions on the basis that the existing proposal is unworkable, for instance, or would damage the economy (Grant 2000: 193).

Although cabinet and parliament are normally accommodating in the case of majority governments, on occasion they may demand changes to the policy proposal in return for their approval. The need for approval by cabinet and parliament sets the broad parameters within which policy change must be limited. It may also influence specific policy proposals by leading the prime minister, responsible minister(s) and, where relevant, the president to tailor these proposals in advance to meet anticipated concerns.

Once policy proposals are approved, they need to be implemented. This often requires the cooperation of a number of policy actors inside and outside government. Local authorities, for instance, implement much central legislation, while interest groups and corporations may have the capacity to wreck implementation through non-compliance or direct action. For this reason the political executive at national level often seeks the prior agreement of policy actors with power over implementation, thus including these actors in the bargaining over the content of policy proposals.

As well as seeking cooperation in approving and implementing public policy, political executives also seek political support from as wide a range of groups and individuals as possible due to their desire to be re-elected. For this reason an ability to give or withhold political support – as distinct from a settled and non-negotiable position for or against the government – constitutes a bargaining chip where a policy actor has popular support that it may be able to influence. Representatives of interest groups and corporations may offer rhetorical support or make donations to political parties, or they may threaten or implement legal action or sanctions in the form of direct action such as strikes, disinvestment or layoffs.

Other politicians, such as party leaders and members of legislative committees, may be included in policy-making because they possess relevant expertise and/or the legal authority to block or amend policy proposals, which comes into play whenever a government lacks a majority, for example because it is a minority government, or where a backbench revolt occurs, and gives the power to legislate to whoever can muster a majority on the relevant issue. Parties holding the balance of power have a particular advantage here. Politicians at other levels of governance, such as European Commissioners and *Land* Minister-Presidents in Germany, have independent legal powers over specified areas of public policy. Certain parliamentarians and other officeholders may be able singly or jointly to refer legislation to constitutional courts, which may disallow it. Politicians at subnational level may be responsible for implementing legislation decided at national level, which can greatly affect how the policy concerned is interpreted in practice. For all these reasons it may be necessary for elected office-holders at national level to make policy concessions in order to have their policies approved and/or implemented in a form that is acceptable to them.

Civil servants possess significant resources: access to ministers and to the prime minister, plus the president where there is one, which gives them frequent opportunities to persuade their political masters that a particular option is the best means of achieving their policy objectives; policy expertise, which can be used to support technical argumentation in favour of preferred options; the role of drafting policy proposals, which gives them the chance to shape the details of major policy proposals if not their main lines and possibly to channel and shape the thinking of the political executive; and the capacity to facilitate or obstruct policy implementation by virtue of their role in translating legislation into programmes and delivering these programmes, which creates an incentive for the political executive to take the views of civil servants into account in order to secure effective implementation. Nondepartmental bodies such as central banks may possess independent legal power in certain areas. Civil servants at EU and subnational level, along with officials of international organizations such as the World Trade Organization, possess similar resources.

Judges, especially those on constitutional courts, may possess the legal authority to block or amend policy proposals on the grounds that they are inconsistent with constitutional law, EU law or other relevant law. While this may not often lead to direct negotiations on the content of public policy, it may well prompt the prime minister, ministers and their civil servants to shape their proposals with the views of relevant judges in mind.

Corporations and interest groups possess a number of important resources that can be used in efforts to influence public policy (Rhodes 1986, Jordan and Richardson 1987, Dowding 1995, Greenwood 1997, Grant 2000). Their expert knowledge about their area of operation gives governments an incentive to give them access to the policy-making process to help ensure that policy proposals are developed with as realistic a view as possible of the likely effects of different policy options, which in turn gives interest groups and corporations the opportunity to use information to support their arguments that their preferred policy options provide the best way to achieve government objectives. (This is also the case with non-government experts such as academics). Money can be used to finance lobbying, publicity campaigns, legal action and direct action. It may also be given to political parties or to relevant politicians and officials in exchange for policy concessions (bribery). In many areas of public policy the cooperation of corporations and interest groups is necessary for policy changes to be implemented effectively, so the threat or actuality of non-compliance gives governments an incentive to make policy concessions to ensure compliance. Corporations and interest groups may be able to give or withhold political support for the government, such as rhetorical support, which gives governments an incentive to make policy concessions to gain or keep political support and thereby maximize their chances of victory at the next election. An important variable here is the significance to the government of a corporation's or interest group's support, which depends on factors such as their size, capacity to deliver on promises and threats, likely electoral impact of their opposition, access to the mass media, and pre-existing popular support. In certain cases corporations and interest groups may be able to challenge proposed or actual policy changes in the courts, including courts in other jurisdictions such as the EU.

Finally, interest groups may be able to challenge proposed or actual policy changes by means of threatening or implementing sanctions in the form of direct action such as strikes, protest marches, boycotts, publicity stunts, blockades, occupations and other disruption, destruction of property, and violence against individuals (Grant 2000: 140), while corporations may threaten or implement disinvestment or layoffs. Again this creates incentives for the government to make appropriate policy concessions.

Media proprietors, editors and journalists in the print and electronic media are well-placed to give or withhold political support in the form of media slant. This is desired or feared by governments, depending on its orientation, because voters' pictures of politics and public policy are obtained almost entirely via the mass media. This means that media slant may have electoral consequences, which leads governments to manoeuvre to try to obtain maximum favourable coverage by taking into account the preferences of media owners, editors, journalists and advertisers when making policy decisions. Media advisers (spin doctors) may be influential here. The importance of media support to governments depends on factors such as the size of the audience for different forms of media, the state of public opinion in the first place and the extent to which public opinion is believed by politicians to be influenced by the positions taken by media owners, editors and journalists.

The primary assets of the electorate, of course, are their votes, but it should be remembered that even outside the polling station people can exert pressure on governments by means such as demonstrations and non-compliance with new laws, as was the case with the poll tax in Britain, for example, as well as via their responses to opinion polls.

3 Evaluation of the effects of each trend on policy actors

According to Sabatier, major policy changes are the result of external perturbations altering the composition and/or resources of contending advocacy coalitions. As noted earlier, for the composition of an advocacy coalition to change there must be a change in the membership of the policy subsystem or a change in the views of one or more policy actors that leads them to switch coalitions. For the resources of an advocacy coalition to change there must either be a change in subsystem membership, a change in the views of one or more policy actors that leads them to switch coalitions, or a change in the resources of one or more policy actors in the coalition. This means that for a king trend to affect the composition or resources of an advocacy coalition, and through this cause a major policy change, it must (a) cause new policy actors to enter policy subsystems or existing ones to leave, (b) alter the views of one or more policy actors, or (c) alter the resources of one or more policy actors.

Once a king trend is identified, therefore, the next step is to investigate the extent to which it leads either to policy actors entering or leaving policy subsystems or to changes in their views or resources. This involves using the official and academic expert literature relating to the king trend under consideration to help extrapolate causal connections forward from the king trend in order to identify impacts on subsystem composition or on the views or resources of policy actors.

A couple of examples will help clarify what this means. The internationalization of production may lead to foreign corporations joining relevant national policy subsystems, and also adds to the political resources of business (capacity to take direct action) by making it easier for companies to leave the country if governments displease them. At the same time scientific evidence concerning climate change has clearly altered the views of many politicians and officials about energy policy.

Since governments often alter public policy in direct response to signals from the electorate such as opinion polls, due to their desire for re-election, it is also necessary to examine the impact of king trends on factors that influence electoral turnout and voter choice, perceptions of which put pressure on government policy-makers to favour or oppose certain policies. The electoral literature suggests that four factors are especially important: (1) the relative size in the electorate of social groups that have distinct material or symbolic interests which are affected by government policy, such as social classes, age cohorts and churchgoers; (2) the extent to which voters identify with particular political parties; (3) the extent of issue-voting, especially economic voting; and (4) the agenda and partisanship of television and the press (Denver 2003). King trends can affect each of these electoral factors. As the population ages, for example, the electoral weight of the elderly and their concerns increases, while party identification may be eroded by rising levels of education, rendering voters open to other influences and undermining the electoral position of governments by increasing electoral volatility.

4   Evaluation of the direction of consequent pressures on public policy

Once it is clear how each trend affects the composition of policy subsystems/ networks and the views and resources of policy actors, the next step is to unpack the implications of these effects for the direction of public policy. The question is therefore how changes in the views and resources of policy actors, and in the composition of policy networks, cause major policy changes, by which I mean changes in policy instruments used to reach existing or altered policy goals, such as introducing means-testing into the pension system, and changes in the settings of policy instruments that are perceived by one or more major policy actors as constituting a major policy change either immediately or over time, such as frequent above-inflation rises in pension rates.

The ACF and policy network theories portray policy change as the outcome of interaction among policy actors, in particular bargaining (resource exchange). In terms of policy network theory this implies that the appearance of a new policy actor, or a significant strengthening of their resources, would lead to pressure for public policy to move in the direction desired by that policy actor, other things being equal. Conversely, the disappearance of a policy actor from a subsystem, or a significant weakening in their resources, would lessen or remove pressure for public policy to move in their direction. Increasing the bargaining power of corporations, for example, would be expected to lead to increased pressure on public policy in move in a pro-business direction, while a decline in the membership of mainstream churches would be expected to reduce pressure for public policy to conform to traditional Christian values.

For Sabatier, however, advocacy coalitions are the focus rather than individual policy actors, and major policy change is seen as the result of changes in the composition and resources of contending advocacy coalitions. This means that before the ACF can be applied, it is necessary to draw out the implications for advocacy coalitions of the impact of king trends on policy actors. For example, the implications of any increase in the policy-relevant resources of corporations would need to be translated into changes in the resources of contending advocacy coalitions in areas such as economic policy and environmental policy. As advocacy coalitions are defined by their policy views, however, and policy views always relate to specific public policies and therefore cannot be characterized in general terms, this part of the analysis can only be carried out in relation to particular policy subsystems/networks in particular policy areas (see Table I.3).

Table I.3 Policy sectors

Policy area	Policy sector	
Defence and foreign affairs	Defence	Foreign affairs
Law and order	Policing and internal security Judicial policy	Penal policy Immigration
Economic policy	Macroeconomic policy Taxation Competition policy Employment policy Investment policy	Business regulation Financial regulation Research and technology Regional policy
Sectoral policies	Agriculture, forestry and fisheries Energy Transport Communications	Information Society Water policy Media policy Environmental policy
Social policy	Health Social security Social services Education	Housing and urban affairs Women Minorities Family policy
Other policies	Culture Sport	Religion

Source: Compston 2004: 2.

Once this is done, conclusions are drawn concerning the pressure exerted by these changes on the direction of public policy. If the resources of an advocacy coalition increase as a result of the impact of long-term trends, we would expect that this would increase pressure for the content of public policy to move closer to that advocacy coalition's policy core, other things being equal. If an advocacy coalition's resources diminish, for example because a member leaves, we would expect a lessening of pressure for public policy to move in its direction.

A similar logic can be applied to changes in the factors that influence electoral turnout and voter choice insofar as these changes are caused by king trends, as these can be translated into greater or lesser electoral pressure for particular types of policies. A growing preponderance of relatively old people in the electorate, for example, would be expected to lead to greater electoral pressure for good quality services for the elderly, other things being equal.

Plan of the book

The book consists mainly of chapters on each of the 19 king trends and their implications for public policy. They can be read separately, if you are only interested in particular trends, but taken together they constitute a synoptic picture of the directions in which public policy is being pressured to move by those major long-term trends that fit the criteria for being a king trend. The findings of these 19 chapters are then brought together in the final chapter to construct an integrated model of the directions in which public policy is being pressured to move by the main long-term trends of our time – the big picture – including consideration of obvious interactions between different pressures on public policy, as these may reinforce, counteract or inflect each other. While this does not permit us to predict policy change in detail, since the interacting chains of cause and effect cascading through time are so complex, and causal factors such as the influence of personalities are impossible to predict, it does provide a picture of the underlying matrix of pressures exerted by major long-term technological, economic, environmental and social trends that interacts with the pressures exerted by shorter-term trends and fluctuations, as well as individual events, to determine the shape of public policy.

Part I
The March of New Technology

It is a truism to note that technological developments have transformed human life and continue to do so in areas ranging from manufacturing to the media to the military. The continuation of technological innovation and the spread of its products is one of the safest predictions one can make for the next 20 years. The causal significance of technological innovation is not that it determines future developments but that it enables people to do different things, or the same things differently. What people actually do with these opportunities is a function of their pre-existent motivations – which incidentally also influence the nature of technological innovation in the first place. In this connection technological developments are important not only as trends in their own right but also as important contributory causes – enablers – of other trends. Better production technology, for example, enables higher productivity and economic growth.

While specific innovations cannot be predicted, it is possible to forecast with some confidence that the use of recent innovations such as the Internet will increase in the years ahead, and that further innovations are likely in many fields. These are being driven by scientific discoveries financed mainly by governments, universities and corporations. And it seems clear that the pace of innovation is increasing. Between 1996 and 2000 patent applications per year rose worldwide from 1 million to 1.3 million, and in Europe from 221,697 to 270,574 (EPO 2001). Research and development investment has been rising by about 4 per cent per year over the past two decades and has been rising especially quickly in the areas of information and communication technology and biotechnology (OECD 2001a: 8). On the basis of this we can predict that the power of humankind to do things for good or evil will continue to increase. The significance of this can hardly be overstated.

The four chapters in this section analyse four major technological trends. The first two are the most important current generic technological trends operating today, namely developments in information and communications technology (ICT) and biotechnology. The other two technological trends relate not to forms of technology as such but to major uses of technology, namely technological applications in the areas of healthcare and defence. To simplify just a little, this means developments in the technologies of life and death.

Other technological trends are dealt with elsewhere in the book in the context of the king trends that they help to constitute. Thus manufacturing technologies are analysed in the context of the growth and diversification of production, energy technologies in the context of the growth of energy use, transport technologies in the context of increasing mobility, and media technologies in the context of the expansion of mass media.

1
Information and Communications Technology

Introduction

Developments in ICT have significant ramifications for policy actors and public policy. Among other things the use of ICT increases the effectiveness of government and thereby their popularity and capacity to do what they want independent of public opinion, pushes governments towards adopting new policy instruments, encourages governments to do what they can to attract and keep ICT investment and to increase business and individual use of ICT, increases the policy leverage of spatially-dispersed groups such as international non-governmental organizations, and elicits more vigorous measures to fight cybercrime. The increasing use of ICT also affects public policy through applications in healthcare and defence as well as through contributing to other king trends, in particular economic growth, the shift to services, the internationalization of production and finance, and the expansion of mass media.

Few people in the developed world can have missed the rise and spread of ICT during the past couple of decades, especially the explosive proliferation of computers and mobile phones. The number of PCs in the EU-15 grew from 25.5 million in 1990 to 107.8 million in 2000, while the number of Internet hosts in the EU-15 grew from just 33,000 in 1990 to 10.9 million in 2000 (Eurostat 2002: 294–5). By 2002 most organizations in Europe were online to some extent, including 94 per cent of businesses, while more than half the adult population used the Internet (European Foundation 2003: 5). The number of mobile phone subscribers in the EU-15 grew from 3.1 million in 1990 to 277.6 million in 2000 – or from less than one per 100 inhabitants in 1990 to 63 per 100 inhabitants now – and is expected to become even more widespread (OECD 2001b: 51, Eurostat 2002: 297, Eurostat 2003a: 44, 78).

But there is more to it than this. ICT can be conceptualized as comprising all technology that facilitates the creation, manipulation/processing, storage and communication of information. Table 1.1 lists some of the main types.

The OECD identifies three main underlying technological trends that are driving developments in this area: rapidly increasing processor and memory

Table 1.1 Major information and communications technologies (ICTs)

Type	Examples
Semiconductor technologies	Integrated-circuit chips that control computerized devices. Discrete semiconductors that process electrical switching and processing. Analogue semiconductors that process signals from phenomena such as light, heat and pressure, and from sound amplifiers, voltage regulators, interface circuits and data converters. Digital semiconductors that process information in binary form: memory chips store data, microprocessors govern how data is processed, logic devices control transmission and interpretation of information. Optical and biochips.
Software	Programs, routines and symbolic languages that control functioning of computer hardware and direct operations via binary on-off switching of certain electronic impulses. System software such as operating systems; utilities; networking software; system management software for data storage and job scheduling; network management software to control computing infrastructure such as network performance; and security software such as firewalls. Programming tools comprise database management system tools; components, objects and development environments; development life-cycle management; and Internet tools. Applications software for specific tasks such as word processing. 3-D techniques, virtual reality, voice recognition.
Data storage	Hard drives, memory cards, holographic data storage.
Network technologies	Provide communication between network components including servers, switches, hubs, routers, network interface cards and storage gear. Recent developments including combining voice, video and data on single networks, in-home networking, wireless networks, optical networks and broadband networks.
Internet technologies	Creation, development and processing of electronic information through a computer network system for purposes such as communication and e-commerce.
Telecommunications	Movement of voice, video and data via fibre optics, copper wire, undersea and coaxial cable, and microwave; wireless services such as mobile phones, video cameras, Global Positioning Systems; satellite services.
Photonic or opto-electronic	Technologies for generating, modulating, guiding, amplifying and detecting optical radiation, such as lasers in fields such as communications and medicine.

(Continued)

Table 1.1 (Continued)

Type	Examples
Sensors	Devices which respond to an input quantity by generating a functionally related output usually in the form of an electrical or optical signal.
Biometric technologies	Measurement of physiological and/or behavioural characteristics for the purpose of identifying individuals, such as retinal scanning.
Robotics	Robots (including remote presence robots) for applications such as tasks in hazardous environments, bomb disposal, surveillance; industrial robots; personal robots such as toys, cleaning robots; surgical robots; autonomous robots.
Artificial intelligence	Games, speech recognition, understanding natural language, computer vision, expert systems such as diagnostic systems, search engines, movie animation.

Sources: NSTC 1999, Brooks 2002, TechsectorTrends 2002, Dicken 2003: 90, McCarthy 2003, MAS 2003.

performance that increase memory and processing power tenfold every five years, declining memory costs, and expanding communications capabilities. As computing power increases, unit price and size decrease and communications capabilities expand, leading to the improvement of computing and communications capabilities and their incorporation into more and more devices. This means more channels of communications between people, between devices, and between people and devices. Recent examples include the development of Internet access via mobile phones and TVs, increased use of wireless communications such as Bluetooth and satellites, and increased use of peer-to-peer communications that enable users to interact directly rather than via a centralized system (OECD 2002: 221–34). It is also likely that 'soft computing' will develop, that is, systems that can tolerate uncertainty and missing information, which would enable the development of computers that can speak, listen and understand (Cabinet Office 2000). Another likely development is the refinement of virtual reality systems, by which is meant three-dimensional interactive computer-based systems that provide a sense of presence in space to the user, at least in respect of sight and sound if not touch and smell: you put on your hi-tech helmet, and perhaps data gloves, and you are able to interact with other objects (or people) through the computer (Gallaire 1998: 65).

There is an extraordinary world on its way.

Applications

ICTs already pervade our lives through applications in government, business and the media as well as through incorporation into consumer goods. There is also a dark side, as ICT enables cyberwar and cybercrime.

Table 1.2 sets out some of this enormous variety of ICT applications.

Table 1.2   Examples of current and possible future ICT applications

Field	Applications
Management and administration	Word-processing, data-processing, automation of processes such as human resources, manufacturing (supply-chain planning, plant operations and production planning); financial and customer relationship management; email, teleconferencing; knowledge management systems; databases; surveillance of processes, employees, consumers.
Manufacturing	Computer-aided design, computer-aided manufacturing and computer-aided engineering: mechanical computer-aided design and engineering, electronic design automation; architecture, engineering and construction; geographical information systems; robots.
Finance	Automatic teller machines; online financial transactions such as banking, share-dealing; international financial transactions and transfers; electronically linked stock markets.
E-commerce	Sale/purchase of goods or services over computer networks, including secure electronic payment tools; online booking and ticketing; automatic billing at checkouts.
Healthcare	Rehabilitation, enablement such as bridging spinal cord damage, and artificial intelligence-based elderly and handicapped support devices, including devices using thought recognition; global networked medical information; automated diagnostics; health monitors; remote provision of information and services such as video consultations, remote diagnostic equipment, telepresence surgery; cybernetic enhancement of athletes.
Media	Digital and interactive television, high-definition television, personalized content TV, e-newspapers, e-books, CDs, DVDs, online and stand-alone games, virtual reality.
Consumers	Chips in vehicles, appliances and toys; mobile phones; Internet access via mobile phones.
Military	Precision guided weapons; electronic warfare, cyberwarfare; sensors; communications and navigation; real-time fusion of multi-sensor information for high assurance recognition of

(Continued)

Table 1.2 (Continued)

Field	Applications
	hostile targets; cryptography; intelligent weapons such as minefields; use of artificial intelligence to enable military devices to gather information and make autonomous judgements in areas such as intelligence, surveillance, target acquisition, reconnaissance and support for decision-making; electronic-brain links to improve ability of the brain to handle, perceive or view data via implanted equipment or links with remote equipment.
Crime	Planting of viruses; illegal interception of telecommunications; computer hacking for vandalism, identity theft, diversion of funds or extortion; unauthorized copying of copyrighted material such as software and music; use of Internet by paedophiles to recruit children; communications among criminals and terrorists; money laundering.
Surveillance	Wiretaps, interception of email, Internet clickstream monitoring, video surveillance with facial recognition, satellite surveillance, biometrics, PINs, ID cards with programmable chips (smart cards), remotely searchable databases constructed by the state (health, tax etc) and businesses (market research etc), data warehousing, data mining, data transfer between state and commercial databases, international transfer of surveillance data.
Other	Research, bio-informatics, e-voting, personal document readers, electronic paper, traffic management, cryptography, natural language recognition, teleworking, tele-education.

Sources: Stix 1995, Gallaire 1998: 66, Grabosky and Smith 1998, Anton *et al.* 1999, Latham 1999, Roberts 1999, Foster and Welch 2000, Nuffield 2000, DERA 2001, Cohen 2002: 250–1, OECD 2002: 221–34, Dicken 2003: 90, Jewkes 2003, Lyon 2003, Kumar 2005: 42.

We are heading towards a society in which virtually everyone can gain access to virtually all publicly available information that exists. Meanwhile ICT in the form of email, the Internet, mobile phones and the increasing number of television channels increases the number of potential connections between people and between people and devices, and increases their speed relative to ordinary mail. This means that more and more can be done at a distance, especially as robots become more capable, including in areas of activity such as management, education, caring and tourism.

However the development of new ICT products and services doesn't necessarily mean that their use will become widespread, as adoption and use of new technology is also influenced by factors such as ease of use, backward compatibility, perceived advantages of use, low- or no-cost ownership, affordability, non-critical failures, the state of the economy (through affecting disposable income), the importance and criticality of adoption compared with viable alternatives, the dependence of firms on market penetration to make money, and dependence for viability on a critical mass of users (Hundley *et al.* 2003: 18).

One view is that entertainment will become the leading edge of new information services in forms such as online computer games with tens of thousands of participants, Web-mediated physical activity such as interactive games requiring strenuous physical responses, interactions with people from different cultures made possible by translation programmes, viewing athletic events from almost any vantage point, video glasses that place images directly before a viewer's eyes, music and movies on demand, e-books, and ubiquitous web cameras providing entertainment, communication and increasingly intrusive surveillance (Hundley *et al.* 2003: 15–16).

One obvious disadvantage of dependence on computers, networks and their software, however, is that disruption of these by accidents, terrorist action or other causes could bring down vital systems such as air traffic control and power generation, including nuclear power plants (Miller *et al.* 1998: 14–15).

ICTs are most vigorously exploited by government and business – and by criminals (cybercrime).

Government

The main applications of ICT in the public sector are to internal administration and the provision of information and services (e-government), the decision-making process including elections (e-democracy), and surveillance.

Governments currently use ICTs mainly for mass processing tasks, payment processes and internal administrative processes such as procurement, payroll and human resource management as well as Internet-based applications such as online filing, communication with citizens and within governments, and the dissemination of statistics and government publications. New online services include portals that bring together information on particular topics or for particular groups and allow identified users to access customized information and services, for example enabling citizens to submit taxation and other forms online, with the intent of providing an interactive one-stop shop for all of a citizen's needs rather than expecting citizens to deal separately with a multitude of difference agencies. Ultimately the aim is to offer a comprehensive electronic service available 24 hours a day 7 days a week that is automatically tailored to each citizen's individual circumstances (Silcock 2001: 89, Hudson 2002: 520, OECD 2003a: 29–35).

The main policy areas affected so far in Britain, France and Germany are taxation, health, social security, education, employment, law enforcement, regulation of business activities, issuing of permits, personal documents such as passports, and libraries. The overwhelming majority of e-government transactions are between citizens and local government rather than national government (Ferguson 2004: 230, 236). ICT applications in healthcare and defence are analysed in the context of developments in healthcare technology and military technology in Chapters 3 and 4 respectively rather than being included here. ICT applications in law enforcement are considered in the section on cybercrime.

One problem with e-government up to now is that its effectiveness has been restricted by the fact that not everyone has access to the Internet, although European governments are putting in place measures to improve access to information to overcome the digital divide between those who have the means and skills to take advantage of ICT and those who don't, for example by providing public Internet access points and ensuring that IT skills are taught in schools and elsewhere (OECD 2003a: 14, Ferguson 2004: 230). Another problem is that one of the main ways in which the use of ICT is expected to reduce costs, namely by facilitating data-sharing and exchange between government departments and agencies, is difficult to reconcile with the protection of privacy and maintenance of trust on which take-up of e-government partly depends (Bellamy 2002: 221).

As well as being employed to improve government operations and services, ICT can be used to improve government policy-making and analysis by making more information more readily available (including knowledge-sharing within government) and by enabling the use of tools such as linear programming, expert systems and computer models (Bellamy 2002: 224, 226). European governments are also attempting to facilitate citizen participation in decision-making by means such as online consultation, online participation in meetings, and electronic voting (Ferguson 2004: 230).

Finally, innovations in ICT facilitate the use of surveillance for law enforcement, security, espionage and other state purposes. The increasing use of ICT in general means that more information is routinely collected about people and organizations by the state, business and other organizations. The use of increasingly sophisticated ICTs by the state makes it easier not only to collect still more information, for example by placing more CCTV cameras in public places, but also to integrate and analyse vast amounts of information from different domestic and foreign public and private databases. State surveillance systems such as the Carnivore and Echelon telecommunications interception systems set up during the Cold War under the UK/USA intelligence gathering agreement, and the EU's Schengen Information System that collects personal data on criminals and suspects, are already very technologically sophisticated (Lyon 2002: 22–3, 118–20). While the existence of improved surveillance technology does not necessarily mean that surveillance will be expanded, over time one would nevertheless expect, other things being equal, some governments to take advantage of its increasing sophistication to collect and analyse more data.

Business

Businesses have been quick to exploit ICT innovation. In fact ICT innovation has been largely financed by business and designed to meet business requirements, and business lobbying has been important in pushing governments to make regulation business-friendly in areas such as technical standards, pricing, access policies, the deregulation and privatization of European telecommunications carriers and the extension of intellectual property rights (Schiller 2000, Webster 2002: 130–1).

The ICT sector

The ICT sector as defined by the OECD consists of manufacturers of products intended for information processing and communication, products that use electronic processing to detect, measure or record physical phenomena or control a physical process, and services that enable the function of information processing and communication by electronic means. ICT products thus include office, accounting and computing machinery, electronic components, television and radio transmitters and apparatus of line telephony and telegraphy, television and radio receivers, sound or video recording or reproducing apparatus and associated goods, instruments and appliances for measuring, checking, testing, navigating and other purposes, and industrial process equipment. ICT services comprise wholesalers of machinery, equipment and supplies, enterprises that rent out office machinery and equipment including computers, telecommunications, and computer and related activities (OECD 2003: 96). Well-known companies in the ICT sector include computer and software companies such as IBM and Microsoft as well as telecommunications companies such as Vodafone and Nokia.

There is abundant evidence that the ICT sector is becoming more important in the economy. Investment in ICTs is growing as a share of investment across the economy due to falling prices and growing demand for ICT applications. A survey of nine OECD countries (the G7 plus Australia and Finland) revealed that ICT investment rose from less than 15 per cent of total non-residential business investment in the 1980s to between 15 and 30 per cent of total investment, depending on the country, in 2000. Investment in software in particular grew significantly between 1980 and 2000, while trade in ICT goods excluding software doubled during the 1990s from 6.5 per cent of OECD merchandise trade to almost 13 per cent before plunging precipitously in 2000 and 2001 as the dot.com bubble burst (OECD 2002: 21, 33, OECD 2003: 74, 101, OECD 2003b: 36–7). Services dominate: in 2000, three quarters of value added was for ICT services and just one quarter for ICT manufacturing. It is also worth noting that the EU runs a trade deficit on ICT: in recent years ICT imports to the EU-15 have consistently outpaced ICT exports (Eurostat 2003: 8, 32).

The OECD expects that the ICT industry will continue to grow because firms using ICT benefit from the increased integration of network technologies and efficiencies it makes possible while prices of ICT goods and services are expected to continue to fall (OECD 2002: 60).

Growing use of ICT by business in general

Growing investment in ICT means growing use of ICT by business. Firm-level studies show that in many OECD countries the use of ICT has a positive impact on firm performance in relation to productivity and can help firms gain market share. The greatest benefits from ICT appear to be realized when ICT investment is combined with organizational changes such as new strategies, new business processes and practices, and new organizational structures. Several studies identify a link between ICT use and the ability of firms to adjust to changing demand and to innovate, which is consistent with the aggregate-level finding that countries that invest most in ICT have the highest shares of patents in ICT (OECD 2003b: 59–73).

ICT has the potential to affect most if not all functions within firms, as well as every industry and service, through its application to scientific and market research, design and development, machinery, instruments and process plant, production systems and delivery systems, and marketing, distribution and general administration (Freeman *et al.* 1995: 588).

In relation to manufacturing the use of ICT not only enables more automation but also makes it easier to alter production process settings to produce customized products at short notice. Computer simulation, rapid prototyping, use of robots, Flexible Manufacturing Systems and Computer Integrated Manufacturing all facilitate the transition to so-called 'agile manufacturing'. This capacity for flexible specialization means that high productivity can be achieved just as well through a diversified set of low-volume products as via standardized mass production, which enables a profitable focus on segmented as well as mass markets (Dicken 2003: 108–9). Developments in manufacturing technologies and their policy implications are explored in detail in the context of the growth and diversification of production and consumption (Chapter 5).

Employment effects of the increasing use of ICTs include new jobs in producing and delivering new products and services and job losses in areas such as telecommunications as new labour-saving equipment is installed (Freeman *et al.* 1995: 589). ICT workers grew from 2.7 per cent of total occupations in the EU in the mid-1990s to 3.2 per cent in 2001 (OECD 2003: 76). Firm-level studies typically find that ICT use increases the demand for skilled workers and reduces the demand for unskilled workers, which is consistent with the aggregate-level finding that investment in ICT is associated with a high share of highly skilled ICT workers in total occupations. Firms using ICT also typically pay higher wages (OECD 2003b: 60, 68).

The increased automation of manufacturing made possible by ICTs implies a loss of manufacturing jobs and in this way contributes to the shift to services discussed in Chapter 8, although it should be noted that ICT-based products can counteract this trend by replacing services (Gershuny 1978). In the entertainment sector, for example, ownership of TV, videos and computer games may mean fewer visits to pubs, restaurants and cinemas and therefore fewer jobs in these service sectors.

Castells postulates a new international division of labour between producers of high value based on informational labour, producers of high volume based on lower-cost labour, producers of raw materials based on natural resources, and redundant producers (Webster 2002: 102). However it is not clear that high value ICT-intensive production will remain in developed countries: much software development is already done in countries with lower labour costs, and it is possible that competition on labour costs will lead companies to relocate ICT-intensive activities to countries such as India, where much of the labour force is highly-educated but receive much lower wages than their European counterparts (May 2003: 77).

A further consequence of ICT innovation has been the development of e-commerce:

> The sale or purchase of goods or services, whether between businesses, households, individuals, governments, and other public or private organizations, conducted over computer-mediated networks. The goods and services are ordered over those networks, but the payment and the ultimate delivery of the good or service may be conducted on or off line (OECD 2002: 131).

Computer-mediated networks include not only the Internet but also EDI, Minitel and interactive telephone systems, although some define e-commerce more narrowly as referring only to Internet transactions (OECD 2002: 131).

One indication of the growth of e-commerce is that the number of servers with secure software suitable for use in e-commerce, e-banking, teleworking and e-government per 100,000 inhabitants grew significantly between 1998 and 2002, by which time the Internet was used by over 60 per cent of businesses with over 10 employees in all EU countries (OECD 2003: 82–3, 88). The most common use of the Internet by businesses in 2002 was to provide and access information. It was also used to a lesser extent for financial transactions, but rarely to send or receive orders for goods. Overall the use of e-commerce remained very low: in the few countries for which data is available, Internet sales ranged between 0.4 per cent and 1.8 per cent of total sales (OECD 2002: 131–46).

However it seems likely that e-commerce will expand. Surveys indicate that the main drivers of e-commerce for business are the desire for greater efficiency through means such as speeding up processing, improvement in service quality, simplification of tasks, cost reductions and simpler business processes, the desire to reach new/more customers and to expand the geographical market, and fear of losing market share (OECD 2002: 148–9). As relevant ICT applications become cheaper, more effective and easier to install and use, and these motivations remain in place, we would expect the take-up of ICT to increase and e-commerce to expand.

One consequence of this is likely to be a continuing process of disintermediation as intermediate agents between producers and consumers are increasingly bypassed (Michalski 1999). Furthermore, the Internet and e-commerce intensify competition among sellers by increasing choice of products and prices for consumers, which increases pressure on business costs, including labour costs, at the same time as it increases demand for employees who can devise new and better products, processes and ways of doing business in general. The implication of this is higher wages for creative people but lower wages and deteriorating working conditions for people in routine jobs who can easily be replaced (Reich 2002).

Regardless of whether firms engage in e-commerce, developments in ICT enable more efficient and effective management and coordination of companies not only through the application of ICT to office processes but also through improved communication and surveillance systems. Improved means of monitoring work practices, for example, imply better control of employees (May 2002: 69–70). The application of ICT to market research facilitates both the collection of data about consumers in the form of records of past transactions, statements of preference on warranty forms and web surfing records, and the analysis of this data in order to segment customers into groups based on profiles (Lyon 2002: 92). Improved ICT also facilitates industrial espionage.

An especially important consequence of ICT innovation is that the global web of telecommunications it makes possible facilitates cross-border operations by corporations by making it easier to monitor, co-ordinate and manage their dispersed activities. The internationalization of production and its implications are analyzed in detail in Chapter 11. More generally the use of ICT increases the span of control for managers of large organizations such as transnational corporations (TNCs), enabling them to become bigger and more complex while still remaining effective.

The application of ICT to financial services enables more sophisticated designing, tracking and forecasting of increasingly complex financial products such as derivatives, while electronic communications facilitate the internationalization of financial markets (see Chapter 12) as well as financial disintermediation (bypassing of financial intermediaries by investors) and electronic trading of financial products (Castells 2000: 152–4).

Developments in ICT have also led to big changes in the media industry. Arguably the most important of these has been digitization, as this brings a common language for all forms of electronic media and thus convergence in the sense that the same media content can be distributed through all forms of media (Gorman and McLean 2003: 206). The growth of multi-channel and digital access platforms such as cable, satellite and digital terrestrial television has also provided consumers with an increasing choice of content by making possible a big increase in the number of television channels (Council of Europe 2000: 2; OECD 2001b: 119; Andersen 2002: 7, 80). At the same time it is also clear that traditional media, including free-to-air TV, will lose audience share due to competition from new media such as the Internet, video on demand, interactive TV, personalized content TV and online gaming (Andersen 2002: 11, 121–7; Gorman and McLean 2003: 204–5). The expansion of mass media is discussed in detail in Chapter 13.

The informationalization and networkization of business

The development of ICT is making knowledge and information more and more important in determining business success or failure, as the application of ICT results in enhanced knowledge creation, greater access to information and knowledge, and expanded capabilities for coordinating and applying information across a widening range of applications and uses, as well as new products in the ICT and other sectors, plus efficiency gains and productivity growth. Computer networks appear to be especially important here, as they make it easier for firms to outsource activities, work more closely with customers and suppliers, and better integrate activities throughout the value chain (OECD 2002: 221, OECD 2003b: 64).

Castells argues that the development of ICT has contributed to the creation of a new informational, global and networked economy during the last quarter of the 20th century. The new economy is informational because the competitiveness of firms, regions and nations increasingly depends on their capacity to generate, process and apply information, which is obviously facilitated by the application of ICT. It is global because it is organized on a global scale, which again is facilitated by ICT. And it is networked because productivity is generated through, and competition is played out in, a global network of interaction between business networks that are largely constituted by computer networks. Networks, defined as sets of interconnected nodes, are seen as the wave of the future because they are well-adapted to the increasing complexity of interactions and to the unpredictable patterns of development arising from the creative power of these interactions and can now be materially implemented due to developments in ICT (Castells 2000: 69–77, 501). The Internet, for example, has the advantages of enabling operations and transactions to be scaled up and down easily via reprogramming (scalability); interactivity in chosen time with customers, suppliers, subcontractors and employees that bypasses vertical channels and improves the flow of information and adjustment to new circumstances; management of flexibility by facilitating strategic guidance and decentralized multiple interactions between partners; branding; and customization via personalized, iterative, online interaction and automated profiling of customer preferences (Castells 2001: 77).

ICT-facilitated business networks include interfirm networking, such as franchising, as well as corporate strategic alliances on specific issues such as R&D. Castells argues that corporations are becoming networks in order to internalize the advantages of network flexibility by decentralizing units and giving them more autonomy. This can go further with the vertical disintegration of production from within a division of a corporation to along a network of firms (Castells 2000: 170–8), although there does not appear to be evidence of any broad-based trend towards vertical disintegration even though it is clear that some firms are moving in this direction. Business networks centred on one or more multinational firms may be supplier networks with subcontractors, producer networks of co-producers, customer networks with forward linkages to distributors, standard coalitions that try to lock firms into proprietary or interface standards, and technological cooperation networks. The new economy is powered by information technology, organized around computer networks and staffed by self-programmable labour. Innovation depends on knowledge generation facilitated by open access to online information, and profits are increasingly obtained by means of designing applications, selling services, packaging and customizing. In other words, successful organizations are those that generate knowledge and process information efficiently, adapt to the variable geometry of the global economy, are flexible enough to change what they do as goals change, and innovate (Castells 2000: 99–101, 188, 207), and for these purposes the network enterprise is seen as the superior organizational form.

While Castells' conceptualization of what is going on is vivid and plausible, however, as yet it remains unproved, and in some respects it is not supported by the evidence. For instance, the increased premium placed by firms on flexibility and adaptability implies the replacement of standard patterns of work with work that is more flexible in terms of working time, less secure, no longer tied to a regular workplace, and based on individual contracts, as this suits employers wanting adaptability and is facilitated by the use of ICTs (Castells 2000: 282–5, 296), but the available evidence does not identify a consistent trend towards non-standard patterns of work in Europe in recent years (OECD 1998a: 157, 160–1, OECD 2002: 133, 319, ILO 2003, European Foundation 2001, European Foundation 2003a). For the moment, therefore, we should be more cautious in our extrapolations.

Cybercrime

ICT innovation has created new opportunities for crime involving ICT, or cybercrime (Table 1.3).

Advances in telecommunications and especially the Internet have provided new opportunities for organized crime groups and expanded the arena in which they can operate. Improved computer and printer technology makes it easier to counterfeit documents and currency, and moving money using computers renders the monitoring of financial transactions more difficult. Organized crime groups have also taken full advantage of mobile phones, in particular pre-paid, pirated or encrypted phones and phone cards, to communicate while reducing the chances of interception (Europol 2003: 12).

The main costs of cybercrime for business, according to a recent British survey, consist of lost revenue, downtime, damage to systems, the cost of security measures and consumer resistance to e-commerce due to security fears (NCIS 2003: 65). The single most important impact of cybercrime on British businesses in 2003 was on the ability of companies to operate and function, with financial and IT organizations also concerned about the impact on corporate reputation and share price. However cybercrime was not considered to have

Table 1.3 Crime in the digital age

Type	Explanation and examples
Interception of telecommunications	Illegal interception of telecommunications for surveillance, law enforcement, espionage and/or crime by means such as phone-tapping, hacking into computer networks or intercepting electromagnetic impulses used in telecommunications
Electronic vandalism and terrorism (including cybersabotage at the workplace)	Hacking into computer networks using a phone connection, username and password obtained by deceit, electronic impersonation, access via other systems or collusion with insider, in order to destroy or encrypt files, overload a system, alter presentation data such as home pages, or access secret information (with possible disruption of vital systems such as communications, military systems and financial systems), by direct manipulation or by introducing software
Extortion	Using information obtained by hacking into computer systems to extort money, for example by threatening to expose security flaws in bank systems; use of the threat of denial-of-service attacks
Electronic fund transfer crime	Hacking into computer systems to divert funds, acquire sensitive data such as payment card details for use in making counterfeit cards or in 'card not present' fraud over the phone or Internet, accessing credit card accounts, securing loans and cashing cheques via theft of personal identity by stealing and counterfeiting credit cards, deceiving or coercing users to disclose PINs, obtaining card details from personal computers, or 'skimming' (copying) credit cards in shops
Telemarketing fraud	Credit card fraud and fraud involving poor-quality or non-existent goods, bogus charities, the manipulation of share prices, and chain letters and pyramids
Spoofing	Duplicating a genuine website using a similar Internet address to deceive customers into supplying card details, account details or other information
Share price manipulation	Planting misleading stories on the Internet to inflate a company's share prices, then selling one's own shares before the ruse is discovered
Electronic money laundering	Concealing income from law enforcement authorities, tax authorities, creditors or estranged spouses by putting money into a legitimate context such as a bank account without revealing its origins (placement), moving the money in a series of electronic transactions to conceal ownership and location (layering), and blending into the mainstream economy (integration)

(Continued)

Table 1.3 (*Continued*)

Type	Explanation and examples
Theft of intellectual property rights	Unauthorized transfer, copying, storage and use of copyrighted material such as software, games, movies and music; cracking security features to enable copying
Stealing telecommunications services	Stealing mobile phones, line interception, billing system fraud such as deceiving people into ringing high cost numbers, exchange fraud such as obtaining services using fictitious names, use of counterfeit phones using details of others
Offensive uses of the Internet	Websites with violent, racist, homophobic or pornographic content; use of the Internet by terrorists, racists, homophobes and paedophiles for recruitment of members; spamming, email flaming, online defamation and stalking
Criminal conspiracies	Facilitated by quicker, more reliable communications, especially when encrypted

Sources: Grabosky and Smith 1998, Jewkes 2003.

much of an impact on company finances. The most common form of cybercrime by far was virus attacks. Theft of data was perceived to have the most impact, but was experienced by very few companies (NHTCU 2004: 9, 15).

Implications

It can hardly be doubted that ICT developments are affecting many areas of life today, and it seems clear that further innovation in ICT will continue to facilitate change in government, the economy and society at large. It is therefore hardly surprising that major policy actors in a very broad range of areas take an interest in ICT and its associated policy issues. Table 1.4 gives an indicative idea of who one would expect to be involved in policy-making relating to ICT.

The main implications of developments in ICT for public policy identified in this chapter are quicker policy change and more sophisticated policies, policies that are more independent of public opinion, a shift to new types of policy instrument, a shift towards policies favoured by the ICT sector, more vigorous policies to encourage ICT use by business, more union-friendly policies in general but less union-friendly policies in relation to manufacturing unions, a shift towards policies favoured by spatially-dispersed groups and non-traditional groups in general, and more vigorous measures to fight cybercrime. The policy implications of ICT developments in healthcare and defence are considered in Chapters 3 and 4, while their indirect implications via contributing to other king trends are considered in the chapters on economic growth (Chapter 5), the

Table 1.4　Generic ICT policy network

Type of policy actor	Specific policy actor
Political executives and associated parties	Chief executives Ministers responsible for e-government, e-commerce, information society, technology Ministers responsible for health, education, taxation, social security, police and internal security, defence Regional and local executives European Commission, especially Commissioner for the Information Society
Non-government politicians	Parliamentary committees relating to ICT, R&D, technology, economic policy, public services, defence
Civil servants and military	Ministries and agencies dealing with e-government, e-commerce, information society, technology Ministries and agencies dealing with health, education, taxation, social security, police and internal security, defence and intelligence European Commission, especially DG Information Society Data protection authorities International organizations such as the World Trade Organization (WTO) and World Intellectual Property Organization (WIPO) Corrupt officials working on behalf of organized crime
Judges and regulators	National and European levels
Business	ICT industry: manufacturers of hardware and software, producers of Internet content, originators of transmissions, telecommunications providers and service providers (especially providers of ICT equipment and services to the public sector) Banks and other financial institutions Transnational companies and other large corporations
Interest groups	Trade unions Civil liberties and pro-privacy groups
Media (television, press)	Media corporations
Non-government experts	OECD Academic experts on ICT, e-government and e-business
Electorate	Citizens who use ICT

shift to services (Chapter 8), the internationalization of production and finance (Chapters 11 and 12), and the expansion of mass media (Chapter 13).

Quicker policy change and more sophisticated policies

One effect of increasing use of ICT should be to improve the efficiency and effectiveness of all organizations that implement it properly. The spread of

ICT increases the amount of information available to all policy actors and in this way facilitates policy learning and quickens the pace of policy change. In other words, the policy process speeds up and becomes more sophisticated. At the same time developments in communications technology make it easier to coordinate action within and between (organizational) policy actors, which also implies a swifter and more sophisticated policy process. This in turn implies more policy change and more effective – and therefore different – public policies.

Policies that are more independent of public opinion

To the extent that ICT operates as intended, its increasing use by public authorities adds to the capacity of governments to do what they want to do in a number of ways.

First, increasing automation of mass processing and internal administration, and better communication and coordination, should mean more efficient internal operations and therefore cost savings that can be spent on improving services, returned to taxpayers in the form of tax cuts, or used to reduce budget deficits. Other things being equal, this should make governments more popular (or less unpopular).

Second, increasing information and better access to outside information should mean better-informed policy-making and more effective policy learning, which implies more effective policies and therefore superior policy outcomes. This also would be expected to make governments more popular, other things being equal. As noted above, more effective policies means different policies, at least at the level of detail.

Third, electronic delivery of services implies better services and/or cost savings that can be spent on improving other services, returned as tax cuts or put towards budget deficits, which again should make governments more popular, other things being equal. However these benefits are limited to the extent that citizens do in fact use the Internet, which provides an incentive for governments to take steps to universalize access to the Internet and therefore to e-government services. Any electoral benefits are also offset from time to time by bad publicity over ICT failures in the form of cost overruns and service delivery failures (OECD 2003a: 16).

Fourth, better means of surveillance and identity verification imply more effective police and security capabilities and therefore lower crime, disorder and terrorism than would otherwise be the case. This too should mean that governments are more popular than they would otherwise have been.

Many if not most of these benefits accrue to local and regional governments rather than national governments, at least in the first instance, due to the very significant role played by these subnational levels of government in delivering public services.

In short, increasing use of ICT in government should increase the popularity of the governments concerned, other things being equal. This reduces the electoral risk of implementing unpopular policies, which should embolden at least some governments to implement more partisan policies than otherwise would be the case and/or to introduce tougher measures to resolve crises than they otherwise would have done.

A shift towards policy instruments more suited to a world permeated with ICT

As time goes on some of the traditional mechanisms of governance are becoming increasingly difficult to apply. E-commerce makes transaction taxes such as VAT more difficult to collect, for example, while existing regulations are ill-suited to new business models, regulation and licensing are more difficult to apply when service providers are beyond national jurisdictions, and limits on offensive or dangerous information, such as bomb making instructions, are not always observed by others (Hundley *et al.* 2003: 35). The fact that this threatens government effectiveness and popularity gives political leaders strong incentives to find and use policy instruments more suited to the environment created by ICT (Hudson 2002: 524), for example by cooperating with other countries to devise common regulations for businesses that use ICT to operate across borders.

A move towards policies favoured by the ICT sector

The increasing economic weight of ICT manufacturing and services in national economies means that the performance of ICT firms is becoming more important in securing economic growth. The desire of governments to achieve economic growth therefore implies that the policy preferences of ICT firms are becoming more important for governments to take into account relative to those of other business sectors. The pressure that ICT corporations can put on governments is increased to the extent that information-based companies find it easier to move elsewhere than industrial firms. This implies increasing pressure on national governments to nurture the ICT sector through means such as facilitating inward foreign investment by ICT companies, boosting incentives for domestic companies to invest in ICT-related R&D, increasing training in ICT skills, and improving the business climate in general for ICT firms.

More vigorous policies to encourage businesses to use ICT

There is considerable evidence that business use of ICT contributes significantly to economic growth. The OECD reports that for the countries for which data is available, ICT investment during the period 1995–2000 typically accounted for between 0.3 and 0.8 percentage points of growth in GDP per capita, and similar studies come up with similar findings (OECD 2003b: 36). Firm-level evidence also suggests that effective diffusion and use of ICT contributes to economic growth (OECD 2002: 22).

Given the importance of economic growth for a government's re-election prospects, this implies that the growing use of ICT by business strengthens the electoral position of governments, other things being equal, which provides incentives for governments to step up the implementation of policies designed to encourage the diffusion of ICT to businesses, individuals and households, for example by funding or providing incentives for R&D in ICT, providing or encouraging training in ICT skills, adapting regulatory frameworks, ensuring interoperability of ICT hardware and applications, adapting and enforcing intellectual property rights, and addressing security, privacy and electronic identification and authentication issues (OECD 2002: 19, European Commission 2004b).

More union-friendly policies

As well as sharing in the benefits brought by ICT to all organizations in the form of better information and more efficient administration, unions can be strengthened by the increasing use of ICT in a number of other ways.

First, the use of websites and email facilitates increased recruitment of new members by lowering the cost of contacting prospective members, making it more convenient for them to access information about unions, and enabling them to sign up for membership online (Diamond and Freeman 2002: 581, Ward and Lusoli 2003: 154).

Second, the use of ICT facilitates the retention and attachment of existing union members by adding to the expertise of local representatives and by lowering the cost of, and improving, services for members through means such as expert systems advice through FAQs, queriable online knowledge base systems and individualized services tailored to the requirements of individual members in areas such as labour law, work-related issues and problems, job training, career advice and job vacancies (Diamond and Freeman 2002: 581–3, 588–90, Ward and Lusoli 2003: 153).

Third, use of websites and email enables unions to get their message direct to members and to the public without having to rely on expensive advertisements or highly filtered and often unsympathetic media reports. It also facilitates the provision of easily accessible material for journalists (Diamond and Freeman 2002: 577).

Fourth, union campaigns can be strengthened by using the Internet to publicize the union case, improve the coordination of campaigns, reduce the cost of canvassing and balloting, and obtain support from elsewhere (Diamond and Freeman 2002: 585–7).

To the extent that ICT has these effects one would expect the political leverage of unions to increase, other things being equal, leading to more union-friendly policies. On the other hand it needs to be borne in mind that ICT use also strengthens employers and governments, so it is not clear that the use of ICT strengthens unions relative to employers or governments.

Less union-friendly policies in relation to manufacturing unions

Despite the creation of new jobs in ICT-related areas, the increasing use of ICT in the economy also leads to job losses where functions are automated, especially in unions' traditional core area of manufacturing. This implies that the increasing use of ICT in manufacturing is eroding the membership of manufacturing unions and thereby their political leverage, which implies less pressure on governments to implement or keep policies favoured by manufacturing unions.

A shift towards policies favoured by spatially dispersed groups and non-traditional groups in general

One of the most important political resources of mass membership non-state policy actors such as trade unions is their capacity to mobilize mass action such as strikes and demonstrations. As mass action is easier to organise where the group members concerned are concentrated in one or a few locations, groups whose members are scattered throughout the country, or over the whole world, have found it difficult to translate their mass membership into an effective political weapon. Although mail, telegraphy and fixed-line telephones did enable groups whose members were spatially scattered to coordinate up to a point, they were obviously at a disadvantage compared to, say, factory workers in large industrial cities. For this reason the increasing capacity for coordination at a distance brought by the use of websites, email and mobile telephones disproportionately benefits spatially dispersed groups. In recent years human rights, women's, environmental, labour, religious and peace movements have all engaged in global coordination and action with the help of the Internet (Cohen and Rai 2000), while ethnic identity movements and nationalist movements are also potential beneficiaries (Castells 2001: 138). One striking example of the Internet empowering new groups was its role in publicizing the cause of the Zapatista rebels in Mexico during the 1990s and coordinating the efforts of their foreign supporters; another was the anti-globalization protest against the 1999 World Trade Organization (WTO) meeting in Seattle (Cleaver 1998, Castells 2001: 141).

This implies that over time the political resources of spatially-dispersed mass membership organizations are increasing more rapidly than those of other groups, other things being equal. This means that we should expect policies preferred by spatially dispersed groups to be implemented to a greater extent than before, again other things being equal, to the benefit of international non-government organizations in particular, such as the anti-globalization movement.

In fact the improved communication and information made possible by ICT lowers barriers to grass-roots mobilization and organization in general, which implies that the coming of the Internet benefits non-traditional groups in general. For this reason use of the Internet is likely to intensify group-centred, pluralistic politics and to lead to more rapid and intense citizen responses to mobilization efforts by linkage groups – accelerated pluralism – which may decrease the coherence and stability of interest group politics as the political process loses some of its dependence on stable public and private institutions and the political system accommodates a broader range of interests and views and becomes more fluid and accessible (Bimber 1998).

Adaptation of laws and law enforcement to the challenge of cybercrime

The emergence and evolution of cybercrime inevitably elicits a response from law enforcement agencies as they transfer their commitment to fighting crime to a new front. This is likely to be supported by increasing pressure exerted directly or indirectly by the increasing number of organizational victims of cybercrime.

One relatively uncontroversial response is to encourage or mandate the development and application by individual and corporate users of available preventive technologies (see Table 1.5) as well as the incorporation of security

Table 1.5　Examples of technical protection against cybercrime

Type	Explanation and examples
Adoption of best practice	Includes regular updating of operating systems and software, strong password policies, locking down systems, disabling all unnecessary services, installation and regular updating of anti-virus software, firewalls and high fidelity intrusion detection systems, encryption, and regular backing up and storing offsite of all vital data
Ingress and egress filtering	For example blocking untrusted source addresses and offensive websites and emails
Parsing all input data	Instructing computers to analyse what incoming messages say rather than simply executing the code directly, then ensuring that no combination of computer responses to this data can affect a core operating programme
Physical disconnection from all other systems	Removes the possibility of access from another system (although even disconnected systems are vulnerable to insiders such as janitors), although going this far substantially reduces the usefulness of computer systems
Anti-piracy measures	Electronic surveillance, restricting access to relevant servers, restricting access to copyrighted works through encryption, electronic locks, digital signatures and digital fingerprinting (steganography), incorporation into copyrighted works of software that restricts copying and usage or which destroys data when unauthorized copying occurs (logic bombs)
Measures against electronic funds transfer crime	Upgrading credit card security, for instance by incorporating biometric means of verifying identity; fraud detection software, improved cryptography
Measures against money laundering	Systematic and automated monitoring of electronic financial transactions to identify those of a suspect nature

Sources: Libicki 1995 ch. 7, Grabosky and Smith 1998, Vatis 2001: 19–20.

considerations into developing technology at the design stage (European Commission 2001: 6, 11, 32, 34).

Another is to adapt existing law to take account of new forms of crime and to ensure that law enforcement and security agencies have the resources and training to take full advantage of ICT in their fight against cybercrime. In finance, for example, the communications technology that facilitates international financial transactions can also be used to monitor them (Sica 2000: 71). To this end the Council of Europe's Convention on Cybercrime obliges signatories to define criminal offences and sanctions for computer-related crimes involving fraud and forgery, child pornography, copyright infringements and security breaches such as hacking, illegal data interception and system interferences that compromise network integrity and availability. It also requires countries to establish domestic procedures for detecting, investigating and prosecuting cybercrime, as well as for the collection of electronic evidence, including the expedited preservation of computer-stored data and electronic communications, system search and seizure, and real time interception of data, within the bounds set by the need to protect human rights and the principle of proportionality (Archick 2004). European and international agreements in recent years have extended intellectual property right protection to cover new ICTs such as computer programmes and the lay-out designs of integrated circuits (European Commission 2004c, WTO 2004b).

In some cases, however, the measures proposed by law enforcement and security agencies come into conflict with the interests of others. Moves to facilitate state access to private computer and telecommunications systems in the pursuit of criminal investigations obviously have the potential to compromise the confidentiality of private and commercial information. Moves to make money laundering more difficult by imposing more stringent reporting requirements on financial institutions mean additional administrative burdens, may compromise commercial confidentiality, and – for the less scrupulous – may lead to a loss of business. Moves to obstruct criminal communications by restricting anonymous access to telephony, such as by banning pre-pay cards, and to the Internet, such as by restricting the use of re-mailers and Internet cafes, are opposed by much of industry and by privacy experts (Grabosky and Smith 1998: 196–209, European Commission 2001: 21). Nevertheless, as cybercrime and its effects increase in magnitude it is reasonable to expect a succession of moves in the direction of increasing state control and surveillance of the Internet and other forms of ICT.

As much cybercrime is unconstrained by national borders, a third response is to improve international cooperation despite the reluctance of national governments to agree to measures such as letting foreign police operate in their countries (Jewkes 2003). The UN Office on Drugs and Crime argues that combating cybercrime effectively necessitates investigative powers that can be used to obtain evidence from anywhere on a computer network, regardless of national jurisdiction, more quickly than offenders can move or erase evidence (UN 2000), while the Council of Europe's Convention on Cybercrime requires signatories to establish a rapid and effective system for international cooperation, including permitting law enforcement agencies in one country to collect computer-based evidence for those in another (Archick 2004).

Putting all this together, we would expect new developments in cybercrime to lead to adjustments in criminal law and law enforcement including heightened surveillance, more restrictive regulation, and international harmonization and cooperation.

Conclusion

Table 1.6 summarizes the implications of increasing ICT use for public policy that have been identified in this chapter. To get an overall view of the policy implications of ICT developments, however, it is also necessary to look at their indirect implications via other king trends, as detailed in other chapters.

Perhaps the most significant of the implications listed here are the succession of pro-ICT regulatory changes we should expect in relation to the ICT sector, the use of ICT by business and individuals, and the fight against cybercrime, and the changes in policy instruments used in areas such as economic policy as governments adapt to the increasingly ICT-rich environment. The implications that international non-government organizations will benefit, and that politics is likely to become increasingly fluid due to the

Table 1.6 Policy implications of developments in information and communications technology (ICT)

Policy implications	Causal chain from trend
Quicker policy change, more sophisticated public policies	More policy learning due to better information, better access to information and better coordination within organizations
More autonomous policies in general	Increasing government popularity as a result of ICT improving public services due to better informed policy-making, better communications and coordination, automation of internal government functions, electronic delivery of services leading to savings that can be spent on improving services, cutting taxes or reducing budget deficits; increasing economic growth due to increasing business use of ICT; and less

(Continued)

44

Table 1.6 (Continued)

Policy implications	Causal chain from trend
	crime, terrorism and disorder due to better surveillance and identity verification
Shift towards policy instruments suited to the environment created by ICT, such as international regulation of business	Applications of ICT in areas such as business make some existing policy instruments less effective: regulation and licensing, for example, are difficult to apply when businesses providing services via ICT are beyond national jurisdiction
Shift towards policies favoured by ICT sector, such as expanding financial incentives for ICT-related foreign investment and R&D	Increasing economic importance of the ICT sector combined with its relative mobility
More vigorous measures to encourage businesses and individuals to use ICT effectively	Evidence that business use of ICT augments economic growth, plus the cost advantages of delivering government services by electronic means
More union-friendly policies	Increased policy leverage for trade unions due to ICT facilitating internal operations, recruitment, retention of members, communications with members, coordination of campaigns and dissemination of the union case to the media and to the public
Less union-friendly policies	Decreasing policy leverage for unions in areas where members are lost due to job losses caused by automation
Shift towards policies favoured by spatially-dispersed groups and non-traditional groups in general	ICT improves the capacity of spatially-dispersed groups to coordinate at a distance, and lowers barriers to grass-roots organization and mobilization in general
More vigorous measures to fight cybercrime, such as tighter regulation, more surveillance and greater international cooperation	The growth of cybercrime elicits growing pressure from law enforcement agencies and the increasing number of victims of cybercrime for governments to take more effective action against it
Indirect effects via other king trends	Developments in ICT improve healthcare technology (Chapter 3) and military technology (Chapter 4), and contribute to economic growth (Chapter 5), the shift to services (Chapter 8), the internationalization of production and finance (Chapters 11 and 12), and the expansion of mass media (Chapter 13)

increasing frequency of flash mobilizations by single-issue groups coordinated by ICT, are also potentially significant, depending on their magnitude. So is the implication that governments stand to gain electorally from the increasing use of ICT and are therefore more likely to implement what they want as distinct from what is electorally expedient, although any such effect is likely to be obscured by the simultaneous effects on government popularity of many other factors.

2
Biotechnology

Introduction

Biotechnology is perhaps the most controversial of the new technologies developing today, and policy-making in this area is largely based around the conflicting imperatives of economic growth and safety. As a consequence the main implications for public policy are greater policy autonomy for governments, more vigorous measures to assist the biotechnology industry, and stricter safety and environmental regulation of some applications of biotechnology.

The OECD defines biotechnology as 'the application of science and technology to living organisms as well as parts, products and models thereof, to alter living or non-living materials for the production of knowledge, goods and services' (OECD 2003). This is commonly identified with genetic engineering but in fact covers a range of biological techniques and processes (Table 2.1).

Business and government are taking advantage of the enabling power of biotechnology where it furthers their objectives by developing and applying its techniques and processes to a growing variety of areas, most notably agriculture and food production, energy production, manufacturing (especially chemicals and pharmaceuticals), environmental care and healthcare (Table 2.2). It is also to be expected that biotechnology will be used both for criminal ends – biocrime – and in law enforcement, as well as for military purposes. As applications of biotechnology to healthcare and defence are covered in Chapters 3 and 4, in this chapter the focus is on other uses. Of these arguably the most significant in economic and political terms is the application of genetic engineering to agriculture.

The few internationally comparable statistics on biotechnology that exist indicate strong growth in this sector. Between 1990 and 1999 the number of biotechnology patents submitted to the European Patent Office grew by 10 per cent per year on average, and biotechnology venture capital increased between 1995 and 2001 in most EU countries. The number of dedicated biotechnology firms founded per year grew substantially between 1976 and 1998 before dropping back to 1994 levels by 2000 (European Commission 2002a: 35, 38,

Table 2.1 Main biotechnologies

Type	Details
Bioprocess or fermentation technology	Growing large numbers of cells under controlled conditions within a containment system (bioreactor) to convert substrates from the surrounding medium via biochemical reactions into: • chemicals such as ethanol, acetone, enzymes, perfumeries and polymers; • pharmaceuticals such as antibiotics, diagnostic agents and vaccines; • fuels such as ethanol, methane and biomass; • food and beverages such as cheese, alcohol, coffee, baker's yeast and food additives; • agricultural products and processes such as feedstuffs, vaccines, ensilage and composting processes, microbial pesticides, and plant cell and tissue culture
Genetics	Manipulation of whole organisms via selection, sexual crosses and hybridization, and mutation by X-rays and mutagenic chemicals, as traditionally practised in fields such as agriculture to improve plants and animals
	Cellular manipulations of DNA by cell fusion or cell culture and regeneration of whole plants from these cells for purposes such as the production of monoclonal antibodies and the cloning of plant species
	Molecular manipulation of DNA and RNA (genetic engineering or recombinant DNA technology) by the addition or deletion of parts of the DNA molecule, which involves isolating DNA from donor cells of plants, animals or micro-organisms, fragmenting it into groups of one or more genes using enzymes, coupling selected fragments to another piece of DNA (the vector) and then passing the vector into the host or recipient cell genome for purposes such as the production of new pharmaceuticals, improved agricultural productivity, better food quality and flavour, and improved pollution control

Source: Based on Smith 2004.

OECD 2003d: 14, 20). Between 1996 and 2003 the area planted with genetically-modified (GM) crops globally increased from 2.8 million to 67.7 million hectares despite very little planting within the EU itself. By 2002 GM crops were being grown on 18 per cent of the total land under cultivation across the globe. GM soya, almost all of which was herbicide tolerant, and GM maize, two-thirds of which was insect resistant and one-third herbicide tolerant, accounted for 80 per cent of this area. Two thirds of all GM crops were being grown in the United States (Food Standards Agency 2003, James 2003). Meanwhile the number employed in the European healthcare biotechnology

Table 2.2 Current and possible future applications of biotechnology

Area	Examples of applications
Mining	Use of microbes to extract metals from ore by solubilization (bioleaching), and use of plants to extract metals from soil (phytomining)
Energy	Energy crops such as sugar cane, harvesting of natural vegetation, conversion of organic wastes into direct energy or energy-carrier compounds such as ethanol, biodiesel (modified rapeseed oil), methane and hydrogen, via direct combustion, anaerobic digestion, destructive distillation, gasification, chemical hydrolysis, biochemical hydrolysis; use of microbes to release petroleum from oil shelf and tar sands
Environmental improvement	Use of microbes to decompose organic waste including sewage, anaerobic landfill technology producing methane, composting of organic waste; clean-up of contaminated water, land or air (bioremediation) by optimizing conditions for microbial biodegradation via adding nutrients, adding new microbes, genetically engineering micro-organisms to be able to degrade resistant organic pollutant molecules; using plants to remove inorganic pollutants from the soil (phytoremediation); detection and monitoring of pollutants by means such as microbial biosensors that produce a reaction on contact such as luminescence (biomonitoring); use of microbes to extract metals from industrial effluent by solubilization (bioleaching); use of clean bioprocesses to replace polluting production processes, such as by replacing hazardous chemicals
Agriculture and forestry	Improvement of plant (and tree) quality and productivity via breeding, cloning of superior plants, mutation, cell fusion between different species and genetic modification (transformation) to improve resistance to specific herbicides (to enable these to be used for weed control), improve resistance to insect pests and microbial diseases, and reduce losses during storage and transport, for example by slowing softening; use of oil-producing plants such as soy bean to produce industrial lubricants, cosmetics and biodegradable detergents; use of natural and GM micro-organisms to control pests; use of drugs to improve health or productivity of animals; selective breeding and genetic engineering to improve the quantity and quality of animal products such as meat and milk, improve disease resistance and produce pharmaceuticals; use of GM hormones and vaccines; improved diagnosis of animal diseases using immunoassays, DNA probes and biosensors
Food and beverages	Production of fermented foods and beverages such as alcohol, tea, coffee, dairy products such as cheese, flavours, sweeteners, enzymes and vitamins; rapid diagnosis of contaminants such as salmonella; use of microbes to produce single cell protein (SCP)

(Continued)

Table 2.2 (*Continued*)

Area	Examples of applications
	from ethanol and organic wastes for animal feed and human food such as protein supplements and meat substitutes; production of food from GM plants and animals
Manufacturing	Use of bioreactors to replace existing industrial processes with more efficient and environmentally friendly processes in areas such as antibiotics, enzymes, chemicals, pharmaceuticals, pulp and paper, textiles, leather; use of plants and animals to produce pharmaceuticals, plastics, industrial lubricants, cosmetics, biodegradable detergents
Healthcare	New antibiotics, vaccines, monoclonal antibodies, biopharmaceuticals such as insulin and human growth hormone; gene therapy (introduction of genetic material into human cells to alleviate/eliminate disease); *in vitro* fertilization, artificial wombs, cloning (fusing genes into a dormant cell to produce a new embryo); pre-implantation embryo diagnosis; designer babies; transplantation of GM animal organs into humans; genetic testing; designer tissues for transplantation; artificial human organs
Other	Biological warfare, DNA fingerprinting for forensic science and paternity testing, bio-crime such as mislabelling of GM products, human cloning, patent infringement, bio-terrorism, genetic typing of individuals, chimeric animals, molecular computers

Sources: Rifkin 1999: 2, 24, 195, Manning 2000, OECD 2001c: Ch 2, DTI 2003a, DTI 2004, Smith 2004.

industry increased from 67,445 in 2000 to 77,907 in 2003, while revenues increased from $9,872 million in 2000 to $13,937 million in 2003 (EuropaBIO 2003).

It seems clear that technological innovation in this area will continue, and the growing diversity of practical applications of biotechnology means that its use is highly likely to expand in scope and value over the next 20 years or so.

Implications

Table 2.3 lists the main policy actors that one would expect to be involved in policy-making as a consequence of the progressive development and application of biotechnology.

The fact that biotechnology, especially genetic engineering, comes with risks as well as benefits means that there is likely to be a range of judgements about the wisdom of going ahead with any given application, especially as in

Table 2.3   Generic biotechnology policy network

Type of policy actor	Specific policy actor
Political executives and associated parties	Chief executives Ministers of agriculture, industry, environment, health, defence, trade and technology European Commissioners for trade, agriculture, environment, health, enterprise, research, technology, food safety
Non-government politicians	Relevant parliamentary committees at national level European Parliament Other EU governments US government
Civil servants and the military	Departments and agencies relating to agriculture, industry, environment, health, defence, trade, technology, food safety, law enforcement European Commission Directorates-General relating to trade, agriculture, environment, health, industry (enterprise), technology US diplomats and civil servants, especially trade representatives
Judges and regulators	World Trade Organization (WTO) European Patents Office (EPO) US Patent and Trademark Office (PTO) Codex Alimentarius Commission (plant health), International Office of Epizootics (animal health), Secretariat of the International Plant Protection Convention (plant health)
Business	Firms with interests in biotechnology research, agriculture, food-processing, food retailing (supermarkets), pharmaceuticals and insurance
Interest groups	Farmers Industry organizations such as EuropaBIO
Other non-government organizations	Anti-biotechnology movement based on environmentalist groups
Media (television, press)	Specialist journalists and publications Mainstream media on specific controversies such as GM food
Non-government experts	Microbiologists, ecological biologists Experts in health, trade
Electorate	Consumers/public opinion

many cases we presently lack sufficient scientific information to be able to estimate the risks with any precision, in contrast to processes and products involving heavy metals, for example, where the dangers are well known (Manning 2000: 28). This sets the stage for the emergence of two opposing advocacy coalitions: one convinced of the benefits of biotechnology and discounting its risks, the other focussing on possible dangers. And this is what we find: a producer-oriented coalition of biotechnology-using firms, such as agri-chemical companies, supported by molecular biologists, economic authorities and the US government facing a safety-oriented coalition of environmentalist groups with support from environmental authorities, professional ecologists and the European Parliament. Farmers and European governments are divided (Patterson 2000, Vogler and Russell 2000: 8).

Since we cannot tell in advance which of these advocacy coalitions is likely to prevail, and the outcomes of their encounters are likely to be different in different areas of biotechnology anyway, it is difficult to reach definite conclusions about the net effects of developments in biotechnology on public policy. However, it is possible to draw out the separate and partly conflicting implications for public policy that, depending on their relative magnitude, will together determine the net policy implications. These are greater policy autonomy for governments to the extent that the growing use of biotechnology by business increases economic growth, more vigorous measures to assist the biotechnology industry in order to maximize its contribution to economic growth and improve the environment, and, by contrast, stricter regulation of some types of biotechnology for safety and environmental reasons.

More autonomous policies

The rapid growth of the use of biotechnology in agriculture and industry (DTI 2003a) means that the performance of biotechnology and biotechnology-related firms is becoming more important to economic growth. According to economic theory, the introduction of new technology should improve economic welfare overall. In relation to agricultural technology, for example, the use of herbicide-tolerant and pest-resistant crop varieties should enable farmers to reduce inputs while increasing yields, which should in turn lead to reduced costs and higher profits for them as well as to lower prices for consumers, assuming a competitive market (Gaisford *et al.* 2001: 7–11). And these are not the only potential benefits for agriculture, as Table 2.4 demonstrates.

The increasing use of biological processes in manufacturing (see Table 2.2) should also contribute to the growth and diversification of production. It is possible that by the end of the 21st century 50 per cent of liquid fuels, 90 per cent of chemicals, and 99 per cent of materials will derive from biosources (Broderick 2002). Increased availability of bio-energy and improved recovery of petroleum are likely to have at least some effect on economic growth by improving energy security and keeping energy prices lower than they otherwise would be, but although more bio-energy reduces the need to use fossil fuels, any consequent beneficial effect on climate change is likely to be partly or wholly cancelled out, or even outweighed, by the increased use of fossil fuels made possible by increased recovery of petroleum.

Nevertheless the increasing use of biotechnology should bring environmental benefits. Biotechnology-based manufacturing can be cleaner than

Table 2.4 Applications of genetic engineering to agriculture

Area	Examples
Plants	The creation of herbicide-resistant plants to enable more effective/less damaging herbicides to be used against weeds, which also makes it easier to conserve the soil by using no-till and conservation tillage systems, meaning less erosion and more wildlife
	Resistance to insect damage, which has the additional benefits of requiring less spraying, which means less contamination, operator poisoning and killing of non-target insects
	Production of bio-pesticides that target specific crop pests but do not harm anything else
	Reducing the need for water and/or fertilizers by improving crop ability to access the nutrients they need
	Longer storage life
	Improved taste and appearance
	Improved nutritional value, for example by reducing lipids that are bad for cholesterol
	Better plant disease diagnosis
	Viral, fungal and nematode resistance
	Improved efficiency of photosynthesis
	Extended ability to fix nitrogen
	Tolerance of high soil salinity and other poor soil conditions including metal contamination, which is of particular relevance to the 3rd World
	Drought, heat and frost tolerance
	Reducing the lignin content of timber, thus reducing the need for processing
Animals and fish	Faster growth, lower fat, increased disease resistance, and docility
	Meat, milk and eggs that are more nutritious
	Increased milk yields and production of designer milk, for example milk without the protein that causes lactose intolerance
	The production of pharmaceuticals in milk for healthcare and, possibly, recreational use
	Animal feed that reduces phosphorus and nitrogen excretion, total manure excretion and offensive odours
	Improved animal health by improving the detection, treatment and prevention of diseases and other problems, for example through improved nutrition, new drugs and vaccines, and identification of genetically disease-resistant animals for breeding (pets too)
	Improved animal welfare by reducing/eliminating need for practices such as castration and dehorning
	Production of animals, such as pigs, with organs that resist rejection by the human immune system and therefore can be used in xenotransplantation
	The creation of GM animals for drug studies

(Continued)

Table 2.4   (Continued)

Area	Examples
Microbes	Use of modified bacteria and yeast in food production processes such as fermentation Production of pharmaceuticals

Sources: FAO 2000, BIO 2003, 2003a; Biotechnology Roundtable 2003, Monsanto 2003, Nottingham 2003.

the alternatives because the chemistry of living organisms is more efficient than that of chemical processes and the wastes generated tend to be recyclable and biodegradable. Energy inputs can be reduced, for example where wood pulp is treated with fungi rather than thermomechanically (OECD 1999). The increasing use of biotechnology to process waste and clean contaminated soil should also lead to a cleaner environment.

To the extent that the use of biotechnology does increase economic growth and improve the environment, this should increase the popularity of national governments, other things being equal, since economic growth means more jobs and higher incomes while a cleaner environment means fewer political problems in this area. This puts them in a stronger position to implement unpopular policies without losing office at the next election. Over time one would expect at least some governments to take advantage of this to implement more partisan policies than otherwise would be the case and/or tougher measures to resolve actual or anticipated crises. In short, the positive economic and environmental effects of applications of biotechnology imply increasing policy autonomy for governments.

More vigorous measures to assist the biotechnology industry

Because governments wish to achieve economic growth for electoral and other reasons, the increasing economic weight of the biotechnology sector implies increasing pressure on national governments to alter regulatory and other policies to benefit biotechnology and biotechnology-related firms in order to maintain and expand their contribution to economic growth, for example by expanding incentives for companies that invest in biotechnology and by adapting existing process and product regulation to biotechnology in ways that facilitate its development and use.

Policies designed to assist the biotechnology sector are not new. Ever since the 1970s biotechnological processes and products such as single-cell proteins, gasohol, self-nitrating plants and fermentation engineering have been promoted by governments as part of establishing a new and environmentally-friendly industry (Bud 1995, Falkner 2000: 144–5). Perhaps the best illustration of how governments have been prepared to assist the biotechnology industry in the past is the extension of the scope of patents to cover biotechnology processes and products in order to encourage innovation in this area by enabling private firms to make money from biological research. This is because a patent is a property right granted by a state authority to inventions that are new, involve an inventive step and have an industrial or other useful capability, in exchange for disclosing full details, a right which excludes others from the use or benefit of the patented invention without the consent of the patent holder, usually for 20 years. Patent holders either provide the product or service covered by the patent themselves, or license others to do so in return for payment (royalty). The broadening of patent rights began with the US Supreme Court's *Diamond v. Chakrabarty* decision in 1980 to permit a genetically modified bacterium to be patented, which led to inventions involving biological material and some life forms being deemed patentable in the US and in a number of other countries, but the 1995 Agreement on Trade-Related Aspects of Intellectual Property (TRIPS) negotiated by WTO member states established minimum standards for patenting for WTO members that include allowing patenting for any technology or process for making things. In relation to biotechnology this means that all micro-organisms and biotechnological processes for producing plants and animals are patentable. The first GM plant was patented in 1985 and the first GM animal in 1988, and since then the number of patents on genetically-modified organisms (GMOs) has increased rapidly (Manning 2000: 16, Williams 2000: 73, Gaisford *et al.* 2001: 22, 37–9, OECD 2002b: 21–7). These moves to broaden patentability have occurred despite opposition on the grounds that genes should not be patentable because they are discoveries rather than inventions, and, in relation to human genes, because they constitute the core of humanity and therefore should not be owned as property. It is also argued that TRIPS benefits TNCs based in industrialized countries at the expense of developing countries, since developing countries are usually in no position to take advantage of the new patent rights while TNCs are free to collect plants from these countries, alter them slightly, then sell them back, a practice labelled bio-piracy by its critics (Williams 2000: 75–6). Other controversies involve the use of blocking or overly broad patents that discourage or limit the use of the inventions they cover, the proliferation of gene patents that raise transaction and financial costs by necessitating the negotiation of multiple licences when developing a new product or process (patent thickets and royalty stacking), and reach-through claims of research tool patents to claim patents on products identified by others using that research tool (OECD 2002b: 11–18, 29).

Stricter regulation of biotechnology

So far we have focussed mainly on the benefits of biotechnology. But there are dangers as well. These relate to laboratory activities, the process plant, the final product and the environment due to factors such as the ability of natural and GM organisms and viruses to cause disease, the use of known dangerous micro-organisms in processes such as vaccine production, toxicity and allergy

Table 2.5 Actual and potential risks of genetic engineering in agriculture

Area	Examples
Ecological risks	GM crops themselves become weeds, for example due to herbicide or insect resistance
	Transfer of genes from GM crops to wild relatives and other plants and organisms (genetic pollution), for example herbicide-resistance, antibiotic-resistance
	Increased use of herbicides due to the availability of herbicide-resistant crop plants
	Crops that incorporate insecticides may kill non-target species or speed up the development of insect resistance to insecticides
	Ecological damage due to GM animals escaping and breeding with wild relatives
	Toxicity of GM crops for wildlife, for example crops designed to produce pharmaceuticals
	Virus-resistant plants create new viruses through recombination and/or transcapsidation
	Impossibility of eradicating GMOs once they enter the environment, especially microbes
	Loss of crop genetic diversity, leading to greater vulnerability to disease and pests
	Engineered fish may alter native ecosystems, driving wild populations to extinction
Animals	Side-effects for GM animals such as arthritis
Risks to human health	Creation or strengthening of a pathogen due to transfer of genes from GM microbes
	Allergic reactions due to the unintended encoding of proteins that cause allergenic responses
	Eating food with antibiotic resistance genes could reduce the effectiveness of antibiotics
	Transfer of antibiotic resistance to human and animal pathogens
	Meat containing drugs designed for farm animals could cause cancer
	Contamination of food supply with drugs from pharmaceutical-producing plants
	Production of new toxins
	Concentration of toxic metals in edible parts of plants meant to isolate these in inedible parts
Ethical issues	Transfer of human genes to animals or food
	Use of genes from animals that are proscribed by certain religious groups
	Transfer into plants or animal feed of animal genes may cause problems for vegetarians
	Xenotransplantation (transplantation of animal organs into humans)
	Moral objections to patenting animals

(Continued)

Table 2.5   (Continued)

Area	Examples
Economic and social issues	Lack of consumer acceptance in Western Europe (but not US)
	Greater dependence of farmers on a decreasing number of large TNCs such as Monsanto not only for GM seeds but also for chemicals and fertilizers that these crops require
	Economic disruption due to substitution of traditional production methods by new methods
	Bio-piracy: altering and patenting organisms from developing countries
	Export crops are displacing crops for local use in the Third World
	Small farmers disadvantaged because only large farmers can afford GM seeds
	GM activities in developing countries that are outlawed in industrialized countries

Sources: FAO 2000, Manning 2000, Gaisford *et al.* 2001: 18, BIO 2003b, UCS 2003, GM Science Review 2003, Nottingham 2003.

associated with microbial production, an increase in the pool of antibiotic resistant micro-organisms, the disposal of spent microbial biomass, the purification of effluents from biotechnological processes, the industrial use of GM micro-organisms, and the contamination, infection or mutation of process strains (Smith 2004: 235–40). In agricultural biotechnology alone there are numerous health and environmental risks associated with genetic modification of plants, animals and microbes (Table 2.5). As more and more GMOs are released, it is almost certain that a small percentage will in fact be damaging for the environment, judging by past experience with the effects of the release of non-indigenous species on indigenous ecologies (Rifkin 1999: 73–9). Bioremediation processes may result in incomplete biodegradation and thus breakdown products that are more hazardous than the starting materials (DTI 2004: Checkpoint H4). Transplanted organs from animals to humans might introduce animal viruses into humans (Rifkin 1999: 104). There is also the risk of bio-warfare aimed at human populations or farm animals and crops (Smith 2004: 235–240), as well as the possibility of bio-terrorism and the certainty of bio-crime. And genetic modification of humans puts into question the future of human nature itself.

To the extent that perceptions of risk become widespread, popular opposition to the forms of biotechnology concerned will grow, weakening the electoral position of governments that ignore this opposition, other things being equal, and strengthening the hand of groups that want to restrict or ban the relevant applications. The result will be increasing pressure to restrict or ban the applications concerned. These effects will be greatly magnified to the extent that applications of biotechnology do in fact cause widely publicized environmental or other disasters.

Leaving aside the issues of human biotechnology and biological warfare, these political effects are best illustrated by the controversy over GM food.

Environmental groups oppose GM foods for health, environmental, ethical and political (anti-corporate) reasons. Greenpeace argues that since GMOs can reproduce and interbreed with natural organisms, their release constitutes 'genetic pollution' as there is inadequate scientific understanding of their impact. Since GM foods are already here, it advocates labelling of GM ingredients and segregation of GM from non-GM crops. It also opposes all patents on plants, animals, humans and their genes. A study of the anti-GM movement in Britain characterizes it as being based on leadership networks of counter-experts in pre-existing anti-biotechnology and seed networks that are critical of GM agriculture due to its risks to health (food quality) and the environment (loss of biodiversity) plus the threat it poses to the autonomy of individuals, communities and nations (farmer control over seeds, national control over indigenous resources) and equity (compensation to developing countries for genetic material taken, altered and sold back) (Purdue 2000, esp. 9, 61–3, Gaisford *et al.* 2001: 30–31, Greenpeace, undated).

A number of GM products were approved for introduction into Europe between 1996 and 1998, but during this period opinion polls showed increasing public opposition in Europe to GM crops and food, and direct action, in the form of uprooting of GM crops, began in 1998 (Purdue 2000: 94, Schurman 2004: 254–5). This increasing consumer concern was reflected in increasingly tough regulatory stances on the part of EU governments, the European Commission and the European Parliament (Patterson 2000, European Parliament 2004). In June 1999 France, Denmark, Greece, Italy and Luxembourg stated that they would block any new EU authorizations until existing EU legislation was tightened up, especially in relation to labelling and traceability of GMOs. This created a *de facto* moratorium on new approvals while EU legislation in this area was being revised (Gene Watch UK 2003b).

The view that public opinion is important in this area is consistent with the fact that regulation in the US, where at least until recently public opinion was supportive of GM food, or at least quiescent, is more industry-friendly and less restrictive than in Europe, although factors such as differences in industry structures and policy-making institutions, the strategic behaviour of the anti-biotechnology movement and recent food safety disasters in Europe also play a role in explaining these international differences (Bernauer and Meins 2003, Prakash and Kollman 2003, Schurman 2004, esp. 245–55). The more industry-friendly regulation of the US appears to be one reason for US dominance of the biotechnology industry, and European biotechnology firms have invested heavily in the US (Falkner 2000: 145–6).

The current mobilization of public concern in Europe about GM food by environmentalist groups means that any political benefit gained by governments as a result of agricultural biotechnology boosting economic growth is offset or even outweighed by the negative effects of antagonizing worried voters. Public support for their position on GM foods gives environmental groups a new bargaining resource with government by providing governments with electoral incentives to make policy concessions to these groups, which implies that authorities become more likely to respond to demands to impose stringent safety regulation.

This can be seen in relation to the regulation of agricultural biotechnology, which is formulated mainly at the EU level and implemented by Member States (DTI, undated). Agricultural biotechnology is subject to regulation mainly in relation to intellectual property, GMO releases, GM processes and products, and trade. Legislative initiatives in recent years have strengthened the legal powers to regulate in this area, established new agencies for this purpose, and strengthened safety regulation. EU legislation on releases of GMOs now requires risk assessments of direct and indirect short- and long-term effects of all GMO releases on health, the environment and biodiversity as well as public consultation before decisions on applications are made. Where consent for a GMO release is given, this specifies labelling and monitoring requirements and may include conditions on marketing the product. GM food, food produced using GM processes and food products that are obtained by novel processes, contain novel or modified molecules, or otherwise differ substantially from established food, must be demonstrated to be safe, not misleadingly presented, and nutritionally comparable when used as replacements for conventional food. Labelling must indicate any characteristic or food property which renders the novel food or ingredient no longer equivalent to an existing one (for example because it differs in composition, nutritional value, nutritional use or intended effects) and the method for obtaining this, and must ensure that the final consumer is informed of the presence of a GMO (DTI, undated – see also Genewatch UK 2003a).

Conclusion

Table 2.6 summarizes the policy implications of increasing use of biotechnology identified in this chapter. The implications of biotechnology application to healthcare and defence, as noted earlier, are analysed in the next two chapters.

In essence, where developments in biotechnology improve economic welfare and the environment and are uncontroversial they strengthen the electoral position of incumbent governments, enabling them to risk implementing policies that are more independent of public opinion than would otherwise be the case as well as encouraging them to move public policy in a more biotechnology-friendly direction. Where public concern is mobilized against a particular use of biotechnology on safety grounds, on the other hand, these effects are countered by pressure to restrict or ban the applications in question.

Table 2.6 Policy implications of developments in biotechnology

Policy implications	Causal chain from trend
More autonomous policies in general	Greater government popularity due to the increasing contribution of biotechnology to economic growth and a better environment
Policy changes to increase the use of biotechnology, attract biotechnology-related foreign investment and benefit the biotechnology sector in general, such as adapting process and product regulation in ways that facilitate the development and use of biotechnology, and expanding financial incentives for biotech-related incoming foreign investment and R&D	Increasing economic and environmental importance of biotechnology
Stricter safety and environmental regulation of certain types of biotechnology, in particular genetic engineering	New developments in biotechnology are at times accompanied by new types of risk and may lead to disasters such as contamination of non-GM crops with GMOs, with associated bad publicity and increased political leverage for anti-biotechnology groups
Indirect effects via other king trends	Developments in biotechnology improve healthcare technology (Chapter 3) and military technology (Chapter 4) as well as contributing to the growth and diversification of production (Chapter 5)

3
Healthcare Technology

Introduction

Technological innovation relevant to healthcare is resulting in a continuous series of new products and processes designed to improve healthcare. Table 3.1 sets out a number of the most prominent current and expected future developments. There seems little doubt that healthcare technology will continue to develop for the foreseeable future.

Among other things the use of new healthcare products and processes is likely to affect the way that healthcare is delivered and experienced. Improvement of screening and treatment of serious conditions is expected to enable a change in emphasis from 'diagnose and treat' to 'predict and prevent'. The increasing sophistication of healthcare provision is expected to lead to a greater concentration of expertise and equipment in a smaller number of larger centres dealing with complex cases, while a growing proportion of common conditions is treated locally in small centres linked telemetrically to specialist centres. Telemedicine implies better access to healthcare from remote locations. Hospital stays are expected to become shorter due to more diagnosis, treatment and monitoring taking place outside the hospital, plus practices such as minimal access and image guided surgery that mean less need for recuperation. Home care and self care are expected to increase in importance due to developments such as better information for patients and public, remote diagnostic equipment and home diagnostic systems such as home blood test kits (Robert 1999).

More importantly, improvements in technology should improve the effectiveness of healthcare itself, thereby prolonging life and improving quality of life. The significance of this for us all can hardly be overstated.

But it comes, literally, at a price. Although the use of new technology can reduce healthcare costs, it is generally agreed that on balance it increases costs. At the same time consideration of new and expected developments in healthcare technology arouses ethical and religious concerns of various sorts. Some of the most prominent of these are set out in Table 3.2.

Table 3.1 Developments in healthcare technology

Area	Products and processes
Information and communication technology	Rehabilitation and enablement such as bridging damage to spinal cords, electronic cornea implants, computer-assisted hearing, artificial intelligence-based elderly and handicapped support devices, disability assistance devices using thought recognition
	Expert systems enabling diagnosis and defining the most applicable treatment
	Minimal access and image guided surgery: endoscopes (including robots), lasers, lithotripsy, and very high energy ultrasound beams (such as to destroy tumours)
	Surgical operations by robots (can be more precise and reliable than human surgery)
	Telemedicine: use of telecommunications technology to provide medical information and services, such as video consultations, remote diagnostic equipment, telepresence surgery (surgeons operating at a distance)
	Better information for healthcare staff via globally-available networked computerized medical information, diagnosis and treatment algorithms (automated diagnostics), patient data and instructional material
	Better healthcare information for patients and the public via the Internet
	Full personal medical records on smartcard
	Personal wearable health monitors
Bioengineering	Pacemakers, artificial hips, knee replacements, shoulder and finger joint replacements, vascular grafts, heart valve replacements, breast prostheses, intraocular lenses, blood, electrical implants to stimulate muscles in disabled people
	Artificial skin, ears, hearts, kidneys, lungs
	Artificial senses through sensors directly stimulating nerves;
	Biosensors, such as for monitoring levels of glucose in diabetics
	Tissue engineering: the combination of living cells with synthetic polymers that ultimately dissolve, leaving behind new versions of functioning biological tissue
	Diagnostics: monoclonal antibody-based tests, genetic probes, DNA amplification, and agents improving *in-vivo* diagnostic imaging
Genetics and allied	Screening of patients to determine susceptibility to diseases and disorders caused by single genes such as cystic fibrosis, chromosome disorders such as Down syndrome, and those caused by particular combinations of genes in concert with environmental factors, such as heart disease, most cancers, and Alzheimer's disease – includes carrier testing, prenatal testing and newborn screening
	Gene therapy: delivery of new genes into patients' cells, for example tumour cells, to replace or supplement defective genes

(Continued)

Table 3.1   (*Continued*)

Area	Products and processes
	Biopharmaceuticals from genetically modified plants, animals and microbes, such as antibiotics, insulin, vaccines, cancer medicines; also nutritional supplements
	Treatment tailored to an individual's genes, for example types and doses of drugs
	Use of stem cells, which can be directed to differentiate into specific cell types, to replace cells to treat diseases such as Parkinson's and Alzheimer's diseases, spinal cord injury, stroke, burns, heart disease, diabetes, arthritis; also for delivery of new genes
	Genetic enhancement, such as using genetic engineering to raise IQ
General	Less toxic anaesthesia
	Transplantation: prevention of rejection of transplants by recipients; ability to transplant organs such as pancreas, small bowel and endocrine organs; cloning of skin and growth of retinal tissue and corneal endothelium; organ and tissue replacements that combine living tissue with artificial components; xenotransplantation: the use of organs from other species; new mechanical devices
	Cyborgs (cybernetic organisms): humans enhanced by engineering, for example athletes
	Extending life by extending cell life
	Cryonics
	New managerial technologies

Sources: Robert 1999, NHGRI undated, Department of Health 2003, Freeman and Moran 2000, DHSS 2001, National Institutes of Health 2002, DTI 2003a, Wellcome Trust and Strategy Unit 2003: 4–5.

Table 3.2   Issues arising from developments in healthcare technology

Type of concern	Object of concern
Ethical and religious concerns	Xenotransplantation (transplantation from animals to humans)
	The use of embryos as a source of stem cells for use in tissue engineering
	Genetic testing: paternity testing, forensic genetic profiling, use of genetic tests by insurers and employers. Concerns include privacy of an individual's genetic information, whether patients should be told that they might be at high risk of developing an illness because of their genetic makeup when there is no effective treatment or cure for that disease now, pre-implantation diagnosis and screening of embryos, the possibility that insurers

(*Continued*)

Table 3.2   (*Continued*)

Type of concern	Object of concern
	might use the results of genetic tests to deny insurance coverage, and the possibility that employers might use the results of genetic tests to refuse or terminate employment
	Human cloning, gene therapy and eugenics, for example the possibility of voluntary or compulsory genetic therapy for gays and others considered deviant, or germ-line engineering of humans leading to consequences such as genetic enhancement or breeding humans for slavery
	New psychotropic drugs, for example drugs designed to control behaviour such as Ritalin
Other concerns	Safety regulation in relation to possible unforeseen effects of new treatments, for example new drugs, gene therapy, xenotransplantation
	Cost and effectiveness of healthcare technologies such as pharmaceuticals, including issues such as price control
	Regulation of standards of telemedicine services, home-care tests and equipment, IT and electronic information, Internet sites
	Gene patents and the potential for excessive ownership rights of sequences or insufficient intellectual property protection to encourage investment; ability of individuals and groups based in rich countries to patent gene sequences unique to poor countries without compensation

Sources: NHGRI undated, Nuffield 2000, Executive Summary: 5, Nuffield 2000, Part 2: 7, Silberglitt *et al.* 2001: xiii, Biotechnology Roundtable 2003, DTI 2003a, Fukuyama 2003: 59, 155–9, 206–7, Wellcome Trust and Strategy Unit 2003: 6–9, 22.

Implications

Among the most prominent policy actors in the healthcare field are doctors, managers, pharmaceutical and medical device manufacturers, and patients in their capacities of citizens, workers and insurance subscribers. The economic and social significance of the healthcare system means that not only health ministers but also finance ministers, heads of government and – in some countries – presidents take an interest. In social insurance systems such as Germany sickness funds administered by employers and unions are also important (Moran 1999, Freeman 2000). Table 3.3 provides a more comprehensive list of policy actors with an interest in healthcare technology and its consequences.

The main policy implications of developments in healthcare technology are adjustments to existing regulation relating to safety and cost–benefit assessment, formulation of new regulation in response to genetic and other technologies that open up options for people that have not existed before, increasing government control over the healthcare system due to better information and communications technology (ICT), more patient-centred

Table 3.3 Generic healthcare policy network

Type of policy actor	Specific policy actor
Political executives and associated parties	Chief executives Minister of health Finance minister Social ministers
Non-government politicians	Opposition leaders and health spokespeople Parliamentary committees relating to health, finance European Commissioner responsible for health Regional and local governments
Civil servants, special advisers and other public sector employees	Department of health Public health services, such as the British NHS, and their constituent and associated organizations, such as hospitals and medical schools Public health insurance funds Regulatory and advisory agencies such as health technology assessment agencies Economic and social ministries Regional and local administrations
Judges and regulators	Commissions of inquiry New field of application for existing courts
Business	Pharmaceutical companies Medical device producers Private health services Private insurance companies Employers in general as contributors to funding healthcare
Interest groups and non-government organizations	Health funds and hospitals administered jointly by employer and employee representatives Organizations representing doctors, dentists, nurses, social workers, technicians and other medical staff Organizations representing managers and white-collar workers Organizations representing ancillary workers such as cleaners Health advocacy groups such as AIDS activists Religious groups
Media	Specialist journals National press and television
Experts	Medical researchers working in government, business and academia Economists, lawyers, health policy analysts
Electorate	Patients/taxpayers/workers/insurance payers

healthcare, greater policy autonomy for governments due to better health-care, less policy autonomy as increased spending on healthcare necessitates efforts to control costs and/or raise taxes, and more business-friendly policies in relation to healthcare technology companies.

Adjustment of existing regulation

The application to new technologies of the concerns sustaining existing safety and cost-benefit product and process regulation is likely to lead to the amendment of this regulation in order to take these new technologies into account. Unless the views and/or resources of the relevant policy actors change for other reasons, the amended regulation is likely to be similar to existing regulation. In some cases, such as regulation of telemedicine, verification of Internet sites relating to health, and standard-setting for information technology and electronic information, the application of concerns about safety and cost-effectiveness is likely to lead to increased demand for international regulation (Nuffield 2000: 5).

Formulation of new regulation

Most new healthcare technologies, if they operate as intended, improve healthcare and its outcomes. Others, such as gene therapy, have implications that range far beyond healthcare. Contemplation of these arouses ethical and religious concerns in a number of quarters and mobilizes religious and other groups whose moral values are or would be violated by use of the technology in question. These concerns are commonly expressed as demands for new forms of regulation designed to control or even block use of the relevant technologies. Such demands are especially prominent in relation to xeno-transplantation, the use of embryos as sources of stem cells, genetic testing, human cloning, gene therapy and the use of new psychotropic drugs.

Xenotransplantation

Xenotransplantation – the transplantation of animal organs into humans – raises a number of concerns. Some object to the use of animals for this purpose in principle, especially if they are genetically modified to ensure that their organs won't be rejected by human recipients. There is also the possibility that being used in this way would cause considerable suffering for the animals involved. Second, there is the possibility that animal organs will pass on animal diseases to humans (Nuffield Council on Bioethics 2004). Third, some religious groups object to the idea of receiving organs from animals, or at least from particular animals such as pigs, although it would seem that this concern can be easily accommodated by ensuring that all prospective recipients are given the right of consent over whether such a transplant is carried out.

Although information on regulation of xenotransplantation is hard to find, it would appear that at present there are few if any legal barriers to trans-planting animal organs into humans if and when this becomes technically feasible. Unless substantial problems arise when this does occur, such as actual transmission of animal diseases, there seems no reason for the use of xeno-transplantation to result in any major policy change.

The use of embryos as a source of stem cells

Stem cells are non-differentiated cells that can give rise to more specialized types of cells. Their medical significance is that they enable cell therapy: the production and implantation of specific types of cell in order to cure or allevi-ate diseases characterized by loss of these cell types. In future it may be possible to grow whole organs from stem cells for use in transplantation, and to use stem cells for rejuvenating therapies. The problem is that at present stem cells are generated from embryos that are destroyed in the process, which many find repugnant, especially those who believe that the embryo has the moral status of a person from the moment of conception (Holm 2002: 494–7, NHGRI 2004).

Current regulation of human embryonic stem cell research in Europe varies from country to country. Some, including Britain, Finland, Greece, the Netherlands and Sweden, allow human embryonic stem cells to be obtained from supernumerary embryos (embryos created for the purposes of *in vitro* fertilization but not used). Others, including Austria, Denmark, France, Germany and Ireland, prohibit the use of supernumerary embryos in this way, although some allow the import and use of embryonic cell lines. Others have no specific legislation on the subject. The creation of human embryos for research purposes and for the procurement of stem cells is prohibited by the 1997 Convention of the Council of Europe on Human Rights and Biomedicine as well as by national legislation in Austria, Denmark, Finland, France, Germany, Greece, Ireland, Italy, the Netherlands, Portugal and Spain, but is permitted in Britain (European Commission 2003c: 38–42).

Genetic testing

The simplest type of genetic test consists of comparing two samples of DNA to determine whether they are from the same person. This is what is done in paternity (parental) testing and in forensic genetic profiling.

Paternity tests can reliably exclude a particular individual as a biological parent of a given child, although they cannot absolutely confirm that the individual concerned is definitely a biological parent (GeneTests 2004). Their use is increasing, due in part to the discovery that the non-paternity rate, which is estimated at 1–5 per cent, is higher than previously thought. Although there are social and ethical issues involved such as the consent of the mother or child (paternity testing only requires a sample of the child's hair, so secret and unauthorized testing is difficult to prevent) as well as privacy and confi-dentiality, the authentication and validation of the tests, and their status in legal proceedings (Martin and Frost 2003: 194–5), paternity testing is an established technology and it is hard to see any major policy changes occur-ring as a result of its increasing use.

Comparison of a person's DNA profile with a DNA sample from the scene of a crime can establish conclusively that the person concerned was not there, although a positive identification cannot absolutely determine that the person definitely was there (Interpol 2000). It can also help to identify human remains and settle probate and immigration disputes (ASLME 2004). Forensic genetic profiling of this sort is an established technology, but the concomitant growth of DNA databases for use in criminal and other investigations represents a threat to privacy if genetic information on anything but identity is released to employers, insurers, schools, adoption agencies or researchers. It also potentially threatens human rights, as it clearly enables a greater degree of social control by governments that could be used as a means of oppressing certain individuals or groups (Genewatch UK 2005). Whether opposition from privacy groups leads to any changes in policy probably depends on unrelated factors such as social and governmental perceptions of the seriousness of security risks such as terrorism.

Genetic testing for medical purposes consists of examining a person's DNA (or indicator proteins) to identify particular genes or gene sequences, and is used to identify single gene disorders, predispositions and pharmacogenetic sensitivities. Single gene disorders are identified by means of prenatal testing (which gives women the possibility of terminating their pregnancy if a disorder is identified), newborn genetic testing (which enables early treatment for certain disorders), diagnostic testing of children (to confirm the presence of a particular disease), and adult presymptomatic and carrier testing (to map the inheritance of serious rare genetic disorders in families in order to improve management of their care and to inform reproductive choices). There are about 10,000 single gene disorders which, taken together, affect up to five per cent of the population. Genetic tests are currently available for about 200 of these. Testing is also beginning to be carried out to identify specific gene mutations that might significantly increase the risk of developing cancer, heart disease and other conditions. Pharmacogenetic testing is designed to identify individual responses to drugs and thereby make it easier to match drugs with patients (Department of Health 2003, Martin and Frost 2003: 189–94).

Genetic tests can also be used for insurance and employment purposes.

Insurers, at least in Britain, want access to the results of genetic tests already taken by applicants because they are concerned that otherwise an increasing number of people will become aware from genetic tests that they are susceptible to an illness likely to lead to premature death or to early claims on critical illness, income protection or long-term care insurance policies and that this will lead them to apply for insurance that they would not otherwise take out, or at higher levels than would otherwise be the case, without telling the insurer, the problem being that this would lead to higher claim costs for the insurer and thus to higher insurance costs for other policyholders. This in turn might deter low and medium risk customers from purchasing policies at all and thereby seriously undermine the finances of insurance companies (Daykin *et al.* 2003: 2, 7, 9, 27).

The problem on the other side is that allowing insurers to require disclosure of the results of genetic tests, or even to require applicants to take genetic tests, will make applicants who 'fail' uninsurable and lead to the development of a significant genetic underclass (Daykin *et al.* 2003: 2). The clash here is between the principle that people should not be treated differently due to different genetic characteristics, and here race is a case in a point, and the principle that people with different risk profiles should be treated differently (Launis 1999). In addition, at present few genetic tests have high levels of reliability or predictive value. Furthermore, if a patient cannot be sure of keeping confidential the results of genetic tests taken for medical purposes, they may be less willing to take them in the first place, which would impede adequate diagnosis and treatment.

In Britain and some other countries the regulatory response has been to permit insurers to ask about the results of previous genetic tests for certain conditions, but only for very large sums assured (Daykin *et al.* 2003: 28). However the 1997 Council of Europe Convention on Human Rights and Biomedicine prohibits discrimination on the grounds of genetic heritage and limits genetic testing to health purposes and to scientific research limited to health purposes. This commits signatories to banning the use of the results of genetic tests by insurers. Countries in which national legislation also prohibits this include Austria, Belgium, Denmark and Luxembourg. In other countries there are either moratoria of the use by insurers of this information or voluntary agreements to restrict its use (Genetics and Insurance Committee 2004, Annex F).

It would seem likely that if insurers do suffer financial problems due to applicants failing to disclose the results of genetic tests, regulation will eventually converge on the British model, as this allows applicants for insurance to keep the results of genetic tests to themselves unless they purchase high levels of insurance. For their part, insurers get protection where it really matters from a financial point of view. On the other hand, improvements in the reliability and predictive value of genetic tests are likely to remove one of the main arguments against their use by insurers and thereby increase pressure for restrictions on their use to be loosened.

Employers may wish to use genetic tests to exclude individuals who may be susceptible to workplace chemicals from jobs where they are likely to be exposed, avoid hiring workers who might need a lot of time off or retire early due to ill health, exclude individuals from health insurance or other employee benefits because they might use these excessively, monitor the health of employees to determine whether they have been exposed to dangerous levels of chemical hazards, or exclude individuals from certain jobs on the basis that they pose a threat to others if they develop a predicted illness suddenly (Genewatch 2003c: 2).

At present very few genetic tests are high in relevance, reliability and predictive value, which means that their use in employment or promotion decisions would obviously be inappropriate and unfair, but this situation may well change in the future. If the use by employers of genetic tests becomes widespread, at least some people will find that their genetic makeup makes it difficult or even impossible to find jobs, especially good jobs, leading to the creation of a genetic underclass that is unemployable as well as uninsurable. Is this what we want? If not, employer use of genetic tests has to be restricted. In some countries, such as Austria, use of genetic data on employees is explicitly prohibited whereas in others, such as Britain, the government's position appears to be that while it is not appropriate for employers to require or request genetic test results to assess the long-term health of employees or job applicants, it might be appropriate to use them to ascertain susceptibility to workplace features that do not present any hazard to most people (Whittaker and Alivizatos 2003: 11, 13, Genewatch 2003c: 6).

However the policy dynamics will change in the future as work-relevant genetic tests become cheaper, more numerous and more accurate and employers become more aware of their advantages – especially if they find foreign competitors using them. The result is likely to be greater pressure by employers on governments to let them use as many genetic tests as possible, starting with tests for sensitivity to workplace hazards.

Human cloning

Advocates of human cloning argue that it can provide genetically related children for those who cannot be helped by other fertility treatment as well as for lesbians and for parents of a child who has died, and claim that it is a reproductive right and should be allowed once it is judged no less safe than natural reproduction. Opponents argue that human cloning is unsafe and would diminish the sense of uniqueness of the individual (CGS 2003). So far opponents of cloning have the upper hand. Human cloning is prohibited by Article 1 of the Convention on Human Rights and Biomedicine of the Council of Europe, which a number of European countries have signed, and explicit laws banning human reproductive cloning, and in some cases therapeutic and research cloning as well, exist in most west European countries (Council of Europe 1997, Global Lawyers and Physicians 2004).

At present very few animal cloning attempts are successful, and cloned animals that do survive often have birth defects or die early (NHGRI 2004), but if and when animal cloning does become safe it seems certain that sooner or later human clones will be born. At this point, if not before, scientists, people who have been cloned, people who would like to be cloned and, later, clones themselves will press for legalization of cloning.

Gene therapy

Somatic gene therapy consists of introducing genetic material into a patient's cells in order to treat or prevent a disease, and at present offers hope mainly to people suffering from single gene disorders for which there are few if any alternative treatments. Gene therapy also has the potential to treat conditions such as cancer and heart disease by enabling cancerous cells to be killed more effectively and selectively, increasing the effectiveness of conventional cancer drugs, boosting the ability of patients' immune systems to recognize and destroy tumour cells, and generating new blood vessels and improving blood flow around the heart (Department of Health 2003: 19–21). Such medical uses appear to be relatively uncontroversial.

Germ-line gene therapy, on the other hand, is dynamite because transferring genes to germ (egg and sperm) cells means that any resulting genetic changes pass on to future generations (NHGRI 2004a).

Advantages of permitting inheritable genetic modification include enabling couples to avoid passing on serious genetic diseases and to produce children who are healthier, longer lived, more athletic, more intelligent and more attractive than would otherwise be the case. Opponents argue that in almost all cases there are other ways to enable parents to avoid passing on genetic diseases and that inheritable genetic enhancement is unsafe. More generally it is argued that inheritable genetic modification would change the nature of human life and society forever and erode our sense of a common humanity. To the extent that it is limited mainly to the affluent, it would also increase social and economic disparities. Furthermore, those undertaking germ-line gene transfer would be doing so without the consent of those affected, who do not yet exist (CGS 2003a, NHGRI 2004a).

So far successful gene transfer techniques have not been developed for either somatic or germ-line transfer, which means that gene therapy for humans is not safe at the moment (NHGRI 2004a). There is moreover widespread agreement that human germline engineering should be banned altogether, and that somatic genetic modification should be limited to clearly medical applications, as distinct from genetic enhancement. The 1997 Convention on Human Rights and Biomedicine of the Council of Europe bans all human germ-line genetic modification, and explicit laws banning this type of gene transfer already exist in Finland, France, Germany, Italy, Norway, Spain and Sweden (CGS 2004, Global Lawyers and Physicians 2004).

But is this stance sustainable? First of all, as time goes on gene transfer techniques are likely to become safer and more reliable. Second, if it is technically feasible, designer babies will be born sooner or later whether it is legal or not. As with cloning, at this point we can expect pressure from scientists, parents and would-be parents of genetically modified children and, in due course, from these children themselves for inheritable genetic modification to be made legal.

New psychotropic drugs

Psychotropic drugs are those that affect the mind. Some are legal, such as caffeine, alcohol and tobacco. Others are illegal, such as cannabis, cocaine and LSD. And there are medical drugs the use of which is only legal under medical authority, such as Valium.

Increasing knowledge of human neurotransmitters such as serotonin, dopamine and norepinephrine, which control the firing of nerve synapses and the transmission of signals across neurons in the brain and thus affect our subjective feelings, has led to the manufacture of new psychotropic drugs such as the antidepressant Prozac and the stimulant Ritalin, which is used to treat attention deficit-hyperactivity syndrome by increasing focus and attention span, creating a sense of euphoria and increasing short-term energy levels. It is expected that as time goes on more new psychotropic drugs will emerge, for example drugs to reduce anxiety, reduce the need for sleep, increase the ability to learn and retain facts, increase stamina and motivation, and decrease sensitivity to pain (Fukuyama 2003: 42–52).

If they appear to be safe, many people are going to want to use them in their daily life for work and/or recreation. In changing how they feel, the drugs will also change what they do and how they do it. Society will be different. And popular demand will grow for these drugs to be made (or kept) legal and available.

Increasing government control of the healthcare system via the use of ICT

The increasing use of ICT facilitates increased central control of healthcare systems. Replacing paper patient records by electronic records, for example, makes it easier to control doctors via mechanisms such as medical audit (Freeman 2002: 763). This opens the way to new policies based on improved information about the health system, such as new ways of organizing the delivery of healthcare.

More patient-centred healthcare

As curative medicine becomes more effective at dealing with acute diseases, patients with chronic diseases and conditions become relatively more numerous. One effect of this is to create a more numerous and durable constituency for patient advocacy groups. The high profile of AIDS activists is a case in point here (Moran 1999: 183–4). Other things being equal, this should result in the inflection of at least some healthcare policies in the interests of patients, as opposed to other groups such as doctors, as well as increasing political support for healthcare spending.

Greater policy autonomy for governments due to better healthcare

Unless something is very wrong, we would expect better healthcare technology to result in better healthcare. To the extent that governments are held responsible for healthcare this implies greater popularity, or at least fewer electoral problems in this area. This in turn reduces the electoral risk of implementing unpopular policies, which would be expected to lead at least some governments to implement more partisan policies than would otherwise be the case and/or to introduce tougher measures to resolve crises than they otherwise would have done.

Less policy autonomy as higher healthcare spending leads to financial problems

Although new technology can in certain instances reduce healthcare spending, for example by curing patients more quickly or by automating medical or support functions, in general the introduction of new medical products and treatments increases the cost of providing healthcare. New medical products such as new drugs are often expensive in themselves. The use of new products and procedures often adds to the cost of existing treatments rather than replacing them. The new opportunities for diagnosis and treatment opened up enable many more patients to be treated than previously and prolong the lives of patients who subsequently require a great deal of support, such as very premature babies. New treatments often require additional investment in specialist personnel (Freeman 2000: 29, Harrison and Dixon 2000: 48, Nuffield 2000, Ham 2004: 73). The cost of pharmaceuticals, for example, is rising: a survey of 14 OECD countries found that between 1970 and 1997 real pharmaceutical expenditure per capita rose by an average of 3.6 per cent per year, resulting in a total rise of 260 per cent. Although pharmaceutical spending declined as a share of total health expenditure between 1970 and 1980, it rose significantly between 1990 and 1998 (OECD 2001d: 46–7). An OECD survey of recent health reforms suggests that technology may explain up to half the total spending growth over the last few decades (Docteur and Oxley 2004: 43, 66).

This means that the electoral benefits for incumbent governments brought by new technology, in the form of better healthcare for citizens, are offset by the financial problems they create in the form of growing deficits in state budgets and/or the finances of health funds, as these pose a serious and recurring problem for governments because almost all possible responses are likely to undermine their electoral support. Doing nothing and letting the deficit grow is likely to make the government unpopular with the economically minded and cannot be sustained indefinitely. Increasing revenue to cover the increased spending, for example by increasing the contributions of employers and/or employees to health funds and/or raising income tax or other taxes, is generally unpopular. Employers in particular oppose rises in their social contributions because they add to business costs. Revenue will rise to the extent that economic growth and high rates of employment expand the tax base, but governments may not be so lucky. And the alternative of cutting spending in healthcare or other areas is likely to be unpopular among patients, their increasingly strong advocacy groups, the huge numbers of people who work in the healthcare system and voters in general, all of whom are likely to be patients at some stage. Nevertheless, over the past few decades government initiatives to contain healthcare costs have included regulation of prices and volumes of healthcare and inputs into healthcare, caps on sectoral or overall health spending, and shifting of costs to the private sector. Technological costs in particular have been tackled by means such as introducing more stringent pre-marketing controls to determine whether a new technology is safe and effective, limits on capital spending on major items of medical equipment and, for pharmaceuticals, price control and stricter controls on cost reimbursement as well as tighter prescribing guidelines for doctors. Governments have sought to minimize any negative electoral effects of cost-saving measures on the quality of healthcare by means such as moving to make healthcare systems more efficient by enhancing the role of healthcare purchasers, improving hospital contracting and payment systems, improving managerial independence and cost accountability of hospitals, and increasing competition among providers (Moran 1999: 183, Freeman 2000: 71, Docteur and Oxley 2004: 44–69).

In short, revenue rises and/or cost control measures necessitated by the tendency of spending on medical technology to grow are likely to undermine the electoral support of incumbent governments, offsetting any electoral benefits accruing from improvements in healthcare made possible by this new technology. Which of these opposed effects is the more significant, however, is impossible to determine.

More business-friendly policies for medical technology companies

The size and economic significance of medical technology industries means that their performance affects economic performance overall and through this the electoral prospects of incumbent governments (Moran 1999: 12). Pharmaceutical production in Europe in 2002, for example, was estimated to be worth about €160 billion, up from just €63 billion in 1990 (EFPIA 2003: 3). Medical technology industries also help to sustain other key economic sectors. Medical device producers, for example, are important customers of the electronics industry, while the pharmaceutical industry has connections with the chemical industry (Freeman and Moran 2000).

The growing economic significance of the healthcare technology sector increases pressure on governments to provide a more business-friendly environment in order to attract healthcare technology R&D and production to their country and keep it there. Because expanding the domestic market for these industries by allowing healthcare services to buy more pharmaceuticals and medical devices is limited by the need to contain costs, governments are generally restricted to helping these industries as exporters, for example by making medicine regulation more industry-friendly by delivering faster approval rates (Lewis and Abraham 2001).

Conclusion

Table 3.4 summarizes the main implications of developments in healthcare technology for public policy.

Table 3.4   Policy implications of developments in healthcare technology

Policy implications	Causal chain from trend
Extension of existing safety and cost-benefit regulation to new healthcare products and processes made possible by developments in healthcare technology, including greater use of international regulation	Advances in healthcare technologies create products and processes that are not covered by existing safety and cost-benefit regulation, including cross-border provision of healthcare and healthcare advice
Increasing pressure from insurers and employers for governments to allow the expansion of genetic testing of insurance applicants and employees	The increasing reliability of genetic testing weakens one of the main arguments against its use and strengthens the incentives for insurers and employers to use it
Increasing pressure on governments to legalize human cloning and inheritable genetic modification	The increasing safety and reliability of animal cloning and inheritable genetic modification weakens one of the main arguments against use of these techniques on humans and increases the number of would-be parents who would like to take advantage of them Eventual birth of human clones and designer babies whether legal or not
Increasing pressure on governments to legalize, or refrain from criminalizing, new psychotropic drugs	Increasing variety of new relatively safe psychotropic drugs increases the number of people who would like to be able to use them for work and/or recreation
More autonomous policies in general	Increasing government popularity due to increasing effectiveness of healthcare services as a consequence of improvements in healthcare technology
Less autonomous policies in general	Decreasing government popularity as adoption of improved healthcare technology increases healthcare costs, leading to government efforts to strengthen cost controls and/or raise additional revenue to compensate
Increasing government control over healthcare	Enabled by developments in information and communications technologies
More patient-centred healthcare	Improving healthcare means an increasing proportion of patients with chronic conditions as opposed to acute diseases, which creates a more numerous and durable constituency for patient advocacy groups such as AIDS activists, thus strengthening the political resources of patients relative to other groups such as doctors
More business-friendly policies in relation to manufacturers of pharmaceuticals and medical devices	Increasing economic significance of the healthcare technology sector

Of these perhaps the most interesting is the likelihood that pressure will increase on governments to legalize human cloning and inheritable genetic modification as the relevant medical techniques become safer and more reliable, as such moves would have far-reaching effects on human societies. Society would also change significantly if the increasing pressure to make new psychotropic drugs legal, or keep them legal, results in their use for work and recreation becoming normal.

Sadly for governments the electoral benefits they would expect as a result of developments in healthcare technology improving healthcare outcomes are offset by the negative effects of the financial problems created by the tendency of healthcare technology costs to rise.

4
Military Technology

Introduction

In this chapter we look at three types of developments in military technology relating to Europe that we can be reasonably certain will continue for the next 20 years or so: innovations in military technology as such, the spread of weapons of mass destruction (WMDs), and the intensification of computer warfare or cyberwarfare. Most of the various implications of these developments for public policy can be grouped together as different aspects of a broader policy trend towards greater assertiveness of state power.

Although the focus of this analysis is on West European countries, in considering trends in military technology it is necessary to place these countries in the context of their alliance with the US, which since the end of the Cold War is generally considered to have a clear edge in terms of military technology over all other countries (CIA 2000: 9, 35). For this reason Western defence thinking since the dissolution of the Soviet Union has tended to concentrate on military action against less technologically sophisticated countries and against non-state groups such as Al Qaeda. The analysis in this chapter assumes that most EU Member States will remain part of a Western military alliance that will remain far more technologically sophisticated that any possible opponent(s) for at least the next 20 years. It begins by looking at recent developments in conventional military technology and their policy implications, then goes on to consider the spread of WMDs and the intensification of cyberwarfare and what these developments are likely to mean for the direction of public policy.

Improvements in military technology

Military advantage is in large part a function of technological sophistication, and over the past couple of centuries warfare has been transformed by technological innovations such as the development of machine guns, railways, wireless communication, tanks, submarines, aircraft, missiles, electronics, computers and nuclear weapons. Technological innovation in this area is currently advancing on a number of fronts, as shown in Table 4.1.

It is widely held among defence experts and the military that the extensive use of computers, satellite-based communications systems, stealth technologies, precision guided munitions and other technologically dense weapons constitutes the latest revolution in military affairs as the attrition-based mass destruction warfighting paradigm epitomized by the two World Wars is replaced by what has variously been labelled 'precision warfare', 'cyberwar', 'information warfare' and 'third wave warfare'. The argument is that from the 1970s increased use of microelectronics, precision munitions, stealth technology, near real-time sensing capabilities and more advanced command, control, communications, computing and intelligence (C^4I) have generated quantum improvements in the ability to grasp the battlefield ('visibility'), destroy or incapacitate the enemy ('lethality') and respond to battlefield developments ('agility'). As a consequence there is now more stress on 'non-linear operations', whereby the set-piece battles along a continuous front line of the past are replaced by high-tempo combat operations conducted simultaneously against targets throughout the battlefield, especially critical logistical and C^4I infrastructures, with the object of paralysing enemy forces (Latham 1999). A former US Chief of Staff summarized the likely battlefield effects of current and likely future improvements in military technology as follows. First, improvements in the ability to deliver long-range lethal fire accompanied by increased dispersion of individuals and units and greater mobility. This places an increased premium on quick demand decisions, coordination of movements and unit cohesion. Second, greater volume and precision of fire. Third, increased integration of reconnaissance and intelligence gathering systems with command and control, fire delivery and manoeuvre capabilities. Fourth, increased ability of smaller units to create decisive effects due to better weaponry combined with the greater speed at which they are able to acquire targets, manoeuvre, employ fires and relocate. Finally, an increase in commanders' capacity to detect the enemy at long range due to advanced technological and human intelligence and better resolution of information gathered, plus near real-time dissemination of the data to the proper levels of land forces, and greater invisibility to the enemy as a consequence of developments in holography, virtual reality, the use of microelectromagnetic systems, nanotechnology, televideo and other information networks (Sullivan and Dubik 1995). This revolution in military affairs also applies to airpower: the US in particular can now carry out much more precise strikes than ever before all over the world, and the increasing accuracy of these strikes means that the destructive power of bombs and missiles does not have to be as great, so that targets can be destroyed with much less collateral damage and casualties than was previously possible (Garden 2002).

The military importance of this shift in military technology and tactics seemed to be demonstrated by the speed with which the 1991 Gulf War was

Table 4.1 Developments in military technology

Type	Examples
ICT-related	Better precision guided weapons
	Intelligent weapons such as intelligent minefields
	Improvements in electronic warfare such as better methods of attacking military and civilian computer systems
	Sensors capable of operating despite countermeasures, for example airborne nanosensors and sensors mounted on mobile microrobots that can penetrate cover
	Improved sensor management via artificial-intelligence algorithms that can help optimize and reconcile sensor coverage
	Jam-resistant communications and navigation
	Increases in computing power to develop capabilities such as the fusion in real time of multi-sensor information to enable high assurance recognition of hostile targets, and quantum cryptography, which offers the prospect of perfectly secure communication
	The use of artificial intelligence to give military devices the ability to gather information and, acting autonomously, to make intelligent judgements, including judgements of risk. This has implications for areas such as military intelligence, surveillance, target acquisition and reconnaissance, and support for military decision-making. It may also mean that in certain circumstances it might be possible to remove human personnel from the front line
	Bionics: electronic-brain links designed to improve the ability of the brain to handle, perceive or view data via implanted equipment or links with surface or remote equipment
Other	Better armour and protection systems
	Better stealth weapons
	Better unmanned aerial vehicles
	Arsenal ships with hundreds of cruise missiles to supplement or replace aircraft carriers
	Militarization of space to improve command, control and intelligence capabilities and to enable global strike and missile defence using directed-energy weapons ranging from electronic jammers to lasers, as well as kinetic-energy weapons and space-based conventional weapons
	Better defences against biological and chemical attacks and more sophisticated biological warfare capabilities, as a result of developments in biotechnology
	New systems of propulsion and power generation, such as electric and solar power, leading to devices such as micro unmanned airborne vehicles
	The use of nanotechnology in sensors, information-processing and communications, and to create clothing, weapons and personal communications that automatically adapt to changing condition, as well as clouds of nanotechnology particles designed to disrupt electronic systems and nano-robots designed for medical use or reconnaissance

Sources: Stix 1995, Latham 1999, Foster and Welch 2000, DERA 2001, MOD 2001, Cohen 2002: 250–1, Lewis 2004: 5, Preston *et al.* 2002: xvi–xix.

won, the success of air strikes in obtaining Serb withdrawal from Kosovo in 1999 (Cohen 2002: 243, Garden 2002: 152–3), and the success of the US invasion of Iraq in 2003.

On the other hand it is unclear to what extent technological developments will in fact make the battlefield transparent, given the difficulties of collating and interpreting the enormous volume of information (data overload), not to mention countermeasures such as concealment and deception, while dependence on technologically sophisticated information and communication systems means that associated military forces would be seriously weakened if these systems were successfully attacked and disrupted (Cohen 1996, DERA 2001). It is unclear to what extent the quick victories in recent wars can be attributed to the new information warfare. Biddle, for example, argues that the speed of victory in the 1991 Gulf War was in large part a result of military errors by Iraqi forces that rendered them vulnerable to punishment by the new weaponry, and that NATO's 1999 air campaign over Kosovo demonstrated yet again that against covered, concealed targets even precise strike technology can inflict little real damage (Robertson 2001: 79, Biddle 2002: 106–10, Garden 2002). Finally, adversaries may avoid direct engagement with US and allied forces in favour of employing unconventional strategies and tactics to negate their technological advantage, such as suicide bombing. Other alternative strategies include attempting to dissuade the use of force by exploiting the sensitivity of public opinion in Western countries to casualties, for example by targeting civilians, siting military targets in civilian areas, and undertaking offensive information operations; launching nuclear, biological or chemical attacks; disrupting communications, transportation, financial transactions, energy networks and/or computer networks via computer warfare; and attacking military capabilities through electronic warfare, psychological operations, the use of new technologies such as directed energy weapons or electromagnetic pulse weapons, and the use of denial and deception techniques (CIA 2000: 35–6, DERA 2001).

Implications

Within each country a number of actors play a role in defence policy-making (see Table 4.2). The vital nature of national defence means that presidents and prime ministers are prominent as well as defence and foreign ministers, their departments and the armed services. Foreign governments such as the US government and other NATO allies are also important, as are defence industry lobbyists.

Developments in military technology are likely to increase pressure on public policy to take a more interventionist foreign policy stance, economize on the purchase of major weapon systems, reduce or erase the traditional boundaries between the military services, and increase the use of surveillance by police and internal security services.

Table 4.2   Generic defence policy network

Type of policy actor	Specific policy actor
Political executives and associated parties	Chief executives Foreign minister Defence minister Finance minister
Non-government politicians	Parliamentary committees relating to foreign affairs, defence, finance Foreign governments, especially the US government and other European governments European Commission
Civil servants and military	Foreign, defence and finance ministries Armed forces: army, navy, air force Security and intelligence organizations NATO and EU officials
Business	Defence contractors
Interest groups/non-government organizations	Returned servicemen Antiwar groups
Media	Owners, editors, and foreign and defence correspondents
Non-government experts	Academics, think tanks
Electorate	Voters

More interventionist foreign policy

It is widely believed that Western electorates will only support the use of force abroad if it promises quick victories with few or no casualties and minimum destructiveness (Goure 1993, DERA 2001, Robertson 2001: 73). Because precision warfare promises exactly this, the potential electoral costs of foreign intervention are reduced. This would be even more the case to the extent that, in the future, technology can replace soldiers on the front line. Another way of putting this is to say that the credibility of the arguments of foreign policy hawks is enhanced by the deployment of systems designed to prosecute precision warfare. Other things being equal, this means more pressure for foreign and defence policy to take a more interventionist course than previously.

Having said this, history shows that in the past technological superiority has in general constituted but a fleeting advantage, and the effectiveness of many new weapon systems has often been negated by single operational or tactical changes (Goure 1993, CIA 2000: 38). If an enemy succeeds in disrupting the new computerized intelligence, command and control systems of Western armed forces, for example, military intervention may not result in victory, and even if it does this may be at the cost of numerous casualties. Such a disaster need only happen once for the credibility of hawks to be weakened substantially, as it was following the Vietnam War. Until and unless this happens, however, and bearing in mind the magnitude of Western military and technological superiority, the progressive development of precision warfare techniques implies increasing pressure for more proactive and interventionist foreign and defence policies.

Measures to economize on the purchase of major weapon systems

The increasingly high costs of developing and deploying new military technology, compounded by more rapid obsolescence, puts structural pressure on the defence budget to expand. To equip most or all soldiers with equipment such as thermal weapon imagery and computers, for example, would be extremely expensive (DERA 2001, Robertson 2001: 75–6). Although world and West European military spending and the arms trade have fluctuated since 1989 (US Department of State 2003, SIPRI 2004 chapters 10, 11), unit production costs of major weapon systems such as combat aircraft are estimated to have risen steadily by about 10 per cent per year in real terms since the end of World War II (Kirkpatrick 2004: 261–3).

This weakens the position of the armed services in pressing for the purchase of new weapon systems because governments incur electoral risk if they have to finance increased spending in this area. Although state revenue rises automatically to the extent that economic growth and high rates of employment expand the tax base, governments may not be so lucky. Both raising taxes and cutting spending elsewhere in defence or in other policy areas to compensate are likely to be unpopular, not least because many people are directly or indirectly economically dependent on the military and associated defence industries (Hartley 2003: 109).

Other things being equal this means that as time goes on countries can be expected to economize on the purchase of major weapon systems. There are a number of ways in which this can be done, although each has its drawbacks. Governments may purchase fewer weapon systems at a time, for example fewer combat aircraft per order, as a number of countries have been doing, although this risks military disaster if war breaks out. They may move to slow the weapon system replacement cycle so that costs are incurred less frequently, although this tends to incur high maintenance costs on old equipment and risks it being outclassed by later systems. Weapon systems may be chosen that are capable of performing several roles despite the fact that consequent design compromises risk compromising their capability in one or more of these roles. Another possibility is to adopt a policy of incremental acquisition whereby a weapon system is brought into service with a limited capability that is then progressively upgraded over time, although this may face technical difficulties and result in spreading the cost of the project rather than reducing it. Finally, governments may choose to share development costs with other countries, as is the case with the current Eurofighter project in Europe, for example, although this may result in delays as collaborating nations disagree on how things should be done (Kirkpatrick 2004: 270–1, Airforce Technology 2005). By making national governments more dependent on the decisions of foreign governments, furthermore, international cooperation in weapon procurement also means that national governments lose a certain amount of authority over defence policy-making to joint decisions with allies, which may result in different policies being implemented than would otherwise be the case.

Increased integration between the armed services

To be used most effectively, innovations in military technology need to be accompanied by matching changes in military doctrine, culture and structures (DERA 2001). While functional need does not necessarily guarantee an appropriate response, it seems reasonable to expect that developments in military technology will lead at least some military strategists to push for these matching changes. Thus one consequence of using new technology to develop more integrated warfighting strategies is likely to be pressure to move away from the traditional division of military forces into armies, navies and air forces towards joint forces in which land, air and sea power is integrated (Cohen 1996).

Increased surveillance

Improvements in surveillance technology made under military auspices have the side-effect of making it cheaper, easier and more profitable for others to use surveillance more extensively. Given that one would expect organizations such as police and internal security services to want to take advantage of this, the likely consequence is that they and others, such as private security firms, are likely to press harder for public policy to become more permissive in this respect in order to enable them to expand their use of surveillance.

Proliferation of weapons of mass destruction

As time goes on it is reasonable to expect that improvements in military technology will continue to spread beyond the Western alliance to other states and to non-state organizations such as armed religious groups and criminals. Export and control regimes and sanctions are thought to be becoming less effective due to diffusion of technology, more porous borders and the dependence of arms manufacturers on foreign sales. IT-driven globalization is expected to significantly increase interaction among terrorists, narcotraffickers, weapons proliferators and organized criminals, giving them better access to information, technology, finance, and deception and denial techniques. This facilitates the proliferation of WMDs and their means of delivery (CIA 2000).

For adversaries of Western forces, WMDs have the advantage of undermining the technologically-based superior conventional capabilities of Western forces, and could be used to deter allied military action as well as in direct attacks on military forces or civilian populations. Biological weapons in particular are seen as the 'poor man's atom bomb' (Davis and Gray 2002: 269, 281). Table 4.3 sets out some of the main characteristics of the principal WMDs.

Table 4.3   Weapons of mass destruction

Type	Characteristics
Nuclear weapons	Atomic bombs use nuclear fission to release explosive energy of up to 50 kT, and up to 500 kT when boosted with fusion material (the bomb that destroyed Nagasaki in 1945 was about 20 kT). Thermonuclear or hydrogen bombs use nuclear fusion and there is no limit to their potential explosive power. Both can be delivered via aircraft bombs, artillery shells, depth charges, torpedoes, land mines, cruise missiles, and ballistic and other missiles.
	The US and Russia are each estimated to possess about 10,000 nuclear weapons, China 400, France 350 and Britain 185. Israel is suspected of having over 200, India over 60, and Pakistan between 24 and 48. Russia has dramatically reduced its nuclear weapons and has taken control of all nuclear weapons stationed in other former Soviet republics. The 2002 Treaty of Moscow committed the US and Russia to reduce their strategic nuclear arsenals to between 1,700 and 2,200 weapons each by 2012, although the US intends to achieve this simply by moving them to a reserve stockpile. Tactical and reserve weapons are not covered by either the START or Moscow treaties, and the Moscow Treaty expires in 2012.
Biological weapons	These are based on bacteria such as anthrax and plague, toxins such as botulinum toxin and ricin, viruses such as Ebola and smallpox, and rickettsiae. Infection can occur via inhalation, ingestion or absorption through the skin. Anthrax is a preferred agent because it is highly lethal, easily produced in large quantities at low cost, can be stored for a long time as a dry powder, and is relatively easy to disperse as an aerosol. Its symptoms are fever, shock, skin pustules, difficulty in breathing, tachycardia, cyanosis and death in 90 per cent of cases if not treated. Genetic engineering can produce biological agents that are more resistant to vaccines and antibiotics, have a higher epidemicity or infectivity, can survive in harsher environments and are more difficult to detect and identify. It will also become possible to target biological weapons on people with a particular genetic identity.
	The Biological Weapons Convention, which by 2002 had been ratified by 145 countries, bans the development, production and stockpiling of biological and toxin weapons and requires the destruction of existing agents, weapons, equipment and means of delivery. The actual use of biological weapons is prohibited by the 1925 Geneva Protocol. However there is no provision for checking

(*Continued*)

Table 4.3   (Continued)

Type	Characteristics
	compliance, and biological agents and toxins that can be described as being for peaceful purposes are not banned. Nor is research. At the beginning of the 21st century it was thought that biological weapons were already held by Iraq, Iran, Syria, Libya, China, North Korea, Russia, Israel and Taiwan.
Chemical weapons	Nerve agents such as sarin attack the nervous system directly and cause convulsions, cessation of breathing, vomiting, paralysis and death within minutes. Blood agents such as hydrogen cyanide attack the ability of blood to process oxygen and cause dizziness, weakness, anxiety, loss of consciousness, convulsions, cessation of breathing, paralysis and death within minutes. Blister agents such as mustard gas attack the epidermis, mucous membranes and tissues, causing large blisters and damage to eyes, airways and internal organs. Pulmonary or choking agents such as phosgene and chlorine attack the respiratory system causing progressive shortness of breath, severe hacking cough and rapid fluid loss. Death occurs when the lungs fill with fluid and the victim drowns. Mental incapacitants such as BZ disorient the mind, producing hallucinations and irrational behaviour.
	The Chemical Weapons Convention, which by 2002 had been ratified by 145 countries, bans the development, production, acquisition, transfer, stockpiling and use of chemical weapons. Although it is policed by inspectors, it also allows research into, and production of, chemical warfare agents for defensive purposes.

Sources: Schwartz 1998, Sidell and Patrick 1998, Garrett 2001, MOD 2001 Chapter 1: 2, US Department of Defense 2001, Davis and Gray 2002: 257, 277–8, Barnaby 2003: 16–23, 43, 55, 100–2, 163–5, CDI 2003, BTWC 2004.

The nature of the threat

Nuclear weapons

Over the next few decades more and more non-nuclear states are likely to develop and deploy nuclear weapons. Up to now most potential nuclear states have chosen not to do so but instead to sign up to the 1970 Nuclear Non-Proliferation Treaty, which bans the acquisition and transfer of nuclear weapons (US Department of State, undated). However about two dozen such countries have research reactors with sufficient highly enriched uranium to build at least one nuclear bomb (Allison 2004).

Terrorists are also likely to obtain the capacity to go nuclear. The simplest way to do this would be to make a so-called 'dirty bomb' by wrapping radioactive waste in conventional explosives so that detonation spreads radioactivity over a wide area. As there is a lot of radioactive material about, it seems likely that sooner or later one or more terrorist groups will obtain the capacity to produce and use dirty bombs. Radioactive waste is held at commercial nuclear power plants all over the world and is often transported in large quantities over long distances. Security in Russia is especially poor. It is reported that over the past decade there have been over 175 instances of terrorists trying to obtain or smuggle radioactive material, and business and research facilities in the US alone have misplaced almost 1500 pieces of equipment containing radioactive materials over the past few years. It is also reported that many portable nuclear generators were abandoned in the former Soviet Union when the Cold War ended. In 1996 Islamic rebels from Chechnya planted a dirty bomb in a Moscow park but did not detonate it, apparently to demonstrate Russia's vulnerability, and it appears that at least until recently Al Qaeda was trying to build a dirty bomb (Blair 2001: 1–2, Burgess 2003).

An attack on a nuclear power plant using heavy munitions or a commercial jet could also cause heavy casualties through spreading radiological contamination if it caused a meltdown of the reactor core similar to Chernobyl or the dispersal of spent fuel waste kept on site (Blair 2001: 2, Burgess 2002, Barnaby 2003: 157–61).

Even more serious is the possibility of terrorists obtaining and using an actual atomic bomb. As it is relatively easy to fabricate a workable atomic bomb once the ingredients are obtained, but relatively difficult to produce plutonium or highly-enriched uranium, the main risk appears to come from the possibility of terrorists obtaining diverted fissile material or a fully-fledged atomic bomb. It might be possible for terrorists to obtain a small tactical nuclear weapon that could be transported in the boot of a car, such as nuclear artillery shells or nuclear landmines, possibly from Russia, as it is not clear that all Russian nuclear weapons are accounted for. Once a bomb was obtained, it could be sent anywhere in a shipping container. Russia's so-called 'suitcase bombs', for example, are thought to weigh about 60 pounds and be the size of a small refrigerator, and it is possible that Russia may have built even smaller bombs similar to the attaché-case size bomb thought to have been built by the US in the late 1970s (Blair 2001, Newhouse 2002: 45–7).

If just fissile material was obtained, a crude atomic bomb based on highly-enriched uranium could be designed and fabricated by just two or three people with appropriate skills, and an explosion equivalent to 100 tonnes of TNT (the largest conventional bombs have explosive powers of around 10 tonnes of TNT) could well be obtained simply by obtaining a critical mass of highly enriched uranium and dropping one half onto the other half. Such a device could be transported and detonated in a small van. As most highly enriched uranium is held by the military, terrorists might find it easier to obtain nuclear material from one of the 438 nuclear reactors existent today by diverting civil mixed-oxide (MOX) from the growing trade in nuclear fuel. MOX consists of a mix of plutonium oxide and uranium oxide from which the plutonium oxide could be relatively easily removed by chemical means and used to fabricate a weapon (Barnaby 2003: 36, 68, 111–17). Alternatively, terrorists might obtain fissile material either from Russia, where there is thought to be at least 1,000 tons of highly enriched uranium and 150 tons of plutonium scattered around, much of it in badly secured storage sites, or from Pakistan, where Islamic radicals have links to the government and military (Blair 2001, Newhouse 2002: 46).

Finally, terrorists might be able to launch one or more US or Russian nuclear weapons by hacking into missile launch-control systems to send false orders or give the impression of an incoming attack. False alarms are a particular problem for the deteriorating Russian warning system (Mintz 2002, Newhouse 2002: 48–9).

Biological weapons

Biological agents can be delivered in aerosol form by ballistic and cruise missiles, battlefield rocket and artillery shells, spray tanks mounted on aircraft, unmanned aerial vehicles, land vehicles and ships, and clandestine portable devices. They can also be dispersed in food or water (MOD 2001 chapter 1: 1, Davis and Gray 2002: 277–8). A study by the Office of Technology Assessment concluded that a single airplane delivering 100 kg of anthrax spores over Washington DC could kill up to three million people (OTA 1993: 54). Such an attack would be extremely difficult to guard against, and even a minor biological attack could create panic that could impact on the economy by means such as by causing a stock market crash (Garrett 2001).

Biological agents are cheaper to produce than nuclear and chemical material because they reproduce themselves, and production is easy to disguise because production facilities, equipment and staff are very similar to those used to produce antibiotics and vaccines. Biological weapons can be produced from scratch by acquiring a biological agent from soil, contaminated food or the corpses of animals that have died from the disease, then isolating it and culturing it in facilities that are relatively cheap and unsophisticated. Terrorists could also acquire them by theft or from a sympathizer working in a production facility. And it is clear that terrorists are interested, as in the past terrorist groups have been found in possession of typhoid bacteria, botulinium toxin, anthrax and – by order from a legitimate supplier – bubonic plague (Barnaby 2003: 48–53, 119–24).

On the other hand, because biological agents are living organisms, they are fragile and can be difficult to deliver. Biological agents can be killed by chlorine in the water supply, for example, and use with explosives tends to destroy all but one to two per cent of the agent (Donovan 2001: 6).

Chemical weapons

Chemical agents are less of a threat to populations than biological agents because those who are affected cannot infect others, but they act more quickly because they do not have an incubation period. They can be spread using shells, mines, missiles, bombs or spray. Volatile agents vaporize on dissemination and are carried on the wind, while persistent agents remain in liquid state and can contaminate areas for long periods. However effective delivery is not easy, as chemical agents can be dispersed or otherwise rendered harmless by natural phenomena such as temperature, sunlight, wind and moisture (Sidell and Patrick 1998, Donovan 2001: 6, MOD 2001 chapter 1: 2).

On the other hand, chemical weapons are easier to produce than either nuclear or biological weapons, as the chemicals used to produce nerve agents, for example, are widely available from legitimate suppliers, no special equipment is required for their production, and the details of their preparation are described in the open literature. They can also be made in plants very similar to those used to produce herbicides (Barnaby 2003: 63, 84, 119).

Is WMD proliferation likely to continue?

Over the next few years more and more states will acquire the technical capacity to develop WMDs, especially biological and chemical weapons, which can be produced at low cost compared to nuclear weapons and are difficult to detect and control because their production can be concealed and many of their components and the equipment needed to produce them also have legitimate uses (Davis and Gray 2002: 278, 281). In 1999 the British military considered that around 20 countries either possessed or were interested in possessing biological or chemical weapons and their means of delivery (MOD 1999 chapter 2).

It is also clear that terrorist groups are attempting to acquire WMDs. A survey of open-source material identified 23 incidents involving use, possession, attempted acquisition, plots and threats of chemical, biological, radiological or nuclear (CBRN) materials in 2002, excluding hoaxes, compared to 25 in 2001, 49 in 2000 and 27 in 1999. Reported incidents include the putative theft of radiological material by Chechen rebels, a plot by the Real IRA to steal plutonium from the Sellafield nuclear power plant in Britain, an attempted acquisition of chemicals by Hamas for use against Israel, and a plot by Al Qaeda to detonate a dirty bomb in the US. CBRN agents were actually used on six occasions, compared with 14 in 2001 and 36 in 2000. The only deaths occurred in Zimbabwe, where seven people were killed and 47 injured in a poisoning incident involving a religious sect (Turnbull and Abhayaratne 2003). In August 2003 the deputy director of the organization that repairs Russian nuclear icebreakers and submarines was arrested for trying to smuggle or steal nuclear material or weapons. It is thought that more than 100 potential weapons in a dozen countries remain in circumstances that leave them vulnerable to theft (Allison 2004: 2–3).

From the point of view of terrorists, chemical and biological weapons are arguably more cost-effective than nuclear weapons: nuclear weapons cause much more property damage and have better target control, but are much more difficult to procure and manufacture and have a higher detection risk (Shubik 1997: 410). However they may hesitate to use biological weapons due to the possibility that people infected with the biological agent might travel to the country of the terrorists' origin during the incubation period before symptoms appear and spread the disease there – although this consideration might not stop millennial groups.

If we accept that more and more states and terrorist groups are likely to acquire WMDs, it follows, other things being equal, that the chances of their use against European countries and/or their nationals and interests abroad will increase. It is therefore reasonable to expect that sooner or later an attack using WMDs will occur, although the chances of a really devastating attack with an atomic bomb or biological agent would appear to remain small. Such an attack would not be expected to come from sovereign states, because this would invite massive retaliation by NATO forces, although the possibility of covert attacks cannot be ruled out. Instead terrorist groups appear to be the more likely source of any attacks, for example religious groups that believe that the end of the world is at hand. It was, after all, the Japanese millenarian cult Aum Shrinrikyo that first used chemical weapons (sarin) in Tokyo in 1995, an attack that killed 12 people and injured about 5,500 (Donovan 2001: 5–6, Kiras 2002: 226). Islamic groups such as Al Qaeda and Hizbollah are also thought to be interested, along with Christian white supremacists (Barnaby 2003: 127–36).

Putting this together, the most likely scenario is that terrorists detonate a dirty bomb, attack a nuclear facility to spread radioactivity, or use chemical weapons. We have already seen that all of these types of attacks have either been considered or actually carried out in the past.

Implications

To the extent that European policy actors conclude that continuing proliferation of WMDs is making their use against European countries and their interests more likely, they will seek greater protection from this possibility by taking countermeasures. If and when actual attacks occur, we would expect more drastic countermeasures. More precisely, policy actors' (and electorates') perceptions of the costs and benefits of current and possible future policies relating directly and indirectly to WMDs change as a direct result of threatened or actual WMD attacks. This adds to the credibility of those who want the countermeasures anyway, perhaps for other reasons. Those who want greater use of surveillance to fight crime, for instance, will find a more receptive audience among policy-makers if fear of WMDs is high, while those concerned about privacy will find it more difficult to have their ideas accepted.

As the attack on the World Trade Centre in 2001 has focused attention on the issue of attacks using WMDs, to see what governments are likely to do in response to this threat it is useful to look at the EU Strategy Against Proliferation of Weapons of Mass Destruction adopted by the European Council in December 2003 and the US National Strategy to Combat Weapons of Mass Destruction, which takes counter-proliferation a few steps further (European Council 2003, White House 2002). Although formally these list policy changes that have already taken place, many of the measures have not (yet) been put into effect, or are in the early stages of implementation. In real terms, that is, many of these policy changes have not yet taken place.

The policy shifts foreshadowed in these documents can be divided into six main types: increased diplomatic efforts to counter WMD proliferation, better security for WMD-related materials, equipment and expertise, improved civil defence, improved control of illegal trafficking, increased efforts to promote international and regional stability, and offensive action against possible users of WMDs.

Increased diplomatic efforts to counter WMD proliferation

This means devoting more bilateral diplomatic attention to dissuading countries from developing WMDs using both positive incentives, such as preferential trade deals and bilateral aid, and, if necessary, sanctions such as arms or trade embargoes.

It also means working for the universalization and strengthening of the main treaties, agreements and verification arrangements on disarmament and non-proliferation such as the Nuclear Non-Proliferation Treaty, International Atomic Energy Agency safeguard agreements, Biological and Toxin Weapons Convention, Chemical Weapons Convention, and coordinated export controls designed to prevent the supply of biological agents, chemicals and associated dual use technologies and equipment (Australia Group, Missile Technology Control Regime, Wassenaar Arrangement, and UN, OSCE and EU arms embargoes).

On some issues it means promotion of new agreements. Specific EU proposals include prohibiting the production of fissile material for nuclear weapons, introducing universal and binding bans on biological and chemical weapons, implementing more intrusive verification and inspection regimes, strengthening export control policies and practices within the EU and beyond, and further restricting the movement of material and expertise relevant to the construction and use of WMDs such as nuclear and nuclear-related items and technology and dual-use technologies. Another element is maintenance of an extensive set of non-proliferation and threat reduction assistance programmes in relation to Russia and other former Soviet states to address the threat posed by the large quantities of Soviet-legacy WMD and missile-related expertise and materials.

One implication of this strengthening of multilateral agreements and regimes in relation to WMDs is further restrictions on the ability of national governments to make autonomous decisions in areas such as export controls, which may result in different policies being put in place than would otherwise have been the case.

Better security for WMD-related materials, equipment and
expertise within the EU

This includes establishing better physical protection for nuclear materials and facilities, strengthening EU and national legislation and control over pathogenic microorganisms and toxins, and improving cooperation between public health, occupational health and safety, and non-proliferation structures. Another possible move here, although not one (yet) adopted by the EU, would be to discontinue reprocessing of spent nuclear fuel to recover the plutonium (Barnaby 2003: 138). A successful attack on a nuclear power plant would be likely to lead to more drastic measures such as reducing or discontinuing the use of nuclear power, or radically altering the location and design of nuclear power plants. One means of preventing terrorists from tricking nuclear powers into launching their own weapons, for example by hacking into command systems, would be to de-alert strategic missiles by separating their warheads from launchers (Newhouse 2002: 49).

Improved identification, control and interception of illegal trafficking

Proposed measures here include the establishment of common EU policies on criminal sanctions for the illegal export, brokering and smuggling of WMD-related material, improved EU and international controls on the transit and transhipment of sensitive materials, and more effective interdiction of the movement of WMD materials, technology and expertise by the military, intelligence, technical and law enforcement communities, including more extensive and intrusive border controls at ports and airports. These controls would be made even more stringent in the event of a WMD or its components being smuggled into a country and used for a successful attack, and could ultimately reduce levels of global trade and travel.

Improved civil defence

WMD consequence management, as it is referred to by the US National Strategy, consists of providing training, planning and other assistance to state/regional and local governments to deal with the medical and other consequences of an attack using WMDs. This may result in substantial changes in what sub-national levels of government are expected to do and how they do it. Better civil defence also implies more surveillance in order to detect attacks as soon as possible, such as monitoring of the air over cities, plus more sharing of data nationally and internationally. Improvements in civil defence will be facilitated by technological advances such as the recent development of a new anthrax vaccine (Office of the Press Secretary 2004).

Increased efforts to promote a more stable international and regional environment

According to the EU Strategy it is important to try to reduce the desire of states and non-state groups to acquire WMDs by means such as fostering regional security arrangements, arms control and disarmament processes. It would also help if the US and European countries addressed at least some of the grievances that increase support for anti-Western states and non-state groups. However it is noticeable that the US National Strategy does not mention this point. One reason appears to be a concern not to give in to terrorism, or to be seen to be giving in: it is important that threatening or using WMDs is not rewarded. Another is that to address these grievances may well involve economic or other losses for the West, such as giving up control of Middle East oil, the life-blood of Western economies, or breaking with Israel. A further reason is the belief, at least on the part of some, that it is impossible to address the root causes of Islamic terrorism, the major perceived threat at present, because it is America and the West as such that is hated (Pillar 2001: 32).

Although, logically, successful attacks using WMDs should strengthen incentives to try to remove the root causes of their acquisition and use, it is clear from experience that anger, retaliation and other draconian measures are much more likely responses. One can see how things might turn out in miniature by looking at Israeli measures against Palestinian attacks, which include not only physical barriers but also draconian restrictions on movement, targeted assassinations and massive retaliation for any bombings.

Offensive action against possible users of WMDs

The US National Strategy goes further than its EU counterpart in foreshadowing offensive action to combat the construction and use of WMDs. Elements here include improving intelligence capabilities, deterrence via the threat to use overwhelming force (including 'all our options') in response to any use of WMDs against the US or its allies, measures to detect and destroy WMD assets before they are used, active defences to disrupt, disable or destroy WMDs en route, and effective retaliation to eliminate future threats. While deterrence is hardly a new policy, the provision for the detection and destruction of WMD assets *before* they are used means reserving the option of making pre-emptive strikes, an option that has already been implemented in the case of the invasion of Iraq in 2003. This is a very aggressive policy stance, and one that is shared by some European countries, such as Britain, at least up to a point.

In this connection one measure proposed by the US is the construction of a missile defence system to defend not only the US but also its allies against incoming ballistic missiles with WMD payloads using interceptor missiles and other defences such as lasers. The aim here is to supplement the deterrent threat of retaliation using nuclear weapons on the rationale that the chief nuclear threat to the West is no longer a massive Soviet nuclear strike but rather a few weapons launched by so-called rogue states (US Department of Defense 2001, Davis and Gray 2002: 270–1, Office of the Press Secretary 2003).

One problem with this reasoning, however, is that nuclear weapons and other WMDs need not be delivered via ballistic missiles, which among other things are very expensive. Alternative means of delivery include aircraft, ship-launched cruise missiles and smuggling through ports. Cruise missiles in particular are thought to be more accurate, easier to obtain or produce and better-suited than ballistic missiles for delivering chemical and biological weapons. Still, at the turn of the century about 36 countries were thought to possess ballistic missiles, including five with intercontinental ballistic missiles, while fourteen are producing them of which three (China, North Korea and the US) export them. Several other countries are thought capable of producing them (Betts 1998, Tanks 2000: 7, Newhouse 2002: 44, Barnaby 2003: 151–2). It is therefore at least possible that eventually a terrorist group will manage to acquire a ballistic missile or two. Another problem is that a space-based missile defence system could be destabilizing, as it threatens the capacity of China and Russia to deter the US from launching a pre-emptive nuclear first strike because a missile defence system might be able to protect the US from a retaliatory strike by the relatively few enemy nuclear weapons that escaped the first strike. And by 2015 a number of non-Western nations are expected to possess satellite capabilities that will enable them to target not only space assets such as weaponry but also Western forces and their deployments on the ground and to degrade these space assets via attacks on their ground facilities, electronic warfare such as signal jamming, directed-energy weapons such as low-power lasers, and denial and deception (Lewis 2004: 6, CIA 2000: 39–40).

Increased powers for police and security services

One of the most striking aspects of Western responses to 9/11 has been the introduction or widening of police powers to imprison people (suspected terrorists) indefinitely without trial and, if media reports are to be believed, the use of torture in interrogation on the rationale that the consequences of failing to obtain information that could stop an attack using WMDs are so grave that all measures to obtain such information are justified. This is perhaps the most worrying response to 9/11 and the threat of WMDs because it means, literally, the introduction of a police state – a democratic police state, to be sure, but still a state in which the police can come and take people away without legal recourse. It is suspected terrorists who are the targets today, but it might be suspected violent animal liberationists tomorrow, or anti-abortionists thought likely to attack abortion clinics, or people with suspected criminal tendencies. Or you or me.

Intensification of cyberwarfare

Cyberwarfare consists of operations designed to monitor, steal, alter, disrupt, deny, degrade or destroy information resident in computers, operations to shut down or take control of computers and their operations, and operations to prevent, deter, defend, mitigate and recover from such attacks (Department of

Defense, undated, Libicki 1995 chapter 7). Cyber attacks are an obvious way for states and groups which are hostile to the West, but unable to compete in terms of conventional military technology, to mount offensive operations, especially as the source of such attacks can be disguised, making it difficult if not impossible for the US and its allies to retaliate effectively (Vatis 2001: 13). Table 4.4 lists ways in which computers and computer systems can be attacked.

Effects of an attack may include denial-of-service, unauthorized use or misuse of computing systems, and loss, alteration and/or compromise of data or software, which can result in financial loss, loss or endangerment of human life, loss of trust in computer systems, and loss of public confidence (CERT

Table 4.4 Examples of types of cyberattack

Type	Details
Virus	A piece of computer code written with the intention of replicating itself and spread by being attached to (hidden in) a host programme that itself is transferred from computer to computer, such as an email attachment; may damage hardware, software or information
Worm	A type of virus that replicates itself from machine to machine across network connections without user action by taking control of features on computers that can transport files or information, often congesting the network as it spreads
Trojan horse	An apparently useful programme containing hidden functions that can exploit the privileges of the user running the programme to do things that the programme user did not intend, such as installing back door programmes that allow intruders covert access or infecting computers with viruses
Distributed denial of service attacks	Actions by distributed computers (often including computers already taken over without their owners' knowledge) that prevent any part of another computer system from functioning in accordance with its intended purpose, for example due to being overwhelmed by requests for the IP address, a 32-bit number that identifies each sender or receiver of information sent across the Internet (ping requests)
Back Door	A hole in the security of a computer system deliberately left in place by designers or maintainers, or established by maliciously manipulating a computer system, that enables intruders to enter the computer system at will
Packet sniffer	A programme that captures data from information packets as they travel over the network, such as user names, passwords and proprietary information, that can then be used to launch widespread attacks on systems

Sources: Summers 1997, CERT 2001, Vatis 2001, CERT 2004, Microsoft 2004.

2003: 4). Semantic attacks subtly alter the content of web pages such as news and government sites in order to disseminate false information. Denial-of-service attacks shut down critical communications nodes such as mail servers, government websites, search engines, e-commerce sites and news services. Attacks on domain name servers (DNS), which provide the numerical addresses of the systems on which web servers runs to users seeking to connect to those web servers, can lead to the DNS servers providing incorrect addresses to users, thus directing them without their knowledge to websites that could contain false information while depriving the correct web sites of traffic. Attacks on Internet routers, which ensure that information gets from source to destination, could bring the Internet to a standstill or cause routers to redirect information into Internet 'black holes' (Vatis 2001: 14–17). Attacks can be launched not only from outside computer systems but also by insiders with authorized access, including janitors and contractors (CERT 2003: 65).

Cyber attacks can target both military systems, such as command and control systems, and civilian systems, such as those that control power plants, although military systems are more difficult to attack because they are not designed for public access and generally build in measures such as redundancy and physical isolation for certain critical systems (Libicki 1995 chapter 7). An unanticipated and massive attack on the computers that control critical infrastructure could be devastating, depending on how dependent the infrastructure systems are on information systems and how open these information systems are to outside entry from the Internet. The US government defines critical infrastructures as 'the public and private institutions in the sectors of agriculture, food, water, public health, emergency services, government, defence industrial base, information and telecommunications, energy, transportation, banking and finance, chemical and hazardous materials, and postal and shipping', and points out that the computer networks that make these institutions work control physical objects such as electrical transformers, trains, pipeline pumps, chemical vats and stock markets (White House 2003: vii–viii). While the networks used by banks and financial institutions are protected in having very little external access, the sensors used in electrical infrastructures and water resource management may be vulnerable along with the systems on which oil and gas infrastructures rely. Successful cyber attacks on these could affect numerous economic sectors including manufacturing and transportation (Vatis 2001: 17–18).

Adversaries may also use computers to conduct espionage against governments, research centres and private companies, and to prepare for cyber strikes by mapping information systems, identifying key targets, and inserting back doors and other means of access (White House 2003: viii). Sabotage of computer systems may be used to blind, intimidate, divert or simply confuse an enemy as a precursor to more open and conventional hostilities (Cohen 1996).

It is clear that both states and non-state actors are developing their ability to use cyber attack in offensive operations. By the turn of the century Russia,

China, India and Cuba had already been identified by US analysts as being countries with acknowledged cyberwarfare policies, while North Korea, Libya, Iran, Iraq and Syria were thought to have some capabilities in this area and France, Japan and Germany were also seen as being active (Office of Naval Intelligence 2000). US intelligence officials believe that certain hardware and software imported from China, Russia, France, Israel and India are already infected with devices that can read data or destroy systems (Robinson 2001). It is also likely that the US is already undertaking offensive operations to obtain information and put itself in a position to wreak devastating damage on foreign computer systems if and when hostilities commence.

Non-state groups also appear to be developing their capabilities in this area. It is thought that at one point the IRA planned to use computers to attack power stations around London (Vatis 2001: 12), and in 2002 it was reported that Al Qaeda had put emergency telephone systems, water storage and distribution, and the power grid and power plants, including nuclear power plants, under surveillance, in particular the digital systems that control emergency dispatch systems and industrial controls (Anderson 2002).

And computer systems are vulnerable. A US military exercise in 1997 found that many government and commercial sites were easily attacked and taken down, including the power grids of nine cities and local emergency service systems as well as 36 Pentagon networks, in which insertion of fake orders and news reports succeeded in sowing mistrust in the command-and-control system (Adams 2001, Hildreth 2001: 3–5). Intrusions over a period of years that were first detected in March 1998, and which may have originated in Russia, involved breaking into hundreds of networks used by the Pentagon, US Department of Energy, NASA and defence contractors and stealing thousands of files (Adams 2001, Vatis 2001: 11). Since 1995 US Department of Defense computer systems have been attacked up to 250,000 times per year (Robinson 2002).

Cyber attacks have also been occurring elsewhere. Tensions between India and Pakistan over Kashmir led to increased pro-Pakistan defacements of Indian websites, while sensitive nuclear data was reportedly downloaded from the Bhabha Atomic Research Centre. Israelis and Palestinians have defaced each other's web sites, conducted coordinated distributed denial-of-service attacks and penetrated computer systems, utilizing worms and Trojan horses in their efforts. During the bombing of Kosovo in 2000, all of NATO's approximately 100 servers were attacked and periodically brought to a standstill by hackers suspected of being in the employ of Serbian military forces, using denial-of-service attacks and thousands of emails, many containing viruses. Following a mid-air collision between an American surveillance plane and a Chinese fighter in 2001, 1200 US sites, including those belonging to the White House, US Air Force and Department of Energy, were defaced or subjected to denial-of-service attacks by hacker groups thought to be at least tolerated by the Chinese government (Vatis 2001: 5–8).

Vatis argues that politically motivated cyber attacks are increasing in volume, sophistication and coordination, and that attackers are increasing attracted to high value targets such as electronic networks, servers and routers, and to economic services such as banks (Vatis 2001: 9–10). Internet attacks are easy, low risk and hard to trace, as they often come via a series of compromised remote systems. Intruder tools are increasingly sophisticated, easy to use, often automated and designed to support large-scale attacks. There are also thousands of exploitable vulnerabilities in technology, vendors continue to produce software with vulnerabilities, including well-known vulnerabilities, and there is a shortage of qualified information security staff and a lack of coordinated effort in organizations to protect, detect, analyse and respond to computer security events. As a consequence, the ability of authorities to react fast enough to major events is thought to be declining significantly (CERT 2003: 8–13, 16, 43–4).

Implications

To the extent that cyber attacks are perceived by state authorities and others as increasingly endangering the national interest, there will be increasing pressure to implement countermeasures. These fall into three main categories: technical measures to improve computer security in the public and private sectors, moves to dissuade, prevent and counter cyber-attacks, and the appropriation of greater powers over telecommunications and the Internet.

Protection of computer systems

There are numerous ways in which computers and computer systems can be protected against cyber attacks. The first is for public and private institutions to consistently follow best practice, including regular updating of operating systems and software, strong password policies, locking down systems, disabling of all unnecessary services, regular backing up and storing offsite of all vital data, and installation and regular updating of anti-virus software, firewalls and high fidelity intrusion detection systems. Other technical measures include ingress and egress filtering, for example blocking untrusted source addresses, and instructing computers to parse all input data, that is, to analyse what the message says rather than simply executing the code directly and then to ensure that no combination of computer responses to this data can affect a core operating programme. Where core operating programmes need to be changed, access can be restricted to a few superusers with tightly controlled access, and digital signatures used that establish a traceable link from input back to the user (Libicki 1995 chapter 7, Vatis 2001: 19–20). Physically disconnecting computer systems from all other systems removes the possibility of access from another system, although going this far substantially reduces their usefulness, but even disconnected systems are vulnerable to insiders such as janitors. Governments can also provide information to the private sector about best practice and likely threats, and distribute tools, tests and code that make it easier to secure their systems.

To the extent that the perceived threat worsens, or devastating cyber attacks actually take place, it is likely that governments will move to make adherence to minimal levels of security a precondition for regulatory approval where relevant, and over time impose increasingly tight regulatory standards on the Internet and its users to put limits on the private sector's practices and markets (Libicki 1995 chapter 7, Molander *et al.* 1996: 20).

Moves to dissuade, prevent and counter cyber-attacks

As well as taking purely defensive measures, governments can go on the offensive by attacking the attackers using cyber or other means and by threatening massive retaliation against any major cyber-attack that does take place and succeeds in causing significant damage (Adams 2001).

Appropriation of greater powers over telecommunications and the Internet

If and when cyber attacks cause major damage, governments are likely to appropriate legal powers to obtain greater access to Internet traffic, including ready access to all messages encrypted or not, in order to monitor and track what is going on – although they are likely to be doing this to a considerable extent anyway with systems such as Echelon (Campbell 2000). This would mean the loss of privacy for communications, which would doubtless elicit opposition from businesses concerned about commercial confidentiality and from individuals concerned about personal privacy. Governments would also be expected to appropriate greater legal powers to impose certain restrictions on telecommunications traffic.

Conclusion

Innovation in military technology will continue to take place, weapons of mass destruction will continue to spread, and cyber-warfare will continue to evolve. Table 4.5 summarises the main pressures on public policy exerted by these trends.

The most striking finding here is the extent to which developments in military technology imply greater assertiveness of state power. Precision warfare reduces the electoral risks of military intervention by facilitating quick victories with few casualties and minimum destructiveness. Improvements in surveillance technology make mass surveillance more effective. Perceptions of increasing threats from the spread of WMDs and, to a less extent, from cyber-attack strengthen incentives to take vigorous countermeasures including increased use of surveillance, greater control of telecommunications, greater powers for police and security services, and military intervention.

Table 4.5 Policy implications of developments in military technology

Policy implications	Causal chain from trend
More interventionist foreign policy stance in terms of threatening and taking military action	Decreasing electoral cost of military action due to developments in military technology enabling precision warfare techniques capable of quick victories with few or no casualties and minimum destructiveness
Stronger policies on WMDs including increased diplomatic efforts to counter proliferation, better security for WMD-related materials, equipment and expertise, improved civil defence, more vigorous efforts to intercept illegal trafficking of WMDs, more vigorous efforts to promote international and regional stability, and more frequent offensive action against WMDs	Government perceptions that attacks using WMDs are becoming more likely as continuing proliferation puts them in the hands of increasing numbers of countries and non-state groups hostile to Western countries
Increasing use of surveillance by police and internal security services	Improvements in military surveillance technology increase the law enforcement and security benefits of surveillance
Stronger policies against cyberattacks, such as mandating measures to improve computer security, taking action to dissuade, prevent and counter cyberattacks, and assuming greater powers over telecommunications and the Internet	Perceptions that cyber-attacks are becoming more common and more damaging as ICT technology continues to evolve and the technical expertise of hostile countries and non-state groups improves
Moves to economize on the purchase of major weapon systems, such as by purchasing fewer weapon systems at a time, slowing the weapon system replacement cycle, choosing second-best multipurpose weapon systems rather than state-of-the-art single-purpose systems, incremental upgrading of weapon systems, and sharing development costs with other countries	Increasing cost of developing and deploying new military technologies combined with their more rapid obsolescence
Less autonomous policies in general due to the unpopularity of raising taxes or cutting spending elsewhere to cover the rising costs of weapon systems	
Reduction or erasure of traditional boundaries between the military services	Military advantages of using new technology in integrated warfighting strategies

Part II
Growing Affluence and Structural Change

These days there is economic news wherever you look, but the economic trends that meet the criteria for being king trends mostly escape much media attention due to their gradual and undramatic nature even though their long-term effects are profound.

Economic growth, and the steady rise in incomes and consumption that it makes possible, is transforming our material lives generation by generation in terms of the amount and diversity of what we buy. Integral to this is increasing use of energy as well as greater mobility of people and goods. As manufacturing productivity grows, in large part as a consequence of the technological trends analysed in Part I, fewer people in EU countries are working in manufacturing and more in services ranging from hotels and restaurants to business services to healthcare. Meanwhile the lives of women are being transformed as more and more enter the paid workforce, with substantial economic and social consequences. All of these trends have significant implications for the content of public policy.

Perhaps the most prominent economic trend in terms of media coverage is globalization, which I refer to as internationalization on account of the fact that it mainly concerns Europe, North America and East Asia rather than the world as a whole. My analysis of this is split into separate chapters for trade, production and finance for the sake of clarity, but it is important to remember that these three phenomena are inextricably intertwined. All three have significant implications for the future of public policy in EU countries. Ironically, however, given widespread rhetoric about the inevitability of globalization, of all the king trends economic internationalization is one of the most fragile in the sense that it could be swiftly halted and reversed by means such as unilateral imposition of trade and investment restrictions if the governments of the more powerful nations decided that it was no longer in their interests.

The final economic trend analysed is the expansion of the mass media: the number of ways in which media content can reach consumers is increasing, the consumption of media content in general is expanding, and the media industry itself is growing and integrating. This too has significant implications for public policy.

Part II
Growing Affluence and Structural Change

5
Growth and Diversification of Production and Consumption

Introduction

Perhaps the most significant economic trend of our times is the almost uninterrupted growth in the amount and variety of what is produced and consumed. We are getting richer all the time, and this is expected to continue. The popularity of economic growth and its effects on income, consumption and the tax base implies greater policy autonomy for governments than if there was no economic growth, but over time the policy autonomy of governments is likely to decrease as a result of the erosive effects on party support of electoral dealignment. Nevertheless, the positive effects of growing affluence lead governments to do what they can to keep the process going by helping business by means such as adapting regulation, improving education and training, encouraging the use of new production technology, and opening up new markets. The political leverage of trade unions and the traditional working class, on the other hand, is being weakened, reducing the pressure on governments to implement union-friendly and worker-friendly policies.

Ever since the Industrial Revolution one of the most striking and consistent long-term trends in Western Europe has been the steady growth in production and consumption that has taken place. Despite periodic fluctuations, the economies of the EU-15 prior to enlargement in 2004 grew in real terms by 2.5 per cent per year between 1970 and 2000, although since 2000 real economic growth in the EU-15 has slowed somewhat to 1.8 per cent in 2001, 1.0 per cent in 2002, 1.0 per cent in 2003 and 2.3 per cent in 2004 (OECD 2001e: 48, Eurostat 2005p). Estimated real GDP per head in the EU-15 nearly doubled between 1970 and 2003 in terms of constant 2000 US dollars from US$12,915 to US$25,336 (OECD 2005: 348–439). Futures studies are confident that GDP will continue to grow over the next 15–20 years due to factors such as rising trade and investment and the diffusion of information technology, unless disrupted by unexpected events such as an energy crisis (DERA undated, Cabinet Office 2000, CIA 2000: 6, DERA 2001a: 22–4).

101

Growth in production is largely the result of growing productivity made possible by improvements in manufacturing technologies. Chapter 1 in this book points out the increasing role of ICT such as computer-aided design, computer-aided manufacturing and computer-aided engineering, along with management applications such as the use of databases, data-processing, email, teleconferencing, websites, knowledge management systems, automation of processes such as human resources, supply-chain and production planning, financial and customer relationship management, and surveillance of processes, employees and consumers. Among other things the use of ICT makes it easier to alter production process settings to produce customized products at short notice. Computer simulation, rapid prototyping, use of robots, Flexible Manufacturing Systems and Computer Integrated Manufacturing all facilitate the transition to so-called 'agile manufacturing'. This capacity for flexible specialization means that high productivity can be achieved just as well through a diversified set of low-volume products as via standardized mass production, which enables a profitable focus on segmented as well as mass markets (Dicken 2003: 108–9). Developments in ICT enable more efficient and effective management and coordination of companies through the application of ICT to office processes, communications and surveillance systems. Improved means of monitoring work practices, for example, implies better control of employees and thus, at least in theory, higher productivity (May 2002: 69–70).

Chapter 2 describes how applications of biotechnology are changing manufacturing processes through the increasing use of bioreactors to replace existing industrial processes with more efficient and environmentally friendly processes in areas such as antibiotics, enzymes, chemicals, pharmaceuticals, pulp and paper, textiles and leather, as well as the growing use of genetically-modified plants and animals to produce pharmaceuticals, plastics, industrial lubricants, cosmetics and biodegradable detergents.

Table 5.1 lists a number of other new and developing manufacturing technologies that are changing both what is produced and how it is produced. Meanwhile old technologies, such as 'old' computer chips, are continuing their 'sidewise' movement into new markets and applications.

Some of the immediate economic consequences of improvements in production technologies are as follows.

First, they facilitate economic growth by reducing production costs and raising productivity. For consumers this means the production of more and cheaper goods, which means that their money goes further: they can buy more and have more.

Second, they lead to greater diversity of production and therefore to greater choice – and greater temptation – for consumers.

Third, flexible specialization implies an improvement in the competitive position relative to large firms not only of small and medium-sized firms but also of substantially independent subsidiaries of large firms because it means that economies of scale are no longer so important (Lash and Urry 1987: 199).

Table 5.1 Examples of developing manufacturing technologies

Type	Description
Materials technology	Manufacture of materials that are smaller, smarter, multi-functional, environmentally compatible, more survivable and customizable, including materials that incorporate chemical switches or mechanical sensors to respond to changing conditions, such as clothes or buildings that adjust to the weather and shape-memory alloys that change shape in response to temperature change; biomimetic materials that mimic natural materials; composite materials such as polymers and ceramic fibres that combine strength with light weight; building materials fabricated from waste or recycled material; and superconductor materials that conduct electricity with little or no resistance, making possible more sensitive, faster, smaller, lighter and more energy-efficient electrical/electronic systems. Combinatorial materials design using computing power to screen many different materials' possibilities to optimize properties for specific applications. Manufacturing methods to include nanotechnology (see below)
Nanotechnology	Fabrication of materials and devices atom by atom and molecule by molecule (1 nanometre = 1 billionth of a metre), such as materials with high performance and unique properties and functions (see above), smaller, faster and cheaper semi-conductors that enable the development of low cost computing and the development of ubiquitous computers in consumer products, appliances and environments, and in the longer term quantum or molecular computers; new chemicals and pharmaceuticals; diagnostic devices, molecular scale surgery and prosthetic and medical implants that interact with the body; catalysts in the petroleum and chemical industries; lighter, faster and safer vehicles; more durable, reliable and cost-effective roads, bridges, runways, pipelines and rail systems; aerospace products; cleaner manufacturing processes; more economical water filtration and desalination; more efficient solar energy conversion; smaller and lighter spacecraft including satellites. Possible future applications include artificial photosynthesis for clean energy, smart camouflage materials, and membranes to collect specific toxic or valuable particles from industrial waste
Manufacturing Process Simulation	Use of computational models to study manufacturing processes for the purposes of research and development

(Continued)

Table 5.1   (*Continued*)

Type	Description
Rapid Prototyping	Automatic fabrication of physical models and prototype parts direct from 3D data by bonding material together in layers to form solid objects, for uses such as prototyping, rapid tooling and rapid manufacturing
Robots and Automated Guided Vehicles	Reprogrammable, multifunctional manipulators designed to move material, parts, tools or specialized devices through various programmed motions for the performance of tasks such as welding, painting, material handling, assembly and inspection; computer-controlled vehicles used to move parts between machines and work centres
Flexible Manufacturing Systems (FMS)	Integrated systems of manufacturing utilizing technologies such as robotics and automated material handling, usually in the form of semi-independent computer controlled workstations with their own material handling and machine loading devices
Computer Integrated Manufacturing	Extension of FMS to include other technologies, such as computer-assisted design (CAD), simulation, and computer-aided planning and control, to form factory-wide integrated systems

Sources: Anton *et al.* 1999, NSTC 1999, TechsectorTrends 2002, MAS 2003.

Fourth, flexible specialization implies changes in employment practices within companies as production process settings continually change and employers consequently place greater emphasis on training and flexibility – although not all the forms of flexibility desired by employers have anything to do with managing new technology.

Fifth, the continual emergence of new products to compete with or supplant existing products means constant economic turbulence at company and industry level as producers of new products benefit at the expense of producers of superseded products.

Sixth, improvements in manufacturing technologies contribute to the long-standing shift in employment away from manufacturing towards services (OECD 2001e: 31–3, 40–1). The increasing automation of manufacturing made possible by ICTs, for example, implies a loss of manufacturing jobs, although it should be noted that ICT-based products can counteract this trend by replacing services in areas such as entertainment (Gershuny 1978). More broadly, better manufacturing technology means fewer jobs in manufacturing because production is limited by demand, which is not rising as fast as manufacturing productivity. Therefore fewer workers are needed to produce the same or more goods. In the period 1995–2000, for example, manufacturing production rose in all West European countries at the same time as manufacturing employment was falling in most of them (OECD 2001f). Since employment in services is increasing, the result is a shift in employment from manufacturing to services. This is analyzed in detail in Chapter 8 as a king trend in its own right.

Another consequence of production being limited by demand is a premium on creating, finding, enlarging or opening up new markets, which among other things helps to explain business advocacy of free trade and globalization.

Finally, lower costs of production due to technological progress mean lower prices for consumers and/or higher profits for employers, and workers can get a share of the profits by securing higher wages. This is in fact what has been happening: real incomes are rising and have been rising for a very long time. By 'real incomes' is meant incomes adjusted for price inflation, so these increases represent real increases in purchasing power. The best available measure of this is wages in manufacturing, which are received by a high proportion of people in paid employment and are more consistent and internationally comparable than other available incomes data. Between 1970 and 2000 real hourly earnings in manufacturing grew significantly in almost all the countries for which statistics are available: Austria (2.4 per cent per year), Belgium (1.9 per cent), France (2.1 per cent), Germany (1.8 per cent), Italy (2.2 per cent), Japan (2.0 per cent), the Netherlands (1.0 per cent) and Norway (2.0 per cent). Statistics are not available for all of this period for Britain, but real hourly earnings grew by 3.4 per cent per year between 1970 and 1973, 2.6 per cent per year between 1979 and 1989, and 1.7 per cent per year between 1989 and 2000. The only country where real wages did not grow was the United States, where real hourly earnings in manufacturing declined by 0.1 per cent per year between 1970 and 2000 (OECD 2001e: 86). ILO figures for 1990–2001 indicate that during this period real manufacturing wages rose gradually in almost all developed countries (ILO 2003).

This trend of increasing incomes is expected to continue: global per capita incomes are predicted to double in the period up to 2030 (DERA 2001a), and there is no suggestion that Europe will not share in this.

An important feature of this rise in incomes is that it has been occurring right across the income distribution: in most European countries the structure of income inequality remained much the same as average incomes rose, so that poor as well as rich were carried upwards even though inequality did rise in a few countries, notably Britain (Förster with Pellizzari 2000, Förster and Pearson 2002, Eurostat 2003, LIS 2003).

Rising incomes, of course, imply rising consumption, and the record shows that individual consumption per head in the EU-15 doubled in real terms between 1970 and 2003 in terms of constant 2000 US dollars from US$9,154 to US$18,772 (OECD 2005: 348–9). As incomes continue to rise, so consumption must be expected to continue to rise too.

Table 5.2   Some consequences of rising affluence for consumers

Area	Examples
Goods	More and better food
	Fewer people suffer from absolute poverty – although perceptions of poverty are largely conditioned by comparisons with middle and higher incomes
	Better health and longer life as fewer people are affected by acute poverty and the health problems associated with it
	More and more varied material possessions chosen from among items such as accommodation (home ownership), home decoration and improvement, cars, and electronic goods such as TVs and computers – consequently greater material comfort and more entertainment at home
	Higher energy use, for example as a consequence of more car and air travel
Services	Rising consumption of services, such as dining out at restaurants
	More frequent travel and travel farther afield
Other	Unless all rises in income are spent immediately, higher incomes mean rising direct investment in shares and property as well as rising savings in banks and other financial institutions
	More savings in pensions insofar as contributions are earnings-related: contributions rose in OECD countries from 5.6% to 9.4% of GDP between 1970 and 1998 (OECD 2000: 74). Higher pensions insofar as these are income-related
	Greater impact on the environment due to growth in production and trade as well as growth in consumer activities such as car use

It is important to appreciate the sheer scale of this rise in affluence: in just one generation we have become *twice* as well-off in terms of real purchasing power. And this is expected to continue into the foreseeable future: in another 30 years it is expected that we shall be twice as well-off as we are now.

This massive and continuing increase in affluence affects our lives in numerous ways, some of which are listed in Table 5.2.

As well as consuming more, what we consume is changing. Reliable and internationally comparable time-series data on consumption in Western Europe is difficult to find, but a study of consumption trends in Britain as measured by the UK Family Expenditure Survey found that between 1975 and 1999 absolute spending grew in all categories of expenditure apart from food and tobacco, with the largest real increases going to holidays and education. While the share spent on durables such as furniture remained steady, there was considerable redistribution of spending away from non-durables, such as food, fuel and clothing, towards services. This took place even though the relative price of services rose while the prices of non-durables remained steady and the relative prices of durables fell. More specifically, relative spending on home-prepared meals fell while spending on food prepared for us rose, spending on private transport (and on motor vehicles) rose while spending on public transport fell, and spending on holidays, entertainment and leisure goods as well as telephone calls also rose (Blow *et al.* 2004).

This picture is broadly consistent with findings for OECD countries as a whole, the citizens of which are spending relatively less over time on food, clothing, furniture and household operation and relatively more on rent, fuel and power as well as on health, services and recreation, including restaurants and hotels. There is also a general trend towards larger houses, more household electrical appliances and greater travel distances, especially for tourism. In the period up to 2020 the share of spending devoted to food is expected to continue to fall while the share devoted to energy, transport and services is expected to continue to rise (OECD 2001g: 69).

One important consequence of the increase and diversification of consumption is a greater choice and diversity of lifestyles. This is because to a significant extent lifestyle is determined by consumption: what you do is influenced by what you buy. Thus labour-saving devices such as dishwashers free up time to do something else, TV-watching takes time from other activities, and devices such as telephones and email influence the conduct of relationships. To the extent that increasing diversity of production is matched by increasing diversity of consumption, rising affluence must lead to a greater diversity of lifestyles defined in terms of food, possessions, clothes, where one lives, accommodation, activities, media consumption, recreation and so on. The extent to which this is actually occurring in practice is difficult to determine, but that it is occurring appears to be pretty much universally accepted by those who think about these things.

Another likely consequence of the growth and diversification of production and consumption is an increasingly home-based society as increasing affluence combined with the availability of new technologies, such as digital television, computer games, home diagnostics, tele-banking and tele-shopping, reduce the need for people to go out for entertainment, healthcare, banking, shopping and so on. Watching TV, for example, now takes about 40 per cent of free time in most EU countries (Aliaga and Winqvist 2003: 3, Kumar 2005: 175–9).

Implications

As most production of goods and services in EU countries takes place in the private sector, businesses individually and collectively have considerable weight in policy-making, balanced to some extent by the influence of their employees organized in trade unions, while in government the maintenance and encouragement of economic growth is a central task of major ministries such as finance, industry, trade and technology. However the growth and diversification of production and consumption are so central to our lives that many policy actors take an interest (Table 5.3).

Table 5.3   Generic economic policy network

Type of policy actor	Specific policy actor
Political executives and associated parties	Chief executives
	Government election planners
	Economic, industry, trade and technology ministers
	Spending ministers in areas such as defence, health, social security and education
Non-government politicians	Opposition leaders and spokespeople
	Opposition party election planners
	Parliamentary committees relating to the economy, industry, trade, technology, social policy and defence
	Regional and local governments
	European Commissioners in areas relating to the economy, industry, trade, internal market, technology, social policy and defence
	Foreign governments such as the US government and other European governments
Civil servants, special advisers and other public sector employees	Economic departments and agencies, in particular finance, taxation, industry, trade and technology
	Spending departments such as defence, health, social security and education
	European Commission Directorates-General relating to the economy, industry, trade, internal market, technology and social policy
	Regional and local administrations
	International organizations such as the World Trade Organization
Judges and regulators	Economic regulators such as competition commissions
Business	Business organizations at all levels
	Firms in general, especially large firms such as transnational companies
Interest groups and non-government organizations	Trade unions, especially manufacturing trade unions
	Social security and health funds
	Non-government organizations in most policy areas
Media	National press and television
	Specialist economic media
Experts	Economists in universities and think tanks
Electorate	Taxpayers/recipients of public transfers and services

The main policy implications of economic growth, the improvements in production technology that underpin it, and the increases in income and consumption that result, are adaptation of product and process regulation, increasing pressure to improve education and training, increasing pressure to support new technology, persistent pressure to enlarge markets, decreasing pressure for union-friendly and worker-friendly policies, increasing pressure to improve public services, greater policy autonomy for governments as a result of economic growth and tax base expansion, and decreasing policy autonomy due to electoral dealignment. Note the inconsistent implications in relation to policy autonomy. The growth and diversification of production and consumption also affects policy-making indirectly through increasing energy use, mobility and environmental damage, in particular climate change. These are analyzed as king trends in their own right in Chapters 6, 7 and 14 respectively. The growth of manufacturing productivity that underpins economic growth also means lower employment in manufacturing relative to services. This shift to services and its policy implications are analyzed in Chapter 8.

Adaptation of product and process regulation

The application of existing safety, product quality and ethical concerns to new production technologies is likely to lead to regulation being modified to ensure that these new technologies are covered, for example by formulating specific safety standards for manufacturing processes that employ nanotechnology.

Increasing pressure to improve education and training

As production technology changes more frequently and becomes more and more sophisticated, advanced and appropriate education and training for workers (and managers) becomes more and more important for manufacturers and other producers. Since companies are reluctant to invest much in education and training themselves, among other things because competitors might poach employees they have spent time and money training, they are instead increasingly likely to press governments to improve education systems through means such as increasing participation in education in general, making education more technologically and vocationally relevant (including by enabling private organizations such as corporations to become accredited educational providers), and improving opportunities for employees to go back for more training as technology changes: so-called life-long learning.

Increasing pressure to support new technology

Continual innovation in new production technology means that companies, industries and countries that produce outmoded products are disadvantaged, to the detriment of the economy and therefore the re-election chances of incumbent governments. For this reason there are strong electoral incentives for governments to take steps to encourage investment in new technology, which implies more business-friendly policies in relation to industries such as ICT. This pressure will increase to the extent that technological innovation becomes more economically important.

Maintenance of pressure to enlarge markets

The fact that production is limited by demand leads firms to put pressure on governments to help locate, create, enlarge or open up new markets, for example by pressing Third World countries to open their markets to foreign firms, although this pressure has been operating for a long time and there is no reason to believe that it is increasing in magnitude.

Decreasing pressure for union-friendly policies

Improvements in manufacturing technology weaken manufacturing unions in at least two ways. First, the contraction of manufacturing employment caused by automation erodes the membership base of manufacturing unions. Second, flexible specialization and the consequent diversification of work, plus the associated increased employer pressure for employee flexibility, make it more difficult for unions to organize the manufacturing workers who remain. Since manufacturing unions have generally been at the heart of national labour movements, this implies a reduction in the political leverage of labour movements in general in the making of public policy (Kumar 2005: 72). On the other hand manufacturing unions that retain the allegiance of the shrinking production workforce should retain huge disruptive power due to the continuing economic importance of goods production, so it is important not to write them off altogether. It is also possible that over time the weakening of manufacturing unions will be offset by a strengthening of unions in the service sector as their membership base grows.

Increasing affluence also weakens unions, as it means that workers have less need of unions for economic reasons and their increasingly diverse lifestyles make it less likely that they will identify themselves primarily as working-class or as a 'union man' (or woman), thus weakening class and union solidarity (Lash and Urry 1987: 228). This again implies a reduction in the pressure on governments to implement union-preferred policies. It is somewhat ironic that the achievement of affluence for most workers, a principal if not the principal aim of unions, should lead to the weakening of the trade union movement itself. On the other hand it might also be argued – especially on the Right – that this demonstrates that unions have now fulfilled their main purpose and are no longer relevant.

Decreasing pressure for traditional worker-friendly policies

The shift in employment from production to services due to improved production technology means fewer blue-collar voters and more white-collar voters, which is likely to affect election results insofar as the political attitudes of blue-collar and white-collar workers are different, for example by reducing the core vote for explicitly labour-based parties (for more detail on the policy implications of the shift to services see Chapter 8).

Increasing pressure to improve public services

Over time increasingly affluent citizens become accustomed to buying higher quality and more diverse goods and services in the private sector. It is reasonable to expect that at least some of these rising expectations will be applied to government services as well, leading citizens increasingly to demand higher quality and tailored services rather than standard one-size-fits all services (Scase 2010: 101). Insofar as this occurs it puts greater electoral pressure on governments to improve services. From a party political point of view this benefits the Left, which wants to improve public services anyway, while making it more electorally difficult for the Right to cut tax instead.

Greater policy autonomy for governments as a result of economic growth and tax base expansion

The growth and diversification of production and consumption implies greater government popularity, and therefore greater policy autonomy, in two distinct ways.

First, economic growth is popular because it means higher incomes and because it has become a symbol of government economic policy success. To the extent that it continues, therefore, the electoral position of incumbent governments will be stronger than it would otherwise be, other things being equal, putting them in a stronger position to do what they want without too many concessions to other policy actors.

Second, economic growth increases the size of the tax base: what can be taxed increases in size, so the government gets more tax revenue as time goes on even if tax rates remain unchanged. This makes it possible for governments to improve benefits and services over time without increasing tax rates. Alternatively, governments are in a position to cut tax rates without cutting government programmes. In general the provision of better services and/or tax cuts would be expected to make governments more popular and therefore render them less likely to make policy concessions to public opinion or to other policy actors trying to use public opinion as a lever to extract concessions. In other words, a growing tax base makes the government better able to do whatever it wishes to do. The converse of this effect can be observed during recessions, when a shrinking tax base combined with higher spending on unemployment benefits (and possibly employment programmes) tends to push budgets into deficit, putting governments under pressure to raise tax rates and/or cut spending on programmes, both of which are unpopular. Rising tax revenue due to economic growth would be expected to benefit both parties of the Left, by expanding the scope for them to spend more without raising taxes, and parties of the Right, by expanding the scope for cutting tax without cutting government programmes. This implies that government policies in relation to tax and spending will be more partisan under conditions of economic growth than would otherwise be the case.

In short, the growth and diversification of production and consumption increases the policy autonomy of governments by making it less electorally risky to implement unpopular policies and by increasing the resources available to improve services or cut tax. This makes it more likely that governments will implement partisan policies regardless of public opinion and other political opposition. It also makes it more likely that they will implement unpopular measures to solve crises. These electoral and policy benefits mean that it is hardly surprising that governments of all complexions place such emphasis on securing and sustaining economic growth.

It is important to note, however, that it is short-term economic growth and its consequences that electorates respond to: long-term economic growth simply means that, on average, governments are more popular than they would have been had there been no economic growth. It is also important to note that there is no reason to believe that the growth and diversification of production and consumption over time is increasing government popularity and policy autonomy over time. For that to occur the rate of economic growth would have to increase, which is not expected.

Decreasing policy autonomy over time due to electoral dealignment

The diversification of lifestyles as a result of the diversification of consumption implies increasing social differentiation and fragmentation, with consequent erosion of traditional cultural identities such as working class identity: we increasingly choose our own lives and identities rather than being born into particular cultures and lifestyles. Among other things this implies electoral dealignment in the sense of less class voting, that is, we would expect fewer people to automatically vote on the basis of their class identity. This implication is consistent with the finding that class voting in Britain, France, West Germany, Sweden and the US as measured by the Alford Index (the percentage of manual workers voting Left minus percentage of the nonmanual workers voting Left) fell steadily during the period 1948–1992 (Inglehart 1997: 254–5 – see also Nieuwbeerta and De Graaf 1999, and Miller and Niemi 2002). This means that political parties and governments cannot take as much of their vote for granted as previously because more and more people are deciding for themselves how to vote. Put another way it means that the potential amplitude of electoral swings is increasing, so that even governments with big majorities who are well ahead in opinion polls cannot feel as electorally secure as they would have in the past in a similar situation.

What this means is that over time the electoral risk of implementing unpopular policies is increasing, other things being equal, which would be expected to lead governments to take fewer policy risks, seek wider support for policy initiatives before deciding to go ahead with them, and therefore implement policies that are more cautious, lowest-common-denominator, centrist and populist as time goes on, other things being equal.

Conclusion

The growth and diversification of production and consumption is a long-standing trend the effects of which permeate most if not all areas of life. In terms of public policy it has a number of significant implications. These are summarized in Table 5.4.

Two of these appear to be especially important.

First, while economic growth and its consequences imply greater electoral support for incumbent governments than if there was no economic growth, so that the electoral risk of implementing unpopular policies is lower than would otherwise be the case, the increasing electoral volatility implied by electoral dealignment means that the electoral risk involved in implementing

Table 5.4   Policy implications of the growth and diversification of production and consumption

Policy implications	*Causal chain from trend*
More autonomous policies than if there was no economic growth	Economic growth and the associated rises in income and consumption, along with the consequent expansion of the tax base that enables governments to improve benefits and services without increasing tax rates and/or to cut tax without cutting public services, makes governments more popular than they would be if there was no economic growth
Decreasingly autonomous policies over time	Increasingly risky electoral position of governing (and other) parties due to increasing electoral volatility as a result of electoral dealignment caused by affluence-related diversification of lifestyles and weakening of class solidarity
Improvements to public services	Increasing pressure to improve public services as affluence leads to higher expectations of public services, to the benefit of the Left
Adaptation of product and process regulation to ensure that new production technologies are covered	Existing safety, product quality and ethical regulation may not cover new products and processes made possible by advances in production technology
Improvements in education and training, for example increasing participation in education in general, making it more technologically and vocationally relevant, and expanding life-long education	Increasing sophistication of production processes increases the importance to business of well-educated and well-trained employees, while the possibility that other firms may poach trained employees discourages extensive company provision of training, which leads to increasing pressure on governments to improve the provision of education and training

(Continued)

Table 5.4   (Continued)

Policy implications	Causal chain from trend
More vigorous measures to encourage and facilitate the use of new production technologies	Increased economic significance of state-of-the-art production technologies in preserving and enhancing business competitiveness and therefore economic growth
Maintenance of policies designed to enlarge domestic and overseas markets, such as aggressive free trade policies	Production is limited by demand, so increasing production requires higher levels of demand, which means larger markets, if industry is to contribute as much as it can to economic growth
Less union-friendly policies	Decreasing policy leverage for unions where members are lost due to job losses caused by automation, such as in manufacturing, plus the increasing difficulty of organizing workers due to the increasing diversification of work and the weakening of union solidarity as growing affluence reduces workers' economic need of unions and increasingly diverse lifestyles make it less likely that employees will identify themselves as working-class or as a 'union man' (or woman)
Less worker-friendly policies	Decline in the number of traditional working class voters due to job losses caused by automation

unpopular policies is increasing over time. Other things being equal we should therefore expect that as time goes on increasingly anxious governments will limit themselves more and more to cautious and/or populist policies and to policies on which compromise has been sought and reached with other political actors, other things being equal.

Second, although union members and workers in general will benefit from continuing economic growth, from a political point of view it is bad news because all of its policy implications for unions and workers suggest decreasing political leverage and therefore decreasing pressure on governments to retain or introduce union-friendly and worker-friendly policies. On the other hand, the increasing pressure on government to improve public services would be likely to be seen as positive by unions and the industrial working class that remains, although any improvements that result will not necessarily be along the lines advocated by unions.

6
Greater Energy Use

Introduction

Energy use is vital to our economies and to our lives. Its use globally and in Europe has been increasing for a long time and looks set to continue to increase for the foreseeable future. This creates pressures on governments not only to ensure security of supply but also to reduce energy-related carbon dioxide emissions, due to their crucial role in causing climate change. There is also the alternative possibility that the real energy king trend is rising oil prices rather than rising energy consumption.

Between 1971 and 2000 total annual world energy demand increased by 84 per cent to 9,179 million tonnes of oil equivalent (Mtoe), and this is forecast by the International Energy Agency (IEA) to increase by a further 66 per cent between 2000 and 2030. The European Commission reaches similar conclusions (IEA 2002: 58, European Commission 2003a: 13, 24–31).

In Europe the pattern is similar but the expected increases in energy use are not as great.

Between 1973 and 2000 total energy demand in the 15 Member States of the EU as it was prior to enlargement in 2004 (the EU-15), plus the Czech Republic, Hungary, Norway, Switzerland and Turkey, increased by 32 per cent to 1,689 Mtoe (IEA 2003: Table A5).

Between 2000 and 2030 gross inland consumption of energy in the post-2004 European Union of 25 states (EU-25) is expected to increase by 19 per cent to 1,960 Mtoe per year according to the European Commission's Baseline Scenario, which is based on trends and policies at the end of 2001 in relation to population, numbers of households, economic growth, sectoral shifts, technological progress, liberalization of energy markets, promotion of renewables, planned changes in power generation capacity, planned nuclear phase-outs in Belgium, Germany and Sweden and, importantly, the assumption that energy supplies will remain adequate at relatively modest cost throughout the projection period. Most of the extra demand for energy is expected to be met by natural gas, use of which is expected to rise by two thirds to constitute 32 per cent of total energy consumption. However oil is expected to remain the single largest fuel at 34 per cent of gross inland consumption despite the fact that oil consumption is only expected to increase in absolute terms by 6 per cent. Solid fuels consumption is expected to fall steeply in the short term but then to rise again as a replacement for nuclear power and as its price competitiveness improves due to increases in gas prices. The nuclear contribution is expected to fall from 14.4 per cent of total energy consumption in 2000 to 9.5 per cent in 2030 as reactors are phased out in several Member States after 2010. Renewables are expected to grow by 76 per cent over this period even though novel energy forms such as hydrogen and methanol are not expected to make significant inroads, but would still only amount to 8.6 per cent of total energy consumption in 2030 (European Commission 2004i: 31–48, 170 – see IEA 2002 for a similar analysis).

The Commission also provides a number of alternative scenarios based on different assumptions, but the only scenario under which energy consumption is projected to fall is the 'extended policy options' case, which assumes policy decisions and other factors lead to faster improvements in energy efficiency, greater penetration of renewable energy, a shift towards railways and public road transport as well as higher load factors on all transport modes, emissions trading, and strong penetration of natural gas, biofuels and hydrogen in the transport sector (European Commission 2004i: 13, 113–15, 156–61). While it is certainly conceivable that this could happen, however, getting all these conditions in place seems unlikely, so continuing increases in energy consumption appear more likely than falls in energy consumption.

Because the Baseline Scenario projects that production of primary energy in Europe itself will fall by about a quarter due to steep declines in fossil fuel and nuclear energy production, the scale of expected increases in energy use implies an increase in imports from 47 per cent of energy consumption in 2000 to 67 per cent in 2030. All scenarios, including those that assume maximum use of nuclear power and renewables, project an increase in import dependency (European Commission 2004i: 40, 161, 170).

The big increases in energy consumption that are projected, and the expectation that by 2030 fossil fuels will still provide for 82 per cent of gross inland consumption, leads the Baseline Scenario to project that carbon dioxide emissions will grow by 17 per cent between 2000 and 2030 to 4,304 million tonnes per year. These increases in emissions are expected to be driven mainly by the power generation sector growing and becoming more carbon intensive as the contribution of nuclear power falls and coal makes a comeback, and by increases in fossil fuel use by transport. The most pronounced increase in carbon emissions occurs in the 'high economic growth' scenario. However scenarios that assume strong action on energy efficiency, renewables and greenhouse gas emission targets project cuts in carbon emissions relative to the Kyoto reference date of 1990 of up to 30 per cent by 2030 (European Commission 2004i: 40–7, 157–70).

One possibility that the Commission does not explore is that oil production may peak well before 2030, as a number of industry analysts predict, especially geologists, on the basis that estimates of oil reserves have in the past been inflated for political reasons while the results of recent oil exploration have been disappointing and the growth of demand for oil has been underestimated by organizations such as the IEA (Goodstein 2004, Hirsch *et al.* 2005: 13–19, Illum 2005). The significance of this is that once production peaks and starts to decline, the continuing growth in demand for oil would be expected to drive up oil prices indefinitely, since for transport in particular there are no ready alternative fuels for motor vehicles, aircraft, trains and ships (Hirsch *et al.* 2005: 27, 64). Under this scenario total consumption of energy could fall during the period up to 2030 as less oil is consumed and the accompanying economic slowdown reduces demand for other types of energy as well. In these circumstances the relevant energy king trend would be rising oil prices rather than rising energy consumption.

Implications

Table 6.1 sets out the main policy actors who take an interest in energy. Fuel producers are central players here, especially companies such as the three oil giants Exon-Mobil, Shell and BP and the growing utilities companies of Europe (Thomas 2003). Energy ministers, their departments and associated agencies are also prominent, and dependence on imported energy, especially oil, gives energy policy a significant international dimension. The main opposition to what might be termed the energy establishment comes from certain environmentalist groups. Voters are important insofar as their experience as energy users affects, or is thought to affect, the way they vote.

The implications of increasing energy use for public policy relate mainly to security of supply and climate change. Rising energy consumption also contributes to the growth and diversification of production and consumption, the policy implications of which are analyzed in Chapter 5, and to the increasing mobility of people and goods, which is the subject of Chapter 7. The policy implications of the possibility that increasing oil prices will be the real energy king trend are explored later in the chapter.

Security of supply

Increasing demand for energy means continued pressure on governments to ensure that energy supply meets demand: both businesses and households want continued and easy access to energy and object to disruptions such as blackouts. They also object to big price rises. Energy disruptions and big energy price rises also lead to economic problems and therefore to electoral problems for governments in power when they occur. This all gives governments powerful incentives to do whatever is necessary to ensure security of supply. Three aspects of this are especially important: increasing pressure on governments to

Table 6.1 Generic energy policy network

Type of policy actor	Specific policy actor
Political executives and associated parties	Chief executives
	Energy ministers
	Environment ministers
	Economic, industry, transport, trade and technology ministers
Non-government politicians	Opposition energy and environment spokespeople
	Parliamentary committees relating to energy, the economy, the environment, industry, transport, trade and technology
	Regional and local governments
	European Commissioners in areas relating to energy and the environment
	Foreign governments such as the US and other European governments
Civil servants, special advisers and other public sector employees	Energy departments and agencies
	Environment departments and agencies
	Economic departments and agencies, in particular finance, industry, transport, trade and technology
	European Commission Directorates-General relating to energy and environment
	Regional and local administrations
	International organizations such as the IEA, OPEC and UN
Judges and regulators	Energy and environment regulators
Business	Fuel producers: oil, gas, coal, nuclear fuel, renewables
	Electricity generators: oil, gas, coal, nuclear, hydro, renewables
	Electrical power plant manufacturers
	Industrial users of energy such as steelworks
	Transport industry
	Business in general
Interest groups and non-government organizations	Business organizations relating to energy, industry and transport
	Environmentalists
	Trade unions
Media	National press and television
	Specialist energy and environment media
Experts	Energy and environmental experts in universities and elsewhere
Electorate	Energy users

ensure that imports of energy are not disrupted, continuing pressure on governments to ensure that global investment in energy production is adequate, and continuing pressure on governments to ensure that domestic utilities deliver power reliably and at affordable prices.

Increasing pressure on governments to ensure that imports
of energy are not disrupted

European dependence on energy imports is projected to increase from 47 per cent of energy consumption in 2000 to 67 per cent in 2030, at which point it is expected that that 88 per cent of oil and 81 per cent of natural gas will be imported (European Commission 2004i: 40), which increases the potential economic damage that would be done if energy imports were interrupted and thereby increases the pressure on governments to do whatever is necessary to avoid import disruption due to terrorist attacks or political instability in energy-producing regions or transit countries.

Self-sufficiency in energy would, of course, make these problems irrelevant, but for most European countries this is impossible. Instead governments seek to minimize dependence on any one energy source by diversifying the types of energy used, their sources and supply routes. They also try to minimize the level of imports needed by encouraging energy conservation and efficiency through measures such as adjusting energy prices, using financial incentives to encourage the use of efficient products and practices, mandating minimum efficiency levels (for example for motor vehicles and buildings), reaching voluntary agreements with big energy users, energy rationing, and encouraging technological innovation in areas such as renewables (IEA 2003: 14–15, 105). The other main set of relevant policy instruments are those of foreign policy: diplomacy, provision of assistance, trade sanctions and – if necessary – military intervention.

Continuing pressure on governments to ensure that global investment in energy
production is adequate

If there is insufficient global investment in energy production, demand will exceed supply, energy prices will rise, economic damage will be done, and governments will fall. This puts pressure on governments collectively to take steps where necessary to ensure that global investment in energy production is adequate.

At present it is estimated that global financial resources will be sufficient to finance the estimated US$16 trillion of investment seen as being necessary over the next three decades, half to replace existing capacity and half to meet rising demand, but there are concerns about the energy sector's ability to access capital. In particular it is expected that there will be a need for industrialized countries to help finance energy investment in areas such as upstream oil and gas projects in regions and countries such as the Middle East and Russia that are intended to export energy to OECD countries such as European countries. This creates continuing incentives for European and other governments to do what they can to mobilize investment by ensuring that business environments in energy-exporting countries are made more investor-friendly by putting pressure on their governments to remove market barriers, establish a transparent, efficient and stable legal, regulatory and institutional framework, harmonize trade and tariff rules, protect the freedom to repatriate capital and profits, protect intellectual property, ensure effective corporate governance, tackle problems of corruption and violence, and put in place sound macroeconomic management as defined by investors (IEA 2003: 63–4, IEA 2003a: 26). It also creates incentives for governments to provide assistance to investors going into such countries. If the threat of inadequate investment were to increase, one would expect the pressure applied to governments in developing countries to take these and other steps would also increase, which from the perspective of European governments would mean more assertive foreign policies.

Continuing pressure on governments to ensure that domestic utilities deliver power reliably and at affordable prices

Blackouts in 2003 in Italy, Canada and the US, plus close calls in several other countries, demonstrated that market forces do not by themselves guarantee adequate investment in energy infrastructure. This creates incentives for governments to take steps to ensure that domestic energy companies act in such a way as to ensure security of supply. In the past this was generally done by delegating responsibility for security of supply across the whole market either to a state-owned monopoly or to a private company with exclusive concession rights. However recent liberalization of key energy sectors such as electricity and gas, which was undertaken largely to improve efficiency and thereby lower energy prices and is expected to continue well into the projection period, means that governments are now increasingly dependent on private companies to do the job. The problem is that these companies may not themselves value security of supply as such, and the unbundling of supply and transportation activities means that investment in capacity may not be sufficient to transport new supplies even when these are adequate. Short of renationalization or formal planning, the IEA recommends that governments clearly articulate security of supply objectives and the roles and responsibilities of market players in meeting these, ensure that government policies encourage investment, and consider some sort of safety net where market responses are slow or inadequate (IEA 2002: 180–2, IEA 2003: 59–61). If measures such as these do not succeed, pressure will build to regulate the energy industry more strictly, reintroduce formal planning and, although this seems unlikely at this stage, renationalize at least some energy producers.

Climate change

So far the pressure on public policy is all in one direction: ensuring that projected increases in demand for energy are met. But there is a problem. One of the main unintended consequences of increased energy use, it is now widely agreed, is climate change caused in large part by the burning of fossil fuels, which is estimated to generate over 80 per cent of greenhouse gas emissions (IEA 2003: 90). Climate change is significant because of the serious and potentially devastating damage it is expected to cause to environmental systems and ultimately to economic systems as well. In relation to Europe these effects are expected to include increased flooding, more frequent and intense extreme weather events such as gales, windstorms, storm surges, intense precipitation events and droughts, plus hotter drier summers in southern Europe affecting agriculture and tourism, and an extension of vector-borne diseases such as malaria from the south. There is also the possibility of a significant slowing of ocean circulation bringing warm water to the North Atlantic, which would have a dramatic effect on the climate of Western Europe (IPCC 2001).

According to the UN Intergovernmental Panel on Climate Change (IPCC) the only way of avoiding these and other consequences, or of mitigating them given that climate change is already under way, is to stabilize and ultimately reduce the levels of greenhouse gases in the atmosphere, which can only be done by reducing greenhouse gas emissions to near-zero levels. As we have seen, however, the European Commission's Baseline Scenario projects that the use of fossil fuels will increase significantly so that between 2000 and 2030 carbon dioxide emissions in the EU-25 are expected to increase by 17 per cent, driven mainly by the power generation sector as nuclear power plants are decommissioned and coal becomes increasingly competitive (IEA 2002: 98, 192–3, European Commission 2004i: 46, 170). Although some of the European Commission's other scenarios project a fall in carbon dioxide emissions, these are based on the assumption that European governments will take significant policy decisions in relation to energy efficiency, renewables and greenhouse gas targets that in fact have not (yet) been taken. For this reason it seems more reasonable to assume that increasing energy consumption will lead to carbon dioxide emissions rising rather than falling.

If global warming is to be arrested, therefore, carbon dioxide emissions from energy use need to be sharply cut from current and projected levels. To the extent that concern over climate change grows, this means that in relation to energy governments will come under increased pressure to take steps to reduce these emissions, other things being equal. There are a number of reasons for this. There is the learning process by which environmental scientists have convinced most policy actors inside and outside government that climate change is real, that it is caused mainly by man-made emissions of greenhouse gases, and that it will have damaging consequences if left unchecked. Leading on from this, climate change will sooner or later cause economic damage that will undermine the electoral position of whoever is in government at the time. And there is pressure exerted by expert opinion and environmentalists as well as by policy actors and voters who would suffer from the effects of climate change or who would benefit from measures to counteract it, such as people living on flood plains or producers of low- or zero-carbon energy. There is also pressure from other domestic and international policy actors and voters who have become convinced of the reality of climate change and want something to be done. This pressure will increase to the extent that new scientific findings increase concern or link natural disasters such as the heat wave of 2003 to climate change.

One side-effect of all this is that the policy leverage of fossil fuel producers and users is likely to be reduced, other things being equal, although our continued heavy dependence on fossil fuels means that they will remain important players. Inside government, environment ministers and their departments and agencies are likely to become more involved in the making of energy policy, along with energy and environmental experts in general.

If reduction of carbon dioxide emissions is added to economic goals as an objective of energy policy, however, then insofar as this affects energy use it follows that in at least some cases the most economically rational energy options will not be chosen. It follows from this in turn that in these cases economic damage will result relative to what would otherwise have happened. At the same time, however, climate change itself also has economically disruptive effects, especially in the long term, so there is an economic price to be paid whatever is done or not done.

The problem is that democratic governments with 3–5 year terms of office have every reason to prioritize the short-term over the long-term except to the extent that long-term threats can be dramatized in day to day political life. Furthermore, the rate of climate change can only be significantly affected if all major carbon dioxide emitting countries, including countries such as the US and China, take concerted action. At present there is little indication that this will happen. This enables those opposed to action to argue that there is no point in Europe going it alone, especially if this involves economic costs, because any effects on climate change will be negligible. The counter-argument, of course, is that we all need to do what we can not only as a contribution to mitigating climate change but also to set an example to other countries and to demonstrate that if they act they will not be alone.

There are in principle four main ways to reduce energy-related emissions of carbon dioxide: capture and store carbon dioxide emissions, reduce use of carbon-intensive energy by improving energy efficiency, reduce the carbon intensity of energy use via fuel substitution, and reduce the use of carbon-intensive energy overall regardless of the economic cost.

Capture and store carbon dioxide emissions (sequestration)

The need to reduce the use of fossil fuels will be reduced to the extent that carbon dioxide emissions from energy generation and use can be captured and safely stored, thereby preventing them from reaching the atmosphere. This can be done by removing greenhouse gases directly from industrial or utility plant exhausts and storing them in secure reservoirs such as deep saline formations, depleted oil and gas reservoirs, unminable coal seams and the ocean. Although these techniques of sequestration are as yet relatively undeveloped, it is hoped that in the future they will play a part in reducing carbon dioxide emissions. There are already a number of international R&D and demonstration programmes such as the Norwegian Sleipnir oil and gas field in the North Sea, where carbon dioxide is compressed and pumped into sandstone about 1,000 m below the seabed (Herzog 2001, IEA 2003: 91). However it should be noted that seques-tration would add to the costs of production of the industrial and utility plants involved, and it seems unlikely to be applied to reducing transport emissions.

Improve energy efficiency

Energy efficiency can be improved by improving energy technology so that less primary energy is needed to fulfil the desired tasks, for example by using more efficient fossil fuel combustion technologies and end-use technologies in the built environment, transport and industry. It can also be improved by measures such as better insulation and building design. Insofar as this means less use of fossil fuels, better fuel efficiency means lower carbon dioxide emissions. Gov-ernments can encourage improved energy efficiency by means such as impos-ing mandatory minimum efficiency performance standards for appliances, office equipment, motor vehicles and buildings, and by agreeing voluntary efficiency programmes with industry, such as the agreement providing for European vehicle manufacturers to improve fuel efficiency of new vehicles (IEA 2003: 105–9). Although implementing such standards is likely to add to business and consumer costs, these will be offset at least to some extent by savings on energy use. Lower demand for energy also implies lower energy imports and therefore improved energy security.

Fuel substitution

There are a number of ways in which governments can attempt to reduce the use of fossil fuels by encouraging or mandating fuel substitution.

First, governments can encourage switching from more to less carbon-intensive fuels, for instance from oil to gas. This is already occurring, and is factored into the European Commission projections for energy use, but could be pursued more vigorously, for example by using taxes to raise the price of oil relative to gas, although the protests in Europe in 2000 against fuel taxes demonstrate the political risks for governments of taking this course (Doherty *et al.* 2003).

Second, governments could encourage the expansion of nuclear power, as this generates less carbon dioxide than fossil fuel use. The European Com-mission estimates that maximizing the use of nuclear energy would result in carbon dioxide emissions being 5.6 per cent lower than those projected by the Baseline Scenario (European Commission 2004i: 157). However nuclear power has problems of its own, in particular the difficulty and cost of disposing of radioactive waste and decommissioning nuclear plants once their operating life is over as well as the possibility that nuclear accidents or terrorist attacks could cause the wide dispersal of lethal radioactivity. These problems have led to con-siderable political opposition to nuclear energy on the part of environmentalists and others, leading to planned phase-outs of nuclear energy in countries such as Germany. There is also the fact that at present nuclear energy is unattractive to investors due to factors such as the minimum 7 year lead time for planning and construction combined with uncertainty about construction and decommissioning costs and about what government policy will be in relation to nuclear power once plants are in operation. The last plant to be completed in Western Europe was Civaux-2 in France in 1999. At the turn of the century there were none under construction (MacKerron 2005: 1960–61, El Baradei 2004).

Third, governments can encourage the development and use of low- or zero-emission renewable forms of energy such as solar energy, burning of biomass, wind energy, bioenergy systems, geothermal energy, hydro power, hydrogen energy, photolytic processes, and ocean energy such as tidal energy, ocean thermal energy and wave energy. Ways in which assistance can be provided include provision of financial incentives for the deployment of low carbon technologies, such as grants, preferential loans, special funds, tax exemptions, tax credits and tax reductions, as well as the imposition of renewable energy mandates such as minimum mandatory quotas of electricity to be produced from renewable sources (IEA 2003: 92, 112–14).

Effects of improvements in renewable energy technologies are likely to include a reduction in the price of renewable energy and an increase in the overall capacity to generate energy from renewable sources. Both of these developments should enable the use of fossil fuels to be reduced. To date the most successful policies in this respect are reported to be those that offer long-term investment security through fixed feed-in tariffs for green electricity, technology-specific remuneration for green power, clear and transparent measures for planning and building approval, fair access to the electricity grid, adaptation of the electricity grid, and steps to secure local support for installations such as wind farms (Reiche and Bechberger 2004: 848).

Fourth, switching from fossil fuels to other fuels can be encouraged by making fossil fuels more expensive relative to other fuels by raising their prices via imposing or raising relevant taxes, although again the fuel protests in 2000 demonstrate the political disadvantages of this course of action. A policy simulation carried out for OECD countries as a whole found that removal of all energy subsidies and the introduction of a 1–2 per cent *ad valorem* tax on fossil fuels would result by 2020 in a 25 per cent reduction in carbon dioxide emissions relative to the level of emissions that would otherwise have occurred (OECD 2001g: 154).

Finally, the use of fossil fuels can be reduced by enabling companies to make money from reducing emissions through emissions trading schemes such as the one implemented in the EU in 2005. This involves introducing capped allowances for emissions for large point sources of climate pollution such as power stations, oil refineries and large industry, which account for about 40 per cent of EU emissions, then allowing companies that beat their cap to sell their unused allowances to companies that exceed their caps, which from 2008 would otherwise need to pay a fine of £70 per tonne of excess carbon dioxide emitted and face a reduction in allowances in the following period

(Worthington 2003: 176). If the overall cap is reduced over time, emissions trading should result in the progressive reduction of emissions where it is easiest and cheapest and least damaging.

Reduce use of carbon-intensive energy regardless of the economic cost

If all else failed, governments could in principle embark on a policy of deliberately restricting the use of fossil fuels even if other sources of energy were not sufficient to replace the shortfall, for instance by sharply raising taxation on fossil fuels. But not only would this be unpopular, as the fuel protests in 2000 demonstrated, it would also constrain economic growth and probably lead to higher unemployment, which would be damaging to the re-election prospects of any government brave enough to take this course. It therefore seems reasonable to exclude this option as a real possibility for the time being.

The view of the IPCC appears to be that all of the approaches sketched above should be pursued as far as possible using taxes on emissions, carbon and energy, tradable and non-tradable permits, subsidies, deposit-refund systems, voluntary agreements, technology and performance standards, product bans and direct government spending and investment (IPCC 2001a). The fact that Commission scenarios that incorporate action along these lines project a decrease in carbon dioxide emissions by 2030 of up to 30 per cent compared to 1990 suggests that appropriate policy decisions in these areas could make a significant difference.

At international level concern about climate change has resulted in the Kyoto Protocol of 1997, which committed signatories to reduce their collective emissions of greenhouse gases by 5.2 per cent compared to the year 1990, calculated as an average over the five-year period 2008–12. The target for reductions for the European Union is 8 per cent, with targets for individual Member States ranging from a reduction of 21 per cent for Germany to an increase of 27 per cent for Portugal (Kyoto Protocol 1997 Annex B, EEA 2004b: 7).

In recent years governments have concentrated mainly on providing incentives for energy efficiency improvements and for the deployment of low carbon technologies, especially renewables. The main policy instruments used have been grants, preferential loans and special funds. Tax credits, exemptions and reductions have also played a role, but electoral sensitivity has deterred governments from using increased prices as a way of reducing demand and shifting it to other sources of energy. So far decarbonization strategies have been most successful in countries relying on nuclear power and hydro power. Energy conservation and efficiency measures are also important, and emissions trading is slowly becoming established in a number of countries (IEA 2003: 89–97, 112–14, Kaivo-oja and Luukkanen 2004: 1527).

If global warming is real and does cause increasing problems, more people will become convinced that something has to be done and pressure will mount for governments to do more. If sequestration becomes technically and economically feasible on a large scale, it could make a significant difference, although it is not clear how much (Herzog 2001). Governments could do more to encourage and enforce improvements in energy efficiency, but past experience suggests that such measures will not be enough to offset the effects of rising demand for energy. The development and use of renewables could be accelerated, but this is starting from such a low base, just 5.9 per cent of total energy demand in 2000 (European Commission 2003a: 111), that it is unlikely that they can make a big difference, at least in the short term. The size of the potential contribution of nuclear energy to the reduction of carbon dioxide emissions means that governments will also be under increased pressure to expand nuclear power despite continuing opposition due to its associated problems. Perhaps the most likely scenario is that all approaches that do not constrain economic growth will be tried but that energy-related carbon dioxide emissions will either still rise, although not by nearly as much as they would have without this effort, or will fall but not by very much.

The oil shortage scenario

As mentioned earlier, a number of analysts predict that oil production will peak well before 2030, leading to steadily increasing oil prices for at least part of the period up to 2030. Should this occur, the relevant energy king trend would be increasing oil prices rather than increasing energy consumption, as in such circumstances it is not at all clear that total energy consumption would continue to rise. Although it is not very satisfactory to have an alternative king trend in waiting in case these more alarmist forecasts are accurate, and official figures do not indicate an oil supply constraint in the period up to 2030, the possibility that oil production will peak earlier cannot be ignored altogether because we cannot be sure that it will not happen.

If it does occur, its impact on European economies will be profound. An oil price increase leads to a transfer of income from importing to exporting countries, the magnitude of which depends on the share of the cost of oil in national income, the extent of dependence on imported oil and the ability of users to reduce their consumption and switch to other forms of energy. It also depends on the extent to which gas prices rise as former oil users turn to gas as much as they can, the extent of gas use, and the impact of higher oil prices on the consumption and prices of other forms of energy. Higher oil prices directly raise price inflation and input costs while reducing non-oil demand and investment. The resulting lower level of economic activity reduces tax revenues and increases the size of budget deficits, which tends to lead to higher interest rates. Employee resistance to loss of purchasing power due to price inflation caused by increasing oil prices puts upward pressure on wages, which together with reduced demand tends to lead to higher unemployment. Oil-importing countries such as EU Member States also experience a deterioration in their balance of payments as a consequence of higher spending on oil (and possibly gas) imports putting downward pressure on exchange rates. To the extent that currency values fall the result is more expensive imports and less valuable exports, leading to a drop in real national income. The experience of the last three decades provides empirical evidence of the damage that oil price rises can cause: economic growth fell sharply in most oil-importing countries following the oil price rises of 1973–74 and 1979–80, and most of the major economic downturns in Europe in recent decades were preceded by sudden oil price increases (IEA 2004: 5–6).

Continuing increases in the price of oil and their economic consequences would have three main implications for public policy.

First, the economic problems that would result from rising oil prices would undermine the electoral position of governments, making it more electorally risky for them to implement unpopular policies and thereby making it more likely that they will seek wide support for policies before implementing them, leading to more cautious, centrist, populist and lowest-common-denominator policies than would otherwise be the case. The economic problems caused by rising oil prices may also lead to less coherent policies due to governments being replaced more frequently by alternative governments with different views.

Second, the economic and electoral damage caused by rising oil prices would strengthen the incentives for governments to do more to improve energy efficiency and foster the development and use of alternative sources of energy such as coal, nuclear energy and renewables. It would also motivate governments to do what they can to reduce the need for transport, for instance by promoting the use of communication using virtual reality technologies as an alternative to personal travel.

Finally, the economic problems caused by continuing oil price rises would increase the incentives for powerful oil-importing countries to use military action to take direct control of as much of the remaining oil as they can so that they can keep oil prices relatively low for their domestic users and thereby avoid or mitigate the economic consequences of rising oil prices, at least for a while. Oil prices for other oil-importing countries, of course, would rise more swiftly. The US is obviously the most likely candidate here, but at least some European countries might also be involved. There is also the possibility of conflict between major oil-importing countries for control of oil-producing regions, for example in central Asia.

Conclusion

Energy use in Europe and globally has been increasing for a long time and looks likely to continue to increase for the next 20 years or so. This creates pressures on governments to ensure security of supply and – somewhat at odds with this objective – to reduce energy-related carbon dioxide emissions due to their crucial role in causing climate change. Table 6.2 summarizes these main pressures.

Table 6.2 Policy implications of greater energy use

Policy implications	*Causal chain from trend*
More vigorous measures to ensure security of energy supply such as: • increasing reserve stocks of oil • diversifying foreign energy sources and supply routes • strengthening measures to encourage or enforce greater energy conservation and efficiency (such as by adjusting energy prices, using financial incentives and mandating minimum efficiency levels) • increasing diplomatic and, if necessary, military pressure on recalcitrant foreign governments Continuing efforts to ensure that global investment in energy production is adequate Continuing efforts to ensure that domestic utilities deliver power reliably and at reasonable prices	Increasing dependence of most EU countries on energy imports as energy use increases and domestic energy production falls, combined with the centrality of energy to economic growth and societal functioning in general and therefore to the electoral prospects of incumbent governments
More vigorous steps to respond to climate change, including: • encouraging sequestration of carbon dioxide from industrial and utility plant exhausts • reducing the use of energy in general by improving energy efficiency via means such as mandatory minimum efficiency standards and voluntary energy efficiency agreements with industry • reducing the carbon intensity of energy use via fuel substitution from oil and coal to gas, the expansion of nuclear power and the development and use of renewable forms of energy, using policy instruments such as tax incentives, higher taxes on fossil fuels and emissions, product bans, and emission trading schemes • funding or carrying out research in all these areas	Increasing evidence that climate change is real and that it is caused largely by the use of fossil fuels, making it clear that urgent steps need to be taken to reduce carbon dioxide emissions from energy use if serious environmental and economic problems in the future are to be avoided Pressure from scientists and environmentalists, as well as from policy actors and voters who would suffer from the effects of climate change (such as people living on flood plains) or who would benefit from measures to counteract it (such as producers of low-carbon energy) Increasing political leverage over energy policy of environment ministers, their departments and agencies, and of environmental experts in general inside and outside government

The policy implications of the possibility that the real energy king trend is rising oil prices are omitted on the basis that the relevant international organizations consider that this is unlikely to be a problem during the next couple of decades. We must hope that they are right.

In some respects the measures implied by pressures to mitigate climate change conflict with those designed to protect economic growth by ensuring energy security. Sequestration of carbon dioxide, for example, would be expensive, while shifting away from coal would be counter-productive from the point of view of energy security because it is so abundant. The US Energy Information Administration estimates total recoverable reserves of coal around the world at 1,001 billion tons, enough to last about 190 years at current consumption levels (US EIA: 50).

At the same time there are also policy measures towards which governments are being pushed by both energy security and climate change mitigation considerations, in particular improving energy efficiency and conservation, encouraging new energy technologies, and expanding nuclear energy. We have already seen action on energy efficiency and new energy technologies, and this is likely to continue, albeit mainly restricted to measures that do not in any way threaten economic growth. Other things being equal we can also expect to see action to expand nuclear energy as well.

7
Increasing Mobility

Introduction

As time goes on, people and goods are moving around more and more both within Europe and between Europe and other parts of the world. Between 1970 and 1998 personal mobility per day doubled from 17 to 35 kilometres (European Commission 2001: 11). Mobility has been growing steadily however measured and is almost certain to continue to increase, especially road, air and sea transport. This is the result of increased demand both for personal travel (commuting and other work-related travel, family and civic excursions such as shopping, and social and recreational travel), and for goods the trade and distribution networks for which are becoming longer and more complex. Increasing mobility puts pressure on governments not only to facilitate movement by reducing congestion but also to reduce transport-related carbon dioxide emissions in order to mitigate climate change. If oil production peaks in the next few years, however, rising oil prices will slow or reverse the trend towards increasing mobility, in which case rising oil prices rather than rising mobility would be the real king trend in this area.

Table 7.1 reveals that between 1970 and 2002 mobility increased in the EU as it was prior to the 2004 enlargement (EU-15) for all forms of transport apart from rail freight. Passenger car transport, road freight and intra-EU sea freight more than doubled and dominate transport in the EU-15. The biggest increase came in air transport, which rose sevenfold, although from such a small base that its share of passenger-kilometres remains small. Meanwhile traffic at airports increased five-fold (European Commission 2004e).

Comparable figures for total sea transport are not available, but over 90 per cent of the EU's external trade goes by sea and between 1997 and 1999 the total tonnage of goods handled in the major maritime ports of the EU-15 increased by just under two per cent. The EU-15 merchant fleet (ships of at least 1,000 gross tonnage) increased in terms of carrying capacity by 29 per cent between 1995 and 2003 (European Commission 2004d, 2004h: Table 3.6.13, Eurostat 2004a).

Table 7.1   Transport trends in the EU-15, 1970–2002

	% Change, 1970–2002	Total in 2002	Modal split 2002 (%)
Passenger transport (billion passenger-kilometres)	+133	4,927	100.0
Passenger cars	+149	3,882	78.8
Buses and coaches	+53	411	8.3
Rail	+40	307	6.2
Tram and metro	+41	48	1.0
Air	+748	280	5.7
Freight (billion tonne-kilometres)	+119	3,076	100.0
Road	+181	1,376	44.7
Rail	−16	236	7.7
Inland waterways	+21	125	4.1
Pipelines	+33	85	2.8
Sea (intra-EU)	+166	1,255	40.8
Number of passenger vehicles	+197	185,839,000	
Passenger cars per 1000 inhabitants	+167	491	
Number of goods vehicles	+194	21,902,700	
Length of motorways (kilometres)*	+230	52,914	
Number of road accidents involving personal injury	−11	1,240,720	
Road fatalities	−50	38,604	

Note: * 1970–2001.
Source: European Commission 2004h: Tables 3.2.2, 3.3.2, 3.5.5, 3.6.1, 3.6.2, 3.6.4, 3.7.3. One passenger-kilometre = one passenger carried one kilometre. One tonne-kilometre = one tonne carried one kilometre.

Mobility in the EU seems set to continue to rise, as indicated by Table 7.2. Between 2000 and 2030 passenger transport in the expanded EU of 25 Member States (EU-25), which is more relevant than the EU-15 when looking ahead, is expected to increase by over 50 per cent. This is a slower rate of increase than over the last 30 years but still substantial. Air transport is forecast to grow much more quickly than other modes: its share of passenger transport is expected to double to 11 per cent. However passenger transport overall is expected to continue to be dominated by private vehicles, the use of which is anticipated to take up three quarters of passenger-kilometres travelled. It is also likely that the number of cars on the road will increase, as EU-15 car density is still a third less than the US car density of 771 per thousand inhabitants (Eurostat 2004).

Between 2000 and 2030 freight transport in the EU-25 is expected to almost double. Road freight transport is anticipated to more than double, increasing its share of freight transport as a whole (European Commission 2003a: 149,

Table 7.2   Transport projections for the EU-25, 2000–2030

	% Change, 2000–2030	Total in 2030	Modal split, 2030 (%)
Passenger transport (billion passenger-kilometres)	+55	8,546.0	100.0
Private cars and motorcycles	+51	6,475.2	75.8
Public road transport	+13	556.1	6.5
Rail	+34	538.0	6.3
Air	+209	922.7	10.8
Inland navigation	+61	54.1	0.6
Freight (billion tonne-kilometres)	+88	4,046.0	100.0
Trucks	+111	3,133.4	77.4
Rail	+23	454.4	11.2
Inland waterways	+54	458.2	11.3
Travel per person (km per capita)	+53	18,653.0	
Passenger transport efficiency (toe/Mpkm)	+26	29.0	
Freight transport efficiency (toe/Mtkm)	+7	50.0	
Energy demand in transport (Mtoe)	+35	449.8	100.0
Private cars and motorcycles	+4	163.5	36.3
Public road transport	−9	6.4	1.4
Trucks	+78	193.8	43.1
Rail	−29	6.4	1.4
Air	+59	72.0	16.0
Inland navigation	+44	7.8	1.7
Carbon intensity (tonnes of carbon dioxide per toe)	−4	2.8	
Carbon dioxide emissions (millions of tonnes of carbon dioxide)	+30	1261.0	

Source: European Commission 2003a: 118–122, 149–151. One passenger-kilometre = one passenger carried one kilometre; one tonne-kilometre (tkm) = one tonne carried one kilometre. Toe = tonnes of oil equivalent. Mtoe = millions of tonnes of oil equivalent. Mpkm = millions of passenger-kilometres. Mtkm = millions of tonne-kilometres.

151). Authoritative estimates of EU seaborne traffic up to 2030 do not appear to be available, but the World Bank estimates that world seaborne trade will expand by 4 per cent per year over the decade up to 2010 (DfT 2004), and it seems reasonable to assume that sea traffic involving EU ports will participate in this trend.

Associated with this rising trend in mobility has been a big expansion of tourism, which is expected to continue. Tourist travel currently represents about 9 per cent of total EU passenger travel, 70 per cent of air travel and 11 per cent of energy use by transport. Between 1970 and 2002 international tourist arrivals per year in Europe increased by 254 per cent to 400 million, and by 2020 are forecast to increase by a further 80 per cent to 717 million. Domestic tourism, which is estimated to constitute about 80–90 per cent of tourism, is also expected to increase (OECD 2002c: 36, EEA 2003: 84–5, World Tourism Organization 2005, 2005a).

According to the European Commission the two key reasons for the expected continued rise in mobility are the spectacular increase in car use and the change from a 'stock' economy to a 'flow' economy in which transport is central. Freight movement has also been increased by other developments in business such as specialization, growth in international trade, internationalization of production and finance, the search for manufacturing scale economies, and the rationalization of production facilities. Economic growth is expected to increase the demand for business and personal travel as well as the requirement for freight movement (European Commission 2001: 12–13, 2004i: 106, DfT 2000). The increase in car use is also attributed to factors such as smaller households, more spread out cities in which facilities are becoming more dispersed (for example by locating large new shopping centres at the edges of cities), more cross-commuting instead of radial commuting, and greater use of cars by the elderly (Banister 2002: 2–14). Reasons for the increase in tourism include greater affluence, shorter working hours, earlier retirement, more retirees, increases in vacation entitlements, a trend away from a single long annual holiday towards multiple short holidays, lower prices and extensive marketing (OECD 2002c: 73–9, EEA 2003: 85).

Increases in mobility are expected to have two main immediate consequences over and above sustaining economic growth and meeting our desire to travel more: increasing congestion, and increasing energy use.

Congestion in the EU-15 is already serious, with about 10 per cent of the road network affected daily by traffic jams, 20 per cent of the rail network classed as bottlenecks, and 16 of the EU's main airports recording delays of more than 15 minutes on more than 30 per cent of their flights. Given the economic importance of transport – total expenditure on transport in the EU in 2001 was estimated to be around €1,000 billion, which is more than 10 per cent of EU GDP – this is a substantial problem for the European economy. And it is likely to worsen: the Commission's White Paper on Transport forecast that with current policies congestion will increase significantly by 2010 and that the economic costs of congestion will increase by 142 per cent to reach €80 billion per year, about one per cent of EU GDP (European Commission 2001: 10–11).

Greater mobility also means increasing energy use (Table 7.2). To some extent increasing energy efficiency is expected to offset the effect on energy use of projected increases in transport usage, especially for passenger transport, but even so the total energy used is expected to rise by about a third by 2030. Most of this increased energy is expected to be used by trucks and airplanes. As fossil fuels are expected to constitute 94 per cent of transport fuel in

2030, this means that transport-related carbon dioxide emissions are expected to rise by about a third to constitute 29 per cent of total carbon dioxide emissions (European Commission 2003a: 118–22, 150–1).

Transport also contributes to other environmental problems, including air pollution, noise, loss of land and blight, so one might expect increases in transport to cause more and more environmental damage, but it appears that in the main this is not occurring. Although nature areas are under increasing pressure from the expansion of transport infrastructure, and noise continues to be a serious problem, in other areas the situation is improving: improved emission standards, for example, have led to a substantial drop in the emission of harmful pollutants from road vehicles (Banister 2002: 246, EEA 2004). One might also think that increases in transport, especially road transport, would increase the number of transport-related deaths and injuries, but on the basis of past experience this is not expected, as between 1970 and 2002 the number of road accidents involving injuries or death declined significantly (Table 7.1).

Official projections of increasing mobility are premised on the assumption that oil prices will remain relatively low because oil production is not anticipated to peak before 2030. However a number of industry analysts predict that in fact oil production will peak well before then, on the basis that estimates of oil reserves have in the past been inflated for political reasons, the results of recent oil exploration have been disappointing, and the growth of demand for oil has been underestimated by organizations such as the IEA (Goodstein 2004, Hirsch *et al.* 2005: 13–19, Illum 2005). The significance of this is that once oil production peaks and starts to decline, the continuing growth in demand for oil relative to supply would be expected to drive up transport fuel prices indefinitely, since there are no ready alternative fuels for motor vehicles, aircraft, trains and ships (Hirsch *et al.* 2005: 27, 64). As the cost of transport continued to rise, the trend towards greater mobility would slow or even reverse. Since no-one knows for sure when oil production will peak, we need to take into account the possibility that it will peak sooner than 2030, possibly much sooner. If this happens the king trend to focus on would not be rising mobility but rising oil prices.

Implications

Transport ministers, their ministries, regional and local governments, the transport lobby and environmentalists tend to be the most prominent policy actors in the transport sector (Table 7.3). Also important are finance, industry and environment ministers. Heads of government are often involved in major policy decisions.

National governments set the broad policy parameters for transport operations and planning, including investment procedures and levels, vehicle and driver licensing, safety standards, fiscal measures such as fuel tax,

Table 7.3   Generic transport policy network

Type of policy actor	Specific policy actor
Political executives and associated parties	Chief executives Transport ministers Ministers for finance, energy, environment, trade
Non-government politicians	European Commissioners relating to transport, energy, environment and trade Parliamentary committees relating to transport, finance, energy, environment and trade Subnational leaders at regional and local level
Civil servants, special advisers and other public sector employees	Transport ministries and associated infrastructure agencies such as port authorities Ministries for finance, energy, environment and trade Publicly-owned airlines and airports, rail infrastructure and operating companies, and bus and coach companies International organizations such as the International Civil Aviation Organization (ICAO) European Commission Directorates-General relating to transport, energy, the environment and trade Subnational authorities such as cities and local councils
Judges and regulators	Competition authorities Regulators of air transport, railways, road transport, water transport Environmental regulators
Business	Private airlines and airports, port authorities, rail infrastructure and operating companies, and bus and coach companies Freight companies using road, rail and water transport Construction companies Manufacturers of motor vehicles, airplanes, trains and ships User firms such as importers/exporters, manufacturers, retailers
Interest groups and non-government organizations	Chambers of commerce and industry, trade organizations Organizations representing infrastructure and operating companies Motoring organizations Transport unions Environmental organizations Local groups, such as protesters against airport expansion
Media	Mainstream and specialist transport media
Experts	Transport specialists in the public and private sector
Electorate	Passengers, motorists, consumers

Source: adapted from Preston *et al.* 2004.

environmental standards, planning standards and regulatory standards. Both national governments and regional and local governments are involved in the direct provision of transport infrastructure such as roads and airports as well as transport operations such as railways and buses, although the extent of this has been diminishing in recent years due to privatization. The European Commission is increasingly becoming involved in areas such as infrastructure provision at European level (Preston *et al.* 2004).

Important groups within the transport lobby include employer and trade organizations, public and private carriers such as airlines and haulage firms, construction companies, vehicle manufacturers and motorists' organizations. Behind these stand all businesses that send or receive products or components. In general the transport lobby thinks that mobility is a good thing and wants transport to be improved (UNICE 2002). Environmentalists, on the other hand, wish to restrict or reverse the growth in transport because it is believed to be a major contributor to climate change as well as to other forms of pollution such as noise (T&E 2001, WWF 2002).

The policy implications of increasing mobility relate mainly to congestion and climate change. The implications of the possibility that increasing fuel prices will be the relevant transport king trend are explored later in the chapter.

Congestion

As congestion grows, businesses and voters are likely to exert increasing pressure on governments to do something about it, other things being equal.

Many if not most businesses have an interest in an efficient transport network. Not only are there companies with an obvious stake in transport, such as airlines and road haulage companies, there are also infrastructure companies such as private airports and construction companies, plus importers and exporters as well as manufacturers and retailers wanting to move goods swiftly and at an affordable price. This means that business in general has an interest in taking measures to ensure that congestion is minimized. If congestion grows, therefore, businesses are likely to devote increasing attention and resources to lobbying public authorities to do something about it on the basis that it harms the economy. As congestion and its economic costs mount, these arguments are likely to become increasingly credible to governments.

Pressure from voters is also likely to intensify: as congestion grows and increasingly inconveniences passengers and motorists, they are increasingly likely to take transport into account when casting their votes (or responding to opinion polls), to the detriment of any incumbent government that is perceived not to be doing enough to solve the problem. While transport is just one issue among many others, elected governments are nevertheless likely to be sensitive to this threat.

There are three main ways in which, in principle, governments can tackle congestion: improve transport infrastructure, improve management of transport, and reduce demand for transport.

Improve transport infrastructure

This is the obvious knee-jerk response to congestion: if there is congestion on the roads, build more roads and improve existing ones; if there is congestion at airports, build new airports and expand existing ones. However finance ministers tend to have reservations about the expense of building large infrastructure projects, while locals and environmentalists object to the environmental damage and may conduct high-profile protests against major new projects. Perhaps the most compelling objection to this option is that building new infrastructure may be futile, as there is evidence that road improvement, for instance, tends to release latent demand – in other words, it appears that better roads often result in more traffic rather than less congestion (Vigar 2002: 2).

Improve management of transport

Another option is to try to reduce congestion by organizing transport management and infrastructure more effectively. Freight and passengers could be shifted from road and air transport to less congested modes, in particular short-sea and inland waterway transport, for example by establishing 'motorways of the sea' with ports connected to the inland rail network. Connections between different modes of transport in general could be improved by giving priority to ports and airports that have good connections with the road and rail networks. And traffic management could be improved by employing new transportation technologies such as sensors and Intelligent Transportation Systems, integrating air traffic control at European level, and reorganizing educational and working patterns to avoid overcrowding roads at particular times (European Commission 2001: 15, 36–52).

Again, however, most measures in this area would cost money and may lead to more traffic rather than less congestion.

Reduce demand for transport

If demand for transport could be reduced, congestion would be reduced without the need for expensive new infrastructure. This option is generally referred to as demand management.

There are a number of ways in which demand could be reduced. In relation to cars and trucks, for example, public authorities could extend measures to restrict access to certain areas by means such as establishing car-free zones, extending parking restrictions and introducing access control to give priority to certain types of users such as essential users, residents, public transport, cyclists and pedestrians. Alternatives to conventional car use could be made more attractive, for example by improving public transport, extending park-and-ride schemes and encouraging high occupancy vehicles and smaller cars, which take up less space on the road. The cost of road transport as such could be increased by raising parking prices and increasing taxes, although the available evidence indicates that motorists do not alter their behaviour much in response to increases in fuel tax. In the longer term, land-use planning could be used to reduce the need for journeys, especially long journeys, by placing facilities closer together and restricting developments such as out of town shopping malls, and by planning for higher-density living (Glaister 1999: 165, Banister 2002: 108–10, 213, 248–58, European Commission 2004i: 105).

Measures could also be taken to reduce demand for air travel, for example by adjusting taxation systems to ensure that the cost of air transport fully reflects external costs such as environmental costs. This implies reduction or elimination of tax breaks and subsidies plus imposition of higher taxes, which would mean higher prices that would at least to some extent discourage people from travelling by air (Whitelegg and Haq 2003: 282–8).

More radically, it might soon be possible to reduce the demand for passenger transport by encouraging the substitution of communications for personal travel, for instance in relation to business meetings and tourism, through the use of improved video and virtual reality technology. For example, it may become possible to tour Florence from one's own home using cameras in Florence transmitting to one's virtual reality helmet.

Measures to reduce demand for transport tend to be supported by environmentalists and their allies but opposed by businesses and by motorists and passengers insofar as they directly limit car or air travel or make it more expensive.

Climate change

It is now widely agreed that climate change is taking place and that it is caused largely by the burning of fossil fuels. Since the transport sector consumes about a third of total energy used in the EU-25 – 31 per cent of total energy final demand in 2000 – and is almost completely dependent on fossil fuels, efforts to tackle climate change must obviously include action in the transport sector if they are to have any chance of success (European Commission 2003a: 118–19). As climate change is analysed as a king trend in its own right in Chapter 14, here the aim is to concentrate specifically on the relationship between transport and climate change.

Climate change is significant because of the serious damage it is expected to cause to environmental systems and ultimately to economic systems as well. In relation to Europe this is expected to include increased flooding, more frequent and intense extreme weather events, hotter drier summers in southern Europe (which among other things will hit tourism), and an extension of vector-borne diseases such as malaria from the south. There is also the possibility of a significant slowing of ocean circulation bringing warm water to the North Atlantic, which ironically would dramatically cool the climate of Western Europe. According to the UN IPCC, the only way of avoiding these and other consequences, or of mitigating them given that climate change is already under way, is to stabilize and ultimately reduce the levels of greenhouse gases such as carbon dioxide in the atmosphere, which can only be done by reducing greenhouse gas emissions to near-zero levels (IPCC 2001).

To the extent that concern over climate change grows, in relation to transport governments will come under increasing pressure to take steps to reduce carbon dioxide emissions. Environmental scientists have convinced most policy actors inside and outside government that climate change is real, that it is caused mainly by man-made emissions of greenhouse gases, and that it will have damaging consequences if left unchecked. It is expected that sooner or later climate change will cause economic damage that will undermine the electoral position of incumbent governments. In these circumstances pressure for action on climate change is increasingly likely to be exerted by policy actors and voters who would suffer from its effects or who would benefit from measures to counteract it, such as people living on flood plains and renewable energy companies. Pressure will also be exerted by experts and environmentalists as well as by voters and other domestic and international policy actors who have become convinced of the reality of climate change and want something to be done. This pressure will increase to the extent that new scientific findings increase concern or link natural disasters such as the heat wave of 2003 to climate change. Among other things this means that environment ministers, their departments and agencies are likely to become more involved in the making of transport policy.

If reduction of carbon dioxide emissions is added to economic goals as an objective of transport policy, however, it follows that in at least some cases the most economically rational transport options will not be chosen. It follows from this in turn that in these cases economic damage will result relative to what would otherwise have happened. At the same time, however, climate change itself also has economically disruptive effects, especially in the long term, so there is an economic price to be paid whatever is done or not done. Since business and governments are concerned first and foremost with the short term, however, measures to combat climate change are likely to be opposed by both insofar as they obstruct the pursuit of economic objectives.

There are five main ways in which transport-related carbon dioxide emissions could be reduced, given that sequestration of carbon dioxide from transport emissions is a remote prospect at present: improve the energy efficiency of transport, switch from fossil fuels to less carbon-intensive fuels, move passengers and freight to less carbon-intensive forms of transport, extend emissions trading to transport, and reduce the demand for transport.

Improve the energy efficiency of transport

Since transport is so dependent on fossil fuels, improving the energy efficiency of transport, so that less primary energy is needed to fulfil the desired tasks, must result in lower levels of carbon dioxide emissions, other things being equal. Governments can encourage improved energy efficiency by means such as imposing or raising mandatory minimum efficiency performance standards for motor vehicles and by agreeing voluntary efficiency programmes with industry, such as the agreement providing for European vehicle manu-facturers to improve fuel efficiency of new vehicles (IEA 2003: 105–9). Although implementing such standards would be likely to add to business and consumer costs, these would be offset at least to some extent by savings on energy use. The European Commission estimates that implementing the EC Action Plan for Energy Efficiency, which includes measures such as pro-viding incentives for optimal occupancy of vehicles, modal shifts and modal integration, completion of the internal market in rail transport and reduc-tions in the carbon dioxide emissions of new cars, would result in energy use by transport in 2030 being 13 per cent less than it would otherwise be, which implies a significant reduction in carbon dioxide emissions (European Commission 2004i: 78–9, 87).

Switch from fossil fuels to less carbon-intensive fuels

To the extent that transport providers switch from fossil fuels to less carbon-intensive fuels, carbon dioxide emissions from transport will be reduced, other things being equal. Governments can encourage this by using finan-cial incentives such as grants, preferential loans, special funds, tax exemp-tions, tax credits and tax reductions to foster the development and use of low- or zero-emission renewable fuels such as biodiesel, ethanol, hydrogen, methanol, natural gas, propane and solar energy, as well as electricity gener-ated from non-fossil fuels such as nuclear energy and renewables (IEA 2003: 92, 112–14).

Move passengers and freight to less carbon-intensive forms of transport

To the extent that transport users and freight shift from modes of transport that are totally dependent on fossil fuels, such as road and air transport, to modes that also use other forms of energy, such as rail, much of which runs on electricity that is produced by nuclear energy and to a lesser extent by renewables, carbon dioxide emissions will be reduced, other things being equal. Governments can encourage this by means such as creating a dedi-cated trans-European rail freight network, upgrading existing lines, raising taxes on road transport and removing the tax exemption on aircraft fuel to make air travel more expensive relative to other modes of transport – although the fuel protests in 2000 demonstrate the political disadvantages of raising taxes in this area (European Commission 2001: 27–32, 39, 50–1, Doherty *et al.* 2003). The European Commission estimates that if measures were taken to ensure that the share of passenger rail, rail freight and public road trans-port remained stable at 1998 levels up to 2010 rather than falling as pro-jected, due to action such as adjusting pricing, revitalizing alternative forms of transport and investing in the trans-European network, then by 2030 energy use by transport, and associated carbon dioxide emissions, would be about 4 per cent lower than they otherwise would be. If in addition load factors for all transport modes increased significantly by 2010, so that all transport became more efficient, it is estimated that energy use and carbon dioxide emissions would be about 9 per cent lower (European Commission 2004i: 105, 110).

Extend emissions trading to transport

Emissions trading schemes such as the one implemented in the EU in 2005 provide for those responsible for emissions to keep within set limits by reducing their own emissions and/or by buying the right to increase emissions beyond this limit from others who reduce their emissions below the limits that apply to them. Although it would be difficult to apply this to private cars, it could be applied to mass carriers such as airlines. If the overall limit is reduced over time, emissions trading should result in the progressive reduction of transport-related emissions where it is easiest and cheapest and least economically damaging.

Reduce demand for transport

Reducing the demand for transport would obviously reduce the use of fossil fuels and therefore carbon dioxide emissions. All the measures listed for reducing congestion by reducing demand are relevant here, but reducing demand in order to reduce carbon dioxide emissions is different in two important respects. First, it is not targeted on certain locations, namely bottlenecks. Instead demand reduction is good wherever it occurs. Second, one means of reducing demand in general is precisely *not* to reduce congestion, as making travel longer and less pleasant should discourage it, at least up to a point.

The oil shortage scenario

If oil production peaks earlier than official studies expect and rising oil prices throw the trend towards greater mobility into doubt, the impact on European economies would be profound. An oil price increase leads to a transfer of income from importing to exporting countries. Higher oil prices directly raise price inflation and input costs while reducing non-oil demand and investment. The resulting lower level of economic activity reduces tax revenues and increases the size of budget deficits, which tends to lead to higher interest rates. Employee resistance to loss of purchasing power due to price inflation caused by increasing oil prices puts upward pressure on wages, which together with reduced demand tends to lead to higher unemployment. Meanwhile higher transport costs lead to lower levels of trade, while oil-importing countries such as EU Member States experience a deterioration in their balance of payments as a consequence of higher spending on oil imports, putting downward pressure on exchange rates. The experience of the last three decades shows just how damaging rising oil prices can be: economic growth fell sharply in most oil-importing countries following the oil price rises of 1973–74 and 1979–80, and most of the major economic downturns in Europe in recent decades were preceded by sudden oil price increases (IEA 2004: 5–6).

The economic and therefore electoral problems that would be caused by rising fuel prices would create incentives for governments to do what they can to mitigate their impact by reducing the use of oil in transport wherever this is economically feasible. Ironically this is also the aim of measures designed to mitigate the impact of carbon dioxide emissions from transport on climate change. This means that rising oil prices would reinforce the pressure exerted on governments by concerns about climate change to do what they can to increase the energy efficiency of transport, switch to other fuels, move passengers and freight to modes of transport that are not dependent on oil, and reduce the demand for transport.

However these measures would be unlikely to prevent the problems that would result from rising oil prices from undermining the electoral position of governments, making it electorally more risky for them to implement unpopular policies and thereby making it more likely that they would seek wide support for policies before implementing them, other things being equal, leading to more cautious, centrist, populist and lowest-common-denominator policies than would otherwise be the case. The electoral problems of governments might also lead to less coherent policies due to governments being replaced more frequently by alternative governments with different views.

Finally, the economic problems caused by continuing oil price rises would increase the incentives for powerful oil-importing countries to use military action to take direct control of as much of the remaining oil as possible in order to take it off the world market and reserve it for their domestic users with the aim of slowing or halting domestic oil price rises and thereby avoiding or mitigating the economic problems that would otherwise ensue, at least for a while. This would mean that less oil was available for other countries, leading to even swifter price rises for them than previously. The US is obviously the most likely country to take action of this sort, with troops already well-placed in the Middle East and other oil-producing regions, but at least some European countries might also be involved. There is also the possibility of conflict between major oil-importing countries for control of oil-producing regions, for example in central Asia.

Conclusion

Transport use in Europe and globally has been increasing for a long time and looks likely to continue to increase. This creates pressures on governments to control congestion for economic and electoral reasons and to reduce transport-related carbon dioxide emissions due to their crucial role in causing climate change. Table 7.4 summarizes these pressures. The policy implications of the possibility that the real king trend in this area will be rising fuel prices are omitted on the grounds that the relevant international organizations consider that this is unlikely to be a problem during the next couple of decades, but should not be disregarded altogether.

In relation to congestion the pressures on governments to do something stem mainly from the increasing credibility of business arguments stressing the economic costs of congestion and the threat of electoral retribution if congestion is allowed to increase. In relation to climate change the pressures emanate mainly from policy actors learning from environmental scientists that climate change is real, damaging and to a significant degree caused by transport-related carbon dioxide emissions.

To a considerable extent these pressures are contradictory, so that it is difficult to determine in which direction policy is likely to shift. Thus pressure to improve transport infrastructure is countered not only by traditional arguments such as cost but also by the evidence that it leads to more traffic rather than less congestion, which from the point of view of climate change is counter-productive. Conversely, stringent measures to mitigate climate change would be likely to lead to lower economic growth than would otherwise be the case due to their effects on business costs, whereas a principal aim of reducing congestion is to increase economic growth. The idea of letting congestion itself discourage transport use runs directly counter to the objective of reducing congestion. For this reason it seems likely that implementation of draconian measures to reduce transport-related carbon dioxide emissions is likely to be limited, although this depends partly on the extent to which extreme weather events and other damage linked to climate change do in fact affect Europe in the years ahead.

In other respects, however, measures to reduce traffic congestion and measures to mitigate climate change point in the same direction. Steps to reduce the demand for transport would both reduce congestion and reduce carbon dioxide emissions – although if these constrained economic growth in any way they would conflict with one of the major objectives towards which congestion reduction is aimed. This implies that we should expect successive policy initiatives designed to reduce the demand for transport in ways that are not economically damaging, for instance by encouraging the substitution of communication for personal travel.

Other policy implications of the concern to reduce transport-related carbon dioxide emissions neither contradict nor reinforce those designed to reduce congestion. These include measures aimed at improving energy efficiency, switching passengers and goods to less carbon-intensive forms of transport such as railways, encouraging motorists and others to switch to non-oil fuels if and when these become economically viable, and extending emissions

Table 7.4 Policy implications of greater mobility

Policy implications	Causal chain from trend
More vigorous anti-congestion measures such as: • improving transport infrastructure • improving the organization and management of transport, for example by shifting passengers and freight to less congested modes by means such as improving intermodal connections with 'motorways of the sea' • reducing the demand for transport in areas where congestion is a problem, for example by restricting access to certain areas, raising selected taxes (for instance on air travel) and placing facilities closer to users • encouraging the substitution of communications for personal travel in areas such as business meetings and tourism using means such as virtual reality technologies	Increasing pressure from business and voters to slow, halt and preferably reduce the increase in traffic congestion due to its growing economic and personal costs
More vigorous steps to respond to climate change insofar as it is caused by transport, for example: • improving energy efficiency by means such as mandatory minimum efficiency standards and voluntary energy efficiency agreements with industry • using grants, preferential loans, special funds, tax exemptions, tax credits and tax reductions to foster the development and use of low- or zero-emission renewable fuels such as biodiesel, hydrogen and solar energy, as well as electricity generated from non-fossil fuels such as nuclear energy and renewables • encouraging transport providers to switch from fossil fuels to less carbon intensive fuels or renewables using means such as fiscal incentives • shifting passengers and freight to low carbon forms of transport such as rail by means such as improving the rail network and using fiscal measures to reduce its prices relative to other modes of transport • extending emissions trading to transport, for example airlines • reducing demand for transport in general, for example by using tax measures to raise the price of transport, placing facilities closer to users, and not taking steps to reduce congestion	Increasing evidence that climate change is real and that transport is a major culprit, so that urgent steps need to be taken to reduce carbon dioxide emissions from transport if serious environmental and economic problems in the future are to be avoided Pressure from scientists, environmentalists and policy actors and voters who would suffer from the effects of climate change (such as people living on flood plains) or who would benefit from measures to counteract it (such as producers of low-carbon energy) Increasing political leverage over transport policy of environment ministers, their departments and agencies, as well as environmental experts in general inside and outside government, due to perceptions that transport-related carbon dioxide emissions need to be reduced

trading to airlines – again providing that such measures do not have economically damaging effects. Perhaps the most likely scenario is that all approaches to reducing transport-related carbon dioxide emissions that do not constrain economic growth will be tried but that emissions will either still rise, although not by nearly as much as they would have without this effort, or will fall, but not by very much. The European Commission's best case scenario for 2030, with strong policies in place to restrict energy use and carbon dioxide emissions, is that energy use by transport would be 21 per cent lower than it would otherwise be, and carbon dioxide emissions 31 per cent lower (European Commission 2004i: 122). Such reductions would be significant, but nowhere near the magnitude of the deep cuts that the IPCC considers are necessary for all countries to make if further climate change is to be prevented.

8
The Shift to Services

Introduction

For decades now employment in EU countries has been falling in agriculture and industry (mining and quarrying, manufacturing, utilities and construction) and rising in services, especially professional and business services, and health and social work. The main political effects of this are likely to be a weakening of trade union and working class influence on public policy, better health and education services, and a decline in the policy autonomy of governments due to lower levels of economic growth.

In 1970 the numbers employed in industry and services in the 15 countries that constituted the EU prior to the 2004 enlargement (EU-15) were about equal while significant numbers continued to be employed in agriculture, but by 2003 employment in agriculture was negligible and services employed over two thirds of the workforce (Table 8.1). This pattern also characterized the value added to production by each sector.

Service sector workers are defined by the OECD as individuals working for pay in a local establishment whose major activity is the provision of services rather than goods. Services are often distinguished from goods on the basis that services are intangible, require direct face-to-face interaction and are difficult to store, although products such as computer software do not fit neatly either side of this distinction. Defining services in this way also excludes service-type work performed within mainly goods-producing firms, such as accountants employed by an airplane manufacturer. This suggests that the available statistics may underestimate the real number of people in service jobs (OECD 2000a: 81).

Within the general services category, which in effect consists of everything apart from agriculture and industry, specific types of services can be grouped in many different ways according to many different criteria. The main goods-producing and services categories used by EU countries are set out in Table 8.2 along with the percentages of employment within each category in 1995, the first year for which full data for the EU-15 is available, and 2003. This

Table 8.1 The shift to services in the EU-15, 1970–2003

	% total employment			
Sector	1970	2000	Change, 1970–2000	2003
Employment				
Agriculture	13.5	4.3	−9.1	3.9
Industry	41.4	29.0	−12.4	27.6
Manufacturing	*30.4*	*19.9*	*−10.5*	–
Services	45.0	66.7	+21.7	68.5
Value-added				
Agriculture	6.7	2.2	−4.5	na
Industry	41.2	28.1	−13.1	na
Manufacturing	*29.3*	*19.6**	*−9.7*	na
Services	52.2	69.7	+17.5	na

Notes: * 1999; na = not applicable.
Sources: OECD 2001e: 40–1, 62–3 (1970–2000), OECD 2004 (2003).

Table 8.2 Employment by sector as percentage of total employment, EU-15, 1995–2003

Code	Description	1995	2003	Change
Goods-producing sectors				
A + B	Agriculture, hunting, forestry and fishing	5.2	4.0	−1.2
C	Mining and quarrying	0.4	0.3	−0.1
D	Manufacturing	21.2	18.9	−2.3
E	Electricity, gas and water supply	0.9	0.8	−0.1
F	Construction	7.8	8.0	+0.2
Services sectors				
G	Wholesale and retail trade, repair of motor vehicles, motorcycles and personal and household goods	15.0	14.7	−0.3
H	Hotels and restaurants	3.8	4.1	+0.3
I	Transport, storage and communications	6.0	6.2	+0.2
J	Financial intermediation	3.5	3.4	−0.1
K	Real estate, renting and business activities	7.0	9.3	+2.3
L	Public administration and defence, compulsory social security	7.8	7.7	−0.1
M	Education	6.6	7.0	+0.4
N	Health and social work	9.1	9.8	+0.7
O	Other community, social and personal service activities	4.5	4.7	+0.2
P	Private households with employed persons	1.0	1.2	+0.2

Source: Eurostat 2005.

shows a sharp decline in employment in the manufacturing sector even over this short period as well as an equally sharp rise in employment in real estate, renting and business activities (OECD 2000a: 81–5).

A more useful classification for analytical purposes is that of Elfring (1988), who groups services according to three criteria: the economic function performed by the service, whether businesses or households are the primary users, and whether market or non-market provision predominates. This yields four subsectors, each consisting of four service activities. Producer services (business and professional services, financial services, insurance and real estate) provide intermediate inputs to further production activities, make extensive use of ICT and high-skilled workers, and are sold mainly to other firms. Distributive services (retail trade, wholesale trade, transportation and communications) move commodities, information and people. Personal services (hotels and restaurants, recreational and cultural services, domestic services and other personal services) are provided direct to households and are characterized by direct contact between the consumer and service provider. Social services (government proper, health, education and miscellaneous social services) are provided mainly by the state direct to households (OECD 2001a: 82–3, 117).

Long-term comparable data on trends within the service sector using these categories is not available for all EU countries, but Elfring's study of Britain, France, Germany, Japan, the Netherlands, Sweden and the US found strong growth during the 1970s and 1980s for producer services and social services and some growth during the 1980s for personal services but little change for distributive services. A follow-up study found that between 1984 and 1998 these trends were true of all OECD countries. By 1998 distributive services and social services each constituted about a third of services employment, with the other third divided equally between producer services and personal services. Producer service jobs were mostly in business and professional services, distributive services jobs mostly in retail, and personal services jobs mostly in hotels and restaurants (OECD 2001a: 82–6).

In recent years this pattern of growth in services employment has continued. Between 1995 and 2003 producer services (J + K in Table 8.2) increased as a share of total employment by 2.2 percentage points. This was due entirely to very rapid growth in employment in real estate, renting and business activities. Distributive services (G + I) again remained fairly stable. For personal services and social services the Eurostat categories cannot be perfectly translated into Elfring's groupings, but employment grew in all their major components: in hotels and restaurants and domestic services for personal services, in education and health and social work for social services, and in other community, social and personal service activities, which in Elfring's schema are split between personal services and social services. These developments are reflected in occupational statistics showing job losses in skilled manual jobs combined with growth in the number of professionals, technicians and other service workers (Eurostat 2005a).

By far the quickest growing services sector is real estate, renting and business activities, which might be more accurately identified as professional and business services as it includes computer specialists, researchers and traditional professionals (lawyers, accountants, architects and engineers) as well as estate agents, renters and people in jobs more obviously identifiable as business services (Table 8.3). By 2003 employment in this sector constituted nearly ten per cent of total employment in the EU-15. Between 1995 and 2002 employment in all its principal sub-sectors grew in all EU Member States, especially employment in computer and related activities, albeit from a very low base. ICT workers more generally increased from 2.7 per cent of total occupations in the mid-1990s to 3.2 per cent in 2001 (OECD 2003: 76, Eurostat 2005, OECD 2005a). The growth of professional and business services represents social progress in that working conditions are relatively good compared to the goods-producing sector and other services sectors in terms of the incidence of unpleasant working conditions, unpleasant work tasks, monotonous work, job insecurity, antisocial hours, limited working time flexibility, limited work

Table 8.3   Professional and business services, EU-15, 2003

Real estate activities with own property, letting of own property, real estate activities on a fee or contract basis

Renting of machinery and equipment without operator and of personal and household goods, including automobiles

Computer and related activities: hardware consultancy, software consultancy and supply, data processing, database activities, maintenance and repair of office, accounting and computing machinery, other computer related activities

Research and experimental development in natural sciences, engineering, social sciences and humanities where not combined with education

Other business activities:
  Legal, accounting, book-keeping and auditing activities; tax consultancy; market research and public opinion polling; business and management consultancy; holdings

Architectural and engineering activities and related technical consultancy

Technical testing and analysis

Advertising

Labour recruitment and provision of personnel

Investigation and security activities

Industrial cleaning

Photographic activities

Packaging activities

Other business activities not elsewhere classified, including bill collecting and credit rating, business brokerage, stenographic, duplicating and mailing activities including typing and other secretarial activities, fashion design, auctioning, editing, telephone answering

---

Sources: OECD 2001h: 70–1, Table 8.2, UN 2004. This is the UN classification for real estate, renting and business activities used by the OECD, which is compatible with the NACE Rev.1 classification used by EU Member States.

autonomy, lack of benefits and work-related health problems. Subjective job satisfaction is also relatively high, as are pay levels (OECD 2001i: 99–106).

Employment also grew strongly in the health and social work sector, which consists of hospital activities, medical and dental practice activities, the activities of other health professionals such as nurses and paramedical practitioners, veterinary activities, social work with accommodation such as homes for the aged and rehabilitation homes, and social work without accommodation such as counseling and prevention of cruelty to children and others. By 2003 health and social work employed nearly ten per cent of the employed workforce, about the same as professional and business services. There was also some growth in employment in education, which by 2003 constituted seven per cent of total employment (Table 8.2, UN 2004).

Most of these jobs, as well as many in professional and business services, mainly involve handling information. This is obvious in the education sector, but is increasingly true of the health sector as well with its increasing use of ICT (see Chapter 3), although perhaps less true of social work. The growth of these three sectors, which together now constitute over a quarter of employment in the EU-15, bears out the view of Aoyama and Castells and others that the economy is increasingly becoming informationalized (Aoyama and Castells 2002). Another similarity with professional and business services is the relatively high pay and job satisfaction enjoyed by those employed in education, health and social work (OECD 2001i: 104, 106).

There were also some increases in employment between 1995 and 2003 in hotels and restaurants, transport, communications and storage, private households with employed persons (domestic services) and other community, social and personal activities. This last category consists of a diverse range of activities that includes waste management, the activities of membership organizations such as trade unions, media and cultural activities, sport and other recreational activities, laundering, hairdressing and funeral activities. However the magnitude of increases in employment in these sectors is not sufficient to enable one to be sure that they are more than random fluctuations, although apart from transport, storage and communications they are consistent with the slow growth in personal services in previous periods. Apart from the cultural components of other community, social and personal activities, jobs in these sectors have relatively little information or ICT component, and the hotel and restaurant sector in particular stands out as having low pay, bad working conditions and low job satisfaction (OECD 2001i: 99, 103, 106).

Will the trend to services continue? One possibility is that advances in ICT will lead to massive job losses by enabling the rapid automation of services, as has happened recently in financial intermediation with the advent of developments such as automatic tellers and Internet banking, although the scope for widespread automation of services appears at this stage to be limited. As health and education are largely provided through the public sector, limits to public financing might limit further rises in employment in these areas.

It seems more likely that this long-established trend will continue. According to the OECD there are two main reasons for the rise in services employment. First, there is the greater scope for technologically driven productivity improvements in the goods-producing sector, as this makes it possible to maintain or even increase goods production while cutting jobs whereas in services more production generally requires more employees. The other reason is increasing demand for services as consumer incomes rise (OECD 2000a: 97–105). Both these trends appear likely to continue. Reich suggests that there are no natural limits on what people want and are prepared to pay others to do for them, and most of the growth domains he lists – health, entertainment, intellectual stimulation, attractiveness to others, contact with others, family wellbeing including education, and financial security – relate to growth sectors in services (Reich 2002: 27–9). Demand for professional and business services seems likely to continue to grow as long as business thrives, and there is no reason to suppose that demand for health services will fall, especially in view of population ageing. Rising incomes (Chapter 5) suggest that demand will continue to rise for hotels, restaurants, entertainment and personal services. Expansion of education, especially higher education, seems likely to continue (Chapter 16) due to its perceived value both for the economy and for personal career prospects.

The view that employment growth will come mostly from services is widely shared among relevant experts. During recent years countries with above-average service sector shares of employment, and in particular countries with high employment in producer and social services, have had above-average rates of employment. More specifically, high employment rates are positively correlated with high rates of employment in business and professional services, real estate, health services and other social services. The higher rate of employment in the US compared to the EU average can be largely attributed to higher employment shares for producer services and for hotels and restaurants. A study of 14 OECD countries attributed almost all net employment growth between 1986 and 1998 to increased services employment, suggesting that services are probably the dominant source of further employment gains (OECD 2001a: 106–13).

In short, the most likely scenario is further losses of jobs in manufacturing accompanied by continuing strong expansion in employment in services, especially in professional and business services and in health and social work. The main limiting factors on this are likely to be automation and, for education and health, the availability of public finance. Employment may also grow in education, hotels and restaurants, entertainment services and personal services proper.

Implications

The policy actors most likely to be interested in policy issues associated with the shift to services are those directly affected, such as companies, trade unions and ministers and departments in areas such as industry, employment and health, as well as those indirectly affected such as economic and finance ministers and departments. Heads of government may be involved in major decisions. Although to a large extent actors in these different policy areas are grouped into different policy networks, for the sake of brevity they are listed together in Table 8.4.

The shift to services is likely to affect policy actors and public policy by leading to more services-friendly policies, less union-friendly policies except in relation to health unions, less worker-friendly policies, less policy autonomy for governments, increased government spending on healthcare leading to corrective measures, and greater efforts to expand education and training and the supply of low-skill service jobs.

Table 8.4   Generic policy network relating to the shift to services

Type of policy actor	Specific policy actor
Political executives and associated parties	Chief executives Ministers for industry and employment Ministers for health Economics and finance ministers
Non-government politicians	European Commissioners relating to industry, employment, health and the economy Parliamentary committees relating to industry, employment, health, finance and the economy Regional and local governments
Civil servants, special advisers and other public sector employees	Ministries of industry and employment Health ministries and authorities European Commission Directorates-General relating to employment, industry, economy, health, research Regional and local authorities
Judges and regulators	Professional regulatory bodies such as health and safety regulators
Business	Manufacturers Services firms, especially business services and similar
Interest groups and non-government organizations	Peak employer organizations Peak union confederations and individual unions Professional organizations such as doctors and lawyers Farmers' organizations
Media	Economic journalists and journals
Experts	Employment and industrial relations specialists, economists
Electorate	Employees in manufacturing, professional and business services, and health and social work

More services-friendly policies

As services become more important in the economy, and manufacturing less important, one would expect governments concerned with the economy to pay more attention to the needs of services firms and less to the needs of manufacturing firms, so that over time public policy becomes more services-friendly and less supportive of manufacturing on issues such as regulation, education and training, access to government services, technical and generic assistance to small and medium-sized enterprises, tax policy, and subsidies and targeted financial support (OECD 2000b: 30–8).

Less union-friendly policies

It is generally acknowledged that industrial workers are more likely than service workers to join trade unions. This is certainly true for the eight European countries for which comparable relevant data is available between the beginning of the 1960s and the middle of the 1990s: Austria, Belgium, Denmark, Germany, Italy, the Netherlands, Norway and Sweden. Measures of union density by economic sector for these countries show that during this period union density in industry was consistently higher than in services, apart from transport (Ebbinghaus and Visser 2000: 64–5).

It follows that the shift in employment from the more unionized industrial sector to the less unionized services sector has led to a loss of members for national trade union movements as a whole in these countries, and that further shifts in this direction will lead to further membership losses for unions. To the extent that any leverage exerted over public policy by national trade union movements is affected by the size of their total membership, this implies a reduction in the pressure that national union movements can exert over public policy, other things being equal. In this way the shift to services implies a shift towards less union-friendly public policies.

It also implies that the influence of manufacturing unions over the policy stances of relevant peak national trade union confederations is likely to fall where there are single confederations, as in countries such as Austria and Britain, or two or more confederations divided along religious and/or political lines, as in countries such as France and Italy. Where confederations are divided by sector, as in Scandinavia, membership losses in manufacturing unions imply a loss of leverage for the blue-collar confederation relative to other confederations.

Conversely, the relative influence of unions representing people employed in professional and business services and in health and social work would be expected to rise insofar as this is determined by membership levels. As health and social work is mostly provided by the relatively highly unionized public sector, whereas most professional and business services fall within the private sector, which has lower levels of unionization (Ebbinghaus and Visser 2000: 64), it is unions in the health and social work sector that are more likely to improve their leverage over public policy either directly or via changing the balance of power within or between peak union confederations.

Less worker-friendly policies

A reduction in manufacturing employment means a reduction in the size of the traditional working-class electorate associated with parties of the Left. Other things being equal this implies a reduction in the share of the vote going to Left parties and/or a shift in party policies away from those preferred by the traditional working class as Left parties try to maintain their share of the vote by appealing to other groups in the electorate. This is consistent with the widely held perception that for some time Left parties have been moving towards the right and becoming less socialist and more pro-business.

In public policy terms it means that governments consisting wholly or partly of Left parties are less likely to come to power, and when in power less likely to implement the sorts of policies preferred by working class voters in the past except to the extent that working class preferences are shared by other targeted groups in the electorate.

To some extent this erosion of support for Left parties is likely to be offset by increasing support from the increasing numbers of voters working in health and social work. This is because healthcare and social work are mainly provided through the public sector, and Left parties tend to be more supportive of the public sector than Right parties, especially economically liberal parties. Professional and business services, on the other hand, are so diverse that it is difficult to see any one type of party benefiting from their growth. This means that the net electoral effect of the shift to services is likely to be less pressure to implement the sorts of public policies favoured by the traditional industrial working class, such as legislation to improve the working conditions of people working in the relatively unpleasant, unhealthy and dangerous jobs that are more characteristic of manufacturing than services (OECD 2000i: 99–104).

Less policy autonomy for governments

Because the productivity increases on which economic growth depends tend to be larger in manufacturing than in services, due to the greater ease with which technology can be used to improve manufacturing productivity, the shift to services implies lower productivity growth across the economy as a whole and therefore lower economic growth as time goes on and the shift to services continues. This in turn implies decreasing electoral support for incumbent governments, other things being equal, since economic growth is a symbol of government success and lower economic growth means lower rises in incomes for voters as time goes on. Lower economic growth also means lower tax revenues and therefore less scope for governments to increase spending without raising tax or to cut tax without cutting government programmes. By reducing their electoral security, lower economic growth caused by the shift to services makes it more likely that governments will seek broad support for policies before implementing them, leading to more cautious, centrist, lowest-common-denominator policies than would otherwise be the case.

Increased government spending on healthcare leading to corrective measures

Employing more staff in health and social work should improve the provision of healthcare and social services provided for citizens, and this in turn should improve the electoral prospects of incumbent governments, other things being equal.

The problem is that employing more staff means spending more money, so that the electoral benefits for governments of increased employment in health and social work are offset by the financial problems they create in the form of growing deficits in state budgets and/or the finances of health funds, as these pose serious and recurring problems for governments because almost all possible responses are likely to undermine their electoral support. Doing nothing and letting the deficit grow is likely to make the government unpopular with the economically minded and cannot be sustained indefinitely. Increasing revenue to cover the increased spending, for example by increasing the contributions of employers and/or employees to health funds and/or raising income tax or other taxes, is generally unpopular. Employers in particular oppose rises in their social contributions because they add to business costs. Revenue will rise to the extent that economic growth and high rates of employment expand the tax base, but governments may not be so lucky. And cutting spending in healthcare or other areas is also likely to be unpopular among patients and their advocacy groups, healthcare workers and their representative organizations, and voters in general, all of whom are likely to be patients at some stage.

Nevertheless, as we saw in Chapter 3 government initiatives to contain healthcare costs have in recent years included regulation of prices and volumes of healthcare and inputs into healthcare, caps on sectoral or overall health spending, shifting of costs to the private sector, more stringent pre-marketing controls on new technology, limits on capital spending on medical equipment and, for pharmaceuticals, price control and stricter controls on cost reimbursement as well as tighter prescribing guidelines for doctors. Governments have sought to minimize any negative electoral effects of cost-saving measures on the quality of healthcare by means such as moving to make healthcare systems more efficient by enhancing the role of healthcare purchasers, improving hospital contracting and payment systems, improving managerial independence and cost accountability of hospitals, and increasing competition among providers (Moran 1999: 183, Freeman 2000: 71, Docteur and Oxley 2004: 44–69).

In short, revenue rises and/or cost control measures necessitated by the tendency of employment in health and social work to grow are likely to undermine the electoral support of incumbent governments, offsetting any electoral benefits accruing from better healthcare provision due to staff increases. Which of these opposed effects is more significant, however, is impossible to determine.

More vigorous efforts to expand education and training and the supply of low-skill service jobs

One effect of the shift from manufacturing to services may be an expansion of unemployment among low-skilled workers, as the ratio of low-skill to medium/ high-skill workers is significantly lower in services, especially the growth sectors of producer services and social services, than in manufacturing (OECD 2000a: 96). Unemployment is an electoral liability for governments, so to the extent that they diagnose the problem in this way governments are likely to try to reduce unemployment by taking steps to improve the skills of hitherto low-skilled workers and potential workers by expanding and reforming systems of education and training. The other likely response is measures to expand the number of low-skilled jobs in services, for example by creating more relatively low-skilled caring jobs in public sector social services such as positions for daycare assistants, facilitating the reduction of wages for workers in areas such as personal services in order to make it cheaper for private employers in these areas to employ more people, and reducing the level of unemployment benefits to increase the willingness of the unemployed to accept low-paid jobs (OECD 2004a: 14).

Conclusion

For decades employment in manufacturing has been falling in EU countries while employment in services has been rising, especially in professional and business services and in health and social work. These trends are likely to continue. Their main implications for public policy, where these are clear, are summarized in Table 8.5.

Table 8.5   Policy implications of the shift to services

Policy implications	Causal chain from trend
Public policy that is more services-friendly and less supportive of manufacturing on issues such as regulation, education and training, access to government services, technical and generic assistance to small and medium-sized enterprises,	Increasing policy leverage for services firms relative to manufacturers due to the increasing economic significance of services relative to manufacturing

(Continued)

Table 8.5 (*Continued*)

Policy implications	Causal chain from trend
tax policy, and subsidies and targeted financial support	
Less union-friendly public policy	Less policy leverage for trade unions due to workers in the growing services sector being less likely to join unions than workers in the shrinking manufacturing sector
Public policy that is less sensitive to the concerns of manufacturing unions and more sensitive to the concerns of healthcare workers	Growth in health unions relative to manufacturing unions
Public policy that is less sensitive to the concerns of the industrial working class, for example less likelihood of legislation to improve the working conditions of people working in the relatively unpleasant, unhealthy and dangerous jobs that are more characteristic of manufacturing than services	Fewer industrial working-class voters, leading to a loss of electoral support for Left parties and/or a shift in the policies of Left parties away from those preferred by the industrial working class
Less autonomous policies	The shift to services reduces productivity growth and therefore economic growth, leading to decreasing electoral support for governments as time goes on
Increased government spending on healthcare leading to corrective measures	Increasing employment in healthcare improves healthcare outcomes but also increases healthcare costs, leading to government efforts to strengthen cost controls and/or raise additional revenue to compensate
Increasing efforts to expand education and training	The desire of governments to reduce unemployment for economic and electoral reasons, plus increasing unemployment among low-skilled workers
Increasing efforts to expand the supply of low-skill service jobs, for example by creating more low-skilled caring jobs in public sector social services, facilitating the reduction of wages for workers in areas such as personal services to make it cheaper for private employers in these areas to employ more people, and reducing the level of unemployment benefit to increase the willingness of the unemployed to accept low-paid jobs	

The dominant impression from this is that the shift to services is likely to lead to public policy becoming less union friendly, less responsive to the concerns of the traditional working class, and more inclined to create low-paid services jobs and force people to take them. On the other hand it also implies better education, health and social services.

The other significant implication is that the shift to services undermines the electoral position of governments by reducing the rate of growth of productivity, thereby reducing economic growth overall, which implies a trend towards more cautious, centrist and consensual policies than would otherwise be the case.

9
The Growth of Women's Employment

Introduction

The growth of women's employment is one of the most significant long-term trends operating today, and one that is likely to result in the progressive implementation of more and more policies designed to improve the position of women not only in relation to employment, such as expansion of child-care provision, but in other areas as well.

Ever since the 1960s women have been entering the paid workforce in increasing numbers. Between 1970 and 2000 the female labour force in the 15 countries of the EU as it was prior to the 2004 enlargement (EU-15) grew by about three percentage points a decade from 32.7 to 43.0 per cent of the total labour force. This was due to a combination of a growing female labour force and a shrinking male labour force (Table 9.1). By 2003 female employment had reached 43.6 per cent of civilian employment in the EU-15 (OECD 2001e: 37–9, 66, OECD 2004: 23). This trend was especially marked for educated women, with employment rates of women with a tertiary qualification being much higher than among women with less than upper secondary education (OECD 2002a: 74).

However the increase in women working does not mean that their economic independence has been secured in all cases. Women spend shorter and more discontinuous periods in employment than men and are largely employed in part-time jobs: in 2004 women's share of part-time employment in the EU-15 was 78.6 per cent, and exceeded 60 per cent in all EU Member States. Part-time employment has the advantage of making it easier for women to combine work and family obligations where childcare is inadequate, but it is also concentrated in low-paid occupations with few opportunities for advancement and is more likely to be temporary in nature and to have reduced access to job-related training and occupational benefits (OECD 2002a: 65, 68–9, OECD 2005d: 254).

At the same time employment remains segregated by sector, with women being underrepresented in the goods-producing sector and overrepresented

Table 9.1   The labour force in the EU-15 by gender, 1970–2000

	1970	*2000*	*Change*
Female labour force as a percentage of the female population aged 15–64	42.5	60.2	+17.7
Male labour force as a percentage of the male population aged 15–64	90.6	79.0	−11.6

Source: OECD 2001e: 37–9.

in the services sector. More specifically, women are overrepresented in clerical occupations, sales jobs and life-science/health and teaching professions, and underrepresented in managerial and top administrative jobs, the physical, mathematical and engineering professions, and manual and production jobs. This means that large numbers of women work as salespersons, domestic helpers and cleaners, secretaries, personal care workers, and primary and secondary school teachers. To some extent these jobs in healthcare, social care and education represent an outsourcing of unpaid women's work from the home to the paid workforce. This gender segregation does not disappear as the gender gap in employment rates reduces, although there is some indication that it is less marked among younger workers (OECD 2001e: 40–41, OECD 2002a: 86–91, OECD 2004).

There is also vertical segregation by occupation, with women being underrepresented in senior administrative and managerial occupations and in jobs with a supervisory role. Possible reasons for this include social and cultural biases, the disproportionate responsibility that women still have for raising children and performing household tasks, and women being located in jobs that offer fewer opportunities for promotion (OECD 2002a: 94–6).

Nevertheless the gap between the earnings of men and women appears to be narrowing: a study of nine OECD countries found that the gender wage gap fell by between 14 and 38 per cent over the 15–20 year period examined, depending on the country analysed, although in 1998 hourly rates of pay for women were still only 84 per cent as much as men's hourly earnings in OECD countries as a whole, ranging from 76 per cent in Switzerland (2001) to 92 per cent in Portugal. In terms of weekly or monthly take-home pay the gender gap is much larger due to the fact that a greater proportion of women work in part-time rather than full-time jobs (OECD 2002a: 97–9).

The impact of parenthood works in opposite directions for women and men: while women's work rates generally decrease, men's work rates increase, in line with traditional gender roles and the idea that the lack of affordable childcare makes it difficult for many mothers to work. This gender gap widens as the number of children increases. More specifically, mothers are less likely to be employed than childless women, and parenthood increases the incidence of part-time work among women but decreases its incidence among men (OECD 2002a: 76–80).

Will this trend towards higher employment rates for women continue? One reason to think that it will is that women are disproportionately employed in the growing services sector whereas men are disproportionately employed in the shrinking goods-producing sector. If these trends continue as expected, women's employment looks likely to continue to rise (OECD 2000a: 109). Reasons cited by the OECD for the growth of women's employment include women becoming more highly educated, the outsourcing of traditional female household activities to the labour market, the diversification of employment and working-time arrangements in areas such as part-time work, the increased importance of women's earnings in household income, increasing aspirations for independence and fulfilment, and the interest of governments in raising female employment for economic reasons (OECD 2002a: 63, 66). Most if not all of these factors remain operative.

But how much further can the level of women's employment rise? If there were complete equality on a headcount basis one would expect that women would constitute around 50 per cent of the workforce, depending on their exact proportion of the adult working age population. In fact we find that female employment appears to reach a plateau at around 46–7 per cent of the workforce: once countries reach this level, the upwards trend ceases. By 2000 women already constituted over 35 per cent of the workforce in all EU-15 countries, and in all three of the countries in which there was no discernible upwards trend – Denmark, Finland and Sweden – rates of female employment already exceeded 45 per cent of the workforce. If we conservatively take 48 per cent of the workforce as the upper limit for women's employment, this means that the upwards trend can continue only in those countries that have not yet reached this level. This implies continued growth in women's employment in most EU countries up to around 2010 but in fewer countries thereafter as more approach the 48 per cent figure. The idea that the growth in the female labour force in the EU-15 is flattening out is consistent with the fact that it grew as a proportion of the total labour force by about 4 per cent per decade between 1970 and 1990 but only by about 2.5 per cent between 1990 and 2000 (OECD 2001e: 37).

In short, women's participation in the workforce is growing, at least on a headcount basis, and is likely to continue to grow for some time even though the rate of growth is slowing. Meanwhile the gender gap in pay is narrowing and there is some evidence that occupational segregation may weaken in the future. On the other hand women's share in part-time employment is nearly four times that of men and is only declining slowly (OECD 2005d: 253–4), which indicates that men continue to dominate the full-time workforce, and women continue to spend shorter and more discontinuous periods in employment than men. Full gender equality in the workforce remains some way off.

Implications

Table 9.2 sets out the main policy actors that take an interest in women's employment and associated policy issues. Among the most important of these are women in public office such as ministers, women in women's policy

Table 9.2   Generic policy network relating to women's employment

Type of policy actor	Specific policy actor
Political executives and associated parties	Chief executives Minister for Women or equivalent Women ministers Ministers for employment, health, education, social welfare
Non-government politicians	European Commissioners relating to women's affairs, employment, health, education, social welfare Parliamentary committees relating to women's affairs, employment, health, education, social welfare Regional and local governments
Civil servants, special advisers and other public sector employees	Ministries and offices of women's affairs or equivalent Equal opportunities bodies Ministries of employment, health, education, social welfare and related public authorities European Commission Directorates-General relating to women's affairs, employment, health, education, social welfare Regional and local authorities
Judges and regulators	Courts on issues relating to women's rights Equal opportunity tribunals and similar
Business	Employers, especially in services sectors
Interest groups and non-government organizations	Women's organizations, especially feminist groups Trade unions, especially those with majority women memberships
Media	Women's magazines, women's pages in newspapers Feminist authors and journalists
Experts	Feminist analysts Equal opportunity specialists Specialists relating to other issues of importance to women, such as childcare
Electorate	Female employees Mothers and fathers

offices and women's movement activists, along with chief executives, other ministers, and party and union leaders (Mazur 2002: 176–97).

Although the growth of women's employment seems likely to level off over the next 20 years or so, its implications for public policy will take time to percolate through the system. In part it affects policy actors and public policy through contributing to two other king trends analysed elsewhere in this book: the growth of women's employment means a larger labour force and thus contributes to the growth and diversification of production and consumption (Chapter 5), while the increasing economic independence of women brought about by joining the paid workforce contributes to reducing the average size of households (Chapter 17) because it enables more women to leave loveless or abusive relationships to form single person and single parent households.

Over and above these indirect effects, the growth of women's employment has three main implications for public policy: more women-friendly employment policies, an expansion of childcare and other family services, and more women-friendly policies in general. How governments respond to these pressures, of course, depends largely on country-specific characteristics such as the nature of existing welfare state arrangements.

More women-friendly employment policies

The increase in women's employment implies that over time more and more women will be affected by work-related problems, including problems that affect women more than men such as sexual discrimination in relation to pay and other matters, sexual harassment and violence, lack of quality affordable childcare or other family benefits and services, and lack of permanent well-paid part-time work with opportunities for advancement. It follows from this that demands for public policy measures to address these problems will be shared by more and more people (women) as time goes on. These demands can be expressed via women's organizations, trade unions and voting as well as by women in positions of influence in government and elsewhere.

Women's organizations are already active in this area, and government awareness of the increasing numbers of women affected by work-related problems should add credibility to the arguments of these organizations concerning the electoral benefits for governments of taking action.

To the extent that women join trade unions, women's issues would be expected to become more prominent among union demands and to be pursued more vigorously than previously. This effect should be strengthened to the extent that women themselves come to hold official positions in unions. This means that government responses to union demands are more likely than previously to include measures to address the distinctive work-related demands of women. Between 1950 and 1997 women increased as a proportion of the membership of the major union confederations in all eight EU countries for which data is available. Figures for the 12 countries of the

EU-15 for which data is available for at least some union centres also indicate an upwards trend during the 1990s, so that by 2003 female union membership ranged from a high of 53.5 per cent of all union members in Finland down to just 28.9 per cent in the Netherlands (Ebbinghaus and Visser 2000: 66–7, EIRO 2004). Women are also making at least some progress inside trade unions, with many unions setting up sectional forms of representation for women, while issues of particular interest to women are increasingly reaching union bargaining agendas in countries such as Britain as unions try to attract new members and the number of women trade unionists and trade union officers increases (Healy and Kirton 2000: 349, Dølvik and Waddington 2002: 367, Heery *et al.* 2003: 84, 92).

A similar pattern applies to the electoral arena: more women working implies greater electoral support for women's work-related demands, which increases the electoral incentives for political parties to promise action in this area when competing for government and to implement appropriate policy measures when in government. Again this effect is likely to be strengthened to the extent that women themselves gain more senior positions in political parties and in the public sector.

The net result of all this is that the growth of women's employment is likely to lead to the progressive implementation of measures such as improved equal pay and equal treatment legislation, better legal protection against sexual discrimination and harassment, an expansion of affordable childcare, improved maternity and parental leave, improved rights for part-time workers, improved provisions for flexible working hours, improved occupational health and safety regulation, and more equal treatment in social security schemes. The specifics of these measures, of course, are likely to differ from country to country. In relation to childcare, for example, some countries are likely to choose to expand universal public childcare while others are more likely to encourage private provision of childcare supplemented with means-tested assistance for those who otherwise could not afford to take advantage of the childcare on offer.

Expansion of childcare and other family services

In 1960 fertility was consistently higher in countries with low female employment than in countries with high female employment, as one might expect, but by 1992 the relationship had been reversed: fertility was higher in countries in which female employment was also relatively high. One explanation for this is that in countries where women in effect have to choose between career and family, due to lack of adequate childcare and other family benefits and services, they now choose career and delay having a family, which results in smaller families than would otherwise be the case. In countries where good quality and affordable childcare and other family services are available, on the other hand, as in Scandinavia, women do not have to choose and therefore start families earlier, which results in larger families than would otherwise be the case. In the long term larger families mean a larger labour force and therefore higher economic growth and better state finances. This implies that governments with an interest in the long term have every reason to want women to have as many children as possible, especially with the prospect of population ageing shrinking the size of the workforce (Chapter 15). What this means is that governments which learn that families are larger when women can combine employment with bringing up a family have a strong incentive to expand the provision of good quality childcare and other family services. Encouraging women's employment in this way also has the advantages of reducing poverty and boosting employment in general as increasing numbers of working women with more money but less time increase their consumption of personal services, for example by eating out rather than buying food and preparing it at home (Esping-Andersen 1999: 68–70, 115, 179, Rubery *et al.* 1999: 101–2). In this connection it is noticeable than in recent years the EU has set a target of raising women's employment to at least 60 per cent by 2010, while also issuing directives in areas such as parental leave and working time and pushing Member States to expand the provision of childcare (Kilkey 2004: 334).

More women-friendly policies in general

Along with the growth of women's employment has come increasing numbers of women in positions of influence, although in almost all cases parity with men has not (yet) been reached. A study of ten West European countries found that between 1945 and 1999 the average proportion of women MPs in national parliaments increased from 5.8 to 25.7 per cent, with substantial increases in every country. Women MPs were most common among MPs from left-wing parties. By spring 2001 the proportion of parliamentary seats occupied by women in the EU-15 averaged 23 per cent, ranging from 44 per cent in Sweden down to just 9 per cent in Greece. Similarly, at the end of 2003 women constituted 26.3 per cent of cabinet ministers in the EU-15, ranging from 50 per cent in Sweden down to a mere 8 per cent in Italy (Henig and Henig 2001: 53, 105, European Commission 2002: 97, Van Biezen and Katz 2004: 921).

While we cannot assume that women in positions of power will necessarily pursue distinctively women-oriented goals, there is evidence that at least in Britain, Norway and Sweden the attitudes of women and men politicians do differ on values directly related to women's interests such as gender equality, affirmative action, equal opportunities policy, family policy and men's and women's roles in the workforce (Wängnerud 2000, Bratton 2002, Lovenduski and Norris 2003). Although holding a certain attitude does not necessarily mean that a person will act on it, one would expect that where that attitude is widespread, at least some of those who share it will act accordingly. To the extent that women in positions of influence in areas such as business and the civil service also hold distinctive attitudes towards issues related to women's interests, therefore, we would expect the increasing numbers of women in influential positions to exert increasing pressure on governments to implement policies to improve women's rights and reduce or eliminate gender-based hierarchies not only in relation to employment, as discussed above, but also in areas such as constitutional provisions relating to the rights of women, the representation of women in elected and appointed office, equal opportunities policy in general, family law (marriage, divorce, family support obligations, parent–child relations and the status of children born outside marriage), reproductive rights policy (abortion, contraception, reproductive technology, sex education, family planning), and sexuality and violence policy (rape, domestic violence, women's shelters and refuges) (Mazur 2002, Kilkey 2004: 332).

Conclusion

As time goes on, increasing numbers of women have been entering the paid workforce, and this trend is likely to continue for some time yet before flattening out as women's employment approaches 50 per cent of total employment in more and more countries. The main implications of this for public policy are likely to be the progressive implementation of policies designed to improve the position of women (Table 9.3). There are also indirect policy implications through increasing economic growth and facilitating the trend towards smaller households.

Table 9.3   Policy implications of the growth in women's employment

Policy implications	Causal chain from trend
More women-friendly policies such as: • greater funding and/or provision of affordable childcare • improvements in equal pay and equal treatment legislation, legal protection against sexual discrimination, maternity and parental leave, rights for part-time workers, provisions for flexible working hours, occupational health and safety legislation • more equal treatment in social security schemes • improved constitutional provisions relating to the rights of women • improved representation of women in elected and appointed office	Greater pressure to respond to work-related and other demands of women as the arguments of women's organizations become more credible as awareness of the increasing number of women affected by work-related problems grows, trade unions pursue women's issues more vigorously as the proportion of female members and officials increases, an increasing proportion of women voters are affected by work-related problems, and more women reach influential positions in government and elsewhere The desire of governments to maximize the size of the labour force by

(Continued)

Table 9.3 (Continued)

Policy implications	Causal chain from trend
• stronger equal opportunities policy in general • more women-friendly family law policy (marriage, divorce, family support obligations, parent-child relations and the status of children born outside marriage) • more women-friendly reproductive rights policy (abortion, contraception, reproductive technology, sex education, family planning) • more women-friendly sexuality and violence policy (rape, domestic violence, women's shelters and refuges)	encouraging larger families, combined with learning that women have larger families when they are able to combine family and career than when they have to choose between them
Indirect effects via other king trends	The growth of women's employment increases the growth and diversification of production and consumption (Chapter 5) by increasing the size of the workforce, and facilitates the trend towards smaller households (Chapter 17) by making it easier for women to leave abusive or loveless relationships

The most likely policies to be adopted would appear to be expansion of affordable childcare and other measures designed to make it easier for women to combine career and family, as these are important objectives both for women, who are likely to exert increasing pressure for such policies through unions, women's groups, political parties and positions of influence, and for economic policy given the perceived importance of maximizing the size of the labour force in the face of population ageing.

10
The Expansion of Trade

Introduction

Trade involving European countries has been growing for many years and looks set to continue to grow for many years to come. The main policy implications of this are greater policy autonomy for governments, more business-friendly policies in relation to export and import-competing producers, more vigorous measures to assist workers displaced by trade-related structural adjustment, more vigorous measures to combat illicit trafficking, and a diminishing likelihood of war between major trading partners.

World trade has been growing ever since the end of World War II. Between 1960 and 2000 world merchandise exports (physical goods) doubled as a proportion of world production from 10 to 20 per cent of world GDP. Although trade in merchandise and services continues to be dominated by developed countries, between 1980 and 2002 their share dropped from 79.1 to 73.2 per cent (UNCTAD 2004: 48–9).

European trade has also been growing strongly. Table 10.1 shows that since 1970 trade in goods and services of the 15 Member States of the EU as it was prior to the 2004 enlargement (EU-15) has increased steadily in terms of value, although this rate of increase has slowed recently.

EU-15 trade also increased as a percentage of GDP (Table 10.2), although at times this trend slowed or even reversed briefly, especially in the 1980s. Nevertheless it is clear that the underlying trend was upwards.

Table 10.1 Average annual percentage changes in EU-15 trade in goods and services, 1970–2006

Indicator	1971–80	1981–90	1991–2000	2001–2006*
Exports	5.5	4.6	6.6	3.7
Imports	4.8	4.6	6.1	3.9

Note: * Estimate.
Source: European Commission 2005: Tables 37, 41. 1995 prices.

Table 10.2 also reveals that most trade in goods (comparable services data is not available) has been between EU Member States rather than with the outside world. Moreover, intra EU-15 trade grew more consistently than extra EU-15 trade as a percentage of GDP, so that extra-EU trade fell from 40 per cent to around 35 per cent of total EU goods trade between 1970 and 1990, at which point it stabilized.

In 2003 approximately one third of extra EU-15 trade was with rich European countries that are not EU Member States, the US and Japan. Nearly 20 per cent of extra EU-15 imports came from China and the so-called dynamic Asian economies of Hong Kong, Korea, Malaysia, Singapore, Thailand and Taiwan, considerably more than the 12 per cent of extra EU-15 exports that went to these countries. Extra-EU trade is dominated by manufactures, especially machinery, transport equipment, chemicals and energy (mainly oil). Import penetration rates were especially high for computers and aircraft, while export ratios were high in shipbuilding, motor vehicles and machinery and

Table 10.2   EU-15 trade as a % of GDP, 1970–2006

Indicator	1970	1980	1990	2000	2006*
Total exports of goods and services (% GDP)	21.7	27.2	28.0	35.9	37.1
Total imports of goods and services (% GDP)	21.4	28.6	27.5	35.2	36.0
Intra-EU exports of goods (% GDP)	9.9	13.3	14.7	19.5	19.8
Extra-EU exports of goods (% GDP)	6.8	8.5	7.2	9.7	10.3
Total exports of goods (% GDP)	16.7	21.8	21.9	29.2	30.1
Extra-EU exports as a % of total exports of goods	40.7	39.0	32.9	33.2	34.2
Intra-EU imports of goods (% GDP)	10.1	13.2	14.8	18.4	19.1
Extra-EU imports of goods (% GDP)	7.9	11.2	8.0	11.0	10.9
Total imports of goods (% GDP)	18.0	24.4	22.8	29.4	30.0
Extra-EU imports as a % of total imports of goods	43.9	45.9	35.1	37.4	36.3

Note: * Estimate.
Source: European Commission 2005: Table 36, 38–40, 42–3. Exports and imports at current prices (national accounts) as a % of GDP at market prices.

equipment. Scientific instruments and aircraft had both high import penetration rates and high export ratios (OECD 2003: 106–7, Eurostat 2004c: 39, Eurostat 2005b).

Most EU trade is in similar goods between similar countries (intra-trade) rather than exchange of completely different types of goods, such as manufactured goods for raw materials. Intra-industry trade in similar finished products and in similar goods at different stages of production has increased significantly since 1970, especially in manufactured goods and in particular in sophisticated manufactured goods such as chemicals, machinery, transport equipment, electrical equipment and electronics. One consequence is greater competition between exporters in different countries producing similar goods (Held *et al.* 1999: 173, OECD 2002d: 70–3, European Commission 2004j: 193).

Trade in services is also increasing, stimulated in part by the General Agreement on Trade in Services (GATS), which came into effect in 1995 and established multilateral rules for international trade in services including the principle of most-favoured-nation treatment, which requires countries to treat all their trading partners equally. GATS also provides for the progressive opening of markets on a negotiated basis (WTO 2004).

Trade in services means the provision of services by citizens or firms of one country to citizens or firms of another country. There are four ways in which this can be done. Services such as consumer advice from call centres can be supplied from the territory of one country to the territory of another (cross-border supply). Consumers and firms can make use of services when temporarily in another country, such as services for tourists (consumption abroad). Firms based in one country, such as banks, may set up subsidiaries or branches in another country to provide services in that country (commercial presence). And individuals such as consultants or construction workers may temporarily travel from their own country to another country in order to provide services there (presence of natural persons) (WTO 2004: 2). Between 1960 and 2000 world services exports are estimated to have risen from 3 to 5 per cent of world GDP. The most important traded services are transport, travel services, communication services, construction services, and financial and insurance services (UNCTAD 2004: 48, 62).

European trade in services is not as well-documented as merchandise trade, but between 1995 and 2000 EU-15 exports and imports of commercial services both grew by 4 per cent per year. Services exports then grew by 1 per cent in 2000 and 3 per cent in 2001 before increasing dramatically to 10 per cent in 2002, while imports grew by 2 per cent in 2000 and 3 per cent in 2001 before increasing by 9 per cent in 2002. Extra-European trade in services was mainly with the US: in 2001 38 per cent of services exports went to the US, which in turn provided 40 per cent of EU services imports. Transportation and travel services together made up about half of total EU-15 trade in commercial services (WTO 2003: 42–4, 61, 160–2).

To sum up, European trade has been growing for decades, especially trade in high technology manufactures and services, but is still dominated by trade between European countries. Extra-EU trade is mainly with other developed countries.

It seems likely that trade will continue to expand over the next 20 years or so at least. World and European trade has already been growing for nearly 50 years, although it is possible that trade figures are a little misleading in that goods are increasingly being produced in processes that span several countries and are therefore exported and re-exported on a number of occasions during the production process before they are finally sold as a finished product (Krugman 1995: 334, Hummels *et al.* 2001). At least some of the factors that are thought to have caused growth in trade in the past are likely to continue to operate into the foreseeable future, in particular the spread of transnational corporations (internal trade within such companies is estimated to account for about 30 per cent of world trade), increases in demand for capital and consumer goods due to rapid income growth, and improvements in communication and transportation. It is also possible that the removal of tariff and non-tariff barriers to trade will continue due to the continued expansion and liberalization of the WTO multilateral trading system and the continued creation and deepening of regional trading blocs such as the EU, although we cannot be sure of this because it is impossible to predict the outcome of international trade negotiations (OECD 2001g: 48). Finally, futures studies predict continued growth in trade (DERA 2001: 22; CIA 2000: 22, Cabinet Office 2000), and the OECD expects reductions in transportation and communication costs, along with increasing demand due to growth in non-OECD countries, to cause OECD exports to increase by at least 2.8 per cent per year over the period 1995–2020 (OECD 2001g: 49–50).

Perhaps the main threat to the continued expansion of trade is the possibility that oil production may peak in the next decade or two, as a number of industry analysts predict on the basis that estimates of oil reserves have in the past been inflated for political reasons while the results of recent oil exploration have been disappointing and the growth of demand for oil has been underestimated by organizations such as the International Energy Agency (IEA) (Goodstein 2004, Hirsch *et al.* 2005: 13–19, Illum 2005). The significance of this is that once production peaks and starts to decline, the continuing growth in demand for oil would be expected to drive up oil prices indefinitely. Because for transport in particular there are no ready alternative fuels for motor vehicles, aircraft, trains and ships (Hirsch *et al.* 2005: 27, 64), the result could be a slowdown or even a reversal of the upwards trend in trade due to falling demand for traded goods as rising fuel prices raise the prices of traded goods and economic demand in general falls as a consequence of the economic slowdown that would almost certainly accompany a steady rise in energy prices. The analysis in this chapter is premised on the assumption that this will not happen.

Implications

Trade policy has been a focus of political attention ever since trade began. Table 10.3 sets out the main policy actors interested in influencing public policy in this area. Within the EU the Single Market provides for the free movement

Table 10.3   Generic trade policy network

Type of policy actor	Specific policy actor
Political executives and associated parties	Chief executives Trade ministers Ministers for foreign affairs, finance, industry, agriculture
Non-government politicians	Liberal parties and politicians Nationalist and protectionist parties and politicians Parliamentary committees related to trade European Commissioners for trade, internal market, industry and agriculture Foreign governments, especially the US government
Civil servants, special advisers and other public sector employees	Trade departments and agencies Trade-related departments and agencies, for example foreign affairs, finance, industry, agriculture EU Directorates-General relating to trade, internal market, industry and agriculture Foreign trade departments and agencies, especially US
Judges and regulators	European Commission European Court of Justice World Trade Organization (WTO)
Business	Exporters, especially transnational companies Importers, especially transnational companies Import-competing industries
Interest groups and non-government organizations	Employer and trade organizations Unions in export and import-competing industries Farmers Environmentalists, anti-globalization groups and Third World advocates such as fair trade organizations
Media	National media Trade-related journals and journals in areas such as economics, labour and the environment
Experts	Trade experts and economists in general Labour and environmental experts
Electorate	Workers laid off, or under threat, for trade-related reasons Voters working in exporting, importing and import-competing industries

of goods and services and most trade decisions are taken at European level and enforced by the European Commission. European countries are represented at international trade negotiations by the European Commission, although national governments remain important in the collective determination of EU trade policy stances. The growing importance of global regulation of trade by the WTO means that foreign governments, especially the US government, are also important influences on the regulation of trade as it pertains to EU countries. Exporters and import-competing producers, especially transnational companies, are also significant policy actors, while farmers, trade unions, environmentalists and other non-government organizations are also active.

The main policy implications of the expansion in European trade are greater policy autonomy for governments, more vigorous measures to help export and import-competing producers and workers displaced by trade-related structural adjustment, more vigorous measures to combat illicit trafficking, and decreasing likelihood of war with trading partners.

Greater policy autonomy for governments

It is widely believed that trade brings numerous economic benefits. To the extent that this is true it strengthens the position of governments because re-election is more likely when the economy and voters are doing well, making it less electorally risky for governments to do what they want regardless of public opinion and thereby increasing their autonomy in policy-making.

First, there are benefits for consumers. To the extent that imports of finished goods are cheaper than their domestic competitors, and the costs of domestic production are reduced by imported inputs being cheaper than domestic inputs, increased trade in a competitive market improves living standards by enabling people on any given income to get more for their money. More imports also mean more choice and a wider range of qualities among goods and services. Domestically produced goods may also become more diverse and of better quality due not only to the incorporation of imported components but also to gains in domestic productivity and efficiency as a result of specialization in export industries, stimulation of technological innovation, and price and quality competition from imports (WTO 2001: 3, WTO 2003a, European Commission 2004k).

Second, the European Commission among others argues that cheaper imported inputs, more efficient technology and access to wider markets increases domestic firms' competitiveness and thus leads to higher investment, growth and jobs. It also asserts that all studies in this area find that more open countries grow faster and attain higher levels of income. A multivariate econometric analysis of the EU-15 carried out for the European Commission found that during the 1980s and 1990s a 10 per cent increase in openness (trade as a percentage of GDP) was associated with an increase in the employment rate of 1–3 percentage points (European Commission

2004j: 79–80, 191–2, European Commission 2004k). The WTO also argues that trade expansion leads to higher economic growth, although it concedes that 'open trade alone has not yet been unambiguously and universally linked to subsequent economic growth'. Increased exports may also mean more good jobs, as jobs in export sectors tend to be relatively well-paid and secure (WTO 2001: 10, WTO 2003a).

Third, according to trade theory increasing exports should mean increasing national income and therefore a larger tax base, which among other things gives governments room to redistribute some of the benefits of trade from those who gain most to those under pressure from increasing imports, for example by funding measures to assist companies and workers to become more productive and competitive or to switch to new activities (WTO 2003a). An increase in the size of the tax base also gives governments room to spend more in other areas, cut tax and/or cut budget deficits.

However whether increased trade results in these benefits depends on circumstances. Real gains may not be forthcoming where markets are dominated by monopolies or oligopolies in other countries that control prices, for example, or where trade is conducted on a non-commercial basis in the form of intra-firm trade with export prices set to minimize tax liabilities, and gains may not stay in the country but instead may be spent on imports or invested overseas (Dunkley 2004: 35–9).

In addition, increased trade implies greater economic volatility due to increased international spillover of economic fluctuations (Held *et al.* 1999: 182): where a recession in major trading partners leads to lower demand for exports and therefore loss of domestic production and jobs, for example, these losses are magnified the more important trade is for an economy.

Furthermore, more trade does not necessarily lead to higher employment. Expanding trade is likely to lead to increasing structural adjustment as the increasing size of international markets enables some exporters to make bigger profits and expand while increasing international competition leads to other exporters and import-competing firms being increasingly out-competed by foreign firms. In recent years this has meant visible and traumatic plant closures and job losses in sectors such as textiles and clothing, steel, automobiles, and electronics and digitizable services (European Commission 2004j: 199–200).

More generally there are fears that losses of labour-intensive low-skilled jobs to low-cost emerging economies are not being balanced by job creation in high value-added sectors because production in these rising sectors is not as labour intensive. According to standard trade theory (Heckscher-Ohlin, Stolper-Samuelson theorems), increased trade leads to inter-industry specialization, which for industrialized countries competing with developing countries with abundant low-cost low-skilled labour implies a relative decrease in the wages of unskilled workers in industrialized countries if wages are flexible or a decrease in employment of unskilled workers by net destruction of jobs or skill mismatch if wages are not flexible (European Commission 2004j: 194–6).

But although employment rates among unskilled workers relative to skilled workers in European and other rich countries did fall during the 1990s, there are also other explanations for this, such as the destruction of unskilled jobs in manufacturing by automation and the creation of new jobs in sectors such as business services, health and education in which the ratio of medium/high-skill workers to low skill workers is much higher than in manufacturing (OECD 2000a: 96, OECD 2003h: 145–51, OECD 2003i: 28–9). In addition, econometric studies of the relationship between trade, wages and unemployment in Europe have so far failed to find much evidence for significant trade effects (see, for example, the articles in Greenaway and Nelson 2001, Bella and Quintieri 2000, Hansson 2000, also Bazen and Cardebat 2001, Cuyvers *et al.* 2002, Landesmann *et al.* 2002). One reason for this is that trade with newly industrializing economies that are well-placed to compete on cost is rather small: imports from China and the other East Asian economies most often mentioned as representing low-cost threats have been rising more strongly than EU exports to these countries but by 2003 still comprised less than 20 per cent of extra-EU imports, or about 2 per cent of EU GDP, and the trade deficit with these countries was equivalent to just 0.7 per cent of EU GDP. The share of new Member States in total EU-25 trade is also small, so any trade-related effects on jobs of their incorporation into the EU seem unlikely to be substantial (European Commission 2004: 201, European Commission 2005: Tables 38–9, 42–3, Eurostat 2005b).

Despite this, however, fears remain that trade may harm employment in the future. A report prepared for the European Commission argues that countries such as Brazil, Russia, India and China will increasingly become able to compete with the EU on the basis of low labour costs on an increasing range of products, including industries such as telecommunications and computers, so that the only European industries to survive will be those that involve processes that are intensive in capital, skilled labour or technology, such as aeronautics, electronic components and the automobile sectors, or which produce goods or services that are difficult to transport (Fontagné *et al.* 2004: 5–6).

In short, the logic of trade theory, rising imports from newly industrializing countries, well-publicized instances of trade-related job losses and fears for the future to some extent offset any positive electoral effects of trade for governments despite the lack of evidence that trade has harmed employment in the past.

Nevertheless, to the extent that trade does result in economic benefits for citizens, as well as improving state finances so that governments are in a stronger position to provide better government services and/or tax cuts, and assuming that convincing econometric evidence does not emerge that demonstrates net negative employment effects, the expansion of trade should strengthen the electoral position of incumbent governments, other things being equal, putting them in a stronger position to do what they want without too many concessions to other policy actors.

The perceived economic and electoral benefits of increased trade also provide an incentive for governments to continue pursuing strongly pro-trade economic policies. It is therefore not surprising that in the early years of the 21st century the EU was pushing for further liberalization of access to markets for goods and services, including the reduction of non-tariff barriers to trade such as technical standards and import/export procedures, plus strengthened coverage in the areas of services, investment, competition, transparency in government procurement, intellectual property and trade facilitation. It is noticeable, however, that this free trade zeal does not extend to areas in which the EU is uncompetitive, such as agriculture (WTO 2001: 3, 5).

More vigorous measures to help export and import-competing producers

As trade expands, exporters face increasing competition for foreign markets and domestic industries face increasing competition from imported products and services. In both cases this can lead to the decline or elimination of industries and sectors, including strategically important industries such as agriculture and defence, leading to economic and social costs such as relocation of employment, long-term unemployment, family disruption, devastation of towns and regions, loss of industry-specific skills, and changes in the nature of society. This increases the economic and electoral incentives for governments to do what they can to assist exporters and import-competing industries to compete with foreign firms. The main implications of this for public policy are more business-friendly policies in relation to infrastructure, education, financial aid and R&D; greater emphasis on policies designed to minimize relevant taxes, minimize labour costs, maximize labour flexibility and strengthen international labour standards; and greater emphasis on minimizing the costs to business of environmental regulation and on strengthening international environmental standards.

Resort to outright protectionism, however, is unlikely. Although import-competing industries in trouble may press for a return to the traditional protectionism of higher tariffs and restrictive quotas, this is likely to be counterbalanced by the increasing government commitment to free trade mentioned earlier as well as by pressures exerted by the expanding export sector. It would also infringe the trade rules of both the EU and the WTO.

More business-friendly policies in relation to infrastructure, education, financial aid and R&D

Authorities at national, European and regional levels can assist exporters and import-competing firms by improving and extending transport and communications infrastructure, improving and extending education and training, providing assistance with R&D, and providing loans, subsidies and tax breaks where allowed by EU law. Such measures are generally uncontroversial, and their costs tend to be viewed as investments to be repaid later in the form of economic benefits.

Greater emphasis on policies designed to minimize taxes and labour costs and maximize labour flexibility

Increasing competition with foreign firms means increasing pressure on exporters and import-competing firms to reduce production costs by minimizing taxes and labour costs and maximizing labour flexibility, which increases pressure on governments from firms and experts to reduce employers' social security contributions and corporation tax, take steps to secure wage restraint, and reform employment regulation in areas such as working conditions, working hours, minimum wages and employment protection in order to reduce compliance costs for exporters and import-competing industries. This can be done either unilaterally, for example by legislating to weaken employment regulation or impose tighter legal restrictions on the activities of trade unions, or in concert with major social interests including trade unions, for example by means of social pacts that exchange wage restraint for policy concessions. Policy concertation has the advantage of minimizing social conflict, voter backlash (especially relevant for pro-welfare state left parties) and the risk of arousing protectionist sentiment (Garrett 1998, Rieger and Leibfried 1998).

It is not clear, however, that the tendency of trade expansion to increase pressure on governments to minimize tax and labour costs and maximize labour flexibility has in fact led to major changes in public policy. In relation to tax, for instance, there were high profile policy changes during the 1980s, such as cuts in top marginal rates of corporation tax, but at the same time tax reliefs were reduced or abolished. Furthermore, revenue from corporation tax and employers' social contributions in the EU-15 continues to rise over time as a percentage of GDP (OECD 2004b: 20, 73, 76).

Greater emphasis on strengthening international labour standards

As well as doing what they can to improve the competitiveness of home-based exporters and import-competing industries, governments can take steps to blunt the competitive edge of foreign firms competing on the basis of lower labour costs due to inferior labour standards by pressing for international labour standards to be strengthened, for example by incorporating minimum labour standards into trade agreements. Although such moves have the advantage of being popular at home, however, they are generally opposed by countries that benefit from the status quo and so far have had little success at WTO level. In relation to intra-EU trade, on the other hand, the EU has moved some way in this direction by establishing a body of EU-wide employment regulation in areas such as health and safety, working time, and fixed-term and temporary employment (Europa 2003).

*Greater emphasis on minimizing the costs to business of
environmental regulation*

Governments can assist exporters and import-competing firms to compete with
foreign firms by minimizing costs associated with environmental regulation
through taking steps such as reforming existing regulation to reduce compliance costs while maintaining the benefits to the environment (for instance
by moving from command-and-control regulation to market instruments
such as emissions trading), downgrading existing regulation (so that environmental protection is reduced along with compliance costs), enforcing
existing regulation less rigorously (for instance by cutting the staff of environmental regulators) and resisting moves to upgrade regulation (regulatory
chill). However although this prospect alarms environmentalists, so far there
does not appear to be any systematic evidence that trade is in fact undermining environmental regulation (Busse 2004).

Greater emphasis on strengthening international environmental standards

An alternative way of protecting exporters and import-competing firms against
competition from firms based in countries with low environmental standards
is to negotiate international agreements that set minimum environmental
standards for trade. Although such agreements are not (yet) an integral part
of the WTO framework of trade rules, there is an extensive body of environmental regulation at EU level in areas such as waste management, noise pollution, water pollution, air pollution and technological hazards that restricts
the extent to which firms based in EU Member States can compete on the
basis of low environmental standards. There is also a growing body of agreements at international level outside the WTO framework, such as the Kyoto
Protocol on greenhouse gas emissions, that to some extent places limits on
competition based on low environmental standards (Europa 2001).

More vigorous measures to help workers displaced by trade-related structural adjustment

Even if the expansion of trade has positive employment effects overall, it is
likely to cause short-term job losses from time to time due to loss of export
markets or competition from imports, and as trade affects more and more of
the economy such job losses are likely to become more widespread and frequent. There are numerous incentives for governments to help workers who
lose their jobs in these circumstances, and these are likely to strengthen as
the number of workers affected increases. Assisting laid-off workers to find
new jobs by means of measures such as help with job search, relocation and
retraining, plus the provision of financial assistance in the meantime, facilitates the transfer of labour from declining sectors to growth sectors, thereby
raising employment levels and economic prosperity. There are electoral
advantages in doing whatever can be done to minimize unemployment and

in being seen to respond constructively when job losses are controversial, for instance when they are the result of plant closures that are highlighted by the media and vigorously contested by trade unions. There is also likely to be genuine concern to help people who lose their jobs through no fault of their own. Measures to assist displaced workers could in effect be financed by the expansion of trade itself through its role in increasing economic growth and therefore the size of the tax base, as this provides governments with extra revenue that could be spent in this area (Pass *et al.* 1995: 191; Dunkley 2004: 27, 31; European Commission 2004k).

More vigorous measures to combat illicit trafficking

Illegal trade in people and goods has probably accompanied legitimate trade for as long as trade has existed. Although its hidden nature makes it impossible to be sure whether it is increasing or decreasing, it seems reasonable to assume that it is just as likely as legal trade to be stimulated by increases in consumer demand due to income growth and facilitated by improvements in transport and communications. It therefore seems likely that illicit trafficking in goods such as drugs and toxic waste, as well as in people, is increasing. Police certainly seem to think so. According to Europol, for example, organized crime groups are becoming more active in cross-border smuggling and illegal migration, and the incidence of organized international vehicle trafficking, and trafficking in human beings, is increasing (Europol 2003: 11, 2004a, 2004b, 2004c).

Given this, and bearing in mind that in the absence of reliable data it is perceptions that matter, it would appear reasonable to conclude that the heightened sense of threat created by perceptions of increased illicit trafficking will lead the police, customs and other law enforcement agencies, as well as groups inside and outside of government with concerns about specific issues such as drugs, prostitution and illegal immigration, to increase their efforts to persuade governments to take further steps to counteract this apparent trend by means such as expanding the use of surveillance, increasing police and customs cooperation, tightening border controls and increasing penalties. The perception that illegal trafficking is on the increase would also be expected to increase the number of people concerned about it. The net result is likely to be increasing pressure from relevant agencies and groups, plus increasing electoral pressure on which opposition parties are likely to try to capitalize, for law enforcement to become more intrusive and repressive in these areas both nationally and internationally.

Decreasing likelihood of going to war with trading partners

Military conflict between nations disrupts trade, which reduces sales for exporters and reduces the availability of imported goods and services for domestic industries and consumers, thereby imposing economic costs on the warring parties. As trade grows, those potentially negatively affected by a war in this way become more numerous and their potential losses become greater. For this reason the expansion of trade increases the economic incentives for governments to avoid going to war with their trading partners, thereby making war less likely. This logic was used explicitly as a rationale for European economic integration after World War II (Schuman 1950), and after 50 years of economic integration war between EU Member States now seems inconceivable. So far the same is true for rich developed countries as a whole, although it would be a mistake to conclude that trade rules out war between major trading partners altogether. And of course this consideration does not apply to countries with which the EU has little trade.

Conclusion

European trade has been growing strongly for decades, especially intra-EU trade, and although the rate of growth has slowed in recent years it seems likely to continue to expand for the foreseeable future. Table 10.4 sets out the main implications of this for policy actors and public policy.

Table 10.4   Policy implications of trade expansion

Policy implications	*Causal chain from trend*
More autonomous policies	Strengthening of the electoral position of governments due to the economic benefits arising from increasing trade, such as cheaper goods, more consumer choice, increasingly productive domestic firms due to import competition, and a larger tax base, tempered by greater economic vulnerability due to increasing dependence on foreign markets, short-term job losses due to structural adjustment and fears of job losses for unskilled workers due to import competition, despite lack of evidence that this is occurring
Increasing assistance to export and import-competing producers, including: • improving infrastructure and education and training, providing assistance with R&D, and providing financial aid • more vigorous measures to minimize relevant taxes and labour costs and maximize labour flexibility, such as cutting employers' social contributions and corporation tax, taking steps to secure wage restraint, and reforming employment regulation	The expansion of trade means that export industries are growing but face increasing competition for foreign markets while import-competing industries face increasing competition from imports, magnifying the economic consequences of success or failure and therefore the electoral consequences for governments

(Continued)

Table 10.4   (*Continued*)

Policy implications	Causal chain from trend
• more vigorous measures to minimize the costs to business of environmental regulation, such as moving to market instruments, downgrading existing regulation or enforcing it less rigorously, and resisting upgrading • more vigorous efforts to strengthen international labour and environmental standards, for example by including them in trade agreements	
More vigorous policies to facilitate structural adjustment by means of measures such as help with job search, relocation and retraining, and the provision of financial assistance	Trade expansion increases the number of workers disadvantaged by trade-related structural adjustment and thus increases pressure on governments to help these workers due to the economic and electoral desirability of maximizing employment in general plus sensitivity about negative publicity associated with mass layoffs
More vigorous measures to combat illicit trafficking, such as increased surveillance, increased international cooperation, tighter border controls and harsher penalties	Increasing illicit trafficking of people and goods elicits increasing pressure from law enforcement agencies, as well as groups with concerns about specific issues, to take stronger action
Less militarily aggressive policies towards significant trading partners	Trade expansion increases the number of individuals and businesses potentially negatively affected by the disruption of trade caused by war and magnifies their potential losses

The main puzzle here is that the expansion of trade implies downwards pressure on tax and on labour and environmental standards while recent studies find little evidence that this has been translated into real tax cuts or actual erosion of labour or environmental standards. This may be because most EU trade is with similar countries in similar products rather than with poor countries competing on cost, so that the downwards pressure on tax and on labour and environmental standards simply isn't very strong, at least so far. It would be difficult to argue that this pressure doesn't exist at all.

11
The Internationalization of Production

Introduction

As time goes on, economic activities in European countries are increasingly coming under the control of foreign firms while at the same time domestic firms expand their operations beyond national borders to control foreign enterprises. The implications of this for public policy are numerous and complex, but in general it strengthens the position of governments and transnational corporations in policy-making while weakening the position of trade unions, and is likely to lead to further internationalization of policy-making.

It is important to be clear about what the internationalization of production is. Perhaps the easiest way in is to start by looking at transnational companies (TNCs) and their role. TNCs are defined by the UN as:

> . . . incorporated or unincorporated enterprises comprising parent enterprises and their foreign affiliates. A *parent enterprise* is defined as an enterprise that controls assets of other entities in countries other than its home country, usually by owning a certain equity capital stake. An equity capital stake of 10 per cent or more of the ordinary shares or voting power for an incorporated enterprise, or its equivalent in an unincorporated enterprise, is normally considered as a threshold for the control of assets. A *foreign affiliate* is an incorporated or unincorporated enterprise in which an investor, who is resident in another economy, owns a stake that permits a lasting interest in the management of that enterprise (an equity stake of 10 per cent for an incorporated enterprise or its equivalent in an unincorporated enterprise) (UNCTAD 2003: 231).

The internationalization of production in the sense of the establishment or extension of transnational links as defined above takes three main forms. Greenfield investments involve setting up new productive facilities in the host country. Mergers and affiliations take place when enterprises merge with, or acquire control of all or part of, another enterprise. Strategic alliances differ from mergers and acquisitions in that the participating firms remain independent, and are designed to enable participating firms to economize on costs of production and research, strengthen market position or access other firms' intangible assets. Alliances can link firms horizontally to similar firms or vertically to suppliers and customers, and can take the form of joint ventures in which a separate corporation is set up by the partners, minority equity investments and equity swaps, or non-equity agreements to undertake joint R&D, joint manufacturing, joint marketing, long-term sourcing arrangements, shared distribution and services, or standards setting. Electronic alliances, such as industry business-to-business exchanges, enable firms to reduce search and transaction costs when looking for suppliers and buyers (OECD 2001j: 13–14, 27).

Enterprises choosing to establish or acquire affiliates in other countries can be divided into four main types. Resource-seekers seek physical resources such as raw materials, cheap and plentiful unskilled or semi-skilled labour, and expertise in areas such as technology, management, marketing or organization. Market-seekers establish overseas affiliates to gain access to new markets, improve adaptation to foreign markets, or reduce production or transaction costs, for example by reducing transport costs, avoiding tariffs or securing investment incentives from the host country. Local market presence may be a prerequisite for serving that market at all. Provision of retail banking, for instance, requires local banking outlets. Efficiency-seekers are interested in exploiting the different factor endowments of different countries, for example by locating R&D in rich countries with well-developed universities and labour-intensive processes in poor countries with low labour costs. Strategic asset seekers use internationalization for strategic purposes, for example as a means of cornering supplies or blocking out competition. Firms may also shift production to escape government restrictions in their home country (or another country), or to provide support services for products such as after-sales maintenance (Dunning 1993: 57–62, Eurostat 2002a: 17).

The principal indicator of the internationalization of production is foreign direct investment (FDI), defined as:

> an investment involving a long-term relationship and reflecting a lasting interest and control by a resident entity in one economy . . . in an enterprise resident in an economy other than that of the foreign direct investor. . . . FDI implies that the investor exerts a significant degree of influence on the management of the enterprise resident in the other economy. Such investment involves both the initial transaction between the two entities and all subsequent transactions between them and among foreign affiliates (UNCTAD 2003: 231).

The minimum ownership level required for a direct investment to be deemed to exist is set by the UN at the same level as that used to define an enterprise as a foreign affiliate of a TNC, namely 10 per cent of the voting shares. FDI is therefore a direct indicator of the transnational links that connect the parent enterprises of TNCs with their foreign affiliates. Foreign control of firms, by contrast, is defined as ownership of 50 per cent or more of ordinary shares or voting power on the board of directors (OECD 2001k: 18, UNCTAD 2004: 32).

FDI stock consists of the value of the share of capital and reserves (including retained profits) of foreign affiliates attributable to the parent enterprise, plus the net indebtedness of affiliates to the parent enterprise. FDI flows consist of equity capital (shares purchased in another country), reinvested earnings by affiliates, and intra-company loans or debt transactions. Non-equity (non-share) forms of FDI mainly comprise subcontracting, management contracts, turnkey arrangements, franchising, licensing and product sharing. FDI also involves packages of assets such as expertise, technology and access to markets (Dunning 1993: 4, UNCTAD 2003: 231–2). It is important to note that FDI flows are not necessarily equivalent to domestic gross fixed capital formation. Transfers to affiliates, for instance, may be used as liquidity rather than real investment, actual investment by affiliates may be financed not only by parent companies but also through capital raised on local markets, and acquisitions of foreign firms are not necessarily connected with any fixed capital formation. FDI measures therefore do not necessarily include expansion of affiliates, and do not necessarily say much about TNC coordination and control (Kozul-Wright 1995: 149–50, Wortmann 2000: 2–3). Nevertheless, FDI is an appropriate indicator of the internationalization of production because it does give a general indication of trends in international financial stocks and flows as they relate to international (foreign) control and coordination of production in terms of what is produced, how and where.

As FDI flows fluctuate considerably from year to year according to short-term economic circumstances, trends in the levels of FDI stocks are the best indicators of long-term trends in the internationalization of production. Between 1980 and 2003 world FDI stock multiplied tenfold to US$8.2 trillion (thousand billion). It is estimated that by 2003 at least 61,000 TNCs were operating, with over 900,000 foreign affiliates (UNCTAD 2004a: 8, Annex Table B.3). In 2002 the value added by foreign affiliates was about a tenth of world GDP, twice the share in 1982. Sales by foreign affiliates were estimated at US$18 trillion, compared with world exports of just US$8 trillion. Nearly a third of world exports of goods and services were thought to be taking place within networks of foreign affiliates (UNCTAD 2003: 23). While many TNCs are essentially national corporations with international affiliates, with most of their assets in their home country, many others have the greater part of their assets, sales and/or employment in countries other than that of the parent enterprise (UNCTAD 2004a: Table III.10, Table A.I.3).

So far the internationalization of production is taking place mainly among rich countries. Between 1985 and 2002 the Triad of the EU, Japan and the US accounted for about 80 per cent of global outward stock and 50–60 per cent of global inward stock, with regional groupings around each member (UNCTAD 2003: 23). This is the main reason for preferring the term 'internationalization' to 'globalization'.

However it is unclear to what extent this internationalization of production consists of a TNC allocating different stages of production chains to different countries (vertical FDI), as distinct from simply duplicating its production chain in one or more foreign countries to improve access to foreign markets (horizontal FDI). If the significance of production chains that are distributed among two or more countries is increasing, we would expect international intra-firm trade also to increase as the trade in part-completed goods that is integral to vertical FDI increases, but although UNCTAD data suggest that intra-firm trade did rise from about 20 per cent of trade during the 1970s to about a third by the early 1990s, estimates of intra-firm trade between 1990 and 2000 in the OECD countries for which reasonably reliable information is available (the US, Canada, Japan, the Netherlands and Sweden) suggest that during this period intra-firm trade fluctuated rather than increased (Kozul-Wright 1995: 153, OECD 2003: 108–9).

Internationalization of services is increasing especially rapidly. Between 1980 and 2002 the global stock of FDI in the primary sector doubled, and FDI in manufacturing nearly tripled, but FDI in services more than quadrupled to 60 per cent of total FDI stock in 2002 (UNCTAD 2004: 34, 2004a: 29–31, Table III.10). One aspect of this is the increased offshoring of corporate service functions to foreign affiliates, local companies in another country, or foreign affiliates of other TNCs. So far this is mainly taking place among rich countries, but poorer countries are increasingly becoming involved (OECD 2004a: 147–53, 164–7).

Production in Europe is also internationalizing as European companies expand into other countries, including other European countries, while non-European companies expand their presence in Europe. Within the EU this has been facilitated by the establishment of the Single Market, which among other things provides for the free movement of capital. Capital movements were completely liberalized within the EU by the early 1990s. The proliferation, growth and spread of TNCs has also been facilitated by the removal of barriers to foreign ownership and by privatizations that opened previously public firms to foreign control (OECD 2003g: 171–2).

By 2002 there were over 30,000 TNCs based in the EU, with over 60,000 foreign affiliates, and half of the top 10 TNCs in terms of foreign assets were European (UNCTAD 2004a: 273, 276). Table 11.1 shows the growth of inward and outward FDI stocks in the EU-15. By 2003 the EU's stock of FDI, including intra-European stock, was estimated at about $3.3 trillion. FDI stocks rose in all 15 Member States apart from Greece, where they remained low and steady at around 10 per cent of GDP, and Ireland, where FDI stocks were high, with inwards stock equivalent to 158 per cent of GDP at its zenith in 1985, but fluctuated considerably. However in some countries this upwards trend slowed or even reversed slightly after 2000 (UNCTAD 2004a: Annex Table B.6).

Table 11.1   FDI stock as a % of GDP, EU-15, 1980–2003

	1980	*1990*	*2000*	*2003*
Inward	6.1	10.9	28.5	32.8
Outward	6.1	11.6	37.5	39.6

Source: UNCTAD 2004a: Annex Table B.6.

Table 11.2 reveals that in 2002 most outward FDI stocks held by TNCs based in EU-15 countries were located in other EU-15 countries. FDI stocks held by EU-based TNCs in non-EU countries were mainly located in other rich countries, while non-EU FDI stocks in Europe were mainly held by TNCs from other rich countries (Eurostat 2005r).

FDI in services is increasingly important, especially in the financial, real estate and business services sectors, which are also the ones in which private sector employment is increasing the most (OECD 2001h: 70–1, Eurostat 2002: 47–8, 75–8, OECD 2003: 76, UN 2004, Eurostat 2005, OECD 2005a).

It is clear that production in Europe and by European-based TNCs has been internationalizing for decades in the sense of steady growth in the extent of cross-national control and coordination of production. This is likely to continue. The internationalization of production is long-standing in nature, there are no obvious obstacles in its path, even though governments could quickly reinstate barriers to foreign investment if they wished, and the incentives for firms to engage in cross-border activities, such as market access and cost

Table 11.2   EU-15 direct investment positions, 1994 and 2002

	1994	*2002*
Outward FDI stocks		
Intra-EU FDI as a percentage of total outward FDI stocks	51	59
FDI stocks in the US as a percentage of total extra-EU FDI stocks	44	38
FDI stocks in China and newly-industrializing countries as a percentage of total extra-EU FDI stocks	13	13
Inward FDI stocks		
Intra-EU FDI as a percentage of total inward FDI stocks	56	70
FDI stocks of American TNCs as a percentage of total extra-EU inward FDI stocks	50	54
FDI stocks of TNCs based in China and newly-industrializing countries as a percentage of total extra-EU inward FDI stocks	2	4

Source: Eurostat 2005r. Newly industrializing countries as defined by Eurostat comprise Hong Kong, Korea, Singapore, Taiwan, Malaysia, Philippines, Thailand, Argentina, Brazil, Chile and Mexico.

reduction, remain in operation. Experts believe that global flows of FDI will increase as intense competition continues to force TNCs to invest in new markets and seek access to low-cost resources and factors of production such as labour. FDI flows would also be expected to be further strengthened by higher economic growth and higher stock markets, and by more favourable FDI policies and cross-border agreements (UNCTAD 2003: xv).

Implications

Table 11.3 sets out the main policy actors currently interested in influencing public policy on foreign investment and TNCs. In the first tier are TNCs themselves, by definition the agents of the internationalization of production,

Table 11.3   Generic policy network relating to international investment

Type of policy actor	Specific policy actor
Political executives and associated parties	Chief executives Trade and industry ministers Ministers in related areas such as foreign affairs, finance, education, research, technology, agriculture
Non-government politicians	Economically liberal parties and politicians Nationalist and protectionist parties and politicians Parliamentary committees related to foreign investment and trade European Commissioners for trade, internal market, industry Subnational governments Foreign governments, especially the US government
Civil servants, special advisers and other public sector employees	Trade and industry departments and agencies, including investment agencies Related departments and agencies, for example foreign affairs, finance, education, research, technology, agriculture EU Directorates-General for trade, internal market, industry, research Foreign trade and industry departments and agencies, especially US
Judges and regulators	European Commission European Court of Justice World Trade Organization (WTO)
Business	Home-based TNCs TNCs based in other EU countries TNCs based outside the EU Domestic suppliers, competitors and customers

(Continued)

Table 11.3　(*Continued*)

Type of policy actor	Specific policy actor
Interest groups and non-government organizations	Employer and trade organizations Trade unions Environmentalists Third World advocates Anti-globalization groups
Media	National media Journalists in areas such as economics, politics, labour and the environment
Experts	Economists, labour and environmental experts OECD
Electorate	Workers affected by foreign investment

and national governments, which have legal authority over all firms based or operating in their country. The second tier consists of domestic suppliers, customers and competitors, foreign governments such as the US government, international and supranational organizations such as the WTO and European Commission, regional governments, and trade unions, environmentalists and other NGOs at national, regional and international levels.

The internationalization of production has a number of implications for policy actors and public policy. Its economic benefits would be expected to increase the policy autonomy of governments and make them more likely to implement TNC-friendly policies. At the same time the increasing economic significance of TNCs implies that governments will become more active in trying to limit locational competition, transfer pricing and other damaging practices of TNCs. There is also likely to be greater assistance for domestic workers disadvantaged by competition from incoming TNCs. Internationalization of production also implies less union-friendly policies. On the other hand the extent of pro-TNC policies is likely to be limited by the opposition of the growing anti-globalization movement. More generally the increasing importance of TNCs in the economy is likely to lead governments to change their preferred economic policy instruments, while perceptions that illegal activities are also internationalizing are likely to lead to greater international cooperation in law enforcement. Finally, the internationalization of production implies decreasing likelihood of war with countries with which EU Member States have extensive investment links.

Greater policy autonomy for governments

It is widely believed that the internationalization of production facilitates economic growth and job creation. According to this view, inward FDI expands the production base of the host country, creates employment and produces multiplier effects by means such as placing orders with local industries. Inward FDI can also lead to technology transfer and to an improvement in other firms' management and marketing skills, general efficiency and product quality (Eurostat 2002a: 17). The obvious example of the economic benefits of this is Ireland, where very high levels of inward FDI have been accompanied by very high levels of economic growth.

By the same logic we might expect outward FDI to reduce growth and employment at home, on the basis that it is replacing investment that would otherwise take place at home, but to the extent that parent companies establish affiliates in other countries in order to access new markets when domestic markets are saturated, outward FDI should not reduce production or employment at home. It is also argued that outward FDI by home-based TNCs leads to increased head office employment, increased exports due to servicing the needs of their foreign subsidiaries, and increased efficiency, cost savings, and more productive investment of savings, which in turn leads to increased growth, employment creation and upgrading of production processes (Dunning 1993: 360–2, European Commission 2004j: 214, 216). Econometric studies generally indicate that outwards investment has only a relatively small impact on the EU-15 labour market. The explanation appears to be that although the location of R&D intensive industries is increasingly influenced by countries' endowments of researchers, the location of non-manual labour-intensive industries by the education levels of the labour force, and the location of manual labour-intensive industries by the cost of labour, while industries higher up the value chain and industries with increasing returns to scale are increasingly locating in central regions, the structural adjustment that this entails is rather slow and is not causing large adjustment costs (European Commission 2004j: 211–18).

Since the economic effects of inward FDI are positive and those of outward FDI are not entirely negative, and possibly positive, it follows that for most countries the net effect of inward and outward FDI on growth and employment should be positive. This in turn should make governments more popular, for two reasons. First, higher growth and more jobs would be expected to assist governments' electoral prospects directly. Second, higher growth and more jobs means an expansion in the size of the tax base, which makes it easier for governments to expand services without raising tax rates or to cut tax without cutting services. This should improve their re-election prospects and thereby strengthen their policy autonomy relative to other policy actors because it means that they are less vulnerable to electoral threats posed by other policy actors.

However the other economic effects of internationalizing production are not always positive.

For a start, greater economic dependence on inward foreign investment also means greater vulnerability to economic developments in other countries, such as recessions that prompt TNCs based in these countries to withdraw investment.

Second, even if inward and outward investment taken together produce net gains in production and employment overall, specific job losses caused by relocation of production are likely to reduce the popularity of governments because they often take the form of highly visible plant closures. The popularity of governments may also be eroded by increasing feelings of economic insecurity due to increasing job turnover (European Commission 2004j: 220–1, Scheve and Slaughter 2004).

Third, even if the internationalization of production has created jobs up to now, there are fears that this may not continue in the future. A report prepared for the European Commission, for example, foreshadows further global reorganization of firms leading to relocation away from Europe motivated by cost considerations due to the emergence of sophisticated competitors with very low labour and environmental standards in countries such as Brazil, India, Russia and China, plus the desire of EU-based TNCs to improve access to the growing markets in these and other developing countries (Fontagné 2004: 6, 19, 80).

A fourth problem is that TNCs may take advantage of their transnational status to out-compete local firms, for example by using predatory pricing and cross-border subsidization of activities in order to drive out competitors (Dunning 1993: 437–8).

Finally, the capacity of governments to collect tax, especially corporate tax, is being undermined by the capacity of TNCs to relocate production to lower tax countries and by transfer pricing, which occurs when the price set by a TNC on an intra-firm transaction deviates from the price that would have occurred if the seller and buyer had not been related, in such a way as to reduce or even eliminate the declared profits on which tax is payable and to increase apparent income in low-tax jurisdictions, so that most if not all declared profits are taxed at the lowest possible rate (Navaretti *et al.*, undated: 59–61).

National governments have historically sought to maximize the benefit of inward FDI through regulation of entry conditions and operating requirements. Restrictions may be placed on the share of companies' equity capital that non-residents are allowed to hold. Obligatory screening and approval procedures may stipulate that incoming foreign investors must show economic benefits, obtain prior approval for all FDI projects, or employ a certain proportion of nationals. There may also be ongoing performance requirements in areas such as local purchasing, exports, intra-firm pricing and technology transfer (Dunning 1993: 559, OECD 2003g: 168–9). In recent years, however, investment policy has increasingly focussed on facilitating the flow of FDI through means such as bilateral investment and double taxation treaties, provision of information and advice to incoming TNCs, and financial incentives for inward investment (UNCTAD 2003: 19–21, 36, Raines 2004: 121–3).

To sum up, the popularity of the economic benefits of the internationalization of production, plus the consequent expansion of the tax base, should strengthen the electoral position of incumbent governments, other things being equal. This puts governments in a stronger position to do what they want without too many concessions to other policy actors. It also provides an incentive to continue pursuing liberal policies in relation to foreign investment.

However the positive electoral effects for governments of internationalizing production are offset to some extent by the negative effects of job losses associated with relocating production, increasing feelings of job insecurity, and fears for the future. In addition, the expansion of the tax base is reduced somewhat by the effects of transfer pricing, while the economic benefits are reduced by the negative effects of distinctive TNC forms of sharp practice. And the internationalization of production means that downturns in FDI due to events in other countries will cause more serious economic problems than would otherwise be the case.

More TNC-friendly policies as a consequence of their increasing bargaining power

As TNCs become more important in the economy and inward investment increases in significance for economic growth and employment, national governments become more dependent on the activities of TNCs to secure prosperity and popularity. The increase in the proportion of economic activities being undertaken by TNCs means that their economic and therefore political importance is rising relative to purely domestic firms. If we assume that it is easier for TNCs to transfer production elsewhere than it is for purely domestic firms, increasing internationalization of production means that an increasing proportion of national production can be transferred elsewhere relatively easily. Inwards FDI in particular provides resources that can be withdrawn at any time, which is especially serious where it has entered via a merger or acquisition or has driven local firms out of business (Dunning 1993: 531). Put another way, expansion of the scale of international production means that the consequences of TNCs as a group disinvesting are increasing as time goes on. In addition, by virtue of their economic weight incoming TNCs are often in a position to participate actively in existing national and sub-national policy networks as major new policy actors on the side of business.

This increasing economic dependence on TNCs, plus their activities as new policy actors, increases the bargaining power of TNCs and therefore means that public policy is likely to become more supportive of the distinctive policy preferences of TNCs, other things being equal, specifically further liberalization of national and international investment regulation and expansion of targeted assistance and incentives for inward FDI, and to move in the direction of the policy preferences that TNCs share with business in general: low inflation, good infrastructure, a good education and training system, availability of government advice and assistance in areas such as R&D, low labour costs, high labour flexibility, low taxes and limited environmental regulation.

Further liberalization of investment restrictions and expansion of targeted assistance and incentives for inward FDI

Inward investment is obviously easier when there are few regulatory hurdles, an abundance of information and advice, and generous financial assistance. In recent years policy measures have increasingly been put in place to facilitate the flow of FDI. Increasing numbers of bilateral investment treaties typically cover the scope and definition of foreign investment, admissions and establishment, national treatment in the post-establishment phase, most-favoured-nation treatment (which means that firms from both countries must be treated equally), guarantees and compensation in the event of expropriation, guarantees of free transfers of funds and repatriation of capital and profits, and dispute settlement provisions between states and between investors and states. Double taxation treaties prevent income and assets being taxed in both countries and set up means to prevent tax evasion, resolve international tax disputes, allocate taxing rights between states and prevent tax discrimination. Inward investment agencies provide information, advice and assistance, including financial incentives such as one-off grants and cheap loans as well as fiscal incentives such as time-limited tax holidays. There may also be non-financial incentives such as guarantees against nationalization and price control. Of the 1,640 changes introduced by 165 countries in their FDI laws between 1991 and 2002, 95 per cent were in the direction of greater liberalization (UNCTAD 2003: 19–21, 36, Raines 2004: 121–3).

We would also expect the increasing leverage of TNCs to lead governments to increase their support for international investment rules that further facilitate foreign investment, such as the WTO's 1994 Agreement on Trade-Related Aspects of Investment Measures (TRIMS), which limited the range of restrictive policy measures available to governments, for example by prohibiting governments from requiring particular levels of local procurement by TNCs. In recent years the EU has been pushing for the WTO to establish more extensive multilateral rules on FDI in order to increase investment opportunities (WTO 2005, European Commission 2000a).

Continued policy emphasis on controlling inflation

Inflation poses problems for TNCs and other companies because, among other things, it reduces the price competitiveness of firms both in export and domestic markets relative to firms resident in low-inflation countries, exchange rates being equal (Pass *et al.* 1995: 115). A reputation for low inflation therefore helps to attract foreign investment. Indicators of safe countries from this point of view include not only a good track record on low inflation but also institutions and policies that are considered optimal for the purposes of controlling inflation, notably central banks that are independent from direct political control, so that electoral considerations cannot interfere with their setting of interest rates, and state budgets in which deficits are kept under control. Eurozone countries already have an independent central bank in the form of the European Central Bank, which has price stability as its sole object- ive, while countries outside the Eurozone have progressively made their own central banks independent as well and the Treaty Establishing the European Community obliges Member States to restrict budget deficits to a maximum of 3 per cent of GDP and debt to a maximum of 60 per cent of GDP (European Commission 2005a), although this has proven difficult to enforce. As TNCs become more important, EU-15 countries would be expected at least to main- tain this emphasis on controlling inflation.

More business-friendly policies in relation to infrastructure, education, financial aid and R&D

Authorities at national, European and regional levels can help attract and keep TNC investment by improving and extending transport and communications infrastructure, improving and extending education and training, providing assistance with R&D, and providing loans, subsidies and/or tax breaks where allowed by EU law. Such measures are generally uncontroversial.

Greater emphasis on policies designed to minimize labour costs and maximize labour flexibility

Increasing competition between countries for inward investment means, among other things, increasing pressure on governments for public policies that minimize labour costs and maximize labour flexibility. This means increasing pressure on governments from firms and experts to take steps to secure wage restraint, reduce or eliminate employers' social contributions, and reform employment regulation in areas such as working conditions, working hours, minimum wages and employment protection. From the point of view of employees in general this means lower wages, higher social contributions and/or reduced pensions and health cover, and more unpleasant working conditions even though jobs in the export sectors in which TNCs are espe- cially active have the reputation of being well-paid and secure relative to local jobs (WTO 2003a). Such policies are therefore unpopular and are actively opposed by trade unions. Although they can be introduced unilat- erally, for example by legislating to weaken employment regulation, the alternative of policy concertation with major social interests including trade unions, such as social pacts that exchange wage restraint for policy conces- sions in other areas, has the electoral advantage of minimizing social conflict and voter backlash (Garrett 1998, Rieger and Leibfried 1998).

It is not clear, however, that pressures to implement such measures have been reflected in the content of public policy in the EU so far. Between 1970 and 2000 real wages in manufacturing grew significantly in all European countries for which data was available. In some respects employment regu- lation has been made more employee-friendly rather than more employer- friendly, for example with the introduction of the 35-hour week in France, the establishment of a minimum wage in Britain, and the growth of employment regulation at EU level. And employers' social contributions in the EU-15 have been rising as a proportion of GDP (OECD 2001e: 86, Europa 2003, ILO 2003, OECD 2004b: 76).

Cuts in corporate taxes

The ability of TNCs to locate investment where their tax payments would be lowest puts pressure on governments to cut taxes insofar as they affect TNCs, in particular corporate tax. Having said this, there is little indication that these pressures have so far had much effect on the tax revenues of EU-15 countries. Despite high profile cuts in top marginal rates of corporation tax during the 1980s, tax reliefs were reduced or abolished at the same time, and between 1965 and 2000 revenue from corporation tax in the EU-15 rose steadily as a percentage of total taxation and as a percentage of GDP, before falling slightly in 2001 and 2002 (OECD 2004b: 20, 73).

Greater emphasis on minimizing the costs to business of environmental regulation

The ability of TNCs to locate where environmental standards are lowest puts pressure on governments to minimize the costs associated with environmental regulation through taking steps such as reforming existing regulation to reduce compliance costs while maintaining the benefits to the environment (for instance by moving from command-and-control regulation to market instruments such as emissions trading), downgrading existing regulation (so that environmental protection is reduced along with compliance costs), enforcing existing regulation less rigorously (for instance by cutting the staff of environmental regulators) and resisting moves to upgrade regulation (regulatory chill). However it is not clear how strong this pressure is, as there does not appear to be much systematic evidence that high-polluting industries are moving away from countries with stringent environmental regulations (Busse 2004), and new environmental legislation continues to be passed at national and EU levels.

Greater international cooperation to limit locational competition

Instead of competing with each other for inward investment by implementing policies that may be damaging in other ways, such as introducing tax cuts that undermine state finances, governments may choose to restrict locational competition by cooperating at international level to establish minimum standards in areas such as labour law, taxation and environmental regulation. The increasing dependence of countries on TNCs and their locational decisions implies increasing incentives for governments with high standards in these areas to press for the strengthening of such standards.

In relation to labour rights this implies greater pressure to strengthen EU-wide employment regulation, which already exists in areas such as health and safety, equal pay, working time, and fixed-term and temporary employment (Europa 2003). It also implies greater pressure to establish enforceable minimum labour standards at global level. Although there is already a substantial body of international labour standards agreed under the auspices of the UN's International Labour Organization (ILO) in relation to labour rights such as freedom of association, the right to organize, collective bargaining, the abolition of forced labour, and equality of opportunity and treatment (ILO 2005), these are not enforceable in the way that trade rules, for example, can be enforced by the WTO.

Competition among countries to attract TNCs by reducing corporate tax could be countered by measures such as agreements on tax rates, cost allowance and auditing standards, but there are as yet no binding international standards for corporate tax even though at EU level there is the precedent of a minimum rate for VAT of 15 per cent (Kudrle 2000: 216, European Commission 2005b, 2005c, OECD 2005b). As potential losses from tax competition grow, we would expect greater pressure to be exerted by countries with high rates of corporate tax for international agreements to be struck in this area.

Pressure to attract inward investment by weakening environmental regulation could also be lessened by upgrading minimum standards at international level. There is already an extensive body of environmental regulation at EU level in areas such as waste management, noise pollution, water pollution, air pollution and technological hazards that restricts the extent to which exporters based in EU Member States can compete on the basis of low environmental standards (Europa 2001), plus a growing number of agreements at international level, such as the Kyoto Protocol on greenhouse gas emissions, that to some extent place limits on competition based on low environmental standards.

Whether the increasing pressure exerted by governments with high labour standards, high corporate tax and high environmental standards will succeed in establishing or upgrading minimum standards in these areas, however, remains to be seen in view of the opposition of countries that are currently using low labour standards, low corporate tax or lax environmental regulation to attract inward investment.

More vigorous policies to limit damaging TNC practices and transfer pricing

Even if the internationalization of production creates higher economic growth and more jobs overall, these benefits are vitiated to the extent that TNCs compete with local firms (and each other) in ways that can be considered unfair and damaging. Distinctive TNC practices in this respect include predatory pricing, use of 'deep pocket' advantages to promote non-price competition through means such as advertising, provision of intra-group services at below marginal costs, willingness of parent companies to accept below normal profits and dividends from affiliates, manipulation of cross-border intra-group prices, cross-border subsidization of activities in order to drive out competitors, limitations on the use of technology, control over the sourcing of inputs, and restrictive use of patents and trademarks (Dunning 1993: 437–8).

As TNC involvement in national economies becomes more significant, the impact of such practices will increase, other things being equal, leading to increasing pressure from domestic industry for governments to take steps to counter them, for example by making competition law more rigorous and by cooperating with relevant authorities in other countries, as already occurs within the EU in the context of the EU's competition policy, although the extent to which such pressures are reflected in the content of public policy will be limited by the desire of national governments not to deter inward investment.

As well as damaging local firms via unfair practices, TNCs may use transfer pricing to evade tax which, other things being equal, reduces the re-election prospects of incumbent governments by undermining tax revenue and therefore their capacity to expand public services or cut tax rates. Transfer pricing occurs when the price on an intra-firm transaction deviates from the price that would have occurred if the seller and buyer had not been related. This practice is difficult to detect, especially where the transferred assets are specialized or intangible, such as technology, but it is generally agreed that many TNCs do undertake transfer pricing to reduce tax by choosing transfer payments that increase apparent costs in high-tax jurisdictions, in order to reduce or even eliminate the declared profits on which tax is payable, and increase apparent income in low-tax jurisdictions so that most if not all declared profits are taxed at the lowest possible rate. In response, national tax authorities use a number of methods to impute the price that would have obtained between independent parties, including using comparable arm's length prices for similar transactions, adding a profit margin to estimated costs, subtracting profits from the eventual sales price, and splitting profits between vendor and purchaser. Tax evasion by foreign earnings concealment can be countered by means such as limiting bank secrecy and sharing information between governments (Navaretti *et al.*, undated: 59–60, Kudrle 2000: 216).

The problem is that it is difficult if not impossible to detect and counteract all instances of transfer pricing. Other things being equal, this means that the more production is internationalized, the greater is the revenue loss from transfer pricing. This puts increasing pressure on host governments to reduce incentives for TNCs to engage in transfer pricing by reducing national differences in relation to tax rates, tax base definitions and capital gains tax (Dunning 1993: 521). In practice this means increasing pressure on high-tax countries either to reduce corporate tax or to put in place international agreements that limit the capacity of tax jurisdictions to set very low (or zero) rates of corporate tax.

Greater assistance for workers displaced by structural adjustment

Increasing internationalization of production means increasing competition for local firms from foreign TNCs and increasing foreign investment by home-based TNCs. Both are likely to lead to changes in what is being produced at home and therefore to job gains in some areas but job losses in others. Competition from incoming TNCs may lead hitherto competitive local industries to reduce production, change what they produce or even close altogether, while home-based TNCs investing in other countries may relocate local production to these countries.

Even if the internationalization of production produces net gains in production and employment, job losses caused by relocation of production or competition from incoming TNCs are likely to reduce the popularity of governments because they often take the form of highly visible plant closures in areas such as textiles and clothing, steel, the motor vehicle industry and, more recently, electronics and digitizable services. The popularity of governments may also be reduced by increasing feelings of economic insecurity due to increasing job turnover, especially among the low-skilled (European Commission 2004j: 220–1, Scheve and Slaughter 2004).

As the internationalization of production increases, we would expect the incidence both of highly visible job losses and of job turnover in general to increase. This implies increasing electoral problems for incumbent governments as more and more people are threatened or affected and the media highlight job losses more frequently. Governments are also likely to come under increasing pressure from more and more firms and trade unions to take steps to avert threatened job losses. Job losses also constitute evidence for anti-globalist critiques of the internationalization of production and contribute to sustaining a global anti-globalization movement the supporters of which exert at least some electoral pressure on governments to limit or reverse the internationalization of production.

All this puts governments under increasing pressure to do what they can to minimize the political cost of job losses associated with the internationalization of production. There are three main ways in which this can be done.

First, governments can try to avoid job losses in the first place by providing affected firms and industries with financial and other assistance to keep them afloat. However for EU Member States the extent to which this can be done is limited by EU rules on state aid (European Commission 2005d). Another problem is that state aid of this sort may result in open-ended subsidies to inefficient firms that will never be in a position to compete effectively.

Second, governments can place further restrictions and conditions on inward investment in order to blunt the competitive edge of foreign TNCs. The disadvantage here is that this risks reducing inward investment and therefore losing the jobs that it brings, which may be counterproductive from the point of view of employment overall.

The third alternative is to let market forces operate, in the interests of an efficient economy and more jobs in the long run, but to assist laid-off workers to find new jobs by means of measures such as help with job search, relocation and retraining, while providing financial assistance in the meantime. This facilitates the transfer of labour from declining sectors to growth sectors and should thereby raise employment levels and economic prosperity in the medium to long term. Measures to ensure that laid-off workers do not lose occupational pension entitlements as well as their jobs are also important. Government measures in this area should be possible to finance from the extra tax revenue collected as a consequence of inward investment increasing the size of the tax base, despite reduced taxes from companies hurt by TNC competition, so in this sense should not represent a net cost to governments.

Less union-friendly policies

If we assume that it is easier for TNCs to transfer production elsewhere than it is for purely domestic firms, increasing internationalization of production means that an increasing proportion of firms in any given country are in a position to transfer production elsewhere relatively easily. Since relocation of production would mean job losses for their members, this weakens the bargaining power of unions by providing more and more firms with an additional bargaining chip or threat to use in negotiations. Put another way, the internationalization of production renders the demand for labour more elastic, in that workers in one country can more easily be substituted for workers in another, and this leads to employers becoming less willing to share non-wage labour costs such as social insurance and to greater volatility in earnings and hours (employment) in response to changes in the demand for labour (Rodrik 1997: 16–26).

To the extent that the capacity of trade unions to exert pressure on employers is a significant resource for unions in their dealings with government, this loss of bargaining power vis a vis business would also be expected to reduce the bargaining power of unions within the policy process. Other things being equal this implies that public policy is likely to become less union-friendly as time goes on.

Less TNC-friendly policies due to the rise of the anti-globalization movement

As we have seen, there are a number of drawbacks associated with the internationalization of production, including increasing economic vulnerability to events elsewhere, job losses, and increasing economic dependence on TNCs leading to increasing pressure on labour and environmental standards and on corporate tax. These have contributed to the formation of a global anti-globalization movement supported by those threatened or already damaged by these developments, such as displaced workers, as well as by trade unions, environmentalists, statist parties and groups, anti-capitalist parties and

groups, women's movements, and third world groups and advocates including peasant organizations and indigenous people's organizations (Green and
Griffiths 2002, Seoane and Taddei 2002).

Other things being equal we would expect the rise of this anti-globalization movement to limit the tendency of public policy to move in a TNC-
friendly direction, as growing opposition to globalization, including the
internationalization of production, could result in a loss of support for parties and governments that support it. The 1998 suspension of OECD talks on
establishing a Multilateral Investment Agreement, for example, which
among other things would have prevented governments from imposing performance requirements on foreign firms, is attributed by some observers
at least in part to the anti-globalization movement (OECD 1998b, Seoane
and Taddei 2002: 104).

Changes in economic policy instruments

Increasing internationalization of production reduces the efficacy of commonly used economic policy instruments in a number of ways. The ability of
TNCs to transfer profits out of the country means that demand management
policies have less impact on unemployment and output than would otherwise
be the case. Monetary policy has less influence on the supply of credit due to
the greater capacity of TNCs to borrow abroad when domestic interest rates are
high and to take advantage of low domestic interest rates to borrow domestic
funds for use elsewhere. The capacity of national governments to manage
their exchange rates is undermined by the capacity of TNCs to influence the
exchange rate via their huge international currency dealings. And national
industrial strategies are undermined by the capacity of TNCs to shift production
from country to country (Cowling and Sugden 1996, Held *et al.* 1999: 277).

It follows that governments trying to steer the economy will increasingly
turn to other policy instruments instead such as the ones discussed earlier
that are designed to encourage inward investment and help business in general. Another option is to pursue international economic integration to
improve business efficiency by stimulating competition and enabling firms
to achieve economies of scale, leading to lower prices and more choice for
consumers as well as to improved export competitiveness. This is already further developed in Europe than anywhere else, with the Single Market and
the single currency in the Eurozone (European Commission 2005e, 2005f).
Among other things economic integration implies economic regulation at
international level, which again is well-developed in Europe with institutions such as the European Commission and European Central Bank. One
possibility for the future would be for exchange rate stabilization and coordination of fiscal and monetary policy to be managed by the G3 (Europe,
Japan and North America), specific dimensions of economic activity such as
foreign direct investment and environmental standards by international
agencies, as the WTO currently regulates trade, and minimum standards in

labour market policy and social protection by regional blocs such as the EU (Hirst and Thompson 1999: 191–2).

Greater international cooperation in law enforcement

So far we have focused on how legitimate economic activities are becoming internationalized, but of course there is also much economic activity that is not legal, namely crime. The clandestine nature of crime means that it is impossible accurately to identify crime trends, but some of the developments that have encouraged the internationalization of production appear also to have created new opportunities for transnational crime, and European law enforcement agencies argue that organized crime in particular is internationalizing in a number of respects.

If it is worthwhile for legitimate firms to internationalize their operations, and easier to do than it used to be, it stands to reason that criminals will also find it profitable to expand internationally. Criminal organizations as well as legitimate firms may seek access to new markets, for example, and the foreign expansion of both is facilitated by advances in telecommunications and transport. Within Europe the creation of the EU common market has provided new opportunities and expanded the arena in which organized crime groups can operate (Europol 2003: 11–12).

According to the European Police Office (Europol), organized crime groups in Europe are intensifying international cooperation and coordinating over a wider geographical area. They are also thought to be internationalizing in the sense that they are becoming less ethnically homogenous, and groups originating in Albania, Russia, Turkey, Nigeria, Morocco, China, Vietnam and the former Yugoslavia are now well-established in EU countries. Enlargement encourages the internationalization of crime because the ability to move between 25 instead of 15 Member States makes it more difficult to detect, control and counter their illicit activities. Areas in which the internationalization of crime is especially prominent include fraud, especially VAT fraud, international vehicle trafficking, illegal migration and trafficking in human beings (Europol 2003: 8–17, 2004a, 2004b, 2004c).

To the extent that international crime is perceived to be increasing, demands on governments from individual and organizational victims to implement more effective countermeasures will become more numerous and vociferous, other things being equal. Policy actors that by function or purpose are concerned about crime, such as the police and socially conservative political parties, would also be expected to become more concerned and therefore more active in pressing governments for action. Ultimately the increase in international crime could lead to electoral damage to incumbent governments.

It follows that perceived increases in international crime increase pressure on governments to internationalize law enforcement, as effective action against international crime obviously requires international cooperation at the least, if not full international integration of national law enforcement agencies. To some extent law enforcement in the EU has already been internationalized with the creation of Europol, a network of judicial national authorities (Eurojust), and EU framework decisions designed to establish common definitions and penal sanctions for offences such as trafficking in human beings, cybercrime and confiscation of the proceeds of organized crime. Europol recommends further legal harmonization and more joint operations against leading drug trafficking networks, euro currency counterfeiting and money laundering. Other possible moves include stricter licensing of all kinds of economic activity, especially banks and other financial services, and a binding international convention on the control of transnational organized crime (Voronin 2000: 5, 10, 19, Europol 2003: 24–6, European Commission 2004l).

Decreasing likelihood of war with countries with which there are extensive investment links

Military conflict between nations disrupts connections between TNC parent enterprises and foreign subsidiaries located in the territories of the warring parties. To the extent that these connections add value, this means losses for the TNCs involved and for their workforces, suppliers and customers. As the internationalization of production grows, those potentially negatively affected by a war in this way become more numerous and their potential losses become greater. One would therefore expect the internationalization of production to lead to countries becoming less likely to go to war against countries with which they have extensive investment links.

Conclusion

Firms in the EU and elsewhere have been internationalizing their production for some time, as measured by stocks of inward and outward FDI, and this looks set to continue. Table 11.4 sets out the main implications of this for the direction of public policy.

Overall the internationalization of production should increase the popularity and policy autonomy of national governments, if its economic benefits are as claimed. The belief that these benefits will accrue, plus the decreasing efficacy of traditional economic policy instruments, are likely to lead governments to implement more TNC-friendly policies as time goes on, albeit limited by the opposition of the anti-globalization movement and tempered by measures to limit the negative effects of TNC activities. Trade unions, on the other hand, stand to lose influence in policy-making. The other noticeable feature is that public policy is increasingly likely to be made at international level.

202

Table 11.4 Policy implications of the internationalization of production

Policy implications	Causal chain from trend
More autonomous policies	Greater government popularity due to the economic benefits of increasing internationalization of production plus associated increased tax revenue, tempered by greater vulnerability to events elsewhere, short term job losses, fears about future job losses, and damaging TNC practices
More TNC-friendly policies such as further liberalization of investment restrictions, greater incentives for inward FDI, continued stress on low inflation, corporate tax cuts, improvements to infrastructure and education, more vigorous policies to cut labour costs and improve labour flexibility, and cheaper environmental regulation	Increasing pressure on governments to encourage inward investment due to the increasing economic significance of TNCs, the increasing proportion of national production that can be relatively easily transferred elsewhere, and the increasing numbers of foreign TNCs active in policy networks
More vigorous policies to limit damaging practices by TNCs and transfer pricing, such as greater international cooperation	Internationalization of production increases the economic significance of damaging TNC practices and the revenue lost due to transfer pricing
More vigorous policies to help workers displaced by structural adjustment, such as help with job search and retraining, and financial assistance	Increasing number of workers displaced by structural adjustment caused by the internationalization of production, plus economic and electoral advantages of getting these workers into new jobs and avoiding adverse publicity
Greater international cooperation to limit locational competition, such as agreements on tax	Increasing economic significance of firms relocating to countries with lower taxes, labour standards or environmental standards, or threatening to relocate
Policies designed to limit the internationalization of production, such as maintenance or upgrading of restrictions on foreign investment	Rise of anti-globalization movement due to the side-effects of the internationalization of production such as pressure on labour and environmental regulation
Less union-friendly policies	Reduced leverage for unions as the increasing significance of threatened and actual disinvestment undermines union ability to exert pressure on governments by putting pressure on employers
A shift in emphasis towards policy instruments such as	Increasing TNC activity reduces efficacy of certain policy instruments: their ability to shift

(Continued)

Table 11.4 (*Continued*)

Policy implications	Causal chain from trend
greater international economic integration and measures to encourage inward investment, improve infrastructure and skills, increase assistance with R&D, improve labour market efficiency and reduce business costs	profits means that demand management policies have less impact, their ability to borrow elsewhere or transfer domestic borrowings elsewhere means that monetary policy has less impact on credit, their currency dealings undermine exchange rate policy, and their capacity to shift production undermines industrial policy
Greater internationalization of law enforcement	Perceptions of increasing international crime elicit increasing pressure from law enforcement agencies, victims and others to take stronger action
Less militarily aggressive policies towards countries with which there are significant investment links	Internationalization of production increases the number of those who would be negatively affected by disruption of international production networks caused by war, and magnifies their potential losses

12

The Internationalization of Finance

Introduction

In recent years cross-border financial flows and holdings have grown dramatically and financial firms have become larger and more internationally integrated. This internationalizing of finance looks likely to continue in the years ahead, with important implications for public policy. In general its economic benefits strengthen the capacity of governments to implement their preferred policies except in the areas such as monetary policy in which the increasing economic importance of international financial flows implies increasing pressure on governments to establish and maintain business-friendly policies as defined by financial markets. At the same time governments are likely to strengthen prudential regulation of international finance and increase international cooperation to limit locational competition and reinforce the fight against international financial crime.

We have seen in Chapter 11 on the internationalization of production that FDI is increasing. The same is true of the other main types of international financial stocks and flows: currency, bank deposits and loans, debt securities (bonds), equity (shares), and financial derivatives. The amount of money traded on foreign exchanges has increased massively in recent years: between 1973 and 1995 the ratio of foreign exchange to trade rose from 2:1 to 70:1, and between 1989 and 1998 average daily global foreign exchange market turnover rose from US$590 billion to US$1,490 billion before falling back to US$1,200 billion in 2001 (BIS 2002: 5, Eatwell and Taylor 2000: 3–4). Table 12.1 shows that the value of international bank investment, debt securities and equities in leading European countries is also increasing in terms of current US dollars, albeit with something of a slowdown for equities between 2000 and 2003 as the technology boom came to an end. Comparison with the GDP deflator demonstrates that the value of these increased in real terms as well. Similar rises have taken place in other European countries.

The value of financial derivatives, such as forwards, futures, options and swaps, is also rising. Derivatives, which derive their value from the price

Table 12.1   International investment, 1980–2003 (billions of current US$)

	Outwards (assets)				Inwards (liabilities)			
	1980	1990	2000	2003	1980	1990	2000	2003
Bank investment								
Britain	352	907	1,580	2,359	374	1,036	1,889	2,887
France	na	389	430	621	132	427	530	787
Germany	69	371	680	1,292	74	222	848	1,144
Debt securities								
Britain	14	204	711	1,006	17	251	588	989
France	na	41	454	949	na	160	447	1,011
Germany	15	140	423	789	27	127	742	1,324
Equities								
Britain	32	195	641	663	11	114	902	874
France	na	40	210	300	na	55	502	502
Germany	5	45	573	577	10	81	301	365
US GDP deflator (2000 = 100)								
	45.04	81.59	100.00	106.30	45.04	81.59	100.00	106.30

Sources: IMF 2002, 2005. International bank investment (IMF codes 79aid, 79lid) comprises all financial instruments other than direct investment, portfolio investment, financial derivatives and reserve assets, thus including trade credits, loans, currency and deposits. International debt securities assets and liabilities (79aed, 79led) consist of bonds, notes and money market instruments. International equity securities assets and liabilities (79add, 79ldd) consist essentially of shares. The US GDP deflator is given to enable comparison of figures with inflation.

movements of some underlying product, were originally designed to enable hedging but can also be used for speculative purposes. Forward contracts, for example, have long been used to fix a product price now for delivery at a specific point in the future in order to insure farmers, for instance, against possible falls in the price of their harvest. The same principle can be applied to financial products such as bonds, shares and currencies. Options, for instance, give the purchaser the right to buy a given product (such as shares) at a certain price at a specific point in the future. If the share price rises above the stipulated price by the due date, the purchaser can buy the shares at the stipulated price and profit by selling them on at the new higher market price (Brett 2000: 288–303).

The notional principal amounts outstanding on global exchange-traded derivatives (futures and options), which means the value of the underlying financial products to which they relate, increased from US$730 billion in 1987 to US$36,734 billion in 2003. For Europe the amounts outstanding rose a thousandfold from US$13 billion in 1987 to US$15,405 billion in 2003 (IMF 2004: 190–1). Information on derivatives traded outside exchanges (over-the-counter or OTC derivatives) is more difficult to obtain due to the decentralized nature of these transactions, but a study of 13 industrialized countries found that between 1992 and 1999 the notional values of OTC derivatives in these countries quadrupled from US$24,600 billion to US$94,600 billion (G10 2001: 459). A separate measure indicates that between June 1998 and December 2003 the notional amounts outstanding on OTC derivatives in G10 countries rose from US$72,134 billion to US$197,167 billion. In all these cases it was interest rate contracts that dominated (BIS 2004, Table 19).

Finance is also internationalizing in the sense that the financial system itself is becoming more internationally integrated in a trend the ultimate destination of which would be a global financial system in which investments were made regardless of borders by global financial firms and institutions operating within a single financial market. An increasing number of firms are listed on more than one national exchange, for example, and the exchanges themselves increasingly have overlapping trading hours, while financial firms are becoming bigger and more internationally integrated by means of mergers, acquisitions, joint ventures and strategic alliances (G10 2001, IMF 2001: 11).

It seems likely that financial internationalization will continue for the foreseeable future. It is a well-established and consistent trend with no obvious obstacles in its path unless a series of financial crises persuade national governments to re-impose national financial controls. In addition, experts in the area generally agree that the trend will continue, and at least some of the causal factors to which it is attributed are likely to continue to operate, including increasing use of ICT, financial liberalization, financial innovation and the growth of funded pension schemes (Walter and Smith 2000: 227–8, Greenspan 2003).

Implications

Table 12.2 lists the main policy actors who take an interest in issues relating to international finance. Among the main players are banks, insurance companies, investment companies and pension funds. These are serviced by other financial firms such as investment banks and debt-rating agencies and regulated by a combination of private and official bodies at national, EU and, to some extent, global levels.

The internationalization of finance has four main implications for public policy. To the extent that it increases growth and prosperity it strengthens the electoral position of incumbent governments and thereby increases the likelihood that governments will implement their preferred policies even if these policies are unpopular. These economic benefits also encourage governments to support liberal policies on international finance. At the same time the internationalization of finance makes financial crises more likely and more severe when they do occur, thus adding to the incentives for governments to take action, including international action, to prevent them and minimize their impact when prevention fails. Third, the increasing economic importance of the internationalization of finance increases pressure on governments for business-friendly policies as defined by financial markets.

Table 12.2 Generic policy network relating to international finance

Type of policy actor	Specific policy actor
Political executives and associated parties	Chief executives Finance and foreign ministers Ministers concerned with law enforcement
Non-government politicians	Liberal parties and politicians Nationalist, statist and protectionist parties and politicians Parliamentary finance and foreign affairs committees European Commissioners for economic and financial affairs, and internal market and services Foreign governments, especially the US government
Civil servants, special advisers and other public sector employees	Finance and foreign ministries European Central Bank and national central banks Law enforcement agencies EU Directorates-General for economic and financial affairs, and internal market and services Foreign finance and foreign ministries and agencies International bodies such as the Bank of International Settlements (BIS) and International Monetary Fund (IMF)
Judges and regulators	Financial regulators at national and EU levels
Business	Banks, investment banks, insurance companies, securities firms, pension funds, mutual funds, asset management companies, accountants, and lawyers Financial exchanges and clearinghouses such as the London Stock Exchange, International Organization of Securities Commissions (IOSCO), and Clearing House Inter-Bank Payments System (CHIPS) Financial and coordination services firms such as debt-rating agencies and Lloyds Standards setting bodies such as the International Accounting Standards Board (IASB)
Interest groups and non-government organizations	Professional associations, trade associations and lobby groups in the finance area such as the Institute of International Finance (IIF) and the Financial Leaders' Group (FLG) Non-government organizations concerned about 3rd World debt and the regulation of cross-border financial flows
Media	National media Specialist finance journals
Experts	Economists, financial analysts Think tanks and research institutes
Electorate	Citizens affected by financial crises, contributors to pension funds, pensioners, wealthy clients of financial firms, employers and employees generally

Sources: These include Porter 1995: 103–8, 110–15, 144–7.

Finally, the increase in international financial crime made possible by the internationalization of finance increases pressure on authorities to take further steps to combat these sorts of criminal activities.

More autonomous policies in general and more liberal policies on international finance

The main economic rationale for the internationalization of finance is that it improves economic efficiency by enabling finance to flow to the world's most productive investment opportunities. From a country-specific point of view, access to international capital markets facilitates economic growth by enabling resident firms to finance their activities without being constrained by the level of savings that the domestic economy can muster. The greater range of finance available should also mean that obtaining finance costs less in terms of interest rates. At the same time domestic savers should be able to obtain higher returns because they can now invest in other countries as well as domestically. It is also claimed that the competitiveness of resident firms, and thus their efficiency and productivity, is improved by having to compete with firms in other countries for investment (OECD 2002f: 14, Walter and Smith 2000: 197, 273).

To the extent that the internationalization of finance has these effects, and in the absence of financial crises, we would expect higher growth than would otherwise be the case and therefore greater electoral support for incumbent governments, other things being equal. We would also expect governments to be able to obtain lower interest rates on government debt, which should be of electoral benefit because lower interest payments means that more money is made available to be spent in other areas or to be returned to tax payers in the form of tax cuts. These economic and financial benefits put governments in a stronger position to do what they want without feeling constrained to make too many concessions to other policy actors for electoral reasons.

The economic and financial benefits of the internationalization of finance also create incentives for governments to support financial liberalization, as they have been doing for some time. Within the EU financial liberalization was encouraged by measures such as the First Bank Directive in 1977, which allowed banks based anywhere in the EU to set up branches or subsidiaries in any Member State, the Second Bank Directive in 1988, which established a single EU banking license, and the Investment Services Directive, which provides for non-banking securities firms based in the EU to be regulated by their home country and to operate anywhere within the EU on that basis. By the early 1990s capital movements within the EU were completely liberalized. One effect of the replacement of national currencies by the euro is that pension funds and other important financial institutions that had been restricted to domestic currency investments are now able to invest in assets anywhere in the EU. The Financial Services Action Plan of 1999 set out further measures designed to establish a genuine single market in financial services (Walter and Smith 2000: 40–1, 82–3, 99, OECD 2003g: 171–2, European Commission 2004m).

More vigorous measures to prevent financial crises and minimize their impact when they do occur

One of the principal characteristics of the international financial system is the regular occurrence of financial crises such as the collapse of international banks in the 1970s, the developing country debt crisis of the early 1980s, the Mexican peso crisis of 1994 and the Asian crisis of 1997–98. Such crises can have devastating effects on the lives of millions. The Asian crisis in particular is considered by some observers to have been the worst world economic crisis since the Depression of the 1930s (Porter 1995: 7, Gilpin 2000: 162).

The problem is that there are good reasons for thinking that the internationalization of finance increases both the likelihood and the severity of financial crises.

First, the increasing integration of international financial markets means that crises in one market or country are more likely to create knock-on crises in other financial markets and countries. It also means that there are more countries in which a financial crisis can originate and then spread. If a country defaults on its foreign loans, for example, this may lead to the collapse of the international banks that provided the loans, which then causes serious problems for other international financial institutions and for firms and governments in other countries.

Second, the increasing scale of international capital stocks and flows exacerbates the consequences for a country of any capital flight, so that attempts by small countries to manage market risk, for example, can be overwhelmed by the scale and speed of capital movements (Eatwell and Taylor 2000: 225).

Third, the growth of derivatives increases the risk of financial crisis due to their volatility, complexity and (mostly) speculative nature. Of particular concern are hedge funds that borrow large sums from banks in order to speculate using derivatives, as this raises the possibility that sudden speculative losses could lead to loan defaults, the collapse of a very large financial conglomerate and substantial damage to the financial system in general (Porter 2005: 73, 78, Coleman 2003: 278–80).

Finally, consolidation in the financial sector may increase systemic risk. The larger and more complex a financial institution becomes, the harder it becomes to resolve any difficulties that may arise and the more serious the consequences of a collapse become. Interdependencies between large and complex financial institutions are thought to be increasing as consolidation increases, for example in the form of interbank loan exposures, market activities such as trading in OTC derivatives, and payment and settlement systems, and this increases the risk that a common shock will be transmitted to many firms. The possibility of contagion is also increased by the blurring of differences between commercial banks, investment banks, insurance companies and other forms of financial intermediary (G10 2001: 15).

Because the knock-on economic effects of financial crises tend to undermine electoral support for incumbent governments, those in power have every incentive to take steps to try to minimize the likelihood of their occurring and, when they do occur, to minimize their impact.

One obvious move is to be very cautious with government finances in order to minimize the possibility of financial difficulties, for example by keeping a tight fiscal policy. In other words, the internationalization of finance provides incentives for governments to become more financially conservative and more oriented to financial stability than to growth and employment than would otherwise be the case due to the potential threat of large capital flows, the belief that these flows are motivated by a particular view of sound finance, and the fear that contagious financial crises may strike without warning (Eatwell and Taylor 2000: 52, 120).

Financial firms such as banks also have incentives to minimize the risk of financial crises, but at the same time they object to regulation that increases their costs or restricts their freedom of action. If national regulators respond to financial threats or crises with unilateral strict regulations, therefore, they may put their financial sectors at a competitive disadvantage *vis a vis* foreign rivals. If all countries have the same minimum standards for prudential regulation, however, this isn't a problem. In other words, by increasing the risk of financial crisis the internationalization of finance increases pressures on national governments to conclude international agreements on prudential regulation.

Such agreements have been around for a long time. The post-war Bretton Woods system included controls on the international movement of capital for precisely this purpose. Since the end of Bretton Woods in the early 1970s the centre for international regulation of finance has been the Bank of International Settlements (BIS) and in particular one of its expert committees, the Basel Committee on Banking Supervision (BCBS), which is made up of central bankers and bank regulators from the G10 countries plus Luxembourg. The first main accomplishment of the BCBS was to prevent banks playing off jurisdictions against one another by making the home regulator responsible for the regulation of worldwide operations of banks headquartered in their country. The Basel Accord of 1988 between G10 countries, which set minimum capital adequacy standards for banks in order to reduce the risk of bank collapse, was widely implemented around the world and followed up in 2004 by the Basel II capital adequacy framework. However international regulation of other areas of finance is weaker, as agreements reached through the International Organization of Securities Commissions (IOSCO) and other public and private organizations are generally rather vague and undemanding. At political level the G7 leaders' meetings have taken the initiative since 1975, while the Financial Stability Forum (FTF) brings together representatives from G7 countries and other countries with representatives from international organizations such as the BCBS, IOSCO, the IMF, World Bank, OECD and European Central Bank (BIS 2004a, Porter 2005: 6, 31–43, 59–70, 80–1).

Within the EU, compliance with EU Directives and Basel principles has led to substantial harmonization of prudential regulation of banks, a partial convergence of prudential regulation of securities markets, some minimum standards in relation to insurance and fairly consistent accounting regulation, and in 2002 a new organizational framework for financial regulation, supervision and stability was adopted (European Commission 2004m, ECOFIN 2002, Flockton *et al.* 2004: 143–4, 151).

While proposals for further international prudential regulation tend to be opposed by the governments of countries that currently attract financial activity and investment by means of light regulation, most notably tax havens such as Luxembourg, one would nevertheless expect that the increasing pressure for international prudential regulation created by the internationalization of finance will result in at least some further progress in this direction. One possibility, currently blocked, would be to discourage frequent speculative international financial transactions by imposing a small tax of 0.25 per cent on each transaction (Tobin Tax). Other possibilities include reimposing capital controls, imposing standstills on outward financial flows in times of crisis to shift the costs more fairly onto the private sector, and regulating hedge funds either directly or by regulating the banks on whose loans they depend (Porter 2005: 145, 200–1).

More finance-friendly policies and/or greater international cooperation to set limits to locational competition

Insofar as government policies are perceived to affect the value of financial assets, investors will take them into account when making their investment decisions. It follows that they will be more likely to invest in a given country when public policy is perceived to be favourable to their interests, other things being equal, than when it isn't. Given that governments have economic and electoral incentives to realize the benefits of financial internationalization, as we have seen, this implies pressure on governments to establish and maintain policies that are optimal from the point of view of international financial markets. Because the increasing scale of actual and potential international financial stocks and flows is magnifying the rewards and punishments for 'good' and 'bad' policies as time goes on, this means that the internationalization of finance is increasing pressure on national governments to adopt policies that are considered to be sound by international financial markets.

What financial markets want from public policy varies as circumstances and ideas vary, but typically includes a strong anti-inflation stance. A recent study of the long-term bond market, for example, concluded that in relation to developed countries bond traders are concerned mainly with short-term inflation risk, as inflation cuts the purchasing power of their assets, and with currency risk, which means fluctuations in the value of local currency-denominated assets, and therefore focus mainly on inflation rates and budget deficit levels when judging governments. This finding is generally but not totally consistent with the author's statistical analysis of 19 developed countries between 1981 and 1995, which found that long-term government bond rates were more strongly associated with inflation rates, US long-term interest rates and the current account balance than with budget balances or other economic or political variables (Mosley 2003: 34, 53–9, 69–101).

European monetary and fiscal policies at national and EU levels are already largely compliant with these priorities. Economic and Monetary Union has brought not only a single currency, which eliminates exchange rate risk between eurozone countries, but also an independent European Central Bank complete with inflation target, and requirements that budget deficits be restricted to a maximum of 3 per cent of GDP and debt to a maximum of 60 per cent of GDP (European Commission 2005a), although the deficit limit has proven difficult to enforce. EU Member States outside the eurozone have similar policies. For European countries in general the internationalization of finance therefore implies maintenance of these policies and continued efforts to keep budget deficits under control.

International financial markets also naturally prefer policies that are advantageous for business generally, such as low tax, low labour costs, high labour flexibility, good infrastructure and education, and limited environmental regulation, but the extent to which these affect investment decisions is not clear. Certainly they can matter on occasion, as demonstrated by the massive capital flight that preceded the introduction of a 10 per cent withholding tax on interest and dividend income in Germany in 1988 and which led to its early demise (Walter and Smith 2000: 241), but Mosley's study of the bond market found that relatively few bond-traders were concerned about tax or government spending as such. High levels of government spending, for example, appear to be acceptable as long as they are properly financed, and her statistical analysis failed to find any strong connections between long-term bond interest rates and tax or patterns of government spending. This picture is consistent with the historical record of continuing diversity in relation to government spending, public employment and tax, and implies that in most areas governments retain considerable policy autonomy as far as international financial markets are concerned (Mosley 2003: 57–8, 90–101).

In relation to the location of financial firms themselves the issues are broadly the same as for the location of transnational firms in general, which are analysed in Chapter 11 on the internationalization of production and include the level of inflation, corporate tax levels, the quality of infrastructure and education, labour costs and labour flexibility.

An alternative to yielding to pressure from financial markets to implement policies preferred by financial markets, or paying the price in terms of lower exchange rates, falling bond prices and higher interest rates (Eatwell and Taylor 2000: 115), is to limit locational competition by striking international agreements that set common rules. We have already seen that global locational competition on the basis of light prudential regulation has been limited by agreements such as those struck within the BCBS and that locational competition between EU Member States is being further limited by the gradual establishment of a single regulatory framework for financial services. However in other areas international agreements have been more difficult to reach, as outside the area of prudential regulation national governments are loath to sacrifice any competitive advantage they may have. In relation to tax, for instance, the European Commission push for a 15 per cent withholding tax on interest income has so far been unsuccessful (Walter and Smith 2000: 241–2).

More vigorous measures to combat international financial crime

The international integration of financial markets, along with developments in ICT and the creation of the EU common market, have made it easier to perpetrate frauds across borders and to launder money by moving it rapidly across several national jurisdictions, and the UN predicts that the increase in electronic commercial activities will create new opportunities for criminals in these areas (UN 2000). Criminals may hack into foreign computer systems to divert funds or acquire sensitive data such as payment card details. They may extort money by threatening denial-of-service attacks or by using information obtained by hacking into foreign computer systems to threaten to expose security flaws in bank systems. Another form of internationalizable financial fraud is to plant misleading stories on the Internet to inflate a company's share prices, and then to sell one's own shares before the ruse is discovered (Grabosky and Smith 1998, Jewkes 2003). Money laundering, which is especially important for criminals because it enables them to spend illegally obtained money legitimately, and invariably includes a cross-border element, takes place in three stages. Placement consists of introducing criminal profits into the financial system, for example by breaking up large amounts of cash into smaller sums and then depositing them into a bank account, or by purchasing bearer monetary instruments such as cheques and money orders to be deposited elsewhere. Layering consists of a series of conversions or movements of the funds to distance them from their source, for example through the purchase and sale of investment instruments or by wiring funds through a series of accounts around the world, especially accounts located in jurisdictions that do not cooperate in anti-money laundering investigations. Integration consists of investing the laundered funds in legitimate assets such as real estate or business ventures (FATF 2003a).

To the extent that international financial crime is perceived to be increasing, demands on governments from individual and organizational victims to implement more effective countermeasures will become more numerous and vociferous, other things being equal. Policy actors that by function or purpose are concerned about crime, such as the police and socially conservative political parties, would also be expected to become more concerned and therefore more active in pressing governments for action.

One relatively uncontroversial government response to these pressures is to encourage the development and application of available preventive technologies and the incorporation of security considerations into developing technology at the design stage, including utilizing fraud detection software, improving cryptography, and systematic and automated monitoring of electronic financial transactions to identify those of a suspect nature (Libicki 1995 chapter 7, Grabosky and Smith 1998, European Commission 2001: 6, 11, 32, 34, Vatis 2001: 19–20).

Perceived increases in international crime also increase pressure on governments to internationalize law enforcement, as effective action against international crime obviously requires international cooperation at the least, if not full international integration of national law enforcement agencies. This internationalization of efforts to fight financial crime is already under way. The Council of Europe's Convention on Cybercrime, for instance, requires signatories to establish a rapid and effective system for international cooperation, including permitting law enforcement agencies in one country to collect computer-based evidence for those in another. It is important to note here that the communications technology that facilitates international transactions can also be used to monitor them (Sica 2000: 71, Archick 2004). To some extent law enforcement in the EU has already been internationalized with the creation of the European Police Office (Europol), a network of judicial national authorities (Eurojust), EU-wide databases, and EU framework decisions designed to establish common definitions and penal sanctions for cybercrime and confiscation of the proceeds of organized crime. Police cooperation already takes place at a broader international level through agencies such as Interpol, while IOSCO has now established a multilateral Memorandum of Understanding that commits signatories to exchanges of information and cooperation in the prosecution of cross-border securities fraud (Elvins 2003, European Commission 2004l, Porter 2005: 80–1). The non-binding but widely accepted Forty Recommendations of the Financial Action Task Force on Money Laundering (FATF) established by the G7 in 1989 specify, among other things, that countries should make money laundering a criminal offence, require financial institutions and others to identify customers, retain identification data and transactions records for at least five years, pay attention to all complex, large and unusual patterns of transactions that have no apparent economic or visible lawful purpose, and report any suspicions. Countries are also required to ensure that financial institutions are subject to adequate regulation and supervision and that law enforcement authorities have adequate resources and the power to conduct inspections, compel production of records held by financial institutions, search persons and premises, and seize evidence (FATF 2003a: 8, FATF 2003b).

However the extent to which this increasing pressure for international cooperation results in further internationalization of law enforcement in this area is likely to be limited by opposition from a number of quarters. Moves to facilitate state access to private computer and telecommunications systems in the pursuit of criminal investigations, for example, obviously have the potential to compromise the confidentiality of private and commercial information, while moves to make money laundering more difficult by imposing more stringent reporting requirements on financial institutions mean additional administrative burdens that may both compromise commercial confidentiality and – for the less scrupulous – lead to a loss of business (Grabosky and Smith 1998: 196–209, European Commission 2001: 21). Nevertheless, perceptions that international financial crime is increasing would be expected to lead to at least some further internationalization of law enforcement in this area.

Conclusion

The internationalization of finance, in the sense of the growth of cross-border financial flows and holdings and the growth and international integration of financial firms, has been happening for some time and looks likely to continue in the years ahead. Table 12.3 summarizes its main implications for the direction of public policy. Perhaps the most noteworthy feature of this is that the pro-market policies that one would expect are likely to be accompanied by increasing assertion of state power on an international level to regulate international finance and fight international financial crime.

Table 12.3 Policy implications of the internationalization of finance

Policy implications	*Causal chain from trend*
More autonomous policies Continued government support for financial liberalization	Increasing government popularity (a) to the extent that the internationalization of finance increases economic growth by enabling resident firms to finance their activities without being constrained by the level of domestic savings and at lower interest rates, plus enabling domestic savers to obtain higher returns by investing in other countries, and, possibly, by improving the competitiveness of resident firms by their having to compete with firms in other countries for investment, and (b) by enabling governments to save money by obtaining lower interest rates on government debt
More business-friendly policies as defined by financial markets, such as continued stress on low inflation and greater stress on good infrastructure and education, low tax, low labour costs, labour flexibility, and limited environmental regulation	The increasing economic importance of international financial markets increases the incentives for governments to conform with their wishes

(Continued)

Table 12.3   (*Continued*)

Policy implications	Causal chain from trend
Increasing international cooperation to limit locational competition for foreign investment in areas such as tax and prudential regulation	Desire of governments to pursue at least some policies that financial markets do not like without being punished as a consequence by lower exchange rates, falling bond prices and higher interest rates
More vigorous measures to prevent international financial crises and to minimize their impact when they do occur, including being cautious with government finances and seeking stronger international prudential regulation of banks and other financial firms, for example by imposing standstills on outward financial flows in times of crisis to shift the costs more fairly onto the private sector or by regulating hedge funds either directly or by regulating the banks on whose loans they depend	The internationalization of finance makes financial crises more likely and more severe when they do occur: • it becomes more likely that crises in one market or country will create knock-on crises in other financial markets and countries, for example via a country defaulting on its foreign loans and causing the collapse of the international banks that provided them • the increasing scale of international capital stocks and thus actual or potential capital flows exacerbates the consequences for a country of any capital flight • the growth of derivatives increases the risk of financial crisis due to their volatility, complexity and (mostly) speculative nature • consolidation in the financial sector may increase systemic risk by increasing financial complexity and thereby making it harder to resolve any difficulties that may arise, while increasing size makes the consequences of a collapse more serious
More vigorous measures to combat international financial crime, in particular the further internationalization of law enforcement	The internationalization of finance increases international financial crime, which increases pressure from victims, law enforcement agencies and others for authorities to take further steps to combat these sorts of criminal activities

13
The Expansion of Mass Media

Introduction

The mass media today are conventionally divided into two main types. First there are the print media: books, journals, magazines and newspapers. The electronic or audiovisual media consist of radio and television (terrestrial, cable and satellite), movies, pre-recorded videos and DVDs, sound recordings such as CDs, and new media such as the Internet and video games (EAO 2002: 50). In recent years the mass media thus defined have been growing in four main respects: the variety of electronic media forms through which media content is made available, the number of TV channels, radio stations and print titles, the consumption of media content, and the size and concentration of the media industry. All these trends are expected to continue. However their policy implications are somewhat contradictory. On the one hand most of them imply a shift towards more business-friendly public policies, but this tendency is countered by the easier mass dissemination of anti-establishment views made possible by the growth of the Internet.

Let's have a closer look at the ways in which the media are expanding.

Proliferation of communications media

The last 20 years or so have seen a dramatic growth in the number of ways in which media content can be brought before consumers. Recent innovations include satellite broadcasting, video, high-definition TV, digital radio and TV, interactive TV, personalized content TV, multimedia computers, email, the Internet, electronic books, palmtop computers, consumer computer networks, online news services, personal digital assistants, laser disks, handheld databanks, videotext networks, wireless communications, CD-ROMs, DVDs, mobile phones with WAP technology, MP3 players, music and movies on demand, webcameras providing entertainment, and online and stand-alone computer games. Arguably the most important recent development has been digitization, as this brings a common language for all forms of electronic media and thus convergence in the sense that the same media content can be distributed through all forms of media: TV programmes, for example, can be delivered via the Internet while online content can be delivered via television (Gorman and McLean 2003: 186–7, 201–6).

Likely future developments include portable electronic newspapers, online computer games with tens of thousands of participants, Web-mediated physical activity such as interactive games requiring strenuous physical responses, interactions with people from different cultures made possible by translation programmes, the ability to view athletic events from almost any vantage point, and video glasses that place images directly before a viewer's eyes. Perhaps the ultimate media experience would be that of virtual reality created by 3D interactive computer-based systems that provide a sense of presence in space to the user, at least in respect of sight and sound if not touch and smell: you put on your hi-tech helmet, and perhaps data gloves, and it is as if you were inside the movie or computer game (Hundley *et al.* 2003: 15–16, Gallaire 1998: 65).

Proliferation of TV channels, radio stations and print titles

TV channels have been proliferating rapidly in Europe as a result of factors such as deregulation and the growth of multi-channel and digital access platforms such as cable, satellite and digital terrestrial television. By 2002 there were 767 private TV programme services with nationwide distribution in the EU-15 along with 109 public TV programme services (Council of Europe 2000: 2; OECD 2001b: 119, 122; Andersen 2002: 7, 80; Eurostat 2003b: Tables 5.13, 5.14). However more channels does not necessarily mean greater diversity of content, as many simply repeat material offered first elsewhere, use the same content over and over again or show similar content to other channels (Croteau and Hoynes 2001: 81, Bruck *et al.* 2004: 24).

The number of radio stations has also increased significantly since 1982, when European countries increased the number of FM frequencies available for broadcasting, and the number of magazine and book titles published each year has been rising in most EU-25 Member States in recent years (Andersen 2002: 81, Rightscom and TSEBA 2004: 34, 39).

Growing consumption of mass media

With more media outlets has come growing consumption of mass media. Table 13.1 shows just how rapidly mass media use has been growing in recent years. By 2001 only 3 per cent of households were without a TV set. Between 1990 and 2001 the share of TV households with cable TV grew from 17 to 30 per cent, while between 1995 and 2001 the share of satellite TV households grew from 14 to 22 per cent of TV households. At the same time, however, between 1995 and 2000 free-to-air stations managed to maintain audience share (Andersen 2002: 8, Eurostat 2003b: Tables 5.17, 5.20).

Table 13.1 also shows that average TV viewing time increased during the short period for which EU-wide figures are available to an average of

Table 13.1   Growth in consumption of audiovisual media, EU-15

Indicator	1980	1990	1995	2000	2001	Average annual growth (%)
Television households (million)	109.52	126.06	139.72	147.86	150.33	1.8
Share of private households with TV set (%)	–	95	95	96	97	0.2
Daily viewing time (minutes)	–	–	187	208	210	2.0
Cable TV households (million)	–	21.57	34.42	45.24	45.09	9.9
Satellite TV households (million)	–	–	20.03	28.52	32.76	10.6
Digital TV households (million)	–	–	2.03 (1997)	15.68	23.80	268.1
Cinema admissions (million)	1,037.6	576.7	641.5	843.0	934.0 (2002)	5.2 (1990–2002)
Admissions per inhabitant	–	1.6	1.7	2.2	2.5 (2002)	4.7
VCR households (million)	–	58.56	89.32	109.51	113.84	8.6
Home videos sold (million)	–	93.9	231.6	303.7	274.8	17.5
Home video rental transactions (million)	–	940.0	621.6	701.1	647.5	−2.8
DVD player households (million)	–	–	0.08 (1997)	4.6	12.9 (2002)	3,122.4
DVDs sold (million)	–	–	1.9 (1998)	52.1	118.0	2,092.0
DVDs rented (million)	–	–	0.3 (1998)	34.7	81.2	9,633.3
Total sound recordings sold (million)	759.3	820.6	922.1	1,024.8	973.6 (2002)	1.3

Source: Eurostat 2003b Tables 5.4, 5.5, 5.15, 5.16, 5.19, 5.20, 3.24, 3.25, 4.9, 4.14, 4.16, 4.2, 4.5, 4.6, 6.3 respectively. Average annual growth refers to the total period shown for each indicator.

3½ hours per day. If TV can affect viewers, 3½ hours per day should be enough for these effects to show up.

This growth in viewing time has benefited commercial broadcasters more than public broadcasters. Until the 1980s, TV in most European countries was dominated by nationally exclusive, non-commercial channels with monopoly status that were mostly publicly financed and regulated. Since then, as we have seen, the number of channels available to European viewers has proliferated. Most of these new channels, however, are private, and available data indicate that a growing proportion of viewers is watching commercial rather than public television. Between 1997 and 2001 the daily audience market share of public TV fell from 45.8 to 44.3 per cent (McQuail 1998: 107–10, 116; Andersen 2002: 80, Eurostat 2003b: 92). One reason for this shift is that its (relative) independence from the state means that it is easier for commercial TV to focus narrowly on doing whatever is necessary to maximize the number of viewers, while public broadcasters are more constrained by requirements to broadcast at least some material that governments and/or media elites consider should be broadcast even if viewers are not that interested. Another is that the financial capacity of public broadcasters to develop programming, acquire sports rights and launch new subscription and pay-per-view channels is limited compared to that of the global media groups that own many European TV channels (Williams 2003: 4).

We are also seeing the commercialization of TV in the sense that public channels are increasingly being financed by advertising, sponsorship and merchandising as well as by traditional sources of funding. Between 1990 and 2000 receipts from public TV commercial income, including advertising and sponsorship, rose by 5.4 per cent per year from €5.0 billion to €7.7 billion, a full third of total spending on TV advertising (Eurostat 2003b: 89, Table 5.11).

The consumption of other forms of electronic media is also rising: sales of CDs and other sound recordings are rising in both legitimate and pirated forms, and the number of video game software and hardware sold rose between 1998 and 2001 from 131 million to 183 million (Eurostat 2003b: 108, Table 8.5).

By contrast there has been a long-term decline in the number of newspaper titles and newspaper circulations in most European countries. Between 1997 and 2001 the number of daily titles in the EU fell by 1.4 per cent while the total circulation of titles fell by 4.3 per cent and the average circulation per title fell by 2.9 per cent (De Bens and Østbye 1998: 16; WAN 2002: 5). There are no clear trends in relation to consumption of books, magazines and directories (Rightscom and TSEBA 2004: 24–44), although this might be considered a strong performance in view of the increasing competition from electronic media.

Growth and consolidation of the media industry

As consumption of mass media rises, the media industry is becoming bigger. The available statistics summarized in Table 13.2 indicate that in recent years the European audiovisual media industry has been growing in terms of

Table 13.2   Audiovisual media industry growth, EU-15

Indicator	1980	1990	1995	2000	2001	Average annual growth (%)
Total turnover of audiovisual services (€ billion)	–	–	73.8 (1997)	91.8	97.8	8.1
Number of motion picture and video enterprises	–	–	32,900 (1997)	40,100	–	7.3
Number of radio and television enterprises	–	–	9,800 (1997)	13,600	–	12.9
Employment in motion picture and video activities	–	–	179,000 (1997)	222,000	–	8.0
Employment in radio and television activities	–	–	243,000 (1997)	333,000	–	12.3
Total advertising expenditure (€ billion)	–	45.4	54.1	99.0	95.0	9.9
• TV	–	11.3	17.5	27.3	25.4	11.3
• Radio	–	2.1	2.9	4.3	4.1	8.7
• Cinema	–	0.3	0.4	0.7	0.7	12.1
• Internet	–	–	0.1 (1998)	0.9	0.8	233.3
Turnover of national public TV broadcasters (€ billion)	–	12.4	15.9	24.0	–	9.4
Turnover of national private TV broadcasters (€ billion)	–	7.5	15.8	30.0	–	30.0
Turnover of public radio broadcasters (€ billion)	–	–	3.9 (1997)	5.3	5.5	10.3
Turnover of private radio broadcasters (€ billion)	–	–	3.2 (1997)	4.3	4.1	7.0
Cinematographic full-length films produced	–	–	443	594	625 (2002)	5.9
Gross box office (€ billion)	1.98	2.40	3.01	4.58	5.17	7.7
DVD sales and rentals (€ billion)	–	–	0.05 (1998)	1.39	3.14	2,125.5
Video sales and rentals turnover (€ billion)	–	3.56	4.62	5.96	5.71	5.5
Turnover from sound recordings sales (€ billion)	3.1	6.5	8.5	9.9	9.5 (2002)	9.4

Source: Eurostat 2003b Tables 2.9, 2.11, 1.3, 2.6, 2.8, 1.7, 1.8, 1.9, 1.10, 1.11, 5.8, 5.9, 5.11, 7.7, 7.8, 3.26, 4.3, 4.10, 6.2 respectively. Average annual growth refers to the total period shown for each indicator.

turnover, numbers of enterprises, employment, advertising and films produced (Eurostat 2003b: Table 8.1).

TV broadcasting dominates: in 2000 the turnover of TV broadcasting constituted 59 per cent of total audiovisual market turnover, well ahead of films at

13 per cent, the radio market and sound recordings both at 11 per cent, and video games at 7 per cent (Eurostat 2003b: Table 1.3).

One striking feature here is that the turnover of commercial TV broadcasters has been rising more rapidly than that of public broadcasters. In 1995 the public and private TV markets were equally large, but since then the private TV market has moved ahead (Eurostat 2003b: 89). Between 1995 and 1999 the operating revenues of private television companies increased by 74.9 per cent: 44.3 per cent for private generalist channels with national coverage and mainly financed by advertising, 60.7 per cent for regional/local channels 60 per cent for film pay-TV, and a massive 120.7 per cent for thematic channels and 346 per cent for teleshopping channels (EAO 2002: 136–7).

The print media industry, on the other hand, was not so buoyant. Although overall turnover and employment have risen somewhat in recent years in most EU Member States, the only solid area of growth appears to be in magazine advertising revenue (Rightscom and TSEBA 2004: 37, 45, 48).

As well as getting bigger, the media industry is becoming more integrated both across media and across countries. One reason for this is that expansion is a profitable strategy due to the nature of the media industry: initial production costs are high but the marginal costs of supplying an extra consumer are low, so profits rise rapidly as audience sizes increase, while diversification into related media areas and into other countries is profitable because it is relatively easy for a media product created for one medium or market to be reformatted for another. Other advantages of concentration include power and prestige for owners, potential influence over public opinion, synergies, market dominance, sharing of skills, diversification of risks, increased possibilities for innovation, career opportunities for employees, and cost savings due to fuller utilization of existing personnel, facilities and 'content' resources (Doyle 2002a: 14–15, Burnett 1996: 20, Herman and McChesney 1997: 53–4).

In recent years opportunities to expand have been increased by factors such as the greatly increased capacity to transmit sounds and images at low cost around the world, deregulation of telecommunications utilities, the creation of an EU Single Market without as many restrictions on the media industry as are typically in place at national level, the emergence of global markets for media products, and the fact that digitization makes it easier to develop, package and promote a single concept across different media (McQuail 2000: 111–12, 202, Doyle 2002: 3–5, 40, Doyle 2002a: 21–2, 75).

The result of all this has been growing integration of production and distribution as well as growing industry concentration via acquisitions, mergers, alliances and joint ventures. This has taken place not only between firms in the same media sector but also between firms in different media sectors and between media firms and firms in other industries such as telecommunications. Where national markets are saturated or concentrated to the maximum extent permitted by national media regulation, international expansion may be the only means of expansion for national media companies. The consequence has been the growth of large integrated and international groups, such as Bertelsmann, that control the whole value chain from rights to production, broadcasting and distribution. In relation to content production, on the other hand, the industry has fragmented despite consolidation of top-end players (Council of Europe 2000: 2–3, Croteau and Hoynes 2001: 74–101, Andersen 2002: 8–9, 75, Doyle 2002: 4–5, 35, Doyle 2002a: 21–2, Gorman and McLean 2003: 209–13, Bruck *et al.* 2004: 7, 10).

The future

It seems likely that the expansion of mass media will continue for the foreseeable future. Media-relevant technological innovation is bound to continue. Media consumption is likely to continue to rise as consumer spending power continues to grow and digitization continues to facilitate the development of new types of media outlet. In some countries the percentage of households connected to cable is still very low, which implies considerable scope for future expansion in this area. There is even more scope for expansion in the number of subscribers to satellite TV, as at the turn of the century the penetration rate was less than 10 per cent in most OECD countries (OECD 2001b: 136–7). As media consumption grows, the size of the media industry is also likely to grow, although we cannot be quite so sure that the process of consolidation will continue.

On the other hand the future growth in the size of the television market may be limited by the lack of scope for increasing audience size and viewing time, as virtually all households in EU countries already have at least one television set and further increases in the time people spend watching television may be difficult to achieve due to competition from new media such as the Internet (OECD 2001b: 120). In fact it seems likely that traditional media, including free-to-air TV, will lose readers/viewers due to competition from new media such as the Internet, video on demand, interactive TV, personalized content TV and online gaming (Andersen 2002: 11, 121–7; Gorman and McLean 2003: 204–5). More generally the growing number of TV channels, radio stations, print titles and new media forms is likely to lead to a more fragmented audience as media consumption is redistributed across more television channels and media and regrouped by tastes, interests and other viewer characteristics (McQuail 1998: 116–17, Council of Europe 2000: 2).

Implications

Table 13.3 lists the main policy actors in this area. Among the most prominent of these are public broadcasters, private media conglomerates and state regulators. More generally a wide range of public and private organizations take an interest due, among other things, to their desire for favourable media coverage.

Table 13.3 Generic policy network relating to the mass media

Type of policy actor	Specific policy actor
Political executives and associated parties	Chief executives Ministers for the media, culture, information and telecommunications Government party leaderships and spokespeople
Non-government politicians	Opposition party leaderships and spokespeople Parliamentary committees relating to the media, culture, information and telecommunications European Commissioner for the Information Society and Media Party leaderships and spokespeople at subnational level
Civil servants, special advisers and other public sector employees	Publicly run and/or funded radio and TV broadcasters Departments and agencies relating to the media, culture, information and telecommunications European Commission Directorate-General Information Society and Media Media, election and public relations specialists working for ministers and official bodies (spin doctors)
Judges and regulators	Media regulators at national and EU levels, including competition regulators
Business	Media companies and their owners: • Print media (newspapers, magazines, journals, books, directories) • Electronic media (television, radio, movies, videos, DVDs, sound recordings, Internet, multimedia entertainment including games) News agencies such as Reuters Advertisers and advertising agencies PR agencies and their clients Telecommunications and computing companies and conglomerates Companies in general wanting favourable media coverage
Interest groups and non-government organizations	Journalists' associations Media watchdog organizations Non-government organizations wanting favourable media coverage
Media	Producers, journalists and editors Specialist journals on the media and communications
Experts	Media and communications experts in universities and elsewhere
Electorate	Audience

The expansion of mass media has three main implications for public policy. First, the increasing economic value of the media industry provides it with increasing leverage in dealing with governments over policies relating directly or indirectly to media industry interests. Second, the growth of commercial TV is likely to gradually shift mainstream public opinion, and therefore public policy insofar as public opinion influences public policy, in a pro-business direction. By contrast the growth of the Internet increases the prevalence of anti-establishment views in the electorate by facilitating the communication of anti-establishment messages not generally carried by the mainstream media.

More media-friendly policies

The increasing size and therefore economic importance of the (private) media industry strengthens the incentives for governments to do what they can to ensure that investment and employment in national media industries are maximized. Other things being equal this implies increased policy leverage for the industry on media policy and in other policy areas that affect its economic interests. This growing economic incentive to give favourable treatment to media companies is in addition to the existing political incentive created by the desire for favourable media coverage. The policy leverage of media companies is strengthened to the extent that the increasing international integration of these companies enables them to exert pressure on domestic authorities via foreign governments, such as the US government, either bilaterally or in multilateral forums such as the WTO. Among other things this increasing leverage for the media industry implies a deregulatory trend in media policy in areas such as ownership and content regulation, as we have seen in recent years (Bruck *et al.* 2004: 15), as well as increasing industry assistance in areas such as domestic programme production.

More business-friendly policies

We have already seen that most of the increase in TV viewing has been of commercial rather than public channels. Other things being equal this implies increasing pressure on public policy to shift in a pro-business direction.

The trend towards greater audience share for commercial broadcasters is mainly relevant to public policy through the nature and content of TV news, current affairs, features programmes and political advertising, as it is through these that politicians and other policy actors mainly communicate with voters, and voters get most of their political knowledge and understanding. The mass media provide an arena and channel for debate, make candidates for office widely known, and distribute information and opinion. Access to the media by policy actors may be direct (party broadcasts), filtered (news) or remade (documentaries) (Watts 1997: 2–3, 72–3, McQuail 2000: 4, 285, 524).

History is replete in examples of media owners using their outlets to promote their own values and interests. Owners may influence news reporting not only via explicit editorial interference but also through the choice of key personnel such as producers, decisions about what to invest in and how much, and decisions about sourcing content (Doyle 2002: 19–20).

But how influential are media owners in reality?

Despite obvious everyday examples of media influence such as adjusting travel plans according to weather forecasts, and the fact that politicians and advertisers among others believe that its influence is important, media research has found it difficult to demonstrate consistent patterns of media effects. Instead effects appear to be determined as much by the receiver as by the sender, with no direct one-to-one link between media stimulus and audience response. This is due to factors such as selective attention, interpretation, response and recall, which are shaped by factors such as social characteristics and individual differences as well as by source characteristics, such as authority, credibility, attractiveness and similarity to the receiver, and content characteristics such as unambiguous and concrete subject matter (McQuail 2005: 456–72). In particular there is a widely shared reluctance to attribute much influence to television, and a view that insofar as there is an impact it is mainly to reinforce the existing views of audiences (Street 2001: 87–8, 239).

One prominent school of media research holds that media effects can be best understood in terms of the framing of media messages. By this is meant the selection of some aspects of a perceived reality to make them more salient – more noticeable, meaningful or memorable – in such a way as to define problems, diagnose the causes of problems, make moral judgements about causal agents and their effects, and suggest remedies. As the process of creating coherent messages necessarily involves making conscious or unconscious framing judgements, media messages inevitably contain frames in forms such as the presence or absence of key words, stock phrases, stereotyped images, sources of information, and sentences that provide thematically reinforcing clusters of facts or judgements. Whether a media message is noticed, interpreted or remembered, according to this view, depends on the extent to which receivers' frames reflect the frames of communicators and messages (Entman 2002).

In other words, media research indicates that media messages rarely change receivers' minds directly but instead operate mainly by selectively reinforcing certain elements of receivers' views. One expression of this is agenda-setting: indicating to the public what the main issues are. This is thought to be most effective when the different mass media share the same priorities (Semetko 2004: 360, McQuail 2005: 512–14).

An important corollary is that exclusion of interpretations by frames is just as significant as inclusion, as effects are more likely when people receive and process information about one interpretation but possess little or incommensurable data about alternatives (Entman 2002).

It follows from this that the increasing audience share taken by commercial channels is likely to affect public policy over the long term rather than immediately.

First, as time goes on a growing proportion of households is watching news that is selected and interpreted through the prism of the economic interests of media companies and associated companies such as advertisers. This means that an increasing proportion of the electorate is unlikely to view content that criticizes companies associated with the channel, such as production companies, infrastructure providers and advertisers, as such content is rarely seen on commercial channels (Bruck *et al.* 2004: 26). The same is likely to be true of viewers of public service channels insofar as these are dependent on advertising for funding. As media businesses become parts of conglomerates that are also involved in other lines of business, or themselves expand into other lines of business, the range of businesses not to be criticized expands. Commercial channels are also likely to downplay or exclude criticism of capitalism in general. This implies that over time the electorate is likely to become less critical of business, other things being equal, which implies less support for policies that restrict business activities, such as strict employment or environmental regulation. To the extent that public opinion influences public policy this in turn implies a gradual shift towards more business-friendly policies such as improvements to infrastructure and education, cuts to corporate tax and employer social contributions, more employer-friendly employment regulation, and less stringent environmental regulation.

Second, as media owners and advertisers by virtue of their positions are likely to support pro-business political parties and policies, and their advertisers wish to attract an affluent and therefore predominantly conservative market (Street 2001: 142), the growth of commercial TV means that a growing proportion of households watches news and comment that is likely to be consciously or unconsciously framed in such a way as to favour conservative views, conservative parties (being the parties most supportive of business) and conservative economic policies such as tight fiscal and monetary policies, low tax, hostility towards trade unions and support for deregulation. Other things being equal this would be expected to (a) increase the likelihood of conservative parties participating in government and (b) shift public opinion in general in a conservative direction. The effect of both of these developments over time would be to shift public policy in a conservative direction.

A shift towards policies favoured by spatially dispersed groups

As pointed out in Chapter 1 on developments in ICT, the increasing capacity for coordination at a distance brought by the use of new media technologies such as the Internet, email and mobile telephones disproportionately benefits spatially dispersed groups. In recent years human rights, women's, environmental, labour, religious and peace movements have all engaged in global coordination and action with the help of the Internet. One example of the Internet empowering new groups was its role in publicizing the cause of the

Zapatista rebels in Mexico during the 1990s and coordinating the efforts of their foreign supporters; another was the anti-globalization protest against the 1999 WTO meeting in Seattle (Cleaver 1998, Cohen and Rai 2000, Castells 2001: 138, 141). This implies that over time the political resources of spatially-dispersed organizations are increasing more rapidly than those of other groups, other things being equal, which means that we should expect policies preferred by spatially dispersed groups such as the anti-globalization movement to be implemented to a greater extent than before, again other things being equal.

Less pro-business and less conservative policies

We have seen that the emergence of the Internet provides an additional medium through which news and other information can be transmitted. While media conglomerates have utilized their vast resources to establish a significant presence on the Internet, so that the most consulted websites are those of large newspapers, telecommunications firms and search engines (Bruck *et al.* 2004: 25), the Internet is fundamentally different from television and other mass media in that it enables senders and receivers of information to bypass the framing of the state and corporate mass media. The significance of this is that it makes it eser for groups and individuals who have little coverage in the mainstream mass media, or negative coverage, to disseminate messages directly from their own websites. It also enables independent news sites to carry stories not included in mainstream media coverage, prioritize stories differently and use different framing in the reporting of these stories. The Internet thereby provides for more differentiated provision of political information, greater access for alternative voices, and new forums for the development of interest groups and the formation of public opinion (McQuail 2005: 135, 539).

Let's look at this in a little more detail.

First, the emergence and growth of the Internet means that there is likely to be a growing variety of policy-relevant ideas in circulation, including ideas that receive little or negative coverage in the mainstream media such as radical anti-capitalist ideas, less radical criticisms of business by the labour, environmentalist and anti-globalist movements accompanied by corresponding proposals for changes in public policy, and ideas that are not covered in the mainstream media because they are generally considered to be unacceptable, such as racist and terrorist ideas, although to the extent that these are illegal their expression will be limited by law enforcement agencies.

One consequence of this is a weakening of the agenda-setting power of the mainstream media, since over time an increasing proportion of the electorate will visit websites that do not share the same set of news priorities or framing as the mainstream media, while certain alternative stories, or alternative versions of stories, may achieve wide circulation despite not being carried on the mainstream media. Other things being equal we would expect this to weaken the impact that mainstream news and information framing would otherwise have on public policy, which implies a weakening in the tendency identified earlier for the expansion of media to shift public policy to the right.

Second, the number of Internet users is likely to increase for some time yet, so if we assume that the proportion of Internet users who look beyond state and corporate websites for news and other political information remains much the same, it follows that a growing percentage of the electorate is likely to be exposed to alternative messages of one sort or another. Other things being equal one would expect that over time this is likely to result in a greater proportion of the electorate sharing at least some of these views. Some of these alternative ideas will be more attractive than others and are therefore likely to win wide and committed support from a significant number of people, leading to the formation of new political groups or the strengthening of existing ones. To the extent that these ideas come to command sufficient attention and popular support to give governments electoral incentives to take them into account, we would expect public policy to move in the direction implied by these ideas, other things being equal.

While we cannot be sure which alternative ideas will become influential, the fact that they are ideas largely or totally excluded from mainstream media coverage, or subjected to predominantly negative coverage, implies that at least to some extent they will be ideas that run counter to the pro-business and pro-conservative orientation of the commercial media and therefore have the effect of counteracting one or more aspects of the tendency identified earlier for media expansion to push public policy in a pro-business and conservative direction.

Conclusion

As time goes on the mass media are expanding in relation to the variety of electronic media forms through which media content is made available, the number of TV channels, radio stations and print titles in existence, the consumption of media (especially commercial TV), and the size and concentration of the media industry. Table 13.4 summarizes the main implications of this for public policy.

To some extent these pressures cancel each other out: while the growth of commercial TV means more exposure to a business-friendly and conservative view of the world, the growth of the Internet means more exposure to alternative framing of events for those who take news and other information from the Internet. Perhaps the safest conclusion is that to the extent that the media affects public policy at all, bearing in mind that media research is equivocal on this point, then other things being equal the expansion of mass

Table 13.4   Policy implications of mass media expansion

Policy implications	Causal chain from trend
Policies more favourable to the media industry, such as deregulation and increased industry assistance	The increasing economic value of the media industry provides it with increasing leverage in dealing with governments over policies relating directly or indirectly to media industry interests
Less restrictive policies in relation to the media industry and business in general	The growth in the proportion of viewers that watches commercial TV reduces the proportion of the electorate that is (potentially) exposed to criticism of media companies, associated companies and capitalism in general
More conservative policies	The growth in the proportion of viewers that watches commercial TV increases the proportion of the electorate that is exposed to media messages framed in such a way as to favour conservative (pro-business) parties and policies, which increases the likelihood of conservative party participation in government as well as shifting public opinion in a conservative direction
Shift towards policies favoured by spatially-dispersed groups	Use of the Internet improves the capacity of spatially dispersed groups to coordinate at a distance
Less pro-business and less conservative policies	The growth of Internet use exposes an increasing proportion of the electorate to ideas and policy proposals that are given little or negative coverage in the state and corporate media, in large part because they are anti-business or anti-conservative, which weakens the agenda-setting power of the mainstream media and in some cases leads to anti-business or anti-conservative ideas gaining sufficient political support to give governments electoral incentives to take them into account in policy-making

media is likely to result in more business-friendly and conservative policies in general, but that this trend will be weakened, halted or even reversed in some areas due to the Internet bringing alternative ideas to the attention of a growing proportion of the electorate.

Part III
Climate Change

Is climate change really the only major long-term environmental trend affecting EU countries? I was surprised too. When I first surveyed the state of the environment in Europe in 1994 most environmental indicators were heading the wrong way, but ten years later the situation is quite different. Industrial pollution has fallen substantially over the past 30 years. The use of fertilizers and pesticides in agriculture is in decline. The production, sales and consumption of ozone-depleting substances has fallen significantly, although their long life in the atmosphere means that the ozone layer will take a long time to recover. Emissions of most forms of air pollution, including acidifying and eutrophying substances and ground-level ozone precursors, as well as levels of urban air pollutants such as particulate matter, nitrogen dioxide and sulphur dioxide, have fallen substantially since 1990. Emissions of heavy metals and persistent organic pollutants are also falling. Meanwhile water quality is improving due to improved wastewater treatment and falls in heavy metal concentrations and oil pollution, although nitrate and pesticide levels remain high (EEA 2003: 35, 44, 112–33, 151, 165; EEA 2004a: 21).

Of the remaining negative environmental trends, only climate change meets our three criteria of being well-supported by evidence, of major significance to a large number of people, and likely to continue for at least the next 20 years or so. It is generally accepted within the scientific community that global warming is occurring and that it will continue for decades at least. Assuming this is true, the lives of all of us will be affected directly by changes in the weather and indirectly by the economic and other impacts of climate change (IPCC 2001, OECD 2001l: 13–18, EEA 2004a: 17, 22–3).

The only other environmental trends that come close to being king trends are the increases in waste generation, soil degradation and loss of biodiversity. However none of these trends meet the criterion of being of major significance to a large number of people.

In the case of waste it is clear that although there is no longer any consistent upwards trend in waste generation overall, there are certain types of waste that are continuing to increase, namely municipal, packaging, manufacturing, and construction and demolition waste, along with discarded cars, electrical and electronic equipment, and sewage sludge (EEA 2004c). But how significant is this really for people's lives? People living close to actual and proposed landfill sites (or incinerators) are obviously affected, but for most of us the impact of accumulating waste is minimal.

The same is true of soil degradation. Although comprehensive and comparable data on its extent is impossible to obtain, due largely to measurement difficulties, it is clear that this is a long-term trend because much of it is irreversible, which means that each year adds to the area of soil degraded. Causes include poor cultivation practices leading to erosion, compaction and other problems including desertification in some areas of the Mediterranean; acidification; salinization; contamination by waste, energy production emissions, transport emissions, industrial emissions, pesticides and heavy metals; soil sealing by urban expansion; and tourism (EEA 2003: 198, 204). But the impact of soil degradation is mainly localized and incremental and directly affects few people apart from farmers, who form a very small part of the workforce. Over the very long term soil degradation could significantly cut agricultural productivity in Europe, but there is no evidence that this is likely to happen during the next 20 years or so. As with waste, soil degradation is a long-term trend but not a major one in terms of its effects on people.

This is also the case with loss of biodiversity, by which is meant reductions in the population of certain species, and in some cases their extinction, due to factors such as habitat loss, the spread of invasive alien species, over-fishing and water pollution (OECD 2001l: 60, EEA 2003: 230–7, EEA 2004a: 9, 13). While there is a general consensus that biodiversity is being lost, despite the lack of accurate and comprehensive figures, again this is a trend that does not directly affect many people in any significant way. Loss of fish stocks due to over-fishing, for example, is having a big impact on the fishing industry, but this employs few people and is a very small part of the European economy. If European catches fall, consumers will turn to imported fish. Other losses, such as reductions in the population of some species of farmland birds, are also of little direct significance for most people's lives.

As far as Europe is concerned, therefore, there is just one long-term environmental trend that is of major significance for people's lives: climate change.

14
Climate Change

Introduction

Climate change is one of the best known king trends operating today. Its main policy implications are more vigorous measures to control greenhouse gas emissions and facilitate adaptation to the effects of climate change, and less policy autonomy for governments.

The idea that the climate is changing as a result of human activities is based on scientific findings that (a) carbon dioxide, methane, nitrous oxide, the chlorofluorocarbons (CFCs) and ozone have the effect of keeping the Earth warmer than it would otherwise be (the greenhouse effect), (b) concentrations of these gases in the atmosphere are rising, (c) these rises are caused primarily by the increasing scale of human activities and in particular by the burning of fossil fuels, and (d) average temperatures are in fact rising as time goes on. Carbon dioxide is estimated to have contributed about 70 per cent of the enhanced greenhouse effect so far, compared to 24 per cent for methane (leaks from gas pipelines and oil wells, rice paddy fields, belching of cattle, and wood and peat burning) and about 6 per cent for nitrous oxide. The concentration of carbon dioxide in the atmosphere is thought to have risen by about 30 per cent since 1700. Increasing emissions of water vapour from aviation also contribute to the greenhouse effect. Although not everyone accepts these propositions, there is a broad scientific consensus, based on very extensive research coordinated and summarized by the UN IPCC, that climate change is occurring as a result of human activities (Houghton 2004: 10, 28–52).

The big increases in energy consumption that are expected to take place in the EU over the next 20 years or so, and the expectation that by 2030 fossil fuels will still provide for 82 per cent of gross inland consumption, leads the European Commission to project under its Baseline Scenario that carbon dioxide emissions in the EU-25 will grow by 17 per cent between 2000 and 2030 to 4,304 million tonnes per year. These increases in emissions are expected to be driven mainly by the power generation sector growing and becoming more carbon intensive as the contribution of nuclear power falls and coal makes a comeback, and by increases in fossil fuel use by transport (European Commission 2004i: 46, 170).

Perhaps the main question mark about projections of increasing greenhouse gas emissions is posed by the possibility that oil production may peak well before 2030, as a number of industry analysts predict on the basis that estimates of oil reserves have in the past been inflated for political reasons while the results of recent oil exploration have been disappointing and the growth of demand for oil has been underestimated. The significance of this is that once oil production peaks and starts to decline, the continuing growth in demand for oil would be expected to drive up oil prices indefinitely, since for transport in particular there are no ready alternative fuels for motor vehicles, aircraft, trains and ships (Goodstein 2004, Hirsch *et al.* 2005: 13–19, 27, 64, Illum 2005). Under this scenario total consumption of energy could conceivably fall during the period up to 2030 as less oil is consumed and the accompanying economic slowdown reduces demand for other types of energy as well, leading to falls in carbon dioxide emissions. However even if carbon dioxide emissions did fall, it seems unlikely that they would fall sufficiently for carbon dioxide concentrations in the atmosphere to stop increasing, so global warming would continue, albeit at a slower pace.

The effects of increasing concentrations of carbon dioxide and other greenhouse gases are expected to be serious. According to the 2001 report of the IPCC, global average surface temperatures increased by about 0.6°C over the course of the 20th century and, if current trends in energy use are not arrested, are likely to increase by between 1.4°C and 5.8°C by 2100 relative to 1990, which at the upper end is comparable with the 5–6°C rise in temperature between the last ice age and the present day. As a consequence sea levels are projected to rise by between 0.09 m and 0.88 m by 2100. Other forecast effects include increases in the frequency and severity of extreme events such as droughts, floods and windstorms, reductions in crop yields in tropical and subtropical regions, and decreased water availability in water-scarce regions, especially in the tropics. The report also raises the possibility of large-scale and irreversible changes to earth systems such as a significant slowing of the Gulf Stream that brings warm water to the North Atlantic (which would have a dramatic effect on the climate of western Europe), large reductions in the Greenland and West Antarctic ice sheets (which would add significantly to sea level rises), and accelerated global warming due to carbon cycle feedbacks, releases of carbon from permafrost and/or releases of methane from coastal sediments (IPCC 2001, Houghton 2004: 123).

Even if these effects do not occur, temperatures in Europe are forecast to increase by between 0.1°C and 0.4°C per decade, with higher rises in the south and east and lower rises along the Atlantic seaboard, leading to hotter summers (including more heat waves and more deaths from heat stress) and fewer cold winters (and thus fewer deaths from cold). Europe is also projected to be in line for increased flooding, especially along the coast, along with more frequent and intense extreme events such as gales and wind-storms, storm surges, intense precipitation events and droughts. Southern Europe is expected to be especially seriously affected, with hotter drier summers leading to problems with agriculture and tourism. There is also expected to be an extension of some vector-borne diseases from the south, such as malaria. Ironically, however, global warming is not forecast to have much effect on transport, energy and manufacturing, the sectors most implicated in causing it in the first place (IPCC 2001). Insurance companies calculate that economic losses from extreme weather events have increased tenfold since the 1950s, and by mid-century such events are expected to lead to annual economic costs of 1–2 per cent of GDP for rich countries such as EU Member States and about 5 per cent of GDP for poorer countries. By 2050 rising sea levels are expected to have displaced about 100 million people, and agricultural changes about 50 million (Houghton 2004: 180–7).

Implications

The wide ramifications of climate change mean that a wide range of policy actors take an interest (Table 14.1). Perhaps the most prominent are environment ministers and economic ministers together with related departments and agencies, climate change scientists, energy producers and, in the context of international negotiations, foreign governments.

The main policy implications of climate change are more vigorous measures to mitigate it and to help citizens and firms adapt to its effects, and less policy autonomy for governments.

More vigorous measures to mitigate climate change

The prime source of pressure on governments to do something about climate change is their becoming convinced that it is a real threat: policy learning. This has been a slow process, and as I write the US government is still holding out, but over the last 20 years or so since scientists first raised the alarm most governments have been persuaded. The same is true of most other major policy actors, including those whose interests could well be threatened by measures against climate change: by the late 1990s even some oil companies, such as British Petroleum, were beginning to acknowledge the role of fossil fuels in climate change and the need to address the issue (Carpenter 2001: 314–18).

But climate change also affects the political resources of policy actors.

First, many voters have become concerned about global warming, which means that the electoral support of national governments has become in part contingent on them doing something about it, thereby creating political incentives for them to act.

Second, climate scientists have already gained a central position in policy-making in relation to climate change policies due to the dependence of

Table 14.1 Generic policy network relating to climate change

Type of actor	Specific policy actor
Political executives and associated parties	Chief executives Environment ministers Economic, industry, energy, transport and technology ministers
Non-government politicians	Opposition environment, energy, transport, trade and technology spokespeople Parliamentary committees relating to the environment, energy, industry, transport and technology Regional and local governments European Commissioners in areas relating to the environment, industry, energy, transport and technology Foreign governments
Civil servants, special advisers and other public sector employees	Environment departments and agencies Economic departments and agencies, in particular energy, finance, industry, transport and technology European Commission Directorates-General relating to the environment, industry, energy, transport and technology Regional and local administrations International organizations such as the IEA, OPEC and UN
Judges and regulators	Environmental regulators Energy and transport regulators
Business	Fossil fuel producers and electricity generators: oil, gas, coal Renewable energy producers and electricity generators Nuclear energy producers and electricity generators Industrial users of energy such as steelworks Transport manufacturers and providers: road, air, rail, water Energy efficiency producers and services Trading firms of all sorts
Interest groups and non-government organizations	Business groups relating to energy, transport and industry Environmentalists Trade unions Motoring organizations
Media	National press and television Specialist environment, energy, transport and industry media
Experts	Climate change scientists Environmental, energy and transport experts in universities, think tanks and elsewhere
Electorate	Energy users, travellers, consumers of products produced using energy

governments on science for the information they need to form the factual basis of their decision-making. As policies in areas such as energy and transport increasingly come into question due to concerns about climate change, so the influence of climate scientists and their judgements can be expected to increase, other things being equal.

Third, the increasing importance of environmental considerations for other policy areas would be expected to increase the leverage in these areas of environment ministers, ministries and agencies relative to economic ministers, ministries and agencies.

Fourth, for EU countries the coordination at the EU level of national efforts to mitigate climate change shifts power from national governments to the European Commission and other EU institutions, while to the extent that national efforts are coordinated at global level, by agreements such as the Kyoto Protocol, foreign governments become more influential in shaping national climate and related policies.

Fifth, climate change would be expected to increase the political leverage of producers of nuclear and renewable energy, and of firms engaged in improving energy efficiency, by making them more important to governments due to the contribution they can make to mitigating climate change. By the same token it would be expected to reduce the leverage of fossil fuel producers such as oil, gas and coal companies, other things being equal, as well as of big energy users such as iron and steel, since the activities of such companies constitute a major cause of climate change and in this respect are part of the problem rather than the solution, although this loss of leverage is offset to some extent by the fact that governments need their cooperation in changing their ways if climate change is to be counteracted most effectively.

The most significant result so far of the increased pressure on governments to do something is the UN Kyoto Protocol of 1997. This commits EU Member States and other OECD countries to reduce their collective greenhouse gas emissions so that average emissions over the five-year period 2008–12 are 5 per cent less than in 1990. How countries meet their individual targets is left to them. The emission reduction target for the EU-15 is 8 per cent, with targets for individual Member States ranging from a reduction of 21 per cent for Germany to an increase of 27 per cent for Portugal (Kyoto Protocol 1997, Houghton 2004: 247, EEA 2004b: 7).

Among other things the Kyoto Protocol provides for emissions trading, which enables countries that emit less than their total allowable emissions to sell all or part of their unused emission quota to countries that are having difficulty meeting their obligations. This is being implemented by assigning tradable emission allowances to companies operating combustion plants, oil refineries, coke ovens, iron and steel plants, and factories making cement, glass, lime, brick, ceramics, pulp and paper. The idea is to assign each company allowances that don't quite cover their current emissions in order to make them choose between investing to reduce their own emissions and buying emission allowances from companies that reduce their emissions sufficiently to leave unused allowances. In this way it is intended that the economic costs of reducing emissions will be minimized by enabling cuts to be made where it is cheapest: companies for whom emission reductions are relatively cheap will reduce their emissions and make money by selling allowances to companies for whom it is relatively expensive to reduce emissions. In addition, countries that finance emission savings or sink enhancements in other countries can credit these towards their own emission reduction targets (Kyoto Protocol 1997, European Commission 2004n).

Unfortunately the emission reductions provided for by the Kyoto Protocol would not by themselves be sufficient to stabilize the climate even if all targets were achieved, which doesn't look likely at this stage given the withdrawal of the US and the fact that even the EU is not currently expected to meet its target. According to the IPCC the only way of avoiding the consequences of climate change, or of mitigating them given that climate change is already under way, is to stabilize and ultimately reduce the levels of greenhouse gases in the atmosphere, and this can only be done by reducing world carbon emissions per unit of GDP very significantly from 1990 levels. The European Commission considers that limiting future global average temperature increases to 2°C above pre-industrial levels, which should enable humanity to avoid the more drastic consequences of climate change, would require global emissions to be reduced by at least 15 per cent compared to 1990 levels (IPCC 2001b: 8, European Commission 2005g: 8, European Commission 2005h).

How can cuts of this magnitude be accomplished? From a technical point of view there are a number of alternatives, as set out in Table 14.2. These are explored in more detail in Chapter 6 on increasing energy use, since almost all of them relate to energy, while measures relating to transport in particular are considered in Chapter 7 on increasing mobility. The important thing for us here is that the technical means for stabilizing greenhouse gas concentrations in the atmosphere do exist. The idea that significant cuts can be made is supported by the fact that Commission scenarios that assume strong action on energy efficiency, renewables, carbon sequestration and greenhouse gas emission targets project a decrease in EU-25 carbon dioxide emissions by 2030 of up to 30 per cent relative to the Kyoto reference date of 1990 (European Commission 2004i: 161).

The main problem is that most measures to mitigate climate change have economic costs that make it difficult for governments to implement them to the extent necessary to stabilize greenhouse gas levels in the atmosphere.

First, measures to combat climate change that impose economic costs are likely to be opposed by those who would bear the costs. Where measures to reduce greenhouse gas emissions appear to threaten the competitiveness of affected industries they are likely to evoke strong resistance on the part of these industries. We therefore see the peak EU employers' organization UNICE, for example, repeatedly condemning the emissions trading scheme for being

Table 14.2 Measures to counter climate change

Area	Examples
Energy conservation and efficiency in buildings	Heat pumps, building insulation, improved efficiency of commercial lighting and air conditioning, improved efficiency of residential appliances and space heating, integrated building design, LED lighting
Transport	Improved energy efficiency, switch from fossil fuels to less carbon-intensive fuels, shift of passengers and freight to less carbon-intensive forms of transport, extension of emissions trading to transport, reduction in demand for transport
Industry	Co-generation of heat and power, increased recycling, use of methane from waste as energy source, switch to less carbon-intensive fuels (such as from oil to gas, or from fossil fuels to nuclear power or renewable energy), elimination of methane venting, increase in power station efficiency
Sequestration of carbon dioxide	Pumping of carbon dioxide into spent oil and gas wells, deep saline reservoirs or unminable coal seams after removal from flue stack of power stations or following conversion of fossil fuel feedstocks to carbon dioxide and hydrogen
Renewable energy	Increased use of energy from hydroelectricity, waste such as methane from fermented wet waste, crops such as willow and poplar coppices, wind, solar energy (such as passive solar design of buildings, generation of steam via using mirrors to focus sunlight, photovoltaic solar cells), fuel cells using hydrogen obtained by means such as electrolysis of water using photovoltaic cells, geothermal energy, ocean energy (tides, currents, waves)
Nuclear energy	Fission (but problems with accidents, terrorism and waste), fusion
Policy instruments	Energy-pricing strategies (such as carbon or energy taxes or subsidies for renewables), reducing or removing subsidies such as transport subsidies, emissions trading, voluntary agreements, utility demand-side energy management programmes, regulations such as minimum efficiency standards, incentives for R&D, market pull and demonstration programmes, renewable energy incentives, incentives for consumers such as accelerated depreciation, consumer information, education and training, technology transfer

Source: Chapters 6 and 7, Houghton 2004: 287–312. Sir John Houghton is an ex-chairman of the scientific working group of the IPCC (Working Group 1).

unilateral and placing European countries at a competitive disadvantage, while big energy consumers such as the iron and steel industry express similar concerns (EurActiv 2005). Consumers also object to additional costs, as the fuel tax protests of 2000 demonstrated (Doherty *et al.* 2003). This means that governments that implement economically costly measures risk electoral retribution.

Second, if reduction of greenhouse gas emissions is added to economic goals as an objective of economic policy, it follows that in at least some cases the most economically rational options will not be chosen. It follows from this in turn that economic growth will be lower than it would otherwise be. This cuts right across what one might call the prime directive of modern democratic government, which is to pursue economic growth at all costs both for its own sake and in order to maximize electoral support. This implies that determined implementation of measures to control and reduce greenhouse gas emissions are likely to cost governments votes, other things being equal, making them less likely to implement such measures.

At the same time, however, climate change itself also has economically disruptive effects, especially in the long term, so there is an economic price to be paid whatever is done or not done. The European Commission argues that the benefits of limiting the global average temperature increase to 2°C, in terms of avoided damages from climate change, outweigh the costs of abatement policies, and estimates that reducing EU-25 emissions by about 1.5 percentage points per year after 2012 would reduce EU-25 GDP in 2025 by just 0.5 per cent relative to the level it would otherwise have reached (European Commission 2005g: 4, 15).

What this means is that to a considerable extent this is a long-term versus short-term problem: long-term economic damage if climate change is allowed to proceed versus short-term economic damage here and now if radical steps are taken to mitigate it. The problem is that democratic governments with 3–5 year terms of office have every reason to prioritize the short-term over the long-term except to the extent that long-term threats can be dramatized in day to day political life.

In addition, the rate of climate change can only be significantly affected if all major carbon dioxide emitting countries, including countries such as the US and China, take concerted action. At present there is little indication that this will happen. This enables those opposed to action to argue that there is no point in Europe going it alone, especially if this involves economic costs, because any effects on climate change would be negligible. The counter-argument, of course, is that we all need to do what we can not only as a contribution to mitigating climate change but also to set an example to other countries and to demonstrate that if they act they will not be alone. One way of bringing developing countries in would be an agreement for global per capita emissions to be equalized by some year between 2020 and 2050 at a level that is consistent with stabilizing greenhouse gas concentrations (Global Commons

Institute 2005), although the chances of this being accepted by developed countries such as the US appear to be slim.

Nevertheless, where it is easy to reduce greenhouse gas emissions or expand greenhouse gas sinks, for instance by improving energy efficiency where this would save money anyway, appropriate measures will no doubt often be taken. This may also be the case where mitigation measures also have other positive effects, such as reducing air pollution in general (IPCC 2001b: 9). Such 'no regrets' measures should reduce the rise in atmospheric greenhouse gas concentrations, although the evidence suggests that they alone will be far from sufficient to halt these rises. In recent years governments have concentrated mainly on providing incentives for energy efficiency improvements and for the deployment of low carbon technologies, especially renewables. The main policy instruments used have been grants, preferential loans and special funds. Tax credits, exemptions and reductions have also played a role, but electoral sensitivity has deterred governments from using increased prices as a way of reducing demand and shifting it to other sources of energy. So far decarbonization strategies have been most successful in countries relying on nuclear power and hydro power. Energy conservation and efficiency measures are also important, and emissions trading is slowly becoming established in a number of countries (IEA 2003: 89–97, 112–14, Kaivo-oja and Luukkanen 2004: 1527).

But this is not the end of it. As time goes on there are likely to be further periodic spurs to action. If climate change is real there will be more frequent and well-publicized extreme and damaging events in European and other countries that can be attributed to climate change and which therefore increase pressure on governments to do something. There may also be further alarming scientific discoveries that have the same effect. We have already seen increased media coverage of climate change and related issues as a result of new scientific findings and the rise in the frequency and severity of erratic weather events and natural disasters (Carpenter 2001: 321–4). And as time goes by the more alarming long-term projections, such as the calculation that without countermeasures the increase in average global temperature could reach 10°C by the 22nd century (Houghton 2004: 135), will become short-term projections that are harder to ignore.

In short, pressure on governments to do more will mount over time. This implies that more and more stringent measures will be put in place as time goes on, other things being equal. What these measures will be is impossible to tell in advance, but there are a number of possibilities. If sequestration becomes technically and economically feasible on a large scale it could make a significant difference (Herzog 2001). Governments could do more to encourage and enforce improvements in energy efficiency beyond the point at which they pay for themselves. The development and use of renewables could be accelerated, but this is starting from such a low base, just 5.9 per cent of total energy demand in 2000 (European Commission 2003a: 111), that it is unlikely that they can make a big difference, at least in the short term. And the size of the potential contribution of nuclear energy to the reduction of carbon dioxide emissions means that governments will come under increasing pressure to expand nuclear power if other measures are falling short despite continuing concerns and opposition due to its associated problems of nuclear waste, accidents and terrorism. If presented with a choice between nuclear energy and cuts in energy supply it seems clear that business would opt for nuclear energy and exert pressure on governments accordingly. The situation is similar for households: despite widespread reservations about nuclear energy it seems reasonable to suppose that many if not most voters would prefer nuclear energy to energy cuts. We shall see.

More vigorous measures to help citizens and firms adapt to the effects of climate change

If scientists are correct, the climate is already changing as a result of increasing human-induced greenhouse gas emissions, and will continue to change. This means that many people are already being directly affected and that many more will be affected as time goes on. Some effects may be positive, for instance the lengthening of the growing season in northern Europe, but many are expected to be negative. Sectors dependent on the weather, such as agriculture, fisheries, forestry and tourism, are expected to be especially severely affected.

In these circumstances those affected, or directly threatened, will exert pressure on governments to provide assistance, and this pressure will grow as the number of people and firms affected grows. Increased flooding, for example, is likely to lead to increased pressure on governments to take action on flood protection as more people and firms are affected. Hotter drier summers in southern Europe and their effects on agriculture and tourism will undermine economic growth in these regions, leading to greater pressure for measures to help those affected to adjust. And any northward spread into Europe of diseases such as malaria would elicit vigorous demands for countermeasures.

Other things being equal we would expect that in the rich countries of the EU this assistance will mostly be forthcoming, although not necessarily on the scale desired by those affected.

Less policy autonomy for governments

From an electoral point of view climate change puts governments in a no-win position. If they do little or nothing they will be criticized by environmental scientists and environmentalists, with the assistance of extensive media coverage of climate change and its likely consequences, while if they take bold steps to reduce carbon emissions they come under attack both from those directly affected, such as motorists faced with higher fuel prices due to higher energy taxes, and from business and economists on the grounds that such measures damage the economy, which may well be true, again with the assistance of extensive media coverage. Taking a middle course means criticism from both sides. In all cases electoral support is likely to be lost, which other things being equal implies that climate change causes the electoral support of incumbent governments to erode more rapidly than would otherwise be the case. Since governments with falling electoral support would be expected to be less likely than more electorally secure governments to risk unpopular policy measures and more likely to play it safe by seeking wide support for policy initiatives, this implies more compromise with other policy actors and with public opinion and thus more cautious, centrist and populist policies than would otherwise be the case.

Conclusion

There is good evidence that the global climate is changing as a result of human activities, especially the burning of fossil fuels, and that this process will continue unless drastic steps are taken to reduce the emission of greenhouse gases. The main policy implications of this are set out in Table 14.3.

Table 14.3   Policy implications of climate change

Policy implications	*Causal chain from trend*
More vigorous steps to respond to climate change, including: • encouraging sequestration of carbon dioxide from industrial and utility plant exhausts • improving energy efficiency via means such as mandatory minimum efficiency standards and voluntary energy efficiency agreements with industry • using grants, preferential loans, special funds and tax breaks to foster the development and use of low- or zero-emission renewable fuels such as biodiesel, hydrogen, and solar energy • reducing the carbon intensity of energy use by encouraging fuel substitution from oil and coal to gas, and the expansion of nuclear power, via means such as higher taxes on fossil fuels and emissions, product bans, and emission trading schemes	Increasing evidence that climate change is real and that it is caused largely by the use of fossil fuels, making it clear that urgent steps need to be taken to reduce carbon dioxide emissions from energy use if serious environmental and economic problems in the future are to be avoided Increasing pressure from scientists and environmentalists, as well as from policy actors and voters who would suffer from the effects of climate change (such as people living on flood plains) or who would benefit from measures to counteract it (such as producers of low-carbon energy) Increasing political leverage of environment ministers, their departments and agencies, and of environmental experts in general inside and outside government

(Continued)

Table 14.3   (Continued)

• shifting passengers and freight to low carbon forms of transport such as rail by means such as improving the rail network and using fiscal measures to reduce its prices relative to other modes of transport • extending emissions trading to transport, for example airlines • reducing demand for transport, for example by improving public transport, using tax measures to raise the price of transport, placing facilities closer to users, and not taking steps to reduce traffic congestion	
More vigorous measures to facilitate adaptation to the effects of climate change, such as improving flood defences and planning for agricultural change	Increasing evidence that climate change is real and that urgent steps need to be taken to mitigate its environmental and economic effects, such as increasing flooding and economic losses in southern Europe in relation to agriculture and tourism due to hotter drier summers
Less policy autonomy for governments	Climate change leads to greater criticism of governments whether they take bold steps to reduce carbon emissions or not, leading to more rapid erosion of electoral support than would be the case without climate change

Even if the EU does manage to cut its own emissions of greenhouse gases significantly, however, it seems unlikely that the US or other major emitting countries will follow suit, although this may change as the situation gets worse. The outlook, in other words, is not encouraging.

Part IV

Ageing, Education and Social Liberalization

The five trends that conclude our survey of king trends and their policy implications are central to our personal lives, dealing as they do with how long we live, how well-educated we are, who we live with, our religious beliefs and our sex lives. Population ageing is perhaps the most prominent of these in terms of apocalyptic media coverage of its presumed economic effects, but rising levels of education are also important not only for economic reasons but because by improving the cognitive skills of the population at large it is transforming the way that people think about politics and electoral choice. The other three trends can be thought of as different aspects of social liberalization in the sense that they all involve increased individualization. The trend to smaller households is well-known to experts but is relatively low-profile in our own lives because it creeps up on us over time. Secularization, by contrast, is one of the mega-trends of modernization theory, but these days has more to do with religious fragmentation than with fewer people believing in God. Sexual liberalization in terms of attitudes and behaviour has been kept to the end but, with sex being vital to life itself, might just as well have been placed at the very beginning.

Part IV

Ageing, Education and Social Liberalization

15
Population Ageing

Introduction

The population of Europe is ageing in the sense that the median age of inhabitants has been rising for a long time and is expected to continue to rise. This is true of all EU Member States and has a number of implications for the future direction of public policy. Perhaps the most significant of these are measures to control the deficits in public finances that population ageing tends to cause.

Table 15.1 sets out past and projected figures for some of the principal aspects of population ageing. Although demographic projections become more uncertain the further one goes into the future, they constitute reliable evidence for continuing population ageing over the next 20 years or so because they depend largely on past fertility rates and the age profile, both of which are known, plus the life expectancy of those currently alive, which only changes gradually (EPC 2001: 13). The focus is on the 15 Member States of the EU as it was prior to the 2004 enlargement (EU-15) because better information is available for these countries than for the EU-25 as a whole.

The ageing of the population in Europe is being driven by two main developments. First, the fertility rate (birth rate per woman) has been falling for decades and is now stabilizing at around 1.6 children per woman, compared to 2.6 in 1960. This has reduced numbers in younger age groups, with the result that each cohort born since the 1960s has been smaller relative to the total population than its predecessor. Second, Europeans are living longer. Over the last fifty years life expectancy in the EU-15 has increased by about ten years to reach 82 for women and 76 for men by 2002, and it is expected to keep on rising. As a consequence all Member States will see big rises in the numbers of people aged 80 or over (EPC 2001: 109–10, Eurostat 2002b: 63, 103, Council of the European Union 2003: 13).

Among other things population ageing means increasing numbers of old people relative to other age groups. Over the 40 years after 1960 the proportion of the population over 65 in the EU-15 rose from 11 to 16 per cent, and this is set to rise to nearly a quarter by 2025. This means that the ratio of the

Table 15.1   Population ageing, EU-15, 1993–2050

Indicator	1993	2004	2025	2050
Population 0–14 as a percentage of total population	17.9	16.3	14.4	13.5
Population 15–64 as a percentage of total population	67.1	66.7	62.8	56.5
Population 65+ as a percentage of total population	15.0	17.0	22.8	30.0
Population 80+ as a percentage of total population	3.7	4.2	6.7	10.5
Male life expectancy at birth	73.4	75.8 (2002)	78.7	80.0
Female life expectancy at birth	79.9	81.6 (2002)	84.3	85.5
Total fertility rate	1.47	1.52 (2003)	1.6	1.7
Total population (million)	368.9	382.7	398.8	384.4
Elderly dependency ratio (population 65+ as a percentage of population 15–64)	23.0 (1995)	25.5	36.3	53.2

Sources: Eurostat. All 1993 and 2004 figures, plus population aged 80 and over as a % of total population 2004, fertility rate 2003 and life expectancy 2003: Eurostat 2005d. Population 2025–2050, population by age 2025–2050 and elderly dependency ratio 2005–2050: Eurostat 2005c. Population aged 80 and over as a percentage of total population 2025–2050, life expectancy 2025–2050 and total fertility rate 2025–2050: EPC 2001: 10, 109–10. Some figures are estimates, provisional or projections. Series do not always match up perfectly at overlapping years but are always close.

population aged 65 and over to the working-age population aged 15–64 – the old-age dependency ratio – is expected to rise significantly, especially as the big generation of so-called baby-boomers born in the years following World War II when birth rates were high are now approaching retirement age. Meanwhile the working-age population is expected to fall as a percentage of the total population in almost all EU-15 Member States, with especially large falls forecast for Italy and Spain (EPC 2001: 12, 109, Eurostat 2002b: 63).

One consequence of all this is a gradual slowing down of population growth in the EU-15 over the last 35 years despite a reduction in infant mortality. It is forecast that the population of the EU-15 will peak around 2022 and fall thereafter. However the picture varies by country: while large falls are forecast for countries such as Italy and Spain, the populations of countries such as Britain and France are expected to rise (EPC 2001: 11, 109, Eurostat 2002b: 61, 103).

To the extent that a reduction in the size of the working-age population relative to other age groups translates into a reduction in the number of people employed as a proportion of the total population it implies less production and therefore lower economic growth than would otherwise be the case. The OECD estimates that demographic changes will cause growth in Europe to decline from around 2 per cent per year during the first few years of the 21st century to just 0.5 per cent per year by 2050 (Sleebos 2003: 11). Among other things lower economic growth implies lower incomes and consumption than would otherwise obtain as well as a reduction in the size of the revenue base and therefore lower state revenues than would otherwise accrue.

Furthermore, increasing numbers of older people mean increasing numbers of pensioners and users of healthcare and old-age care services and therefore increasing government spending in these areas, other things being equal. A study by the EU's Economic Policy Committee (EPC) estimates that average spending by EU Member States on public pensions in the EU-15 will rise from 10.4 per cent of GDP in 2000 to 11.5 per cent in 2020 before peaking at 13.6 per cent in 2040 and then falling slightly to 13.3 per cent in 2050, and reports that population ageing is the main driving factor. This means an average rise in public pension expenditure of 3.2 per cent of GDP by 2050. The biggest rise is expected to take place in Greece, where spending is projected to increase by 12.2 per cent of GDP. The only Member State in which pension spending is projected to fall is Britain, where it is expected to decline from 5.5 per cent of GDP in 2000 to just 4.4 per cent of GDP in 2050 (EPC 2001: 19–24).

Projections of spending on healthcare and long-term care are more tentative because the EPC study does not explicitly model non-demographic drivers of health and long-term care expenditure, such as developments in new technology, and does not include the possible macroeconomic feedback effects of a larger healthcare and long-term care sector. This is important in view of the fact that between 1960 and 1990 ageing was not nearly as significant in driving increases in health expenditure as factors such as expansion of coverage of public provision of healthcare and health insurance, increased consumption of healthcare due to increased prosperity, increased use of new and more expensive technology, and high medical price inflation. In addition, healthcare spending over the lifetime of an individual tends to be concentrated at the end of life irrespective of the age of death, which means that increasing life expectancy may not cause significant increases in health spending per individual. At the same time changes in spending on long-term care are driven not only by ageing but also by trends in disability, institutionalization, changes in the way care is delivered and changes in policy on the provision of care (EPC 2001: 33–40).

Bearing all this in mind, between 2000 and 2050 average spending on healthcare in the EU-15 excluding Luxembourg is projected to rise by 1.3 per cent of GDP per capita to 6.6 per cent of GDP, ranging from a rise of 0.7 per cent of GDP per capita in Denmark to 1.7 per cent of GDP per capita in Austria, Greece and Spain. This is expected to result in overall levels of public expenditure on healthcare in 2050 ranging from 5.6 per cent of GDP (Britain and the Netherlands) to 8.2 per cent of GDP (Ireland) (EPC 2001: 44).

Average spending on long-term care between 2000 and 2050 in the nine Member States for which data is available is projected to rise by 0.9 per cent of GDP per capita to 2.2 per cent of GDP. This is expected to result in overall spending levels ranging from just 0.9 per cent of GDP (Ireland) to 5.5 per cent of GDP (Denmark). By far the largest part of the projected increase in spending is attributed to increased spending on those aged 80 or more (EPC 2001: 44–7). The demand for formal care services may be further increased by a reduction in the care-taking potential within society and within the family due not only to a fall in the number of children as a consequence of recent falls in fertility but also to increased geographical mobility and rises in female labour force participation (Sircelj 2002, OECD 2005c: 110).

Putting this together, population ageing is projected by the EPC to lead to an increase in average spending on public pensions, healthcare and long-term care in the EU-15 over the period 2000–2050 of approximately 5–6 per cent of GDP, other things being equal. A slightly more recent study of OECD countries in general comes to similar conclusions (OECD 2003j: 7–9, 35–7).

If we juxtapose this with the tendency for population ageing to reduce the relative size of the labour force and therefore economic growth and the size of the revenue base, so that state revenue is lower than it would otherwise be, the result is a tendency for deficits to emerge and grow either within the state budget or in public finances defined more broadly to include the finances of statutory social insurance funds. This is why we hear such a lot about the threat posed by population ageing.

Implications

The wide ramifications of population ageing mean that a wide range of policy actors take an interest in this and associated issues (Table 15.2). Perhaps the most prominent of these are social and finance ministers plus associated departments and agencies, with employers and trade unions also being important in countries in which insurance-based healthcare and pension provision dominates.

The main policy implications of population ageing are more favourable policies towards older people, less policy autonomy for governments, more vigorous policies to raise labour productivity and expand labour force participation, rises in taxes and social contributions, cuts in spending in age-related areas, more labour-friendly policies, better wages and conditions for military personnel and/or increasing use of military technology, and less stress on fighting crime.

More favourable policies towards older people

The increasing proportion of older people in the population implies increasing pressure on governments to implement policies that are favourable towards older people. There are two reasons for this.

First, an increase in the proportion of older people in the population means an increase in the proportion of older voters, which might be expected to give

Table 15.2 Generic policy network relating to ageing

Type of policy actor	Specific policy actor
Political executives and associated parties	Chief executives Ministers for health, social affairs, finance, employment and education
Non-government politicians	Parliamentary committees relating to health, social affairs, employment, education and the economy European Commissioners relating to health, social affairs, employment, education and the economy Regional and local governments, especially in relation to service provision for older people
Civil servants, special advisers and other public sector employees	Departments of health, social affairs and associated authorities Public health and pension funds Economics and finance departments Departments for employment and education plus associated authorities European Commission Directorates-General relating to employment, industry, economy and health Regional and local authorities, especially in relation to service provision for older people
Judges and regulators	Professional regulatory bodies
Business	Private health and pension funds Private doctors and other medical professionals Private care providers for older people Healthcare firms Health insurance companies Employers as pension providers
Interest groups and non-government organizations	Health, pension and care insurance funds administered jointly by employers and trade unions Employer organizations Trade unions Organizations representing professionals such as doctors and social workers Groups representing older people Women's groups
Media	National media Economic, health and social affairs journalists
Experts	Gerontologists, demographers, social policy experts, economists, actuaries, OECD
Electorate	Working-age and older voters

governments greater electoral incentive to respond to the demands of older people in relation to age-related issues such as pensions, healthcare and other services for the aged, especially in view of the fact that older voters are more likely to vote than younger voters (Denver 2003: 40–3).

However there is little sign of age-related voting at present. While there is some evidence that the political attitudes of older and younger people differ somewhat in relation to issues such as pensions, tax, crime and morality (although on morality this may be a cohort effect rather than an effect of age as such), in general older people are just as divided along class and other structural lines as younger people and tend to keep on voting for the same party they voted for when they were younger. In addition, retirement affects older people in different ways according to their prior socio-economic status, so that even on age-related issues their interests are not necessarily the same. One indication that age-related voting is rare is that pensioner parties have had limited electoral success (Binstock and Day 1996: 364–6, Walker and Maltby 1997: 125, Walker 1998: 18–26, Park 2000). Furthermore, younger people expect to get old in due course themselves and therefore have an interest in ensuring that they are comfortable when they retire. This means that at least some so-called 'aged issues', such as pensions, are in fact issues for the entire electorate.

Nevertheless, the sheer scale of the increase in the proportion of older voters is such that if even a small fraction of them vote on age-related issues, for example in response to government efforts to control pension costs, it could make a difference to election results. For this reason we would expect politicians to feel at least some increased pressure to implement policies that are beneficial to older people and to avoid policies that damage their interests.

The second reason why pressure is likely to increase on governments to implement policies that are beneficial for older people is that as the proportion of older people in the population increases one would expect the membership of groups representing their interests to increase too, which in turn should enable them to intensify activities such as lobbying and thereby exert greater pressure on governments for policies that are desired by older people. The leverage of such groups should also be increased by their being able to point to the increasing risk of electoral retribution from the increasing numbers of older voters in the electorate if governments fail to meet their demands.

In fact groups representing older people are already becoming more important. During the last two decades of the 20th century the number, membership, visibility and political activities of groups representing older people expanded significantly. By the mid-1990s age-based political parties and groups had been formed in Belgium, Britain, Denmark, Italy, Germany and the Netherlands, while in countries such as Luxembourg and Spain this surge of political activity was channelled through existing pressure groups and trade unions. In countries such as Austria and Germany there are also groupings representing older people affiliated to major political parties (Binstock and Day 1996: 370–2, Walker and Maltby 1997: 111–16, Walker 1998: 18–19).

However the pressure that such groups can exert on governments is limited. Older people are not easy to organize politically, as they generally don't meet regularly as a group as industrial workers do, for example, and many suffer from poor health and disability. It is therefore not surprising that Eurobarometer data indicates that the levels of active engagement of older people in political and pressure group activity in Europe during the 1990s were very low. In addition, older people are divided among themselves on many issues (Bond and Coleman 1993: 344, Walker and Maltby 1997: 110, Walker 1998: 22). Perhaps most significant is the fact that there are few sanctions that groups representing older people can apply to governments: electoral threats have limited plausibility, as we have seen, and being retired means that older people lack the option of taking industrial action to press their case.

In short, population ageing may increase the pressure on governments to implement policies that are beneficial for older people, through expanding the number of older voters and the membership of organizations representing older people, but the magnitude of this increase is unlikely to be great.

Less policy autonomy for governments

Population ageing is likely to lead to lower government popularity than would otherwise be the case, for two reasons. First, we have seen that population ageing means a smaller labour force and therefore lower economic growth, lower incomes and lower consumption than would otherwise be the case. The electoral significance of economic growth and material well-being implies that in these circumstances the electoral support for incumbent governments is likely to fall, other things being equal.

Second, we have also seen that lower economic growth implies lower state revenues than would otherwise accrue. Combined with the tendency of population ageing to lead to increasing spending on pensions, healthcare and long term care, this creates a tendency for deficits in public finances to emerge and grow. Since growing deficits cannot be ignored indefinitely, over time economists and others involved in economic policy-making become more united and vociferous in pressing governments to find ways to increase revenue and/or cut public spending. As it is difficult to do either without losing popularity, however, reduced electoral support is again the likely result.

Since governments with relatively low levels of popular support would be expected to be less likely than more popular governments to risk unpopular policy measures and more likely to play it safe by seeking wide support for policy initiatives, falling electoral support for governments implies more compromise with other policy actors and with public opinion and thus more cautious, centrist and populist policies than would otherwise be the case.

More vigorous measures to expand labour force participation and raise labour productivity

The economic and electoral problems created for governments by the reduction in the size of the labour force relative to the population increases the incentives for them to do what they can to increase the size of the labour force by means such as measures designed to increase fertility, delay retirement, increase the participation of women in the workforce, and increase immigration (see Table 15.3), and to try to compensate for the negative effects of labour force reduction on growth by increasing productivity through human capital development and increases in physical capital. A number of European governments are already moving to introduce reforms along these lines (OECD 2003j: 19–22, European Commission 2004o: 15).

Higher taxes and social contributions and/or cuts in pensions, healthcare and long-term care

We have already noted that measures to fix the deficits caused by population ageing are likely to erode government popularity. But what are these measures likely to be?

The first possible response is to increase revenue to cover the increasing spending. One option here is to increase revenue by expanding the tax base via raising employment rates and economic growth, as discussed in the previous section. Delaying retirement would have an especially significant impact because it would simultaneously cut pension spending and raise labour force participation. However it seems unlikely that such measures will be sufficient by themselves to enable governments to meet the full cost of the likely increases in pension and other spending on older people, which means that substantial increases in social security contributions and/or tax would also be needed.

But there are two problems here. First, moves to raise tax or social contributions are likely to be unpopular, with employers in particular opposing rises in their social contributions on the grounds that they add to business costs. Second, raising sufficient revenue to cover the projected spending would be especially difficult not only for countries in which spending is forecast to rise over the period 2000–2050 by more than the expected EU average of 5–6 per cent of GDP but also for countries where public expenditure already approaches or exceeds 50 per cent of GDP, as at these levels even classic big-spending governments such as the Social Democrats in Sweden tend to want to call a halt to the expansion of public spending (Stephens 1996: 43).

Governments therefore have to look at the alternative of slowing, halting and preferably reversing the tendency of age-related spending to rise. Spending could also be cut in other areas, such as education and defence, but this would not address the fundamental issue of the tendency of age-related spending to rise over time if nothing is done.

Table 15.3 Measures designed to increase the size of the labour force

Purpose	Examples
Increased fertility	Financial incentives for families and individuals with children, such as cash payments, tax breaks and subsidies for housing, education, medical and dental services, public transport and recreation services
	Improved maternity and parental leave
	Expansion of free or subsidized childcare
	More flexible working hours for parents, including improved provision of part-time work
Later retirement	Later retirement ages for pension schemes
	Making pensions less generous, for example by switching from indexation by wages to indexation by prices, altering the reference earnings in respect of which pensions are calculated, and switching from earnings-related to flat-rate benefits
	Limitation or abolition of early retirement schemes, restriction of access to disability pensions, and cuts to unemployment benefit levels and benefit periods plus more stringent job search criteria
	Maintenance of demand for older labour by avoiding or abolishing employment protection legislation that constrains employers to retain workers once hired, or by providing wage subsidies to make it easier for employers to cut the wages of older workers as they become less productive
	Legislation against age discrimination in the workplace, including measures to ensure that older workers are not excluded from training programmes
	More flexible working hours, including gradual retirement
Greater female participation in the workforce	Anti-discrimination legislation
	Policies that enable work to be combined with parenthood, such as free or subsidized childcare, improved maternity and parental leave, and more flexible working hours for parents, including part-time work
Increased immigration	Expansion of immigration quotas for working-age people, especially skilled immigrants
	Relaxation of eligibility conditions for long-term residence for employment purposes and for citizenship acquisition, especially for skilled immigrants

Sources: Council of the European Union 2003: 6, OECD 2003j: 19–23, Sleebos 2003: 34–42.

There are numerous ways in which spending on pensions, health and long-term care can be cut, including subjecting pensions to income- or means-testing, extending the qualifying period for a full pension, extending the period used for the calculation of the reference salary to a worker's whole career, indexing pensions to prices rather than wages, and raising the retire-ment age so that workers don't draw pensions for as long. Initiatives to con-tain healthcare costs have included regulation of prices and volumes of healthcare and inputs into healthcare, caps on sectoral or overall health spending, and shifting of costs to the private sector. Governments have also sought to make healthcare systems more efficient by enhancing the role of healthcare purchasers, improving hospital contracting and payment sys-tems, improving the managerial independence and cost accountability of hospitals, and increasing competition among providers. Strategies to limit the cost of long-term care include not only relatively uncontroversial policies such as extending home and community-care programmes in order to stabilize or reduce the number of people receiving care in institutions, and reinfor-cing programmes designed to prevent or delay the onset of disability in old age, but also policies that would impose costs on disabled old people such as increasing private cost-sharing (including the use of supplementary private insurance) and using income- and means-tests to restrict benefits mainly to those most in need (Docteur and Oxley 2004: 44–69, OECD 2005c: 14).

The political problem here is that reforms along these lines tend to be resisted not only by current pensioners and older people receiving health-care and long-term care but also by carers and relatives, organizations representing the interests of older people, and younger people thinking about their future, which means organizations such as trade unions as well. To the extent that people change their vote on this issue, therefore, governments will pay an electoral price for pushing such measures through. Governments also risk mass protests and industrial action. In France, for example, mass union-based protests in 1995 led the Gaullist government to withdraw part of their proposed reforms, while in Italy in 1994 a general strike forced the Berlusconi government to drop its pension reform plans altogether (Bonoli 2000: 163).

What are governments likely to do in this situation? First, other things being equal we should expect vigorous implementation of measures that are rela-tively uncontroversial, such as reinforcing policies designed to stimulate eco-nomic growth and expanding home and community care programmes to reduce the costs of institutional care. After this the name of the game for elected governments is to select those measures that reduce the deficit in a way that minimizes the risks of electoral losses and mass protest. To a significant extent this makes welfare reform an exercise in blame avoidance. Options include try-ing to introduce changes on the quiet, for example by making changes the effects of which are hard to identify or making a sequence of small changes as opposed to a radical one-shot reform, and trying to shift the blame onto other policy actors such as the EU (Pierson 1996: 145, 173–8). Where veto points in political systems give opponents opportunities to block reform, such as powerful parliamentary upper houses or mechanisms that enable citizens to demand referendums on newly-passed legislation, governments have to make policy concessions to the relevant policy actors if their legislation is to go through. In addition, the sensitivity of trade unions to this issue, and their capacity in at least some EU Member States to take direct action to press their case, creates incentives for governments to seek union agreement, or at least acquiescence, by incorporating provisions that accord with trade union goals. In recent years we have seen this occur in a number of European countries (Pierson 1996: 147, 156, Bonoli 2000: 38–50, 150–73).

In sum, the electoral problems involved in increasing revenue and cutting spending in order to control the financial deficits caused by population ageing are likely to lead to measures that are uncontroversial, incremental and/or put together into policy packages that may involve significant changes to taxes, social contributions, pensions, health or long-term care but which also include policy concessions to opponents of reform.

More labour-friendly policies

Other things being equal a reduction in the size of the labour force relative to the demand for labour implies lower unemployment and therefore a stronger bargaining position for labour and trade unions relative to employers. To the extent that this translates into bargaining power in policy-making, for example by making it easier for unions to bring members out on strike on political issues, this implies a tendency over time for public policy to become, or remain, more labour-friendly than it would otherwise be, again other things being equal.

Better wages and conditions for military personnel and/or greater use of technology to improve their military efficacy

The projected reduction in the percentage of young men in the population, combined with the shift from conscription to all-volunteer armed forces, implies increasing recruitment difficulties for the military. Unless decreasing military efficacy is acceptable, therefore, the armed forces are likely to have to improve wages and conditions for recruits in order to keep numbers up and/or compensate for the lack of personnel by stepping up the use of technology to improve the military efficacy of individual military personnel.

The problem, of course, is that both these courses of action imply increasing military spending, which as with pension spending weakens state finances and the electoral position of governments and thereby makes them more likely to implement cautious, centrist and populist policies overall, other things being equal.

Less stress on fighting crime

Since it is generally agreed in the criminological literature that most crime is committed by young men (Entorf and Spengler 2002: 23), it follows that the projected decline in the numbers of young men in EU Member States should lead to a fall in crime, other things being equal. This implies a lessening of electoral and other pressure on governments to fight crime more effectively, which in turn implies less pressure to spend money in this area.

Conclusion

The ageing of the population in the EU has a number of implications for the direction of public policy, some of them contradictory. These are summarized in Table 15.4. While the effects of increasing numbers of older people on state finances has received the most publicity, other effects such as the reduction in the size of the working-age population, and in particular in the number of young men, are also likely to have a substantial impact on the economy, society and public policy.

Table 15.4   Policy implications of population ageing

Policy implications	*Causal chain from trend*
Policies that are more favourable for older people in age-related areas such as pensions, healthcare and other services for the aged	Increasing numbers of older voters as a proportion of the electorate, plus increasing membership of groups representing older people
Less autonomous policies	Falling electoral support for governments due to reductions in the working age population undermining economic growth and state revenue, and the unpopularity of raising revenue and/or cutting spending in order to control deficits caused by the combination of lower revenue and higher spending on pensions, healthcare and long-term care
More vigorous measures to improve labour productivity and maximize labour force size by means such as measures designed to increase fertility, delay retirement, increase the proportion of women working and increase immigration	
Higher taxes and social contributions, and more vigorous measures to improve labour productivity and maximize labour force size	Tendency for deficits in public finances to emerge and grow due to population ageing simultaneously increasing the proportion of older people in the population, and therefore the cost of age-related programmes, and reducing the proportion of working-age people in the population, which reduces the size of the revenue base and therefore state revenue
Cuts in age-related spending, for example by:	
• increasing use of income- or means-testing, extending the qualifying period for a full pension, extending the period for calculating the reference salary, indexing pensions to prices rather than wages, raising retirement age	
• regulating prices and volumes of healthcare and inputs into	

(*Continued*)

Table 15.4   (Continued)

Policy implications	Causal chain from trend
healthcare, capping spending, shifting costs to the private sector, and efficiency measures such as enhancing hospital cost accountability, the role of healthcare purchasers and competition among providers • extending home and community-care to reduce the number of people in institutions, reinforcing efforts to prevent or delay disability, and increasing private cost-sharing	
Measures to be uncontroversial, incremental and/or part of policy packages that include policy concessions to opponents	Unpopularity of steps to raise revenue and/or cut spending
More labour-friendly policies	Greater political leverage for unions due to lower unemployment as population ageing reduces labour force size relative to the demand for labour
Improving wages and conditions of military personnel and/or increasing use of new technology to improve their military efficacy, leading to higher spending and thus to financial and electoral problems and less policy autonomy	Reduction in the number of military age males
Less stress on fighting crime	Lower crime rates due to decreasing proportion of young men in the population

16
Rising Levels of Education

Introduction

As time goes on the average length of formal education that citizens of EU Member States receive is increasing. Among the main implications of this are greater policy autonomy for governments as increasing economic growth due to rising levels of education reduces the electoral risk of bold policy-making, more women-friendly policies as levels of education rise more rapidly among women than among men, more centrist and populist policies as the increasing capacity of citizens to think for themselves undermines authority and party identification, more liberal policies due to the spread of more liberal attitudes as a result of rising levels of education, and less leverage over public policy for trade unions and churches but more leverage for employees and the media.

The proportion of school-age people receiving at least an upper secondary education has been rising for decades, as shown by the fact that the proportion of adults with at least an upper secondary education falls with age. This is true of all EU Member States and means that the overall percentage of the population who are upper secondary graduates will continue to rise over time as older less-educated cohorts die and are replaced by younger cohorts with higher graduation rates. Secondary graduation rates are continuing to increase: in the 15 Member States of the European Union as it was prior to the 2004 enlargement (EU-15) the proportion of people aged 20–24 who had completed at least an upper secondary education rose from 69 per cent in 1995 to 74 per cent in 2004, although rises did not take place in all Member States. By 2004 over 70 per cent of people aged 20–24 had received an upper secondary education in all Member States apart from Spain, Portugal and Luxembourg. And while in the past women have had lower levels of secondary education than men, by 2003 51 per cent of upper secondary students were girls (Eurostat 2002: 95, Eurostat 2005f, 2005g, European Commission 2005i: 307–10).

Tertiary education has also been expanding rapidly, especially since the 1960s: the proportion of people in the EU-15 with tertiary qualifications falls with age, indicating that the proportion of people who have received a tertiary education has been rising for decades and that the proportion of tertiary graduates will continue to rise over time as older less-educated cohorts are replaced by younger more highly educated cohorts. This pattern is broadly true of all EU-15 countries. Eurostat estimates that even during the short period between 1998 and 2003 the graduation rate rose from 37.9 to 50.3 per 1,000 inhabitants aged 20–29, while between 1999 and 2003 the number of students participating in tertiary education rose from 12.4 million to 13.6 million. Tertiary education is rising especially rapidly among women: by 2003 women made up 55 per cent of all EU-15 tertiary students and now outnumber men among tertiary graduates in all EU-15 countries (Wolf 2002: 169–74, European Commission 2005i: 29, 313–17, Eurostat 2005i, 2005j, 2005k).

Within this general increase in tertiary education the relative numbers of graduates in different fields is changing, as indicated by Table 16.1, although the very short time period for which this information is available means that these trends need to be treated with caution. It is noticeable that several of these fields of study are gender-biased, with women outnumbering men in education, humanities and the arts, and health and welfare while the reverse is true for engineering, manufacturing and construction, and science, mathematics and computing (European Commission 2005i: 319–20).

By contrast enrolments in vocational education are in decline. On the other hand the percentage of the adult population aged 25–64 in the EU-15 engaged in lifelong learning, defined as participating in education and training in the four weeks preceding the survey, is estimated to have nearly doubled between 1996 and 2004 from 5.7 to 10.7 per cent, with clear rises in all but two Member States (Eurostat 2005h, 2005j), although again the lack of long-term data in this area makes it difficult to be confident that this is a firmly established trend.

Table 16.1   Tertiary education graduates by field of study, EU-15, 1998–2003

Field of study	% of all fields, 2003	Change in % of all fields, 1998–2003
Agriculture and veterinary	1.5	−0.2
Engineering, manufacturing and construction	14.1	−1.1
Science, mathematics and computing	12.0	+0.7
Education and training	10.0	+0.6
Health and welfare	16.1	+1.0
Services (personal, transport, environmental, security)	3.3	+0.7
Social sciences, business and law	31.0	−0.4
Humanities and arts	12.0	−1.3
Total	100.0	

Source: Eurostat 2005i.

The trend towards higher levels of education is virtually certain to increase over coming decades. Average levels of education are bound to continue to rise for decades to come due to the cohort effect even if expansion of educational provision ceases. The only way that this trend could be reversed would be via shrinkage in educational provision, which seems unlikely. In addition it seems likely that the proportion of people completing upper secondary education will continue to rise, as it has been rising for a long time and the fact that in Sweden the proportion who have completed at least an upper secondary education had reached 86 per cent by 2004 suggests that there is room for this trend to continue for some time in most other Member States. The same is true of tertiary education: participation and graduation rates have been rising strongly for decades and the fact that in 2003 the number of graduates per 1,000 of inhabitants aged 20–29 ranged from a low of 28.8 per cent in Austria to a high of 82.6 per cent in Ireland indicates that there remains plenty of room for further expansion in most EU-15 countries. Wolf suggests that further expansion of education provision will be driven by pressure exerted on elected governments by voters and potential voters due to their perception that tertiary education is now essential if they or their children are to have any sort of chance of obtaining a good job (Wolf 2002: 174–8, Eurostat 2005f, 2005i).

Implications

Its significance both for individuals and for the economy means that education is of concern to a wide range of policy actors centred on national education systems presided over by education ministers and ministries. Table 16.2 lists the types of policy actors that tend to be involved in education policy-making.

The trend towards increasing levels of education has a number of implications for public policy. By increasing economic growth it would be expected to strengthen the electoral position of governments and therefore their capacity to implement their preferred policies. The more rapid rise in education levels among women than among men would be expected to improve their capacity to exert pressure on governments to move public policy in a women-friendly direction. Increasing independence of mind among citizens and voters as a result of rising levels of education is likely to lead to less policy autonomy for governments, offsetting the effects of economic growth, and to policies that are more liberal, more favourable towards the media and employees, and less favourable towards trade unions and churches. Increasing independence of mind would also be expected to result in higher levels of white-collar crime and therefore more vigorous law enforcement measures in this area.

More autonomous policies due to higher economic growth

Among the chief merits of education from the point of view of governments is that it is thought to facilitate economic growth and in so doing increase the size of the revenue base. Both are good for the electoral standing of

Table 16.2 Generic education policy network

Type of policy actor	Specific policy actor
Political executives and associated parties	Chief executives Ministers for education Ministers for employment, finance and research
Non-government politicians	Parliamentary committees relating to education, finance, employment and research European Commissioners relating to education, employment, the economy and research Regional and local governments
Civil servants, special advisers and other public sector employees	Departments of education and associated authorities Departments of finance, employment and research plus associated authorities European Commission Directorates-General relating to education, employment, research and the economy Regional and local authority bodies relating to education Schools, universities and other education providers
Judges and regulators	Professional regulatory bodies
Business	Private education providers such as private schools Major employers and employer associations
Interest groups and non-government organizations	Churches and church schools Professional associations in the education area Trade unions in the education area Parent organizations
Media	National media Education and economic journalists
Experts	Educationists, economists
Electorate	Parents and post-secondary students School pupils as potential voters

incumbent governments and therefore put governments in a stronger position to do what they want while also strengthening their incentives to continue expanding education provision.

Expanding education is thought to facilitate economic growth for a number of reasons. By increasing the number of graduates with specific vocationally relevant skills, additional education helps to ensure that current and future labour market demand for employees with these skills is met. Over and above this it is thought that more highly educated individuals are more productive in whatever jobs they are doing due to their being able to deploy superior cognitive and other general skills to improve productivity by means such as improving managerial practices, making organizational changes and devising new ways of producing goods and services. Increasing the pool of highly educated employees is also thought to increase economic growth by facilitating research and development and the creation of new ideas in general (Temple 2001: 60–2, OECD 2003h: 173).

There is a certain amount of evidence to support these views. The idea that the expansion of education is responding to labour market needs is consistent with the fact that the recent short-term trends in the relative numbers of graduates in each field shown in Table 16.1 broadly reflect the ongoing shift to services in the labour market whereby there is a long-term trend for employment to fall in agriculture and industry while rising in services, especially in the category of real estate, renting and business activities, which includes professionals such as accountants and computer specialists, as well as in the categories of health and social work, education, and other services such as personal services (Eurostat 2005).

Furthermore, education does appear to increase cognitive sophistication in general: American studies up to the 1990s on the effects of college (university) on students typically find not only substantial advances in subject-specific knowledge and in speaking and writing skills but also improvements in more general intellectual skills including abstract and symbolic reasoning, solving problems or puzzles within a scientific paradigm, using reason and evidence to address issues and problems for which there are no verifiably correct answers, intellectual flexibility in the sense of seeing both the strengths and weaknesses in different sides of an issue, and the capacity to cognitively organize and manipulate conceptual complexity. Among other things this suggests that tertiary education enables people to adapt more rapidly and efficiently to changing cognitive and non-cognitive environments (Pascarella and Terenzini 1991: 558–67). More generally it indicates a greater capacity to think for oneself.

On the other hand it has proved difficult to establish empirically that education expansion does in fact lead to higher economic growth, although there is general agreement among economists that for individuals more education does mean higher pay and higher employment rates (Temple 2001: 63–4, Eurostat 2005l, OECD 2003h: 156–7). There are a number of reasons why it is difficult to be sure that education is linked to economic growth. First, the lack of direct indicators of productivity means that studies of the effects of education on productivity typically have to use earnings as a proxy for productivity even though earnings levels are only partly determined by productivity. One problem with doing this is that there could be a significant correlation between extra education and extra earnings even if the extra education didn't improve productivity at all but merely signalled to employers who the most able prospective employees were. Second, any correlation between education and growth may indicate that growth leads to education expansion rather than vice versa, since growth boosts state revenues and thus the ability of governments to fund expansion of the education system (Temple 2001: 64–7, 77). Third, more people spending more time in education means fewer people in the workforce, which implies lower production and lower growth. Finally, even if education expansion has increased economic growth in the past it is unclear to what extent it will do so in future, as there is evidence that in countries such as Britain there are already significantly more graduates than graduate-level jobs (Wolf 2002: 51–2, Keep and Mayhew 2004: 302).

On the other hand it would seem unlikely that extra years of education add nothing at all to average individual productivity and many if not most studies in this area, using a variety of methods, do find that at least some growth in output can be attributed to extra years of education (Temple 2001). It is also possible that an apparent oversupply of graduates is an advantage rather than a problem. A recent report for the European Commission argued that Europe's economic future depends on creating and expanding high-value, innovative and research-based sectors of production, and that in the future up to 30 per cent of the working population will be working directly in the production and diffusion of knowledge while much of the rest of the workforce will need to be no less agile and knowledge-based in order to exploit the new trends (Kok 2004: 19).

Perhaps the most reasonable conclusion to draw from all this is that expanding education does facilitate economic growth, but perhaps not by as much as some people think. To the extent that this is the case governments stand to benefit, as economic growth is not only generally agreed to be good for a government's electoral standing but also expands the size of the revenue base and thereby makes it easier for governments to court voters by improving benefits and services without raising tax rates or by cutting tax rates without cutting government spending. Expansion in the size of the tax base also implies that the growth in the provision of education is in effect at least partly self-funding. The result is that expanding education puts governments in a stronger position to do what they want without making too many concessions to other policy actors.

The other policy implication here is that the anticipated electoral benefits of rising levels of education provide strong incentives for governments to keep on expanding education provision.

More women-friendly policies

One of the distinctive features of the current expansion of education is that women are becoming more highly educated at a greater rate than men. We have seen that from a low base relative to men both the proportion of women receiving secondary education and the proportion receiving tertiary education have risen so that in the most recent cohorts to have reached their mid-20s female graduates now outnumber male graduates. To the extent that education improves cognitive skills this implies that the cognitive skills of women in the population as a whole are rising more rapidly than those of men as older cohorts, in which education levels among women are low relative to men, die and are replaced in the adult population by cohorts in which women are more highly educated than men. Assuming that cognitive skills improve political efficacy, this implies a relative improvement in the capacity of women to exploit whatever opportunities are open to them, for example as a result of their positions in organizations once they are in the workforce, to influence public policy in a women-friendly direction.

In short, the more rapid expansion of education among women than among men implies greater pressure on governments to implement policies preferred by women. Other things being equal one would therefore expect more women-friendly policies in areas such as employment regulation, childcare, social security, the representation of women in elected and appointed office, equal opportunities policy, family law, reproductive rights policy including abortion, and policies on violence towards women such as rape and domestic violence (Mazur 2002, Kilkey 2004: 332).

Less policy autonomy for governments due to increasing independence of mind among voters

One logical consequence of people becoming better able to think for themselves due to rising levels of education is a reduction in the acceptance of received ideas. This implies greater questioning and criticism of governments and public policy, which in turn implies that the electoral support of newly-elected governments is likely to erode more rapidly than previously, other things being equal. It also implies greater support for radical anti-establishment parties.

The increasing ability of people to think for themselves would also be expected to reduce the proportion of voters who vote according to party identification, the habitual and relatively unthinking allegiance to a political party that leads people to vote for that party right or wrong unless extraordinary circumstances intervene. Among other things this means that rising levels of education are likely to lead to identity-based responses to class-based parties being replaced by the expression of preferences based on issues and calculation, so that as time goes on an increasing proportion of voters become floating voters. There is considerable evidence that this phenomenon, known as electoral dealignment, has been in progress for decades. What it means is that the core vote on which established parties have depended in the past is dwindling and that therefore the size of potential vote gains and losses at elections is increasing, rendering all parties, including government parties, more electorally vulnerable (Dalton 2002: 191, 201, Miller and Niemi 2002: 177).

In short, rising levels of education lead to increasing independence of mind among voters and therefore to greater electoral vulnerability for governments. Other things being equal one would expect governments in these circumstances to become more risk averse in their policy-making as they try harder to avoid antagonizing voters and organizations that may be able to influence voters. For this reason one would expect governments to become increasingly prepared to make policy concessions to public opinion and other policy actors in return for their political support, which implies more cautious, centrist and populist policies than would otherwise be the case.

More liberal policies

Another likely consequence of increasing questioning of authority is increasing pressure to relax constraints on personal action, with liberalism to hand as a supporting philosophy. Logically this should increase support for liberal political parties and policies, which implies that over time public policy is likely to become more liberal, other things being equal. Among other things this implication is consistent with the fact that in recent years public policy has become more liberal in areas such as regulation of sexual behaviour (see Chapter 19).

There is also evidence that tertiary education in particular leads to more liberal attitudes in a wider sense. American studies up to 1990 indicate that college (tertiary) education leads to greater openness and tolerance for diversity, stronger 'other-person orientation', greater concern for individual rights and human welfare, and a general increase in liberal political and social values as well as a decline in doctrinaire religious beliefs and traditional attitudes to gender roles. In relation to morality there was found to be a shift away from obedience to rules and authority towards principled reasoning (Pascarella and Terenzini 1991: 559–63). A more recent British study found that tertiary education made graduates more tolerant towards other races, less blindly accepting of authority and less politically cynical (Bynner *et al.* 2003: 3), while a recent Dutch study found that more culturally liberal values were associated not so much with tertiary education in general as with tertiary education in fields of study that prepare for jobs in which interaction is important (Van de Werfhorst and de Graaf 2004). More broadly the World Values Study reveals that education is linked with Postmaterialist values defined as support for a less impersonal society, more say in government, more say on the job and greater freedom of speech, which are rather similar to what other observers call liberal values (Inglehart 1997: 109, 152). Electoral studies also find that education is linked with having relatively liberal political attitudes at least in Britain, where education dominates analyses of the liberal-authoritarian value dimension despite not being prominent as a major determinant of party choice (Heath *et al.* 1991: 90–1, 115, 174–5, 206; NES undated, Franklin 1985: 62–65, Rose and McAllister 1986: 107, see also Denver 2003). Again this implies increasing support for liberal parties and increasing electoral pressure on public policy to move in a liberal direction.

More media-friendly policies

The fact that the core vote on which parties can reliably depend is dwindling means that to win elections party leaders increasingly need to woo relatively uncommitted voters through words and actions. Because political communications with voters are almost exclusively via the media, especially newspapers and television, while electoral dealignment means that the scale of any vote losses that might result from unfavourable coverage is increasing over time, it follows that politicians in and out of government are becoming more dependent for electoral success on how they – and others – are portrayed in the media, and therefore on the goodwill of those who control media coverage. This implies greater policy leverage for media owners, editors and journalists and therefore a tendency for public policy to move in the policy directions favoured by these people. Details of what this means are given in Chapter 13 on the expansion of mass media. Insofar as it means more leverage for the commercial media it implies policies that are more favourable to the media industry, such as deregulation, as well as more pro-business and conservative policies, although pressure to move public policy in this direction is offset at least to some extent by the fact that the growth of Internet use exposes an increasing proportion of the electorate to ideas and policy proposals that are given little or negative coverage in the mainstream media, which weakens the agenda-setting power of the mainstream media and in some cases may lead to anti-business or anti-conservative ideas gaining sufficient political support to give governments electoral incentives to take them into account in policy-making.

Less union-friendly policies

Increasing independence of mind due to rising levels of education implies a loss of membership for traditional mass organizations that depend on member discipline for their political efficacy. For this reason we would expect rising levels of education to lead to a loss of membership for trade unions along with diminishing solidarity among their remaining members, which is a serious drawback for organizations that historically have depended on disciplined mass action as their main weapon against employers and, on occasion, governments. This picture is consistent with the impression of declining union power in many European countries in recent decades. Other things being equal it implies a decline in the ability of trade unions to pose a threat to governments in terms of industrial action and mobilization of large blocs of voters. For this reason we would expect a reduction in the pressure that unions can exert on public policy and therefore a shift away from union-friendly policies in areas such as employment regulation and social security.

More employee-friendly policies

As the employer-employee relationship is very much one of authority and obedience, increasing questioning of authority due to rising levels of education would be expected to lead to increasing questioning by employees of management decisions of all sorts. To the extent that these decisions relate to concerns that employees have in common, such as the desire for good working conditions, this would be expected to lead to increasing militancy at the workplace and greater support for trade unions, other things being equal. To the extent that this militancy can be used by trade unions to increase the pressure that they can exert on governments, for example by increasing their capacity to take industrial action in support of political objectives, one would expect public policy to move in the direction of being more employee-friendly in areas such as employment regulation and social security.

However it is not at all clear that this is happening. In particular there is little indication that employees are increasingly questioning the authority of their employers, although this lack of evidence might be due simply to a lack of relevant data. If it isn't, and there is no trend towards increasing questioning of employer authority, then either the argument that rising levels of education lead to increasing questioning of employer authority is flawed or there are countervailing factors in operation. One possibility is that the trend towards increasing questioning of employer authority is being allayed by the tendency of real incomes to rise over time. Another is that questioning of employer authority is in fact increasing but is masked by the decreasing willingness of employees to express their concerns through trade unions because their authority too is increasingly being questioned.

Less church-friendly policies

As traditional Christian churches are organizations the members of which are expected to defer to the authority of the Bible and the clergy, increasing independence of mind among citizens due to rising levels of education would be expected to lead to a reduction in the proportion of the population that are regular churchgoers. In fact secularization in this sense is a well-established trend, so much so that it is analysed in Chapter 18 as a king trend in its own right. Other things being equal this implies that government policies will increasingly depart from those preferred by churches as time goes on. Details of how this would be expected to work are given in Chapter 18, but the policy implications include an erosion of state support for churches and church schools as well as the removal of policies that support or enforce traditional Christian morality where these conflict with widely held secular norms, for example in relation to sex, reproduction and the role of women.

More vigorous measures to combat white-collar crime

A further implication of people becoming better able to think for themselves due to rising levels of education is an increase in the number of people who decide for themselves whether to obey inconvenient laws rather than simply obeying them because they are the law. Other things being equal this implies an increase in the sort of white-collar crime characteristic of educated people, such as tax evasion, computer crimes and fraud. This would be expected to elicit more numerous and vociferous demands for action against white-collar crime from victims, law enforcement agencies and other interested groups, which, other things being equal, would be expected to result in governments implementing more vigorous measures against these sorts of criminal activities.

Conclusion

Rising levels of education among the population, especially women, have far-reaching implications for public policy. These are summarized in Table 16.3.

Table 16.3   Policy implications of rising education levels

Policy implications	Causal chain from trend
More autonomous policies Continued expansion of education	Increasing electoral support for governments as rising levels of education lead to higher growth and better state finances by producing employees with the specific skills to meet labour market demand and by raising the level of cognitive skills more generally, in this way facilitating productivity improvements, increased research and development and the creation of new ideas in general
Less autonomous policies	Increasing independence of mind among voters as a result of rising levels of education lead to established parties becoming more electorally vulnerable due to greater questioning and criticism of governments and public policy plus lower levels of party identification and higher levels of issue voting
Move towards policies favoured by mass media	Lower levels of party identification and higher levels of issue voting, due to increasing independence of mind as a result of rising levels of education, make governments more electorally dependent on favourable media coverage
More women-friendly policies	More rapid increases in levels of education among women than among men lead to more rapid improvements in cognitive skills among women and therefore an improvement in their relative capacity to pursue policy goals distinctive to women
More liberal policies	More liberal attitudes and greater support for liberal parties and policies due to increasing independence of mind among citizens and voters as a result of rising levels of education
Less union-friendly policies	Increasing independence of mind due to rising levels of education undermines union membership and solidarity

(Continued)

Table 16.3   (Continued)

Policy implications	Causal chain from trend
More employee-friendly policies	Increasing questioning of authority due to rising levels of education would be expected to lead to increasing questioning of employer authority by employees, which would be expected to strengthen trade unions relative to governments by increasing their ability to take effective mass action in pursuit of employee-friendly policies
Move away from policies preferred by major churches	Increasing independence of mind due to rising levels of education undermines church membership and solidarity
More vigorous measures against white-collar crime	Increasing independence of mind due to rising levels of education leads to increasing numbers of people deciding for themselves whether to obey inconvenient laws and therefore to increasing white-collar crime, leading to increasing pressure for action from victims, law enforcement agencies and other groups

While the implications for the policy autonomy of governments are somewhat contradictory, what stands out is the significance for public policy of the role of rising levels of education in improving the capacity of people to think for themselves. In this respect the clear winners in policy terms, to the extent that these implications are reflected in reality, are women, the media and liberals. Churches and unions, on the other hand, stand to lose influence on public policy. This logic also suggests that public policy should be becoming more employee-friendly at the expense of employers.

17
Smaller Households

Introduction

One of the less-noted trends of our time is the tendency for households to get smaller: between 1961 and 2001 the average number of people per household in the 15 Member States of the EU as it was prior to the 2004 enlargement (EU-15) declined from 3.3 to 2.4. Every Member State has experienced a decline in average household size (Eurostat 2003c: 114, Eurostat 2003d).

Among other things this means that more people are living alone. Between 1961 and 1995 the number of one-person households in the EU-15 tripled from 14 million to 42 million. By 2025 there are expected to be between 50 and 70 million one-person households. The proportion of people living on their own rose from 8 per cent in 1981 to 11 per cent in 1999. Over a third of those living alone are women aged over 65 (Eurostat 2003c: 115, Eurostat 2003d).

It also means that there are fewer couples with children. Between 1988 and 2001 the proportion of the population living in families composed of two or more adults and dependent children fell from 52 to 46 per cent. There are also more one-parent families. Although just 4 per cent of the total population live in one-parent families, the proportion of all dependent children aged 0–14 living with just one parent rose from 6 per cent in 1990 to 10 per cent in 2000, and many more people have lived or will live in one-parent families than are living in them at any one time. The overwhelming majority of lone parents are women (Fox Harding 1996: 63, Eurostat 2003c: 115).

This reduction in the average size of households is attributed mainly to four factors. First, there are fewer and later marriages, and more marital breakdowns. The number of marriages per 1,000 inhabitants fell from almost 8 in 1970 to 5 in 2000, while between 1980 and 2000 the average age of marriage increased from 26 to over 30 for men and from 23 to 28 for women. At the same time the divorce rate doubled from 15 per cent of marriages entered into in 1960 to 28 per cent of marriages entered into in 1980, although there are wide discrepancies between individual countries. However to some extent the impact of fewer and later marriages on household size has been offset by an increase in cohabitation outside marriage: by 1998 8 per cent of all couples were cohabiting (Eurostat 2003c: 114).

Second, people are having fewer children. Although the long-term drop in the fertility rate appears to have come to an end, it remains low at 1.5 children per woman in 2000 compared to 2.6 in 1960 (Eurostat 2002b: 61, 63). This means fewer households with children, and fewer children in households where there are children.

Third, it is thought that more women are having children by themselves. Although precise data on this across EU countries is not available, between 1992 and 2003 the proportion of live births outside marriage, which includes births to lone mothers as well as to cohabiting couples, rose from 21 per cent to 31 per cent of all live births (Fox Harding 1996: 85, Eurostat 2005m).

Finally, population ageing reduces average household size because older people are more likely than working-age people to live in couples or alone, since any children have generally left home and at some point one spouse dies, leaving the other one widowed and alone.

Although we cannot be sure about future trends in marriage, divorce and cohabitation, and the downwards trend in fertility appears to have flattened out, population ageing will continue to reduce the average number of people per household by increasing the proportion of the population living alone or in couples. Eurostat projects that average household size will decline to about 2.3 persons by 2010 and to about 2.2 persons by 2025 (Eurostat 2003d).

Implications

The main policy implications of the trend towards smaller households are maintenance of policies designed to expand the supply of housing, tax rises and/or spending cuts, less policy autonomy for governments, steps to improve the provision of childcare and make employment regulation more family-friendly, more vigorous measures to support one-parent families while maintaining support for two-parent families, and more vigorous measures to combat crime.

It is these implications that largely determine the state and non-state policy actors that take an interest in policy-making in this area. These are listed in Table 17.1.

Maintenance of measures designed to expand the supply of housing

One of the main consequences of the trend towards smaller households is that the absolute number of households is increasing strongly despite the slowdown in population growth. Between 1961 and 1995 the number of households in the EU-15 increased from 92 to 148 million, an increase of 61 per cent, whereas the population increased from 319 to 372 million, an increase of just 17 per cent (Eurostat 2003d, 2005q). The trend towards smaller households therefore means more households than would otherwise be the case and

Table 17.1 Generic policy network relating to the trend toward smaller households

Type of policy actor	Specific policy actor
Political executives and associated parties	Chief executives Ministers for family policy, finance, employment, housing, social security, social services, education and health Social liberal parties Social conservative parties
Non-government politicians	Parliamentary committees relating to family policy, housing, employment, social security, social services, education, health and finance European Commissioners relating to family policy, housing, employment, social security, social services, education and health Regional and local governments in relation to housing, childcare and social care
Civil servants, special advisers and other public sector employees	Departments of family policy, housing, employment, finance, social security, social services and associated authorities European Commission Directorates-General relating to family policy, housing, employment, social security, social services, education and health Regional and local authority bodies relating to family policy, housing, education and social care
Judges and regulators	Professional regulatory bodies Family courts
Business	Private childcare providers Private providers of elderly care services House builders and landlords
Interest groups and non-government organizations	Parents' groups, including lone parent groups Women's organizations Churches Social workers' organizations and unions
Media	Women's media Housing and social policy journalists
Experts	Experts on family policy, housing and social care Conservative and liberal think tanks Economists
Electorate	Parents, including single parents, married couples, divorcees House buyers, home owners and tenants

therefore greater demand for housing than would otherwise be the case. Other things being equal this implies continuing pressure on governments to take steps to ensure that additional housing is constructed each year, especially housing suitable for those living alone, by means such as providing tax incentives or cheap loans or by making additional land available to developers.

Tax rises, spending cuts and decreasing policy autonomy for governments

One effect of the decreasing size of households is an increase in the demand for state benefits and services, although in some cases this increasing need for assistance will be met by friends and relatives rather than by the state. Because living alone or heading a one-parent family means that there is no adult on hand to look after you if you become ill or disabled, the increase in the number of people living alone and in one-parent families implies an increase in the demand for formal social care services such as residential services, community services and home-based care services. For one-parent families the absence of a partner who can provide childcare means that the increase in the number of such families increases the demand for childcare if lone parents are to work. To the extent that lack of childcare prevents single parents from working, increasing numbers of one-parent families increase the demand for state financial support due to the fact that absent partners are often either unable or unwilling to provide adequate financial support even when legally required to do so.

While childcare provision should increase the size of the tax base by enabling more women to work, so to some extent is self-funding, in other respects the increasing take-up of state benefits and services adds to the cost of providing them, creating a tendency for deficits in state finances to emerge and grow. To the extent that this cannot be ignored it creates pressure on governments to raise tax and/or cut spending in this or other policy areas. Another option would be to take steps to increase pressure on absent parents to provide adequate financial support for their children.

The problem, of course, is that both raising taxes and cutting government programmes tend to erode the electoral support for incumbent governments, other things being equal. This increasing electoral vulnerability is likely to lead governments increasingly to avoid taking electoral risks with bold policy initiatives that may be unpopular in favour of trying to preserve their electoral support by restricting policy changes to those that have wide support, which means more policy concessions to public opinion and other policy actors and more cautious, centrist, consensual and populist policies than would otherwise be the case.

Steps to improve childcare provision and make employment regulation more family-friendly

From the point of view of economic growth, state finances and therefore the electoral standing of governments it is more advantageous to have lone parents in the workforce producing goods and services and paying tax than for them to be at home dependent on state benefits to survive. This means that as the number of one-parent families grows the potential economic, financial and electoral gains for governments of enabling lone parents to work also grow. The problem is that lack of a partner makes it even more difficult for single parents to combine work and caring for children than it is for the caring partner (usually the woman) in two-parent families, since two working parents can share the caring burden and with two incomes are in a better position to afford formal childcare. For these reasons the increasing numbers of one-parent families increase the incentives for governments to make it easier and more lucrative for lone parents to work by taking steps to expand the provision of affordable childcare and by making employment regulation more family-friendly by means such as extending maternity and parental leave and giving part-time workers the same employment and pension rights as full-time workers.

More vigorous measures to support one-parent families while maintaining support for two-parent families

Empirical findings that children brought up in one-parent families are disadvantaged relative to those brought up by both biological parents imply that rising numbers of one-parent families increase the incentives for governments not only to continue to support two-parent families as the preferred model but also to provide additional assistance to one-parent families in order to help minimize any disadvantages that their children may suffer.

If outcomes for children are affected by parenting then logically two parents should be better than one, so it is not surprising that many if not most empirical studies find that children do worse in one-parent families than in families in which both biological parents are present. Problems identified by these studies include lower academic achievement, poorer health, increased incidence of psychological problems such as anxiety and depression, increased rates of teenage pregnancy, increased rates of accidental death, greater likelihood of living in poverty or being homeless, greater involvement in crime, greater use of illicit drugs, and greater marital instability (Morgan 1999, Saunders 2000, Wasoff and Dey 2000: 61–9, OECD 2003k: 18–19).

For governments this implies long-term increases in the demand for state benefits and services. It may also reduce levels of employment and economic growth (Temple 2001). As noted earlier, this creates a tendency for deficits to emerge and grow in state finances, which in turn leads to tax rises and/or spending cuts, erosion of the electoral position of governments and more cautious, centrist, consensual and populist policies than would otherwise be the case, other things being equal.

One logical response to the evidence on the negative consequences for children of being brought up in one-parent families would be to try to reverse the trend towards increasing numbers of one-parent families. Conservatives such as the American Charles Murray recommend doing this by cutting off all state support for one-parent families, which would obviously discourage their formation but at the expense of casting many current and future one-parent families into destitution. More humane conservatives tend to restrict themselves to recommending measures such as disseminating information to ensure that all current and prospective parents are aware that two-parent families are best for children, providing equal or superior state benefits and services to married two-parent families, and taking steps to make marriage more attractive and divorce more difficult (Morgan 1999: 117–18, 192, Wosoff and Dey 2000: 59).

However even though the evidence that children do better in two-parent families is becoming more widely accepted even by organizations representing one-parent families (OPFS 2001), liberals, feminists and many women voters oppose the idea of reversing the trend towards more one-parent families by means such as making divorce more difficult or discriminating against one-parent families in the provision of state benefits and services on the grounds that this would necessarily damage the welfare of women by making it harder for them to leave marriages in which they are subordinated to their husbands or which are loveless or abusive. In other words, the rise in the number of one-parent families is an unavoidable consequence of the increasing liberation of women from the traditional patriarchal family (Fox Harding 1996: 96, Jagger and Wright 1999, Wasoff and Dey 2000: 11, Millar 2003: 155, Williams 2004: 20).

For this reason it seems unlikely that pressure to reverse the trend towards one-parent families will outbalance the increasing pressure on governments to provide support to lone parents both for electoral reasons, with rising numbers of single parents in the electorate, and in order to enable lone parents to do the best they can for their children in the circumstances in which they find themselves and thereby compensate as much as possible for any negative consequences for children that may result from being brought up in one-parent families. Other things being equal we would therefore expect governments not only to continue to disseminate the message that two-parent families are best and ensure that such families are not discriminated against but also to take steps to make it easier for lone parents to improve their economic circumstances by combining work and caring, for example by expanding childcare and making employment regulation more family-friendly, and to provide sufficient financial support to ensure that children in one-parent families are not left in poverty when their mother/father is not working or has a low-paid job. Evidence from recent years indicates that moves in these directions have been occurring for some time in EU Member States (Williams 2004: 26–9).

More vigorous measures to combat crime

The finding that children from one-parent families are more likely to commit crime implies that the growth of one-parent families leads to an increase in crime, other things being equal. There is also the view that young men who are not married are more likely to commit crimes than those who are married, since marriage has the effect of bringing young men under control (Morgan 1999: 186), which implies that the decline in marriage increases the incidence of crime. To the extent that this is the case we would expect in response more numerous and vociferous demands for action from crime victims, law enforcement agencies and other interested groups. Other things being equal this would be expected to result in governments implementing more vigorous measures against crime.

Conclusion

As time goes on the average size of households in the EU is falling due to fewer and later marriages, more marital breakdowns, people having fewer children and later in life, more women having children by themselves, and increasing life expectancy. Among other things this has resulted in increasing numbers of people living alone, fewer couples with children and more one-parent families. The main policy implications of this are summarized in Table 17.2.

Perhaps the most significant of these is the tendency for the trend towards smaller households to raise government spending, creating financial and

Table 17.2 Policy implications of the trend towards smaller households

Policy implications	*Causal chain from trend*
Higher taxes, cuts in state spending and/or measures to require absent parents to provide more support for their children	Rising numbers of people living alone and in one-parent families increases demand for state benefits and services due to the absence of a second adult in the household to provide childcare and/or care in the case of illness or injury, and thereby creates a tendency for spending to increase, leading to problems with deficits in state finances
Less autonomous policies as governments make more policy concessions to public opinion and non-state policy actors due to a weakening in their electoral standing caused by efforts to rectify deficits	Empirical evidence suggests that children in one-parent families are disadvantaged in later life, so that increasing numbers of one-parent families leads over time to higher demand for state benefits and services, and possibly to lower employment and economic growth as well, and thereby to a tendency for spending to increase and for deficits in state finances to emerge and grow
Increasing funding and provision of affordable childcare, plus measures to make employment regulation more family-friendly by means such as extending	Having lone parents in employment increases economic growth and tax revenue while reducing spending on state benefits, thus bolstering the electoral support of governments, so rising numbers

(Continued)

Table 17.2 (*Continued*)

Policy implications	Causal chain from trend
maternity and parental leave and giving part-time workers the same employment and pension rights as full-time workers	of one-parent families, plus the fact that lone parents find it difficult to work while also bringing up a family, increase the incentives for governments to make it easier for lone parents to combine work and caring
Continued state support for two-parent families combined with increasing support for one-parent families	Empirical evidence suggests that children in one-parent families are disadvantaged in later life, so that increasing numbers of one-parent families leads over time to higher demand for state benefits and services, and possibly to lower employment and economic growth as well, and thereby to a tendency for spending to increase and for deficits in state finances to emerge and grow, but moves to reverse this trend, for example by making divorce more difficult, would face vigorous political opposition not only from the rising numbers of voters who are, or have been, lone parents but also from feminists, liberals and women voters in general
Maintenance of measures to ensure that the supply of housing continues to rise, especially housing suitable for people living alone	The trend towards smaller households means continuing demand for new housing despite the slowdown in population growth
More vigorous measures to combat crime	Increasing numbers of one-parent families imply rising crime because children from these families are more likely to commit crime, while the decline in marriage is also likely to lead to rising crime because young single men are thought to be more likely to commit crimes than young married men, leading to more numerous and vociferous demands for action from crime victims, law enforcement agencies and other interested groups

electoral problems for governments that lead to a reduction in their effective policy autonomy. We also see yet another spur for governments to make it easier for parents to combine working and caring for children. No doubt the increase in one-parent families will remain controversial due to its negative consequences for children, but electoral considerations are likely to keep government responses sympathetic and helpful rather than punitive.

18
Secularization

Introduction

Secularization, as Norris and Inglehart put it, is a multidimensional phenomenon. Indeed Shiner identifies no fewer than six different meanings for the term, while Dobbelaere distinguishes between the secularization of society, religious institutions and individuals (Hamilton 2001: 187, Dobbelaere 2002, Norris and Inglehart 2004: 40). While good direct cross-national evidence is not available on the progress or otherwise of secularization in all these senses over the past 20 years or so, there is persuasive evidence that secularization is proceeding in the 15 Member States of the European Union as it was prior to the 2004 enlargement (EU-15) in the sense of a decline in self-declared religious affiliation and attendance at religious services. However this evidence also indicates that the long-term decline in religious belief may have come to an end, so that what we have is the decline of mainstream organized Christianity rather than the decline of religion as such. What this implies for public policy is less state support for churches and church schools, a move away from policies that support or enforce traditional Christian morality, and more vigorous measures to control crime and anti-social behaviour.

There is abundant evidence that affiliation with mainstream Christian churches is falling in Europe. Figures from national censuses and social surveys show that between 1960 and 1990 declared religious adherence fell in all 14 European countries for which data is available. This trend appears to have continued in the 1990s, as the International Social Survey Programme reports that over the period 1991–98 the proportion of the population who identify themselves with a denomination fell in all of the European countries covered. World Values Survey data for 11 of the EU-15 Member States plus Northern Ireland and covering various periods between 1981 and 1997 indicate declines in self-reported affiliation to Christian denominations in 10 of these countries, while affiliation remained steady in Finland and rose slightly in Sweden. These results are corroborated by figures put together by the Center for the Study of Global Christianity on a best-available-estimate basis, as these indicate a steady decline over the entire 20th century in the proportion of Christians in all regions of Europe apart from former communist Eastern Europe (Crouch 1999: 272–3, De Graaf and Need 2000: 127, World Values Study 2004, CSGC 2003).

There is also abundant evidence that religious participation in EU-15 countries has fallen in recent years. Eurobarometer data for 12 EU Member States summarized in Table 18.1 indicate that between 1970 and 1998 the proportion of people reporting that they attended religious services at least once a week fell in all 12 countries. The decline between 1970 and 1998 was statistically significant for all countries apart from Italy, where religious participation rose slightly between 1981 and 1998. Falls in attendance were especially large in a number of Catholic countries in which attendance had previously been relatively high. As the table makes clear, however, large national differences in religious attendance remain. The World Values Surveys of 1981, 1990 and 2001 also report that the proportion of people reporting that they attend religious services at least once a week fell or remained stable in all 11 of the EU-15 countries covered apart from Italy, where the proportion rose 8 percentage points. This downwards trend is also evident for the sub-period 1990–2001 considered alone. Again falls were greatest in Catholic countries, Italy apart. The International Social Survey Programme surveys for 1991 and 1998 show small falls in the percentages of respondents attending church at least once a month in 10 of the 13 rich countries covered and very small rises in the other three. There is also evidence that participation in religious rites of passage is in decline,

Table 18.1 Percentage of respondents attending religious services at least once a week, EU, 1970–98

Country	1970	1981	1998	Change 1981–98
Spain		47	20	−27
Belgium	52	36	10	−26
Ireland		91	65	−26
Luxembourg		36	17	−19
Netherlands	41	29	14	−15
Northern Ireland		59	46	−13
Portugal		39*	30	−9
France	23	13	5	−8
Greece		27	21	−6
Germany	29	20	15	−5
Denmark		7	4	−3
Britain		7	4	−3
Italy	56	35	39	+4

Note: * 1998.
Source: Norris and Inglehart 2004 Table 3.5 (Mannheim Eurobarometer Trend File 1970–1999). No data was available for Sweden.

as national census and survey data reveal a fall in the number of religious weddings as a proportion of total weddings between 1960 and 1990 in all 11 countries for which there exists data at both time points, while the number of baptisms fell in four of the five countries for which this data is available (Crouch 1999: 267–9, De Graaf and Need 2000: 127, Norris and Inglehart 2004: 72–3).

Another approach to determining whether secularization is occurring is to use religious attendance by age as an indicator on the rationale that religious values are shaped early in life and then persist, so that the religious partici-pation of each generation is an indication of the level of religious participation in general when they were young. If religious participation is in fact falling over time, therefore, one would expect to find a positive correlation with age. And this is exactly what the World Values Survey does find: the proportion of people reporting that they attend religious services at least once a week is higher among older people. The alternative life cycle explanation of this find-ing, namely that people get more religious as they get older, is rejected on the basis that if this were so it would be true of all countries when in fact it is only true of rich countries (Norris and Inglehart 2004: 76–8).

By contrast the long-term decline in religious belief may have come to an end. On the one hand figures from national censuses and social surveys show that between 1960 and 1990 'in almost every country for which we have data for both periods, there is a clear increase in the proportion of Western Europeans . . . not associated with any religion at all' (Crouch 1999: 272–3). In addition, the International Social Survey Programme reports small falls between 1991 and 1998 in the percentages of respondents who believe in God apart from in Eastern Germany, where there was a small rise, and the European Values Study reports that between 1981 and 1999 belief in a per-sonal God fell slightly in eight of the ten EU-15 countries for which data is available, with a slight rise in West Germany and a substantial rise in Italy. However, although the data from a combination of Gallup opinion polls and the World Values Survey summarized in Table 18.2 indicate that between 1947/68 and 2001 belief in God declined in all ten EU Member States covered, during the period 1990–2001 belief in God rose in six of the nine countries for which data was available at both time points. The same pattern is true of belief in life after death: a long-term decline over the period 1947–2001 as a whole but a rising trend during the 1990s (De Graaf and Need 2000: 129, EVS 2003, Norris and Inglehart 2004: 89–91). These results may be due to a short time period catching a short-term fluctuation rather than a continuing long-term trend, but we cannot be sure of this.

What we can conclude is that while there is strong evidence that people are becoming less involved with organized Christianity, we cannot be sure that the long-term decline in religious belief is continuing. For our purposes here, then, secularization means declining religious affiliation and participation. While there are also developments in other aspects of religious life in Europe,

Table 18.2 Percentage of respondents who believe in God, EU, 1947–2001

Country	1947	1968	1990	2001	Change 1990–2001
Britain		77	72	61	−11
Netherlands	80	79	61	58	−3
France	66	73	57	56	−1
Greece		96		84	nd
Belgium			65	67	+2
Denmark	80		59	62	+3
Finland	83	83	61	72	+3
Austria		85	78	83	+5
West Germany		81	63	69	+6
Sweden	80	60	38	46	+8

Source: Norris and Inglehart 2004 Table 4.1 (Gallup Opinion Index 1947, 1968, 1975 from Sigelman 1977, World Values Study 1981–2001). No data was available for Ireland, Italy, Luxembourg, Portugal or Spain.

such as immigrant religiosity and New Age religion, none of these are broadly enough based to constitute EU-wide trends.

Will secularization continue over the next 20 years or so? There are two main reasons to think that it will.

First, religious affiliation and attendance at religious services has been declining for a long time, so in the absence of positive reasons as to why this would come to an end it is reasonable to suppose that it will continue. There is plenty of room for further falls in a number of countries, judging by the high levels of religious affiliation and attendance that remain, and for religious attendance in particular the very low level to which it has fallen in countries such as France, Denmark and Britain demonstrates that further falls in other countries are certainly within the bounds of possibility.

Second, whether secularization in our sense will continue depends on what is driving it in the first place. This is not the place to adjudicate between rival theories of secularization but it is noticeable that at least some of the main causal factors identified by scholars in this area appear to be still in operation, which implies that secularization will indeed continue. A few illustrations will suffice to demonstrate this.

One of the main theories of secularization is that the advent of rationalism and especially science undermine traditional Christianity by rendering at least some of its central empirical claims implausible, while the growing scientific mastery of nature demonstrates the clear superiority of science and technology in practical terms (Norris and Inglehart 2004: 7–8). Despite efforts by some Christians to fight back in areas such as evolution, for example by pushing the counter-theory of 'intelligent design', there is little sign of any real challenge in Europe to the dominance of the rationalist scientific way of explaining and manipulating the natural world.

Related to this is the idea of scholars such as Berger and Bibby that secularization is largely mediated by societal values becoming increasingly incompatible with Christian values, leading to cognitive dissonance which is increasingly resolved in favour of societal values (Dobbelaere 2002: 141). As there seems little indication that societal values are likely to become more similar to Christian values, it appears that this factor will continue to drive secularization as much as it ever has in the past.

Another widely held view is the idea that the functional differentiation of society, which among other things has involved churches handing over much of their responsibility for functions such as education and social welfare to separate secular bodies, has stripped churches of much of their social purpose and thereby rendered them less relevant to the lives of most people (Norris and Inglehart 2004: 9). While churches are still involved in areas such as education, at least up to a point, there seems little likelihood that this will increase.

There is also the view that the emergence of religious pluralism due to the breakup of European Christendom in the Reformation and the later acceptance of religious freedom undermined the idea that there is one religious truth and thereby sowed the seeds of scepticism about religion. Dobbelaere points out that in the past exclusive religions have generally been the result of imposition by rulers. As this is most unlikely to happen in Europe in the near future, religious pluralism seems certain to continue. The counter-argument, namely that religious pluralism stimulates religious faith by forcing religious bodies to compete for adherents, is not confirmed by international comparisons (Hamilton 2001: 207, Norris and Inglehart 2004: 12–13).

Another theory is that religion is in large part a response to existential insecurity, since people living on the edge need reassurance that a higher power will ensure that things work out and that if you follow the rules everything will turn out well in this world or the next. This implies that greater economic security lessens the need for religion, which in turn implies that growing affluence is a major driving force behind secularization. This view is supported by World Values Study findings that secularization is more advanced in rich countries, among rich people, and, for post-industrial nations such as most of the EU-15, in recent times (Norris and Inglehart 2004). Given that economic growth is expected to continue (see Chapter 5), we should therefore expect secularization to continue except to the extent that growing inequality means that an increasing proportion of the population is left behind, as appears to have occurred in the US.

These considerations do not prove that the long-term decline in religious affiliation and participation will continue, but they do indicate that at least some of the causal factors thought to underpin it in the past continue to operate. Given this, plus the long-term nature of the trend in the past, the scope for further falls in religious affiliation and participation in EU-15 countries and the absence of any compelling reason to think that the trend is likely to come to an end, it seems reasonable to suppose that secularization in our sense is indeed likely to continue for the next 20 years at least.

Implications

Table 18.3 sets out the main policy actors affected by secularization. As well as major churches and ministers of religious affairs, plus their departments, these include the parties and interest groups that are most and least sympathetic to churches as well as policy actors in education, due to the involvement of churches in education, and in health, due to issues such as abortion and stem cell research.

The decline in the proportion of the population reporting affiliation with a denomination implies a decline in the proportion of the population whose political identity is at least in part based on religious affiliation, while fewer people participating in religious practices means that fewer people are subject to regular reinforcement of religious beliefs and values or to explicitly

Table 18.3 Generic policy network relating to secularization

Type of policy actor	Specific policy actor
Political executives and associated parties	Religious affairs, education and health ministers
	Christian and conservative parties
	Socialist and liberal parties
Non-government politicians	Parliamentary committees relating to church affairs and other religious issues, education and health
Civil servants, special advisers and other public sector employees	Departments of religious affairs, education and health
Judges and regulators	Courts in areas such as abortion
Business	
Interest groups and non-government organizations	Catholic and Protestant churches and schools
	Other religious groups
	Humanist and secularist groups
	Women's groups
	Homosexual groups
	Doctors and other health professionals in areas such as abortion provision
	Organizations representing scientists in areas such as stem cell research
Media	Religious media
Experts	
Electorate	Active and inactive Christians, adherents of other religions, non-religious voters

political instruction by the clergy where this still takes place, which reduces the opportunity for mainstream Christian churches to influence the beliefs and actions of the population.

Other things being equal this implies that the proportion of the population with political beliefs and values closely aligned with those of mainstream churches is falling. More specifically they imply a decline in the vote for right wing parties, as it is with right-wing political views and voting that religious affiliation and participation are correlated. The World Values Study finds that in postindustrial (rich) countries religion is consistently related to Right ideological self-placement. The Comparative Study of Electoral Systems finds that for 32 industrial and postindustrial countries during the mid- to late-1990s, people who attended religious services at least once a week were much more likely to vote for parties of the right than less religious people, and a study of eight EU-15 countries between 1970 and 1997 based on Eurobarometer data found a strong and consistent correlation between self-reported religious affiliation with the main Christian denomination in each country and voting for religious and conservative parties (Knutsen 2004, Norris and Inglehart 2004: 201–8).

Election results indicate that it is religious rather than secular parties of the right that are in decline, as one would expect: between 1945 and 1994 the share of the vote taken by overtly religious parties declined significantly in eight of the twelve EU-15 countries in which such parties exist, while rising slightly in the other four (Lane *et al.* 1997: Table 7.5a).

Other things being equal the impact of secularization on voting therefore implies a smaller role in government for parties of the right, in particular overtly Christian parties, and therefore a reduction in political pressure to keep or extend Christian-based policies. More generally the shrinking Christian electorate means less electoral incentive for political parties and governments to support the sorts of policies that churches want. In these circumstances Christian and conservative parties might be expected to dilute the extent to which their policies are distinctively Christian in order to broaden their electoral appeal and thereby avoid electoral decline. This can be seen in Germany, for instance, where the role of religion in the programme of the CDU has declined significantly over the past half century (Roberts 2000a: 65–6).

Another implication of declining religious affiliation and participation is a decline in the capacity of churches to mobilize mass direct action, since fewer people are likely to respond to calls to action. This, coupled with declining influence over how people vote and over Christian-based and conservative parties, implies declining political leverage for churches as policy actors dealing direct with governments in the policy-making process.

We would also expect declining religious affiliation and participation to reduce the proportion of the electorate who send their children to church schools, other things being equal, which implies progressive erosion of electoral support for religious involvement in education.

To the extent that falling religious affiliation and participation means rejection of church authority on morality, one would expect that the proportion of the population behaving in ways defined by Christian values as being immoral is increasing as time goes on. In Catholic countries, for example, we would expect an increase in sexual activities forbidden by the Church, such as sex outside marriage and homosexual sex. This is consistent with the fact that the evidence presented in Chapter 19, which analyses sexual liberalization as a king trend in its own right, shows that in recent decades people have been having sex earlier, with more people over the course of their lifetimes, using more varied sexual positions and techniques, and increasingly outside the confines of marriage. People are also becoming more tolerant of sexual activity in general and of homosexuality, premarital sex, cohabitation and prostitution in particular. We would also expect that rejection of Church morality would in the case of some people weaken inhibitions on anti-social and criminal behaviour.

Finally, falling religious affiliation and participation implies smaller families. Norris and Inglehart argue that virtually all traditional religions aim at strengthening the family by encouraging women to stay at home and raise children while forbidding anything that interferes with high rates of reproduction, such as contraception and abortion, in line with optimum survival strategies in traditional poor societies. Secularization thus implies smaller families as people increasingly ignore religious teachings on these matters and take advantage of modern contraception and abortion to limit fertility (Norris and Inglehart 2004: 23). This is consistent with the fact that the evidence presented in Chapter 17 on the trend towards smaller households shows that families have indeed been getting smaller in the EU-15.

In sum, and leaving the issues of smaller families and sexual liberalization to Chapters 17 and 19, the trend towards lower levels of religious affiliation and participation implies falling electoral support for parties of the right, in particular Christian parties, as well as dilution of the Christian content of the policies of these and other parties, erosion of the capacity of churches to mobilize direct action, falling support for church schools, and an increase in behavior that violates Christian norms.

This has three main implications for the content of public policy: erosion of state support for churches and church schools, a move away from policies that support or enforce aspects of traditional Christian morality that conflict with widely held secular norms, and more vigorous measures to control crime and anti-social behaviour.

Erosion of state support for churches and church schools

The declining political leverage of churches and allied parties implies a reduction in political and in particular electoral pressure to maintain state support for churches and their activities in fields such as education.

In a number of EU-15 countries there is an established national church that is given special privileges, but even where this is not the case national governments often provide support for churches such as tax concessions and direct funding. In countries such as Britain and Germany the state also grants legal powers to churches and provides religious education in state schools (Madeley and LeBlanc 2004: 383). The declining political leverage of churches implies that over time state support in these and other forms is likely to be eroded.

Similarly, to the extent that secularization is leading to fewer children attending religious schools, we would expect political support for such schools in the electorate to fall as well, other things being equal. This implies that the political pressure on governments to keep supporting church schools is weakening, which in turn implies that over time we would expect public policy to move in the direction of reducing state support for church schools, for example by reducing financial aid for these schools.

Having said this, it is also clear that governments which mount frontal assaults on the role of churches can run into serious difficulties. During the 1980s, for example, state challenges to church schools in France and Spain elicited major protest movements (Crouch 2000: 93, Soper and Fetzer 2002: 170, 187). Whether state support for churches and church schools is in fact in decline is difficult to tell because reliable internationally comparable data on this is not available.

A move away from policies that support or enforce aspects of traditional Christian morality that conflict with widely held secular norms

Falling religious affiliation and participation implies that as times goes on fewer and fewer people feel bound by the moral teachings of mainstream Christian churches, which means that more and more people are likely to act in ways that contravene these teachings.

In some areas traditional Christian morality is increasingly out of line with widely shared secular norms. In relation to sexual behaviour Christian churches in Western Europe have traditionally taken a restrictive position that is no longer shared by large sections of the population. The Catholic Church forbids any action specifically intended to prevent procreation as well as prohibiting abortion, homosexuality, masturbation and prostitution (Parrinder 1996: 237–9). Other areas in which Christian morality has come into conflict with modern secular norms include marriage and divorce, family policy and the role of women in general, euthanasia, and certain aspects of biotechnology and medicine such as the use of human embryos in medical research.

The increase in the number of people who act contrary to Christian morality in these areas, or who want to, implies that other things being equal popular pressure will build over time to liberalize or remove laws enforcing those aspects of Christian morality that are no longer in accord with broad societal norms. At the same time the declining political leverage of mainstream churches, in conjunction with the declining proportion of the population that shares traditional Christian norms, means that resistance to liberalization in these areas is weakening. This implies that we should expect a progressive weakening or removal of state regulation designed to enforce Christian morality where this conflicts with widely shared secular norms. Among other things this implies liberalization of laws relating to contraception, abortion, homosexuality, divorce, euthanasia and the use of human embryos in medical research. And this in fact is what has been happening, at least up to a point. A study of 19 rich Western democracies based on World Values Surveys found that between 1981 and 1998 low levels of churchgoing were consistently associated with liberal abortion laws in the 13 EU-15 countries included in the study. Recent examples of legislative reversals for Christian morality include the legalization of gay marriages in Belgium, Spain and the Netherlands as well as easier divorce in Spain plus authorization of stem cell research – although in Italy the Vatican was able to defeat a recent referendum that would have made fertility treatments more accessible (Minkenberg 2002, Knox 2005). Further examples of the liberalization of sexual regulation are given in Chapter 19.

More vigorous measures to control crime and anti-social behaviour

Most forms of behaviour that are generally considered to be criminal or otherwise unacceptable contravene not only the law but also both widely-held secular norms and mainstream Christian morality. Insofar as Christian morality adds to the inhibiting effect of the law and secular norms, it follows that increasing rejection of Christian norms would be expected to weaken inhibitions on criminal and anti-social behaviour and therefore cause an increase in the proportion of the population that behaves in a criminal or anti-social manner. To the extent that the incidence of crime and anti-social behaviour is increasing we would expect more numerous and more strident demands from individual and organizational victims for governments to implement more effective countermeasures, other things being equal. Policy actors that by function or purpose are concerned about crime, such as the police and socially conservative political parties, would also be expected to become more concerned and therefore more active in pressing governments for action. Other things being equal we would therefore expect more vigorous measures to control criminal and anti-social behaviour, for example greater powers for the police or more severe penalties for criminal acts.

Conclusion

It is clear that religious affiliation and participation are declining in EU-15 countries apart from Italy, the headquarters of world Catholicism, and that this trend is likely to continue. This implies falling electoral support for parties of the right, in particular Christian parties, as well as dilution of the Christian

Table 18.4   Policy implications of secularization

Policy implications	Causal chain from trend
Incremental erosion of state support for churches and church schools, such as removal of tax concessions and reductions in direct financial aid	Falling religious affiliation and participation implies: • falling electoral support for parties of the right, in particular Christian parties, leading to a smaller role in government for these parties as well as to dilution of the Christian content of the policies of these and other parties • erosion of the capacity of churches to mobilize direct action • falling enrolments in church schools as well as falling electoral support for church schools
Removal of policies that support or enforce traditional Christian morality where this conflicts with widely held secular norms, for example in relation to sexual behaviour, marriage and divorce, contraception, abortion, family policy, the role of women, euthanasia, and medicine and biotechnology	Increasing electoral pressure to remove policies that support or enforce traditional Christian morality due to more and more people acting, or wanting to act, in ways that contravene traditional Christian morality but do not conflict with widely held secular norms, combined with weakening resistance to such moves due to the erosion of the capacity of churches to mobilize direct action and falling electoral support for parties of the right, in particular Christian parties, leading to a smaller role in government for these parties as well as to dilution of the Christian content of their policies and those of other parties
More vigorous measures to control crime and anti-social behaviour, such as making penalties for criminal behaviour more severe	Increasing crime and social disorder due to increasing rejection of Christian morality weakening inhibitions on crime and anti-social behaviour, leading to increasing pressure for more vigorous anti-crime measures from individual and organizational victims of such behaviour as well as from policy actors that by function or purpose are concerned about crime, such as the police and socially conservative political parties

content of the policies of these and other parties, erosion of the capacity of churches to mobilize direct action, falling support for church schools, an increase in behaviour that violates Christian norms, and smaller families. The implications of these developments for public policy are summarized in Table 18.4 apart from their indirect implications via the trend towards smaller families, which are analysed in Chapter 17. Arguably the most significant of these are those relating to the legal regulation of our personal and family lives, as these reflect and promote changes in some of the most fundamental parameters of human existence.

19
Sexual Liberalization

Introduction

It is widely held that in recent decades there has been a sexual revolution. Despite the biological and emotional centrality of sex to the lives of all of us, however, reliable internationally comparable time-series evidence about trends in mass sexual behaviour and attitudes towards sex is hard to find. For this reason this chapter necessarily focuses on those sexual trends for which reasonable evidence does exist for a significant number of the 15 Member States of the EU as it was prior to the 2004 enlargement (EU-15). This reveals a long-term process of sexual liberalization in the sense of people having sex earlier, with more people over the course of their lifetimes, using more varied sexual positions and techniques, and increasingly outside the confines of marriage. People are also becoming more tolerant of sexual activity in general and of homosexuality, premarital sex, cohabitation and prostitution in particular. The main implications of this for public policy are liberalization of laws regulating sexual activities, liberalization of abortion laws, and improved sex education and availability of contraception.

To identify trends in sexual behaviour and attitudes I rely mainly on information collected for the country chapters of the International Encyclopaedia of Sexuality built up between 1997 and 2004 (Francoeur 1997, 2001, 2004). The twelve EU-15 countries covered comprise Austria (Perner 2001), Britain (Wylie 2004), Denmark (Graugaard *et al.* 2004), France (Meignant *et al.* 2004), Finland (Kontula and Haavio-Mannila 2001), Germany (Lautmann and Starke 2001), Ireland (Kelly 2001), Italy (Wanrooij 2001), the Netherlands (Drenth and Slob 2001), Portugal (Nodin 2001), Spain (Nieto *et al.* 2001) and Sweden (Trost and Bergstrom-Walan 2001). The following account is based on these country chapters except where otherwise indicated. All share the same format but nevertheless differ somewhat in what is reported and in how much detail. The important thing, however, is that on nearly all issues on which relevant information is reported the trends recorded are in the same liberalizing direction.

Trends in sexual behaviour

There is substantial evidence that sexual activity is starting earlier. In five of the six EU-15 countries for which information is provided the age of first heterosexual intercourse is reported to be falling. In Portugal it is reported that the average age of first intercourse for women fell from 21.5 in the mid-1960s to 19.8 in the mid-1990s while remaining steady for men at 17.5. The age of first heterosexual intercourse in Finland and Italy is also reported to have fallen in recent decades. Evidence can also be obtained by looking at generational differences, because if the age of coital debut is falling over time it follows that it should be lower among younger people than among older people. This is indeed the case for the two countries for which this information was provided. In Britain a survey carried out in 1990–91 found that the median age of first heterosexual intercourse for women has fallen from 21 for those born in the 1930s and 1940s to 17 for those born between 1966 and 1975. For men the age of first intercourse fell from 20 to 17 (Wellings *et al.* 1994: 38, 84). In Denmark a survey undertaken during the 1990s found that the median age of coital debut among men and women born in 1960 or later was 16, compared to 20 and 21 respectively for men and women born before 1920. Less specifically it is reported that in Ireland and Spain sex among children and adolescents has greatly increased and that in the Netherlands there appears to be an expanding period between the beginning of adolescent sexuality and entering a steady relationship open to procreation. There is no evidence that the age of sexual debut is increasing anywhere in the EU-15, although it is possible that the trend towards earlier sexual initiation may be flattening out, as in Denmark two further surveys found that after 1980 no further decrease took place, while in Germany the age at which males and females have sexual intercourse for the first time has remained constant at about 17 for about a decade.

People are also having sex with more partners over the course of their lifetimes. The 1990–91 survey in Britain found an increase over time in the average number of sexual partners that people have over the course of their life, while a follow-up survey found that between 1990 and 2000 the average number of lifetime heterosexual partners rose from 8.6 to 12.7 for men and from 3.7 to 6.5 for women, while the number of heterosexual partners over the previous five years rose from 3.0 to 3.8 for men and from 1.7 to 2.4 for women (Wellings *et al.* 1994: 98, Johnson *et al.* 2001: 1839). The discrepancies between the average number of partners reported by men and women, when logically they should be the same, demonstrate that people do not always give honest answers to sex surveys. In Finland between 1971 and 1992 the number of lifetime sexual partners was reported to have risen from seven to ten. In Britain, Denmark and Germany there is reported to be a trend away from lifetime marriage towards serial monogamy, which implies more sexual partners. In Germany there is also reported to be a tendency towards very frequent change of sexual partners and the lack of a steady relationship.

Further evidence is provided by generational differences, since if the average number of sexual partners over a lifetime is rising over time it follows that younger people should have more sexual partners than older people. For Denmark at least this is the case: the median number of lifetime sexual partners for people born before 1920 was 3 for men and 1 for women compared to 7 for both men and women born in 1960 or after. There were no reports of exceptions to this trend.

Among other things having more partners means having more sex outside marriage in the form of premarital sex, sex within marriage-like cohabitation and sex outside one's main relationship.

In relation to premarital sex the evidence is a little equivocal: while in Spain the incidence of premarital relationships is reported to have increased during the 1980s, and in Sweden it is reported that all couples who get married engage in premarital sex beforehand, in Finland the percentage of women dating (that is, unmarried) who had had sexual intercourse rose to nearly 90 per cent by the end of the 1970s but then fell to about 80 per cent in the early 1990s.

Cohabitation in the sense of couples living together as man and wife without being married is reported to have increased in the three EU-15 countries for which information was provided, namely Finland, the Netherlands and Sweden. In addition, European Community Household Panel figures indicate that in EU-15 countries in 1998 an average of 9 per cent of couples lived in what the EU refers to as consensual unions. This figure exceeded 10 per cent in Britain, Denmark, France and the Netherlands and topped 20 per cent in Finland and Sweden. For younger cohorts the figures were even higher: a third of couples aged 16–29 were living in consensual unions in the EU-15 as a whole, while in Sweden the figure had reached 70 per cent. In the Mediterranean countries of Spain, Portugal, Italy and Greece, on the other hand, the proportion of couples in the population as a whole living in consensual unions did not exceed 5 per cent (European Commission 2003b: 181). In short, cohabitation appears to be increasing but not in all EU-15 countries.

There is also a certain amount of evidence that sexual contact outside the main relationship is increasing. In Britain the proportion of respondents reporting concurrent partnerships over the past 5 years rose between 1990 and 2000 from 11.4 to 14.6 per cent of men and from 5.4 to 9.0 per cent of women (Johnson *et al.* 2001: 1839). In Germany during the 1980s the incidence of sex outside the main relationship is reported to have doubled for men and quadrupled for women, while in Finland between 1970 and 1992 the number of sexual relationships outside the main relationship is reported to have doubled and survey results in Denmark from the early 1980s showed a rise in unfaithfulness among three female cohorts from the oldest to the youngest. No counterexamples were reported.

Finally, there is evidence of an increase in the incidence of non-standard sexual practices. In Britain the incidence of oral and non-penetrative sex was reported to have increased during the 1950s and 1960s up to a steady level of over 80 per cent (Wellings *et al.* 1994: 162), while between 1990 and 2000 the incidence of oral sex is reported to have risen from 69.7 to 78.1 per cent of men and from 65.6 to 76.9 per cent of women, while the incidence of anal sex is reported to have risen from 7.0 to 12.3 per cent of men and from 6.6 to 11.3 per cent of women (Johnson *et al.* 2001: 1839). In Germany oral sex has become 'a customary practice'. In Finland between 1970 and 1992 the variety of positions used in intercourse increased significantly. In addition the percentages reporting masturbation in the previous month rose from 28 to 42 per cent for men, and from 16 to 25 per cent for women. Happily an increase in sexual satisfaction was observed, especially for women, which the authors of the Finnish chapter attribute largely to reduced fear of pregnancy.

Trends in sexual attitudes

As with sexual behaviour, empirical evidence on trends in attitudes to sex is fragmentary. Nevertheless there is reasonable evidence that attitudes have become more tolerant towards sexual activity in general and towards homosexuality, premarital sex, cohabitation and prostitution in particular. At the same time there is increasing openness about coercive sex such as child sexual abuse and rape. However there are no discernible trends in attitudes to infidelity or sex under the legal age.

Data from the World Values Survey indicates increasing tolerance of sexual activity in general: between 1981 and 1995 the proposition that individuals should have the chance of complete sexual freedom met rising approval, or at least falling disapproval, in all six of the eleven EU-15 countries for which there was a consistent trend, namely Britain, Denmark, Germany, the Netherlands, Belgium, and Spain (World Values Study 2004).

Although for Ireland it is reported that sexual activity is still supposed to be restricted to marriage, with the Catholic influence meaning that for many people sex is associated with fear and guilt, in Austria, Italy, Germany, Greece and Portugal sex is reported to be tied not to marriage but rather to love within a long-term monogamous relationship, married or unmarried. However, in the Netherlands it is reported that although almost all men and women still believe that sex is best within a loving relationship, there is also growing tolerance towards the uncoupling of sex and love. This is also true of Finland: in 1971 sexual intercourse without love was considered wrong by 42 per cent of men and 64 per cent of women, but by 1992 these proportions had fallen to 29 per cent of men and 43 per cent of women.

There is little information on trends in the sexual activities of homosexual men and lesbian women except for Britain, where between 1990 and 2000 the proportion of respondents reporting homosexual partners rose from 3.6 to 5.4 per cent of men and from 1.8 to 4.9 per cent of women, while the proportion reporting homosexual partners over the previous five years rose from 1.5 to

2.6 per cent of men and from 0.8 to 2.6 per cent of women (Johnson *et al.* 2001: 1839). However although in Britain, Ireland, Portugal and no doubt elsewhere homosexuals continue to experience discrimination, there is good evidence that attitudes towards homosexuality are becoming more tolerant. Between 1981 and 1995 the percentages of World Values Survey respondents saying that homosexuality is never justified fell in nine of the eleven EU-15 countries included (Belgium, Britain, Finland, France, west Germany, Italy, the Netherlands, Spain and Sweden), while rising in just two (Denmark and Ireland) (World Values Study 2004). Separate survey evidence for Finland and the Netherlands corroborate this finding. In Finland the percentages regarding homosexual behaviour among adults as a private affair in which officials and legislation should not interfere increased between 1970 and 1992 from 44 to 59 per cent of men and from 45 to 72 per cent of women, while in the Netherlands the percentages believing that homosexuals should be restricted in leading their own way of life fell from 36 per cent in 1968 to stabilize at around 6–7 per cent during the period 1980–87. Even the onset of HIV/AIDS in the 1980s does not appear to have inflected this trend despite the fact that transmission of this illness was linked with the sexual practices of homosexuals.

In relation to sex outside marriage it is reported that there is growing toleration and acceptance of premarital sex in Ireland, Greece and Portugal, while in Britain acceptance of sex before marriage is reported to have become almost universal (Wellings *et al.* 1994: 244). Another indication of changing attitudes is that in Finland the proportion of women setting the promise of marriage as the condition for beginning a sexual relationship fell from two-thirds in 1971 to just 16 per cent in 1992. It is also reported that there is growing acceptance of cohabitation in Italy and Portugal despite the fact that living together without being married is not widespread in these countries. On the other hand marriage does not appear to be on the way out, as although the proportion of respondents agreeing with the idea that marriage is an outdated institution rose between 1981 and 1995 in six of the eleven EU-15 countries covered (Britain, Germany, the Netherlands, Belgium, Finland and Sweden), it fell in four (Denmark, Italy, Spain and Ireland) while remaining essentially unchanged in France (World Values Study 2004).

In general most people disapprove of sex outside one's main relationship, and there is little evidence that this is changing. The World Values Study found that between 1981 and 1990 there was little change in the percentages saying that it is never justified for married men and women to have an affair (Inglehart 1997: 366–7). At the same time national studies yield conflicting findings: between 1968 and 1981 attitudes towards extramarital sex became more tolerant in the Netherlands, but in Finland the proportion of respondents saying that one must be able to accept a spouse's temporary infidelity fell between 1971 and 1992 from 28 to 22 per cent of men and from 29 to 21 per cent of women.

By contrast attitudes towards prostitution have become less disapproving. Although in most countries disapproval of prostitution remains high, between 1981 and 1995 the percentages of World Values Survey respondents saying that prostitution is never justified fell in eight of the eleven EU-15 countries included (Belgium, Britain, France, west Germany, Italy, the Netherlands, Spain and Sweden), while rising in Denmark and fluctuating in Ireland and Finland (World Values Study 2004). This is consistent with the finding that in Finland support for the introduction of public brothels as a means of minimizing problems associated with prostitution, such as sexually-transmitted diseases and illicit drugs, rose from 20 per cent in 1974 to 30 per cent (42 per cent of men but just 17 per cent of women) in 1992.

Although the reluctance of victims to report child sexual abuse, rape and sexual harassment means that it is impossible to identify with any confidence any general trends in their incidence, it is reported that awareness of the extent of coercive sex and preparedness to report it to the authorities is increasing in Austria, Britain, Denmark, Ireland, Greece and the Netherlands. This is sexual liberalization not in the sense of greater tolerance of coercive sex but rather as a process of removing taboos on talking about it.

The future

Will liberalization of sexual attitudes and behaviour continue? It seems likely that it will: it has been in progress for a long time, there remains scope for further liberalization, the political leverage of organized religion is in decline, and there is no counteracting factor in sight.

Despite the fragmentary nature of the evidence it is clear that sexual liberalization is a well-established trend that has been in progress for decades in that people have been starting sexual activity earlier, having sex with more partners over their lifetimes, using more varied sexual positions and techniques, and increasingly having sex outside marriage, while at the same time attitudes to homosexuality and prostitution as well as to premarital sex and cohabitation have been softening and there is increasing openness about coercive sex.

There is also considerable scope for further liberalization of sexual behaviour. As many people still do not engage in sexual intercourse until their late teens or even later, it seems clear that there is scope for more people to engage in sex in their early teens, bringing down the average age of first intercourse further, although we have seen that in Denmark and Germany there is evidence that this trend towards earlier sexual debut may be coming to an end, and strong disapproval of sex among children, and especially sex between adults and children, is likely to inhibit further falls in the lowest age at which people first have sex. There is also scope for a further increase in the proportion of people engaging in premarital sex even though in some countries the incidence of this is now very high. In Germany almost all adolescents practise premarital sex, for example, while in Sweden most if not all couples start with premarital cohabitation and in Finland around 80 per cent of dating women have sexual intercourse. In addition there is considerable scope for further increases in cohabitation as well as in the number of sexual partners that people have during their lifetimes and the use of more varied sexual positions and techniques. However although there is some evidence that the incidence of concurrent sex outside one's main relationship is increasing, the fact that attitudes to this remain solidly antagonistic would be expected to inhibit further increases in the future.

In terms of attitudes the current high levels of disapproval of homosexuality mean that there is plenty of scope for the trend towards greater tolerance of homosexuality to continue, although the experience of Canada seems to indicate that this trend can be reversed when controversy arises over issues such as homosexual marriage (Barrett *et al.* 1997, World Values Study 2004). The same is true of prostitution: high levels of disapproval mean that there remains plenty of room for attitudes to continue to soften. There also appears to be scope for further increases in openness about the extent of coercive sex, exemplified recently by the large amount of media attention devoted to child sexual abuse, and also for increased reporting of sexual attacks to the authorities.

The evidence also indicates, however, that the liberalizing trend in sexual attitudes is not without limit, as none of the surveys referred to above found that attitudes have softened towards sex involving children, coercive sex or sex outside one's main relationship: there appears to be a new sexual morality based on acceptance of all monogamous sexual activity between consenting adults but rejection of all other types of sex.

Another reason to expect sexual liberalization to continue is the declining political leverage of mainstream Christian churches detailed in Chapter 18, as this weakens the political position of those who want to keep the old Christian model of sexual morality.

Finally, there is no counteracting tendency in sight. Even the onset of HIV/AIDS in the 1980s did little to slow the process of liberalization.

In short, sexual liberalization seems likely to continue. The general consensus of writings in this area seems to be that there is a trend away from approving only monogamous sex within lifelong marriage, the traditional Christian moral position, towards tolerance of any sexual activity between consenting adults that takes place within steady, monogamous, loving but not necessarily long-term relationships. Here the words 'consenting', 'adults', 'monogamous' and 'loving' seem to delineate the new moral dividing line. In this light what appears to be happening is that EU-15 countries are moving along a trajectory from the Christian model to a liberal model of sexual behaviour and attitudes, with northern countries in the lead and Mediterranean countries following.

Implications

We have seen that there is a continuing liberalizing trend in relation to the age of sexual debut, number of lifetime sexual partners, sex outside marriage and use of non-standard sexual positions and techniques, plus increasing acceptance of homosexuality and prostitution. Table 19.1 sets out the main policy actors in areas affected by this. Of these arguably the most significant are the parties on opposite sides of the political dispute over sexual liberalization: the socially liberal parties that welcome it, and the Christian and other socially conservative parties that wish to retain the old Christian model.

Sexual liberalization as defined above has three main implications for public policy: liberalization of sexual regulation, liberalization of laws relating to abortion, and improvements in sex education and in the availability of contraception.

Liberalization of sexual regulation

The liberalization of sexual attitudes and behaviour would be expected to increase political pressure to liberalize legal regulation of sexual activities. Sexual liberalization in the electorate implies more support for parties that

Table 19.1   Generic policy network relating to sexual liberalization

Type of policy actor	Specific policy actor
Political executives and associated parties	Ministers for health, education, family policy and interior Christian and socially conservative parties Liberal parties
Non-government politicians	Parliamentary committees relating to social affairs, health and family policy
Civil servants, special advisers and other public sector employees	Departments of health, education, family policy, interior and associated agencies such as censorship boards European Commission Directorates-General relating to health, education and social affairs Police
Judges and regulators	Courts in areas such as abortion and censorship
Business	Sex industry
Interest groups and non-government organizations	Churches and other religious groups Women's groups Homosexual groups Prostitutes' groups Doctors and other health professionals in areas such as abortion provision
Media	Mainstream media Sex-oriented media such as pornographic websites and videos
Experts	Health professionals, sexologists and social policy experts Conservative and liberal think tanks
Electorate	Socially conservative and liberal voters

advocate liberalization and less support for parties that support the old Christian sexual morality, such as Christian Democratic parties. This logic is consistent with the fact that religious parties are in electoral decline: between 1945 and 1994 the share of the vote taken by overtly religious parties declined significantly in eight of the twelve EU-15 countries in which such parties exist while rising slightly in the other four (Lane *et al.* 1997: Table 7.5a). The electoral decline of religious parties implies a smaller role in government for them and therefore a reduction in political pressure within governments to keep or extend policies designed to enforce Christian sexual morality. More generally it means less electoral incentive for parties and governments of all complexions to support such policies. In these circumstances Christian parties might be expected to dilute the extent to which their policies are distinctively Christian in order to broaden their electoral appeal and thereby avoid electoral decline, which again would make it easier for governments to liberalize state regulation in this area.

Greater political support for liberalizing laws regulating sexual activities, and weaker opposition, implies that among other things we should expect increasing pressure to extend to cohabiting couples at least some of the legal protections and privileges accorded to married couples in areas such as taxation, inheritance and division of property when relationships end. This could well have the knock-on effect of increasing still further the proportion of couples who choose to cohabit rather than marry. In relation to homosexuality the liberalizing sexual trends of the past 30 years or so have already been accompanied by liberalization in the law: homosexual acts have been legalized in all EU-15 countries and in a number of these there have been moves to outlaw discrimination against homosexual men and lesbian women, reduce the age of consent for homosexuals to the heterosexual age of consent and introduce legal recognition of homosexual unions (Francoeur 1997, 2001, 2004). In 1989, for example, Denmark pioneered the introduction of legal registration for same-sex unions (Graugaard *et al.* 2004). We would expect more countries to move in this direction in the future.

More liberal abortion laws

Earlier sexual debut, more sexual partners and more sex outside marriage would be expected to increase the number of unplanned pregnancies, other things being equal, and therefore increase the demand for cheap, accessible, safe, legal abortions, which in turn would be expected to strengthen electoral pressure to liberalize abortion laws. This logic is consistent with the fact that abortion laws in most if not all EU-15 countries have become more liberal during the last 20–30 years (Francoeur 1997, 2001, 2004).

Improvements in sex education and availability of contraception

Earlier sexual debut, more sexual partners and more sex outside marriage imply not only an increase in unplanned pregnancies but also an increase in the incidence of sexually-transmitted diseases (STDs), other things being equal, including HIV/AIDS. Given that both unplanned pregnancies and STDs are seen as problems, the issue for policymakers is what to do about them. One possibility would be to try to reverse the trends that are fuelling increases in unplanned pregnancies and STDs, but as we have already noted electoral pressures favour more liberal policies, not more restrictive ones.

However there is an alternative that is much more in line with the tenor of the times, namely to implement policies designed to increase the extent to which sexually active people use contraception, especially condoms, as wider use of appropriate contraception should reduce rates of unplanned pregnancies and STDs. What this implies is policies designed to improve the availability of contraception, such as widening the range of retail outlets, plus policies designed to improve knowledge about contraception, in particular expanded public education programmes and improvements in sex education in school. In the past programmes such as these have often been weakened or blocked by inhibitions about talking about sex, but these should be weakening as sexual liberalization proceeds, clearing the way for more determined efforts. Even in Ireland, where Catholic influence has long obstructed the use of contraception, a survey by *The Irish Times* in 1990 found that 88 per cent of 18–65 year olds favoured provision of information on contraception in schools (Kelly 2001).

Conclusion

Analysing the implications of sexual liberalization for policy actors and public policy suggests that the most likely effects, other things being equal, are liberalization of sexual regulation, liberalization of abortion laws, and improvements in sex education and availability of contraception (Table 19.2).

Sexual liberalization would also be expected to be politically relevant through increasing the number of one-parent and blended families, as the fact that on average people have more sexual partners over their lifetimes implies that more relationships break up, including relationships that have produced children. One indication of this is that between 1992 and 2003 the number of divorces per 1,000 persons rose in Austria, Belgium, Denmark, Germany, Greece, Luxembourg, Portugal, Italy and Spain while remaining steady in Finland, the Netherlands and Sweden and falling only in Britain. Figures were not available for Ireland (Eurostat 2005o). The implications for public policy of increasing numbers of one-parent families are detailed in Chapter 17 on the trend towards smaller households.

Another point is that insofar as earlier sexual debut, more sexual partners and more sex outside marriage lead to more births, sexual liberalization moderates population ageing, although the magnitude of population ageing (see Chapter 15) indicates that this effect is not very significant.

Table 19.2   Policy implications of sexual liberalization

Policy implications	Causal chain from trend
Liberalization of regulation relating to sexual activity such as outlawing discrimination against homosexuals and extending to unmarried homosexual and heterosexual cohabiting couples at least some of the legal protections and privileges accorded to married couples	The spread of more liberal attitudes towards sexuality implies increasing electoral support for socially liberal parties, decreasing electoral support for Christian and socially conservative parties, electorally-motivated moderation of Christian and conservative party policies on sexual regulation, and weakening electoral incentives for governments of all complexions to keep laws enforcing Christian sexual morality
More liberal abortion laws	Increasing electoral demand for abortion due to: • increasing numbers of unplanned pregnancies as a consequence of earlier sexual activity, more sexual partners and more sex outside marriage, and • increasing electoral support for socially liberal parties, decreasing electoral support for Christian and conservative parties, electorally-motivated moderation of Christian and conservative party policies on sexual regulation, and weakening electoral incentives for governments of all complexions to keep laws enforcing Christian sexual morality
Improved availability of contraception, especially condoms, plus expanded public sex education programmes and improvements in sex education in schools	Increasing rates of unplanned pregnancies and sexually transmitted diseases, including HIV/AIDS, due to: earlier sexual activity, more sexual partners and more sex outside marriage, increasing electoral support for socially liberal parties, decreasing electoral support for those who wish to solve these problems by restricting sexual activity, in particular Christian and conservative parties, electorally-motivated moderation of Christian and conservative party policies on sexual regulation, and weakening electoral incentives for governments of all complexions to keep laws enforcing Christian sexual morality

Perhaps the most significant policy implication of sexual liberalization is the tendency towards more liberal regulation of sexual activities, as this not only results from past liberalization of attitudes but also facilitates further sexual liberalization in the future. The question is, just how far can sexual liberalization go?

Part V
The Big Picture

Chapters 1–19 have identified the implications for public policy on an other-things-being-equal basis of each of the 19 king trends considered individually. It is now time to draw these findings together in order to look at the big picture of what king trends as a whole imply for the future of public policy and in this way obtain for the first time a synoptic view of the long-term directions in which public policy in EU countries is likely to move.

20
The Shape of Things To Come

Introduction

The purpose of this study is to obtain a synoptic view of the future directions in which public policy in EU countries is likely to move by using two of the most widely accepted contemporary theories of policy-making to deduce the implications for public policy of king trends: those technological, economic, environmental and social trends that can be empirically verified, affect the lives of large numbers of people and are expected by relevant experts to continue for at least the next 20 years or so (Table 20.1). Both policy network theory and advocacy coalition theory state that major policy changes are caused mainly by external events affecting the outcomes of implicit and explicit bargaining over public policy by altering the views and/or political resources of individuals and groups involved in policy-making. Although most such events cannot be predicted, it is possible to predict the events that constitute trends. This means that identifying how king trends affect the views and/or resources of policy actors enables us to deduce the directions in which these trends are pushing public policy.

Using this procedure in the previous 19 chapters has yielded over a hundred findings concerning the policy implications of each king trend considered individually on an 'other things being equal' basis. In this chapter these findings are put together into a single list that constitutes an integrated baseline projection of the directions in which king trends considered as a whole are pushing public policy before these pressures are inflected by events, personalities and other short-term and unpredictable factors. This is as close as we can get to a synoptic view of the long-term future direction of public policy in EU countries.

The classification on which this list of anticipated policy directions is based is aimed at grouping them into as few categories as possible so as to simplify exposition and understanding. The individual items are not all mutually exclusive, and some are more complex and significant than others, but taken together they do cover all the policy implications of king trends that have

Table 20.1   Identifiable king trends (again)

Type	Trend
Development and spread of technological innovation	1 Information and communications technology 2 Biotechnology 3 Healthcare technology 4 Military technology
Economic trends	5 Growth and diversification of production and consumption 6 Greater energy use 7 Increasing mobility 8 The shift to services 9 The growth of women's employment 10 The expansion of trade 11 The internationalization of production 12 The internationalization of finance 13 The expansion of mass media
Environmental trends	14 Climate change
Social trends	15 Population ageing 16 Rising levels of education 17 Smaller households 18 Secularization 19 Sexual liberalization

been identified in Chapters 1–19 apart from those that cancel each other out or are very minor.

Before setting out this list, though, it is important to be quite clear what it represents. It is not a list of observed current trends extrapolated into the future but a list of the policy implications of king trends. And it is not a prediction of future trends in public policy but a list of those we would expect insofar as policy network theory and advocacy theory correctly specify how king trends influence public policy and this influence is not obscured by other factors.

Another way of putting this is to say that the list describes the directions in which public policy would move if only the 19 king trends were in operation, governments took the line of least resistance and nothing else changed much, with short-term fluctuations cancelling each other out and no major disruptive events such as an energy crisis. The actual future of public policy as it emerges can be thought of as a variation of this scenario.

Baseline projection of future policy directions

At the most general level, and at the cost of doing considerable violence to their diversity and specificity, the net policy implications of the 19 king trends can be loosely summarized as more assertive security policies, more business-friendly economic policies, more liberal social policies and increased public spending. To understand what this means, however, it is necessary to look beyond these four general headings to the 12 specific policy implications that they cover.

More assertive security policies

1. More assertive foreign and security policies

EU governments have both the incentive and the opportunity to implement more assertive foreign and security policies in coming years except in relation to major trading partners. The perceived threats posed by the proliferation of weapons of mass destruction, cyber-attacks on vital computer systems and dependence on energy imports are growing, while ever-increasing levels of production create a constant need to open up new markets in other countries. At the same time the development of precision warfare techniques capable of quick victories with few or no casualties and minimum destructiveness reduces the electoral cost of military action. The result is likely to be more aggressive and interventionist foreign and security policies except in relation to major trading partners, as the expansion of international trade and production networks with these countries increases the domestic economic costs of their being disrupted by military action.

2. More intrusive and internationalized law enforcement

EU governments also have both the incentive and opportunity to implement more vigorous measures against crime. The king trends operating today imply rising crime in a number of respects. There is the perception that developments in ICT are leading to increasing levels of computer crime. The expansion of trade and the internationalization of production and finance are thought to increase the incidence of international crime such as fraud and money laundering. Increasing independence of mind due to rising levels of education implies rising levels of white-collar crime as increasing numbers of people decide for themselves whether to obey the law. There is evidence that children brought up in one-parent families are more likely to commit crime than children from two-parent families, which implies that the increasing incidence of one-parent families means rising crime, other things being equal, although this tendency is offset somewhat by the declining proportion in the population of the category of people most likely to commit crime, namely young men, due to population ageing. And secularization weakens inhibitions against crime and anti-social behaviour by weakening the hold of Christian morality. At the same time the potential effectiveness of law enforcement is being increased by improvements in surveillance technology. The likely results are moves to tighten regulation of ICT, implement tighter border controls, permit law enforcement agencies to increase their use of surveillance of people and systems, introduce harsher penalties for criminal acts, and expand international cooperation in law enforcement.

More business-friendly policies

The king trends operating today strengthen the economic and electoral incentives for governments to shift public policy in a more business-friendly direction in a number of ways, although not all of these are motivated solely by a concern to help business and their effects are not necessarily beneficial only to business. We begin by looking at the policy implications relating to specific types of firms and sectors.

3. *More favourable policies towards expanding firms and sectors*

As time goes on some types of business become more significant for growth and employment, thus increasing the economic and electoral incentives for governments to do what they can to assist them and take advantage of what they do, while others become less economically significant and therefore of lesser political importance except to the extent that their difficulties cause economic or social disruption. The main types of expanding firms and sectors are hi-tech firms, the services sector in general, TNCs, exporters, international financial institutions and media companies. Increasing international competition means that import-competing firms are the ones most at risk of sudden meltdown.

The increasing significance of technological developments in areas such as ICT, biotechnology and healthcare strengthen the incentives for governments to implement more vigorous measures to assist firms in these areas, for instance by expanding financial incentives for technology-rich incoming foreign investment, adapting process and product regulation in ways that facilitate the development and use of new technologies (for example by loosening restrictions on the use of genetic tests by insurers and employees as these tests become more reliable), and expanding direct financial incentives such as tax breaks for R&D. The growing economic significance of new technology also provides incentives for governments to encourage other businesses to use these technologies, to expand education and training so that employees are appropriately skilled in their use, and to intensify efforts to protect business from cybercrime.

The increasing economic importance of services relative to manufacturing strengthen the incentives for governments to make public policy more services-friendly in areas such as regulation, education and training, access to government services, technical and generic assistance to small and medium-sized enterprises, tax policy, and financial support. Similarly, the increasing economic value of the media industry increases the incentives for governments to make public policy more favourable towards media interests in areas such as regulation and industry assistance.

The increasing economic importance of export industries, combined with growing competition for foreign markets and increasing competition from imports for domestic import-competing industries, strengthen the incentives for governments to assist export and import-competing producers by means such as improving infrastructure, expanding education and training, providing additional assistance with R&D, increasing direct financial aid, implementing more vigorous measures to open up new markets in foreign countries, cutting employers' social contributions and corporation tax, taking steps to secure wage restraint, reforming employment regulation to increase labour flexibility, reducing the costs to business of environmental regulation and strengthening international labour and environmental standards, for example by including them in trade agreements.

The increasing economic importance of TNCs and inward foreign investment, plus the increasing ability of resident companies to move production elsewhere, strengthen the incentives for governments to implement policies designed to benefit TNCs in particular such as further liberalization of investment restrictions and greater incentives for inward foreign investment as well as the policies already mentioned in the areas of technology, tax, education, infrastructure, labour costs, employment regulation, environmental regulation and trade policy. At the same time the pressure exerted on public policy by TNC threats to withhold investment or move it elsewhere can be countered by using international agreements to limit locational competition by means such as harmonizing tax regimes, investment regulation and labour and environmental standards, although progress in this area is likely to be limited by the opposition of current 'winners' in these fields to signing international agreements that remove their comparative advantages.

The increasing economic importance of TNCs also implies a change in the economic policy instruments used by governments, since the ability of TNCs to shift profits undermines tax revenue and means that demand management policies have less impact, while their currency dealings undermine exchange rate policy, their capacity to shift production elsewhere undermines industrial policy, and their ability to borrow elsewhere or transfer domestic borrowings elsewhere means that monetary policy has less impact on credit. In these circumstances measures to stimulate business activity, such as the ones listed above, become increasingly important as policy instruments.

The increasing economic importance of international financial markets, combined with the financial importance for governments of minimizing interest rates on government debt, increase the incentives for governments to implement more business-friendly policies as defined by financial markets. Apart from the pro-business policies listed above this means strict policies to control inflation, which are already in place in the EU, and further international financial liberalization. However the extent to which governments will pursue further financial liberalization is limited by the fact that increasing financial internationalization increases the likelihood and severity of international financial crises by tightening international links that facilitate the transmission of financial shocks, increasing the scale and speed of international financial flows, expanding the interdependencies between increasingly large and complex financial institutions, and facilitating the growth of financial derivatives. For these reasons, and because there have been a number of serious international financial crises in recent years, governments are increasingly likely to act together to strengthen prudential regulation of financial institutions, as they have just recently with the Basel 2 agreement.

So far it sounds like business has it all its own way, but in fact it is not all one-way traffic due to the emergence and growth of the anti-globalization movement in response to growing awareness of the downside of increasing economic internationalization (globalization), such as downward pressure on labour and environmental standards, threats to welfare states and economic damage to poor countries. For this reason the movement is likely to grow as economic internationalization develops just as trade unions expanded as industrialization progressed. Furthermore its political efficacy is increasing as developments in ICT improve the capacity of spatially-dispersed groups to coordinate at a distance, as this implies a shift towards policies favoured by spatially-dispersed groups in general including international non-government organizations and movements. The consequence of this is increasing pressure on governments to counter the perceived ill effects of economic internationalization, for example by expanding the use of international agreements to regulate locational competition. Although there is little indication that this will be sufficient to neutralize the pressures exerted on public policy by the economic and electoral implications of the growth of export industries, TNCs and international financial institutions, in part because, as we shall see, the policy leverage of trade unions is being eroded, it is likely to reduce their impact in areas such as tax, trade policy and employment and environmental regulation.

4.   *Priority for securing energy supplies over mitigating climate change*

The increasing dependence of most EU countries on energy imports as energy use increases and domestic energy sources dwindle, combined with the centrality of energy to economic growth and societal functioning in general, increases the economic and electoral incentives for governments to implement more vigorous measures to ensure security of energy supply. This spur to action will be greatly strengthened if official forecasts that oil production will not peak until 2030 are wrong and in fact production peaks before then, as the continued increase in demand for oil combined with falling supply would lead to steadily rising oil prices that would raise price inflation and input costs while reducing non-oil demand and investment, leading to lower levels of economic activity and lower tax revenues, which in turn tend to lead among other things to bigger budget deficits, higher interest rates, higher unemployment, a deterioration in the balance of payments and lower exchange rates.

At the same time there is increasing evidence that climate change is real and that it is caused largely by the use of fossil fuels. This means increasing pressure on governments to take steps to reduce carbon emissions so as to avoid serious environmental and economic problems in the future, which implies increasing pressure on EU and other governments to reduce the use of fossil fuels.

Since economic growth is so vital to the short-term electoral prospects of governments, however, along with providing consumers with cheap energy for their homes and cars, measures to mitigate climate change are likely to be restricted to those that do not significantly constrain economic growth by making energy more expensive. At the same time governments will want to avoid measures that expand energy supply but exacerbate climate change. This means that the policies of choice are likely to be those that contribute both to energy security and to mitigating climate change at the same time, in particular policies designed to improve energy efficiency (as distinct from restricting its use), encourage the development and use of alternative energy sources including nuclear power and renewables, shift passengers and freight to low carbon modes of transport, and encourage the substitution of communications for personal travel.

Ultimately, however, the priority given by EU and other governments to economic growth and re-election means that other policies will also be used to ensure energy security regardless of environmental considerations, such as increasing reserve stocks of fuel and taking steps to secure supplies of fossil fuels through diversifying foreign energy sources and supply routes and increasing diplomatic and military pressure on recalcitrant foreign governments.

What this means is that it is very unlikely that enough will be done to halt climate change. This in turn means that from time to time there will be natural disasters that can be attributed to climate change, each of which will stimulate adoption of more vigorous measures to mitigate climate change providing that these do not significantly obstruct economic growth. It also means that over time increasing pressure from those who are directly disadvantaged by climate change will lead governments to adopt more vigorous measures to adapt to actual changes in the climate, such as by improving flood defences.

5. *More vigorous measures to increase the size and quality of the labour force*

One of the principal implications of population ageing is a reduction in the working-age population as a proportion of the total population. Other things being equal this implies a smaller labour force relative to the population as a whole and therefore lower economic growth and state revenue than would otherwise be the case. For this reason population ageing strengthens the incentives for governments to do what they can to counteract this effect by improving labour productivity and maximizing the size of the labour force. The concern to improve labour productivity, combined with the increasing economic significance of technology and growing unemployment among low-skilled workers, plus the fact that company provision of training is discouraged by the possibility that other firms may poach trained employees, strengthens the incentives for governments to expand education and training, while the desire to increase the size of the labour force strengthens the incentives for governments to implement more vigorous measures to increase fertility, increase the proportion of women working, delay retirement and increase immigration.

6. More vigorous measures to facilitate structural adjustment

The increasing disruption of employment caused by expanding trade and the internationalization of production and finance strengthens the economic and electoral incentives for governments to help employees displaced by these processes by doing more to facilitate structural adjustment. One way of doing this is to provide more help with job search, retraining and financial assistance. Another option, and one that is particularly relevant in view of the fact that unemployment is higher among low-skilled workers, is to expand the supply of low-skilled service jobs by creating more low-skilled caring jobs in public sector social services and/or by facilitating the reduction of wages for workers in areas such as personal services in order to make it cheaper for private employers in these areas to employ more people.

7. More business-friendly policies in general

In addition to the pressures to make public policy more business-friendly in specific areas there is also increasing pressure on governments to implement more business-friendly policies in general.

First, the growth in the proportion of viewers who watch commercial TV increases the proportion of the electorate that is exposed to media messages framed in such a way as to favour business and conservative (pro-business) parties and policies. Although experts in this area stress that media effects on the way that people think are likely to be significant only in the long term, and possibly not even then, to the extent that they do exist they imply a gradual increase in the vote for pro-business parties, other things being equal, and therefore a larger role in government for such parties. More generally the growth of pro-business views in the electorate would be expected to increase the electoral incentives for political parties and governments of all sorts to espouse more pro-business policies, resulting in increasing pressure on public policy to move in a pro-business direction. This media effect would be magnified by the fact that increasing levels of education imply increasing independence of mind on the part of voters and therefore that an increasing proportion of voters are casting their votes on the basis of media coverage of politics rather than habitual party identification. Although the growth of the Internet is likely to offset any pro-business effect to some extent by exposing a greater proportion of the electorate to anti-establishment views not normally carried on mainstream mass media, which would be expected to lead to growing public support for unorthodox policies such as the ones favoured by the anti-globalization movement, this is unlikely to neutralize the otherwise pro-business policy implications of the growth in the proportion of voters who watch commercial TV because news on the Internet as elsewhere is always likely to be dominated by organizations that have abundant resources, which means the state and private companies.

The second reason to think that governments are becoming more likely to implement pro-business policies in general is the declining political leverage of trade unions, the traditional antagonists of employers on labour matters, as a consequence of membership losses due to job losses caused by automation, the decline of manufacturing (union density is lower in most areas of services), the increasing difficulty of organizing workers due to the increasing diversification of work, growing affluence that weakens workers' economic need of unions, rising levels of education that increase independence of mind and thereby undermine union membership and solidarity, increasingly diverse lifestyles that make it less likely that employees will identify strongly with unions, and declining leverage *vis-à-vis* employers due to the fact that the increasing internationalization of production increases the credibility of disinvestment threats by firms. Although there are also ways in which king trends might be expected to strengthen trade unions, their effects are unlikely to be substantial. Rising use of ICT improves union efficacy in areas such as recruitment, communications, coordination of campaigns and dissemination of the union case but this is counterbalanced by the fact that employers can use ICT to their advantage too. Increasing independence of mind among employees due to rising levels of education should make them more prepared to challenge the authority and decisions of employers, but as we have already noted this increasing independence of mind also undermines union membership and solidarity, and in any case it is not clear that employees are in fact becoming more prepared to challenge the boss. The other way in which king trends might be expected to strengthen trade unions is by making employees bolder due to a reduction in unemployment, and in the fear of unemployment, as a consequence of reductions in the size of the labour force due to population ageing. Although it is difficult to compare the magnitudes of the likely positive and negative effects for unions, it seems unlikely that the positive effects will outweigh the negative effects of all the factors listed above, although they should reduce the net erosion in the policy leverage of trade unions to some extent. The net effects of king trends on trade unions are therefore likely to result in decreasing pressure on governments to implement union-friendly policies and decreasing union resistance to the implementation by governments of more business-friendly policies.

The third reason to think that pressure to move public policy in a business-friendly direction in general is increasing is that working class influence on public policy is weakening due to a steady reduction in the proportion of traditional working class voters in the electorate as a consequence of automation and the decline of manufacturing employment. Other things being equal this implies a reduction in the vote for labour parties, a smaller role in government for such parties and diminishing electoral incentives for political parties and governments of all sorts to support the sorts of policies that benefit working class people where these conflict with the interests of employers. The belief that labour parties in particular are shifting to the right is widely shared in EU countries. Again the result is likely to be more business-friendly policies than would otherwise be the case.

To sum up, there are numerous reasons to believe that king trends are pushing governments to step up the implementation of business-friendly policies such as the ones listed in Table 20.2.

Table 20.2   Business-friendly policies

Area	*Examples*
Business in general	Expansion of education and training
	Improvements to infrastructure such as transport and communications links
	Expansion of financial and other assistance, such as tax breaks for R&D
	Cuts in corporate tax and employers' social contributions
	More vigorous steps to secure wage restraint and to reform employment regulation in order to increase labour flexibility
	Cuts in the costs of environmental regulation such as by moving to market instruments, downgrading existing regulation or enforcing it less rigorously
	Extending international economic integration to improve business efficiency by stimulating competition and facilitating economies of scale
	Liberalization of restrictions on the use of genetic tests by insurers and employers
Policies specific to hi-tech firms	Expansion of financial incentives for technology-rich incoming foreign investment
	Adaptation of process and product regulation to facilitate use of new technologies
	Measures to encourage R&D such as grants and tax breaks
	Measures to encourage businesses to use new technologies and to protect business from cybercrime

(Continued)

Table 20.2   (*Continued*)

Area	Examples
Policies specific to the services sector	More services-friendly regulation in relation to education and training, access to government services, technical and generic assistance to small and medium-sized enterprises, tax policy, and direct financial support
Policies specific to exporters and import-competing firms	Measures to open up new markets in foreign countries Measures to strengthen minimum international labour and environmental standards, for example by including them in trade agreements.
Policies specific to TNCs	International agreements to limit locational competition by harmonizing tax regimes, investment regulation, and labour and environmental standards
Policies specific to financial markets	Stress on controlling inflation and support for further international financial liberalization *but* strengthened prudential regulation
Policies specific to the energy and transport sectors	Improving energy security by increasing reserve stocks of fuel and taking steps to secure supplies of fossil fuels through diversifying foreign energy sources and supply routes and increasing pressure on recalcitrant foreign governments Policies designed to improve energy efficiency, encourage alternative energy sources including nuclear power and renewables, shift passengers and freight to low carbon modes of transport, and encourage communications over travel Measures to adapt to actual changes in the climate, such as better flood defences
Labour force size and quality	Measures to increase fertility, increase the proportion of women working, delay retirement, increase immigration and expand education and training
Structural adjustment policies	Increasing help with job search, retraining and financial assistance, plus expansion of low-skilled public sector caring jobs and/or imposition of wage cuts to make it cheaper for private employers to employ people in areas such as personal services

More liberal social policies

8.   *Less church-friendly policies*

Secularization in the form of falling religious affiliation and participation implies falling electoral support for parties of the right, in particular Christian parties, leading to a smaller role in government for these parties as well as dilution of the Christian content of the policies of these and other parties. It also erodes the capacity of churches to mobilize direct action. This in turn implies diminishing pressure on governments to maintain financial and other assistance for churches and church schools and therefore a gradual erosion of state support as time goes on. Secularization also means that more and more people are acting, or wish to act, in ways that contravene traditional Christian morality but do not conflict with widely held secular norms, which strengthens the incentives for governments to remove laws that support or enforce traditional Christian morality in areas such as sexual behaviour, marriage and divorce, abortion, family policy, the role of women, euthanasia and healthcare.

9.   More women-friendly policies

As time goes on the political leverage of women is increasing. The fact that levels of education are rising faster for women than for men implies that the cognitive skills of women are rising relative to men. Increasing numbers of women are working, which means that an increasing proportion of women voters are affected by work-related problems, trade unions pursue women's issues more vigorously as the proportion of female union members and officials increases, and more women are reaching influential positions in government and elsewhere. Governments wishing to maximize the size of the labour force by encouraging larger families are becoming convinced that women are more likely to have children when they are able to combine family and career than when they have to choose between them. And secularization is eroding the political leverage of churches and other policy actors that support the traditional Christian model of women as primarily wives and mothers.

In other words, the capacity of women to pursue their goals is growing, governments increasingly see advantage in making it easier for women to combine work and having a family, and support for the traditional Christian model of the role of women is weakening. This means that over time we should expect governments to implement more women-friendly policies, in the sense of more liberal feminist policies, in areas including reproductive rights (including more liberal laws on abortion), childcare, family law, violence against women, employment regulation, equal rights in general, and the allocation of elected and appointed public positions.

10.   More liberal policies on sexuality

The spread of more liberal attitudes towards sex, reinforced by the weakening of the hold of Christian sexual morality due to secularization, implies increasing electoral support for socially liberal parties, decreasing electoral support for Christian and conservative parties, electorally-motivated moderation of Christian and conservative party policies on sexual regulation, and weakening electoral incentives for governments of all complexions to keep laws enforcing Christian sexual morality. As a consequence we should expect the progressive liberalization of regulation relating to sexual activity, such as the outlawing of discrimination against homosexuals and the extension to unmarried homosexual and heterosexual cohabiting couples of at least some of the legal protections and privileges accorded to married couples in areas such as taxation, inheritance, and division of property when relationships end.

We should also expect wider availability of contraception, better sex education and more liberal abortion laws as governments respond to the tendency of sexual liberalization, in the form of earlier sexual activity, more sexual partners and more sex outside marriage, to increase rates of unplanned pregnancies and sexually-transmitted diseases, including HIV/AIDS, in the context of increasing openness about sex.

11.   More liberal policies on the cloning and genetic modification of humans, and on psychotropic drugs

One of the reasons that human cloning and inheritable genetic modification is illegal throughout the EU is that animal testing shows that these procedures are not safe. As technology develops, however, this is likely to change, thereby increasing the number of would-be parents who would like to take advantage of them. It also seems clear that sooner or later human clones and designer babies will be born whatever the legal situation. Both these developments will increase pressure on governments to legalize the cloning and inheritable genetic modification of humans.

A similar argument applies to psychotropic drugs: as scientists develop an increasing variety of relatively safe psychotropic drugs the number of people who would like to use them for work and/or recreation is likely to increase, leading to increasing pressure on governments to make these drugs legally available.

Increased public spending

12.   Quasi-automatic increases in spending on health, social security and defence

Spending on health, social security and the armed forces has a tendency to increase by itself independent of discretionary decisions made by governments due to the increasing cost of healthcare technology and military technology, the increasing demand for pensions, healthcare and services for older people caused by population ageing and the consequent increase in the political leverage of older people, and the increasing demand for childcare, residential services, community services and home-based care caused by more people living alone or heading single-parent families and therefore lacking a second adult in the household to provide care in the case of illness or injury or, in the case of single parents, childcare.

Other implications

Not all of the likely effects of king trends on public policy imply any particular direction for policy change.

First, technological innovations often elicit regulatory adjustments the specific direction of which cannot be predicted with any confidence. Technological developments in areas such as ICT, biotechnology and healthcare can render existing safety regulation inadequate for its purpose and raise new ethical issues that arouse concern and even hostility on the part of religious and other groups, for example in relation to human cloning. New commercial products and processes made possible by technological developments in areas such as nanotechnology may not be properly covered by existing product and process regulation. More generally, new technologies and their applications may alter the efficacy of existing modes of regulation. Regulation and licensing, for example, are more difficult to apply when businesses providing services via ICT are beyond national jurisdiction.

All these factors stimulate participants in the relevant policy arenas to review, update, extend and transform regulation in order to ensure that new technologies and their applications are adequately covered. International agreements, for example, can ensure that businesses providing cross-border services via ICT are adequately regulated. The problem is that it is not possible in advance to specify the particular policy directions that major regulatory changes will take because the outcomes of struggles over the regulation of technologies are impossible to predict.

Second, a number of king trends have significant positive and negative effects on government popularity but it is impossible to tell whether king trends overall are making governments more or less popular.

Where king trends do make governments more popular, so that office-holders feel more electorally secure and more prepared to take electoral risks, it follows that governments are more likely to implement policies that are more autonomous from the wishes of the electorate and other policy actors than would otherwise be the case. In such circumstances governments are more likely to implement relatively partisan policies – such as nationalization for the left and privatization for the right – as well as policies deemed to be necessary despite being unpopular, such as tax rises. Perhaps the most powerful cause of increasing government popularity is economic growth, the rising incomes and consumption that result and the associated expansion of the tax base that makes it possible for governments to court popularity by increasing spending without raising tax rates and/or by cutting tax rates without cutting spending. King trends that (in general) contribute to government popularity by contributing to economic growth include increasing use of ICT and biotechnology, rising levels of education, the expansion of trade and the internationalization of production and finance. Governments should also benefit electorally through ICT improving the efficiency and effectiveness of government services by enabling better informed policy-making, better communications and coordination, automation of internal government functions, and electronic delivery of services, leading to savings that can be spent on improving services, cutting taxes or reducing budget deficits. Technological innovations should also improve healthcare services, which again should help governments to maintain and possibly improve their electoral standing.

Other king trends, however, make governments less popular, less electorally secure and thereby more likely to make policy concessions to public opinion and to other policy actors as they attempt to shore up their electoral support. Population ageing undercuts economic growth by reducing the size of the working-age population. Spending on health, social security and defence tends to increase by itself, creating a tendency for deficits to emerge that need to be addressed by raising revenue and/or by cutting spending, both of which are unpopular. Increasing affluence puts pressure on governments by raising expectations of government services. Climate change leads to increasing criticism of governments whether they take substantial counter-measures or not. Rising levels of education increase independence of mind and thereby render established parties more vulnerable to big vote losses due to greater questioning and criticism of public policy, lower levels of party identification and higher levels of issue voting. Electoral volatility is further boosted by affluence-related diversification of lifestyles and the associated weakening of class solidarity.

Which of these effects overall is the more powerful? There seems no way of telling, and the answer may well vary over space and time.

There are, however, two developments on the horizon that seem certain to make governments less electorally secure: the energy crisis that starts when oil production peaks, and increasing environmental and economic damage caused by climate change.

Conclusion

The 12 points of the baseline projection of the policy implications of king trends, which are summarized in Table 20.3, constitute a synoptic account of the future directions of policy change insofar as they are determined by major long-term technological, economic, environmental and social trends. This is the first time that such an account has been constructed. The actual future of public policy will differ somewhat from the picture presented here due to the influence of other factors, but if the king trends are correctly specified and the logic is valid it should be similar in many respects. To the extent that it isn't, it should be possible to identify other factors that are blocking or inflecting the pressures exerted by king trends.

Table 20.3 Net policy implications of king trends

General categories	Implications
More assertive security policies	1 More assertive foreign and security policies
	2 More intrusive and internationalized law enforcement
More business-friendly economic policies	3 Increasingly favourable policies towards expanding firms and sectors
	4 Priority for securing energy supplies over mitigating climate change
	5 More vigorous measures to increase the size and quality of the labour force
	6 More vigorous measures to facilitate structural adjustment
	7 More business-friendly policies in general
More liberal social policies	8 Less church-friendly policies
	9 More women-friendly policies
	10 More liberal policies on sexuality
	11 More liberal policies on the cloning and inheritable genetic modification of humans, and on psychotropic drugs
Increased public spending	12 Quasi-automatic increases in spending on health, social security and defence

The significance of this account is not so much in any particular finding about how king trends are likely to affect public policy, as many of these are already well-known, but in the fact that it provides for the first time a holistic picture of the long-term parameters of policy change that need to be taken into account in any serious thinking about where public policy is going or ought to go.

References

Adams, James (2001), 'Virtual defense', *Foreign Affairs* 80(3), May–June.

Agrafiotis, Dimosthenis, Elli Ionnadi and Panagiota Mandi (2004), 'Greece', in Francoeur, *The International Encyclopedia of Sexuality*.

Airforce Technology (2005), 'Eurofighter Typhoon Multi-role Combat Fighter, Europe', <www.airforce-technology.com/projects/ef2000/> [4 Feb. 2005].

Albers, Jens and Guy Standing (2000), 'Social dumping, catch-up or convergence?: Europe in a comparative global context', *Journal of European Social Policy* 10(2): 99–119.

Aliaga, Christel and Karin Winqvist (2003), 'How women and men spend their time: results from 13 European countries', <epp.eurostat.cec.eu.int/cache/ITY_OFFPUB/KS-NK-03-012/EN/KS-NK-03-012-EN.PDF> [12 Feb. 2005].

Allison, Graham (2004), 'How to stop nuclear terror', *Foreign Affairs* 83(1), Jan.–Feb.

Andersen (2002), *Outlook of the Development of Technologies and Markets for the European Audio-Visual Sector up to 2010*, <europa.eu.int/comm/avpolicy/stat/tvoutlook/tvoutlook_finalreport_short.pdf> [3 Apr. 2004].

Anderson, Kevin (2002), 'US "fears al-Qaeda attack"', BBC News Online, 27 June, <news.bbc.co.uk/1/low/sci/tech/2070706.stm> [7 July 2004].

Anton, P.S., R. Silberglitt and J. Schneider (2001), *The Global Technology Revolution*, National Defense Institute, RAND.

Aoyama, Yuko and Manuel Castells (2002), 'An empirical assessment of the informational society: employment and occupational structures of G-7 countries, 1920–2000', *International Labour Review* 141(1–2): 123–59.

Archick, Kristin (2004), 'Cybercrime: the Council of Europe Convention', *CRS Report for Congress* RS21208, <www.fas.org/irp/crs/RS21208.pdf> [16 Oct. 2004].

Arquilla, John (2003), 'What's next for war?', in Zolli, *Catalog of Tomorrow*.

ASLME (American Society for Law, Medicine and Ethics) (2004), 'DNA fingerprinting and civil liberties project', project funded by the National Human Genome Institute of the NIH, <www.aslme.org/dna_04/description.php> [29 Jan. 2005].

Bagdikian, Ben H. (1990), *The Media Monopoly*, 3rd edn, Boston: Beacon Press: 4–5, cited in W.A. Meier and J. Trappel (1998), 'Media concentration and the public interest', in *Media Policy*, ed. D. McQuail and K. Siune, London: Sage.

Banister, David (2002), *Transport Planning*, 2nd edn, London: Spon Press.

Barnaby, Frank (2003), *How to Build a Nuclear Bomb and Other Weapons of Mass Destruction*, London: Granta.

Barrett, Michael, Alan King, Joseph Lévy, Eleanor Maticka-Tyndale and Alexander McKay (1997), 'Canada', in Francoeur, *The International Encyclopedia of Sexuality*.

BATA (British Air Transport Association) (2001), *The Future of Aviation: Response by the British Air Transport Association*, <www.bata.uk.com/documents/The%20Future%20of%20Aviation.pdf> [6 Mar. 2004].

BATA (2003), 'Air transport and the environment', <www.bata.uk.com/environment.htm> [6 Mar. 2004].

Baylis, John, James Wirtz, Eliot Cohen and Colin S. Gray (2002), *Strategy in the Contemporary World*, Oxford: Oxford University Press.

Bazen, S. and J.M. Cardebat (2001), 'The impact of trade on the relative wages and employment of low skill workers in France', abstract, *Applied Economics* 33(6): 801–10.

BBC News (2003), 'Where supermarkets stand on GM foods', 21 Oct., <news.bbc.co.uk/1/hi/uk/3211510.stm> [29 Feb. 2004].

Bell, D. (2002), *French Politics Today*, Manchester: Manchester University Press.

Bella, M. and B. Quintieri, 'The effect of trade on employment and wages in Italian industry', abstract, *Labour* [Italy], 14(2): 291–310.

Bellamy, Christine (2002), 'From automation to knowledge management: modernizing British government with ICTs', *International Review of Administrative Sciences* 68: 213–30.

Benson, J.K. (1982), 'A framework for policy analysis', in *Interorganizational Coordination: Theory, Research and Implementation*, eds D.L. Rogers and D. Whetten, Ames: Iowa State University Press.

Bernauer, Thomas and Erika Meins (2003), 'Technological revolution meets policy and the market: explaining cross-national differences in agricultural biotechnology regulation', *European Journal of Political Research* 42: 643–83.

Betts, Richard K. (1998), 'The new threat of mass destruction', *Foreign Affairs* 77(1), Jan.–Feb.

Biddle, Stephen (2002), 'Land warfare: theory and practice', in Baylis *et al.*, *Strategy in the Contemporary World*.

Bimber, Bruce (1998), 'The Internet and political transformation: populism, community and accelerated pluralism', *Polity* 31(1).

Binstock, R.H. and C.L. Day (1996), 'Aging and politics', in *Handbook of Aging and the Social Sciences*, eds R.H. Binstock and L.K. George, San Diego: The Academic Press.

BIO (Biotechnology Industry Organization) (2003), *Issues and Alternatives: Food and Agriculture*, <www.bio.org/foodag/> [23 Oct. 2003].

BIO (2003a), *Agricultural Production Applications*, <www.bio.org/er/agriculture.asp> [23 Oct. 2003].

BIO (2003b), *Transgenic Animals: Frequently Asked Questions*, <www.bio.org/animals/faq.asp> [23 Oct. 2003].

Biotechnology Roundtable (2003), <www.biotechroundtable.org/industry.htm> [25 Oct. 2003].

BIS (Bank of International Settlements) (2002), *Triennial Central Bank Survey: Foreign Exchange and Derivatives Market Activity in 2001*, <www.bis.org/publ/rpfx02t.pdf> [22 Sept. 2004].

BIS (2004), *Derivatives Statistics*, <www.bis.org/statistics/derstats.htm> [29 Sept. 2004].

BIS (2004a), 'G10 central bank governors and heads of supervision endorse the publication of the revised capital framework', *BIS Press Release*, 26 June, <www.bis.org/cgi-bin/print.cgi> [25 Sept. 2004].

Blair, Bruce (2001), 'What if the terrorists go nuclear?', <www.cdi.org/terrorism/nuclear-pr.cfm> [28 June 2004].

Blow, Laura, Andrew Leicester and Zoë Oldfield (2004), *Consumption Trends in the UK, 1975–99*, London: Institute of Fiscal Studies.

Bond, John and Peter Coleman (1993), 'Ageing into the twenty-first century', in *Ageing in Society*, eds John Bond, Peter Coleman and Sheila Pearce, London: Sage.

Bonoli, Giuliano (2000), *The Politics of Pension Reform*, Cambridge: Cambridge University Press.

Boot, Max (2003), 'The new American way of war', *Foreign Affairs* 82(4), July–Aug.

Brant, K. and K. Siune (1998), 'Politicization in decline?', in *Media Policy*, eds D. McQuail and K. Siune, London: Sage.

Branwyn, G. (2003), 'Cyborgs: are we assimilated yet?', in Zolli, *Catalog of Tomorrow*.

Bratton, Kathleen A. and Leonard P. Ray (2002), 'Descriptive representation, policy outcomes, and municipal day-care coverage in Norway', *American Journal of Political Science* 46(2): 428–37.

Brett, Michael (2000), *How to Read the Financial Pages*, 5th edn, London: Random House.

Brierley, Peter (1999), *UK Christian Handbook: Religious Trends 2, 2000/01*, London: Christian Research.

Brierley, Peter (2002), *Religious Trends 4, 2003/04*, London: Christian Research, <www.christian-research.org.uk/intro.htm> [12 Mar. 2004].

British Social Attitudes: 20th Report (2003), London: Sage, cited in *The Independent*, 9 Dec. 2003: 10.

Brockerhoff, Martin P. (2000), 'An urbanizing world', *Population Bulletin* 55(3), <www.prb.org/Template.cfm?Section=PRB&template=/ContentManagement/ContentDisplay.cfm&ContentID=9829> [24 Oct. 2004].

Broderick, A. (2002), *Emerging Environmental and Industrial Applications of Biotechnology*, Summary, SRI Consulting Business Intelligence, <www.sric-bi.com/BIP/summaries/2385.shtml> [25 Oct. 2003].

Brooks, Rodney A. (2002), *Robot: the Future of Flesh and Machine*, London: Penguin.

Bruck, Peter A., Dieter Dörr, Mark D. Cole, Jacques Favre, Sigve Gramstad, Maria Rosaria Monaco and Zrinjka Peruško Čulek (2004), *Transnational Media Concentrations in Europe*, report for the Council of Europe, <odin.dep.no/filarkiv/228985/Report_transnational_media_concentrations.pdf> [21 June 2005].

BTWC (Biological and Toxin Weapons Convention website) (2004), <www.opbw.org/> [3 July 2004].

Bud, Robert (1995), 'In the engine of industry: regulators of biotechnology, 1970–86', in *Resistance to New Technology: Nuclear Power, Information Technology and Biotechnology*, ed. Martin Bauer, Cambridge: Cambridge University Press.

Burch, Martin (1997), 'The United Kingdom', in *Cabinets in Western Europe*, 2nd edn, eds Jean Blondel and Ferdinand Müller-Rommel, London: Macmillan.

Burgess, Mark (2002), 'A nuclear 9/11: imminent or inflated threat?', <www.cdi.org/nuclear/nuclear-terror-pr.cfm> [28 June 2004].

Burgess, Mark (2003), 'Pascal's new wager: the dirty bomb threat heightens', <www.cdi.org/nuclear/dirty-bomb-pr.cfm> [28 June 2004].

Burnett, R. (1996), *The Global Jukebox*, London and New York: Routledge.

Busse, M. (2004), 'Trade, environmental regulations and the WTO – new empirical evidence', *Journal of World Trade* 38(2): 285–306.

Bynner, John, Peter Dolton, Leon Feinstein, Gerry Makepeace, Lars Malmberg and Laura Wood (2003), *Revisiting the Benefits of Higher Education*, Bedford Group for Lifecourse and Statistical Studies, Institute of Education, <www.hefce.ac.uk/Pubs/RDreports/2003/rd05_03/> [9 Aug. 2005].

Cabinet Office Strategy Unit (2000), *The Future and How to Think About It*, <www.cabinet-office.gov.uk/innovation/2000/strategic/future.shtml> [19 May 2003].

Campbell, Duncan (2000), 'Inside Echelon', Heise Online, <www.heise.de/tp/english/inhalt/te/6929/1.html> [4 July 2004].

Carpenter, Chad (2001), 'Businesses, green groups and the media: the role of non-governmental organisations in the climate change debate', *International Affairs* 77: 313–28.

Castells, Manuel (2000), *The Rise of the Network Society*, 2nd edn, Oxford: Blackwell.

Castells, Manuel (2001), *The Internet Galaxy*, Oxford: Oxford University Press.

CBACI (Chemical and Biological Arms Control Institute), *Bioterrorism in the United States: Threat, Preparedness and Response*, <www.cbaci.org/> [28 June 2004].

CDI (Center for Defense Information) (2003), 'The world's nuclear arsenals', <www.cdi.org/issues/nukef&f/database/nukearsenals.cfm> [28 June 2004].

CERT (2001), 'Home network security', <www.cert.org/tech_tips/home_networks.html> [5 July 2004].

CERT (2002), 'Overview of attack trends', <www.cert.org/archive/pdf/attack_trends.pdf> [9 July 2004].

CERT (2003), 'CERT/CC overview: incident and vulnerability trends', <www.cert.org/present/cert-overview-trends/module-2.pdf> [5 July 2004].

CERT (2004), 'Frequently asked questions about malicious web scripts redirected by web sites', <www.cert.org/tech_tips/malicious_code_FAQ.html> [6 July 2004].

CGS (Center for Genetics and Society) (2003), 'Reproductive cloning arguments', <www.genetics-and-society.org/technologies/cloning/reproarguments.html> [20 Jan. 2005].

CGS (2003a), 'Inheritable genetic modification: arguments pro and con', <www.genetics-and-society.org/technologies/igm/arguments.html> [20 Jan. 2005].

CGS (2004), 'Therapy versus enhancement', <www.genetics-and-society.org/technologies/igm/therapy.html> [20 Jan. 2005].

Chennells, Lucy and Rachel Griffiths (1997), *Taxing Profit in a Changing World*, London: Institute for Fiscal Studies.

CIA (Central Intelligence Agency) (2000), *Global Trends 2015: A Dialogue About the Future with Nongovernment Experts*, <www.cia.gov/cia/publications/globaltrends2015/index.html> [24 May 2003].

Cleaver, Harry M. (1998), 'The Zapatista effect: the Internet and the rise of an alternative political fabric', *Journal of International Affairs* 51(2).

Cohen, Eliot (1996) 'A revolution in warfare', *Foreign Affairs* 75(2), Mar.–Apr.

Cohen, Eliot (2002), 'Technology and warfare', in Baylis *et al.*, *Strategy in the Contemporary World*.

Cohen, Robin and Shirin M. Rai (2000), *Global Social Movements*, London: The Athlone Press, cited in Castells, *The Internet Galaxy*: 143.

Coleman, William D. (2003), 'Governing global finance: financial derivatives, liberal states and transformative capacity', in *States in the Global Economy*, ed. Linda L. Weiss, Cambridge: Cambridge University Press.

Compston, Hugh (ed.) (1996), *The New Politics of Unemployment*, London: Routledge.

Compston, Hugh (2002), 'The direction of public policy in Western Europe: an advocacy coalition approach', *European Politics and Area Studies Seminar Paper*, Cardiff University.

Compston, Hugh (2004), 'Introduction: the nature of public policy in Britain, France and Germany', in Compston, *Handbook of Public Policy in Europe*.

Compston, Hugh (ed.) (2004a), *Handbook of Public Policy in Europe: Britain, France and Germany*, London: Palgrave Macmillan.

Coombs, W.T. and S.J. Holladay (1995), 'The emerging political power of the elderly', in *Handbook of Communication and Aging Research*, eds J.F. Nussbaum and J. Coupland, Hove: Lawrence Erlbaum Associates.

Council of Europe (1997), *Convention for the Protection of Human Rights and Dignity of the Human Being with Regard to the Application of Biology and Medicine: Convention on Human Rights and Biomedicine*, <conventions.coe.int/treaty/en/treaties/html/164.htm> [25 Jan. 2005].

Council of Europe (1998), *Recent Demographic Developments in Europe*, Strasbourg: Council of Europe.

Council of Europe (2000), *Report on Media Pluralism in the Digital Environment*, <www.coe.int/T/E/Human_Rights/media/4_Documentary_Resources/CDMM(2000)pde_en.asp> [5 Dec. 2005].

Council of the European Union (2003), *Joint Report by the Commission and the Council on Adequate and Sustainable Pensions*, <europa.eu.int/comm/employment_social/social_protection/docs/cs7165_03_en.pdf> [18 July 2005].

Cowling, K. and R. Sugden (1996), 'Capacity, transnational and industrial strategy', in *Creating Industrial Capacity*, eds J. Michie and J. Grieve-Smith, Oxford: Oxford University Press, cited in Held *et al.*, *Global Transformations*: 276–77.

Croteau, D. and W. Hoynes (2001), *The Business of Media*, California: Pine Forge Press.

Crouch, Colin (1999), *Social Change in Western Europe*, Oxford: Oxford University Press.

Crouch, Colin (2000), 'The quiet continent: religion and politics in Europe', in *Religion and Democracy*, eds David Marquand and Ronald L. Nettler, Oxford: Oxford University Press.

CSGC (Center for the Study of Global Christianity) (2003), *World Christian Database*, <worldchristiandatabase.org/wcd/> [5 Sept. 2005].

Cuyvers, L., M. Dumont, G. Rayp and K. Stevens (2002), 'International trade with newly industrialised countries: impact on wages and employment within the European Union', abstract, *Economisch en sociaaal tijdschrift* 56(2): 153–80.

Dalton, R.J., S.C. Flanagan and P.A. Beck (1984), 'Political forces and partisan change', in *Electoral Change in Advanced Industrial Democracies*, eds R.J. Dalton, S.C. Flanagan and P.A. Beck, Princeton: Princeton University Press.

Dalton, Russell J. (2002), 'Political cleavages, issues and electoral change', in *Comparing Democracies 2*, eds Lawrence LeDuc, Richard G. Niemi and Pippa Norris, London: Sage.

Davis, Malcolm R. and Colin S. Gray (2002), 'Weapons of mass destruction', in Baylis *et al.*, *Strategy in the Contemporary World*.

Daykin, C.D., D.A. Akers, A.S. Macdonald, T. McGleenan, D. Paul and P.J. Turvey (2003), 'Genetics and insurance – some policy issues', paper presented to the Institute of Actuaries, 24 Feb., <www.ukfgi.org.uk/Sessional%20Paper.pdf> [27 Jan. 2005].

De Bens, E. and H. Østbye (1998), 'The European newspaper market', in *Media Policy*, eds D. McQuail and K. Siune, London: Sage.

De Graaf, N.D. and A. Need (2000), 'Losing faith: is Britain alone?', in *British Social Attitudes: the 17th Report*, eds R. Jowell, J. Curtice, A. Park, K. Thomson, L. Jarvis, C. Bromley and N. Stratford, London: Sage.

Denver, D. (2003), *Elections and Voters in Britain*, Basingstoke: Palgrave.

Department of Defense Directive 3600.1 (undated), cited in Hildreth, 'Cyberwarfare': 17.

Department of Health (2003), *Our Inheritance, Our Future: Realising the Potential of Genetics in the NHS*, <www.dh.gov.uk/assetRoot/04/01/92/39/04019239.pdf> [20 Jan. 2005].

DERA (Defence Evaluation and Research Agency) (2001), *The Future Strategic Context of Defence*, <ww.mod.uk/issues/strategic_context/index.htm> [24 May 2003].

DERA (2001a), *Strategic Futures Thinking: Meta-Analysis of Published Material on Drivers and Trends*, Ministry of Defence, DERA/DSTL/CROO979/2.0, <www.number-10.gov.uk/su/strategic%20futures/meta.pdf> [24 May 2003].

DERA (undated), 'The economic dimension', in *The Future Strategic Context of Defence*, Ministry of Defence, <www.mod.uk/issues/strategic_context.economic.htm> [24 May 2003].

DfT (Department for Transport) (2000), 'Transport Ten Year Plan 2000: background analysis', <www.dft.gov.uk/stellent/groups/dft_transstrat/documents/page/dft_tran sstrat_503943.hcsp> [6 Mar. 2004].

DfT (2003), 'British shipping: charting a new course', <www.dft.gov.uk/stellent/groups/dft_shipping/documents/page/dft_shipping_505251.hcsp> [8 Mar. 2004].

DfT (2003a), 'Key facts – aviation in the UK', from *The Future of Air Transport*, <www.dft.gov.uk/aviation/whitepaper/key/pdf/aviation_uk.pdf> [8 Mar. 2004].

DfT (2003b), '*The Future of Air Transport* – summary', <www.dft.gov.uk/aviation/whitepaper/summary/index.htm> [8 Mar. 2004].

DHHS (Department of Health and Human Services) (2001), *Stem Cells: Scientific Progress and Future Research Directions*, <www.nih.gov/news/stemcells/scireport.htm> [30 Oct. 2003].

Diamond, W.J. and R.B. Freeman (2002), 'Will unionism prosper in cyberspace? The promise of the Internet for employee organization', *British Journal of Industrial Relations* 40(3): 569–96.

Dicken, Peter (2003), *Global Shift*, London: Sage.

Dobbelaere, Karel (2002), *Secularisation: An Analysis at Three Levels*, Brussels: PIE-Peter Lang.

Docteur, Elizabeth and Howard Oxley (2004), 'Health-system reform: lessons from experience', in OECD, *Towards High-Performing Health Systems: Policy Studies*, Paris: OECD.

Doherty, Brian, Matthew Paterson, Alexandra Plows and Derek Wall (2003), 'Explaining the fuel protests', *British Journal of Politics and International Relations* 5(1): 1–23.

Dølvik, Jon-Erik and Jeremy Waddington (2002), 'Private sector services: challenges to European trade unions', *Transfer* 3/02: 356–76.

Donovan, Michael (2001), 'The mass casualty threat of biological and chemical warfare agents', Center for Defense Information, Washington DC, cited in Newhouse, 'Assessing the threats': 53–4.

Dowding, Keith (1995), 'Model or metaphor?: A critical review of the policy network approach', *Political Studies* 43: 136–58.

Doyle, Gillian (2002), *Media Ownership*, London: Sage.

Doyle, Gillian (2002a), *Understanding Media Economics*, London: Sage.

Drenth, Jelto J. and A. Koos Slob (2001), 'Netherlands and the Autonomous Dutch Antilles', in Francoeur, *The International Encyclopedia of Sexuality*.

DTI (Department of Trade and Industry) (2003), 'Frequently Asked Questions', <www.foresight.gov.uk/servlet/Controller/ver=1458/userid=2/> [7 June 2003].

DTI (2003a), *UK BioPortal*, <www.i-bio.gov.uk/UkBioportal/Beginners/html/biotechnology.html> [19 October 2003].

DTI (2004), *UK Biotechnology Regulatory Atlas*, <www.dti.gov.uk/ibioatlas> [29 Feb. 2004].

Dunkley, Graham (2004), *Free Trade*, London: Zed Books.

Dunning, John (1993), *Multinational Enterprises and the Global Economy*, Wokingham: Addison-Wesley.

Dunning, John (2000), 'Globalisation and the new geography of foreign direct investment', in *The Political Economy of Globalisation*, ed. Ngaire Woods, London: Macmillan.

EAO (European Audiovisual Observatory) (2001), *2001 Statistical Yearbook: Film, Television, Video and New Media in Europe*, Strasbourg: Council of Europe.

Eatwell, John, and Lance Taylor (2000), *Global Finance at Risk*, Cambridge: Polity.

Ebbinghaus, Bernhard, and Jelle Visser (2000), *Trade Unions in Western Europe since 1945*, London: Macmillan.

ECMT (European Conference of Ministers of Transport) (2003), *Trends in the Transport Sector 1970–2001*, <www.cemt.org/pub/pubpdf/Depl7001E.pdf> [24 February 2004].

ECOFIN (Economic and Financial Affairs Council) (2002), *2471st Council Meeting, Brussels, 3 December 2002*, <ue.eu.int/ueDocs/cms_Data/docs/pressData/en/ecofin/73473.pdf> [14 Nov. 2005].

EEA (European Environment Agency) (2001a), 'Household number and size, 2001', <themes.eea.eu.int/Sectors_and_activities/households/indicators/consumption/index_html> [3 May 2004].

EEA (2001b), 'Indicator Fact Sheet Signals 2001 – Chapter Households', <themes.eea.eu.int/Sectors_and_activities/households/indicators/consumption/hh03householdnumbersize.pdf> [3 May 2004].

EEA (2002), *Hazardous Waste Generation in EEA Member Countries*, <reports.eea.eu.int/topic_report_2001_14/en> [30 June 2005].

EEA (2003), *Europe's Environment: the Third Assessment*, <reports.eea.eu.int/environmental_assessment_report_2003_10/en> [30 June 2005].

EEA (2004), 'Transport and environment in Europe', *EEA Briefing* 2004/03, <reports.eea.eu.int/briefing_2004_3/en> [2 Mar. 2005].

EEA (2004a), *EEA Signals 2004*, <reports.eea.eu.int/signals-2004/en> [30 June 2005].

EEA (2004b), *Greenhouse Gas Emission Trends and Projections in Europe 2004*, <reports.eea.eu.int/eea_report_2004_5/en/tab_content_RLR> [24 Feb. 2005].

EEA (2004c), *Waste and Material Flows 2004*, <waste.eionet.eu.int/reports/wp2_2004> [30 June 2005].

EFPIA (European Federation of Pharmaceutical Industries and Associations) (2003), *The Pharmaceutical Industry in Figures*, <www.efpia.org/6_publ/Infigures2003.pdf> [3 Mar. 2004].

EIRO (European Industrial Relations Observatory) (2004), 'Trade union membership 1993–2003', <www.eiro.eurofound.eu.int/2004/03/update/tn0403105u.html> [1 Dec. 2004].

El Baradei, Mohamed (2004), 'Nuclear power: a look at the future', *Statements of the Director General*, International Atomic Energy Agency, <www.iaea.org/NewsCenter/Statements/2004/ebsp2004n005.html> [24 Feb. 2005].

Elfring, T. (1988), *Service Employment in Advanced Economies*, Aldershot: Gower.

Elvins, Martin (2003), 'Europe's response to transnational organized crime', in *Transnational Organised Crime: Perspectives on Global Security*, eds Adam Edwards and Peter Gill, London and New York: Routledge.

EMCDDA (European Monitoring Centre for Drugs and Drug Addiction) (2002), *2002 Annual Report on the State of the Drugs Problem in the European Union and Norway*, <annualreport.emcdda.eu.int/en/page24-en.html> [17 July 2003].

Entman, Robert (2002), 'Framing: towards clarification of a fractured paradigm', in *McQuail's Reader in Mass Communication Theory*, ed. Denis McQuail, London: Sage, reprinted from *Journal of Communication* 43(4), 1993: 51–8.

Entorf, Horst and Hannes Spengler (2002), *Crime in Europe: Causes and Consequences*, Berlin: Springer.

EPC (Economic Policy Committee) (2001), *Budgetary Challenges Posed by Ageing Populations*, <www.efrp.org/downloads/eu_publications/ Budgetary_challenges.pdf> [13 May 2004].

EPO (European Patent Office) (2001), 'Trilateral Statistical Report', <www.european-patent-office.org/tws/tsr.2001> [24 Mar. 2002].

Esping-Andersen, Gøsta (1996), 'After the Golden Age? Welfare state dilemmas in a global economy', in *Welfare States in Transition*, ed. Gøsta Esping-Andersen, London: Sage.

Esping-Andersen, Gøsta (1999), *Social Foundations of Postindustrial Economies*, Oxford: Oxford University Press.

ETC (Action Group on Erosion, Technology and Concentration) (2001), 'New enclosures', *ETC Communique* 73, <www.etcgroup.org/documents/NewEnclosuresFinal.pdf> [28 Feb. 2004].

EurActive (2005), 'EU post-2012 climate change policy', Monday 4 July, <www.euractiv.com/Article?tcmuri=tcm:29-137310-16&type=LinksDossier> [4 July 2005].

Eurobarometer 58.0, 2nd edn: 21 Mar. 2003, <europa.eu.int/comm/public_opinion/archives/eb/ebs_177_en.pdf> [28 Feb. 2004].

Europa (2001), 'Environment: introduction', <europa.eu.int/scadplus/leg/en/lvb/l28066.htm> [21 Apr. 2005].

Europa (2003), 'Employment rights and work organisation', <europa.eu.int/scadplus/leg/en/cha/c00005.htm> [21 Apr. 2005].

EuropaBIO (2003), 'Biotech in figures', <www.europabio.org/documents/EY2003 report.pdf> [17 Dec. 2004].

European Commission (2000), 'Economic impacts of genetically modified crops on the agri-food sector', Directorate-General for Agriculture Working Paper, <europa.eu.int/comm./agriculture/public/gmo/ch4.htm> [28 Feb. 2004].

European Commission (2000a), 'Trade and investment: exploring the issues relating to trade and investment', <europa.eu.int/comm./trade/issues/sectoral/investment/conswtoag_inv.htm> [27 Aug. 2004].

European Commission (2001), *European Transport Policy for 2010: A Time to Decide*, <europa.eu.int/comm/energy_transport/library/orientations-lb-en.pdf> [8 Mar. 2004].

European Commission (2002), *The Social Situation in the European Union 2002 in Brief*, <europa.eu.int/comm/employment_social/news/2002/jun/inbrief_en.pdf> [23 Oct. 2004].

European Commission (2002a), 'Innovation and competitiveness in European biotechnology', *Enterprise Papers 7*, <europa.eu.int/comm/enterprise/library/enterprise-papers/pdf/enterprise_paper_07_2002.pdf> [17 Dec. 2004].

European Commission (2003), *Energy and Transport in Figures 2003*, <europa.eu.int/comm/dgs/energy_transport/figures/pocketbook/index_en.htm> [24 Feb. 2004].

European Commission (2003a), *European Energy and Transport: Trends to 2030*, <europa.eu.int/comm/dgs/energy_transport/figures/trends_2030/1_pref_en.pdf> [20 Feb. 2004].

European Commission (2003b), *The Social Situation in the European Union 2003*, <europa.eu.int/comm/employment_social/social_situation/socsit_en.htm> [23 Sept. 2005].

European Commission (2003c), *Report on Human Embryonic Stem Cell Research*, Commission Staff Working Paper SEC(2003) 441, <europa.eu.int/comm/research/conferences/2003/bioethics/pdf/sec2003-441report_en.pdf> [27 Jan. 2005].

European Commission (2004), 'Protecting privacy and fighting spam', <europa.eu.int/information_society/doc/factsheets/024-privacy_spam-october04.pdf> [29 Nov. 2004].

European Commission (2004a), 'A three-pronged approach to the Information Society', <europa.eu.int/information_society/doc/factsheets/002-3pillars-october04.pdf> [29 Nov. 2004].

European Commission (2004b), 'Towards 2010: renewing Europe's Information Society Policy', <europa.eu.int/information_society/doc/factsheets/006-eeurope_next-november04-1.pdf> [29 Nov. 2004].

European Commission (2004c), 'Intellectual property: introduction', <europa.eu.int/scadplus/leg/en/lvb/126021.htm> [30 Nov. 2004].

European Commission (2004d), 'Maritime transport', <europa.eu.int/comm/transport/maritime/index_en.htm> [25 Feb. 2004].

European Commission (2004e), 'Overview of air transport', <europa.eu/int/comm/transport/air/index_en.htm> [8 Mar. 2004].

European Commission (2004f), 'Air transport and the environment', <europa.eu/int/comm/transport/air/environment/index_en.htm> [8 Mar. 2004].

European Commission (2004g), 'Air transport', <europa.eu/int/comm/transport/air/rules/competition_en.htm> [8 Mar. 2004].

European Commission (2004h), *Energy and Transport in Figures 2004*, <europa.eu.int/ comm/dgs/energy_transport/figures/pocketbook/2004_en.htm> [28 Feb. 2005].

European Commission (2004i), *European Energy and Transport Scenarios on Key Drivers*, <europa.eu.int/comm/dgs/energy_transport/figures/scenarios/index_en.htm> [2 Mar. 2005].

European Commission (2004j), *Employment in Europe 2004*, <europa.eu.int/comm/ employment_social/employment_analysis/employ_2004_en.htm> [11 Mar. 2005].

European Commission (2004k), *Trade FAQs*, <europa.eu.int/comm/trade/gentools/ faqs_en.htm> [21 August 2004].

European Commission (2004l), 'A common EU approach to the fight against organised transational crime', <europa.eu.int/comm./justice_home/fsj/crime/fsj_crime_ intro_en.htm> [13 Oct. 2004].

European Commission (2004m), 'Financial Services Action Plan (FSAP)', <europa.eu.int/scadplus/printvbersion/en/lvb/124210.htm> [25 May 2005].

European Commission (2004n), 'Questions and answers on emissions trading and National Allocation Plans', <europa.eu.int/rapid/pressReleasesAction.do? reference= MEMO/04/44&format=HTML&aged=1&language=EN&guiLanguage=en> [4 July 2005].

European Commission (2004o), *The Social Situation in the European Union 2004*, <europa.eu.int/comm/employment_social/news/2004/oct/socsit_2004_en.pdf> [18 July 2005].

European Commission (2005), *Statistical Annex of European Economy*, <europa.eu. int/comm/economy_finance/publications/statistical_en.htm> [4 Apr. 2005].

European Commission (2005a), 'Excessive deficit procedure', <europa.eu.int/comm/ economy_finance/about/activities/sgp/edp_en.htm#top> [4 May 2005].

European Commission (2005b), 'EU policy and law: Value Added Tax', <www. eurunion.org/legislat/VATweb.htm#Background> [5 May 2005].

European Commission (2005c), 'Harmful tax competition', <europa.eu.int/comm/ taxation_customs/taxation/company_tax/harmful_tax_practices/index_en.htm> [5 May 2005].

European Commission (2005d), 'European competition policy: a brief overview – state aid control', <europa.eu.int/comm/competition/state_aid/overview/> [7 May 2005].

European Commission (2005e), 'Why the European Union?' <europa.eu.int/abc/ 12lessons/index1_en.htm> [10 May 2005].

European Commission (2005f), 'Overview of the European Union activities: internal market', <europa.eu.int/pol/singl/overview_en.htm> [12 May 2005].

European Commission (2005g), *Winning the Battle Against Global Climate Change*, <europa.eu.int/comm/environment/climat/pdf/comm_en_050209.pdf> [3 July 2005].

European Commission (2005h), 'Greenhouse gas emissions in the Community', <europa.eu.int/comm/environment/climat/gge_press.htm> [3 July 2005].

European Commission (2005i), *Key Data on Education in Europe 2005*, <www. eurydice.org/Documents/cc/2005/en/FrameSet.htm> [2 Aug. 2005].

European Council (2003), 'EU strategy against proliferation of weapons of mass destruction', <ue.eu.int/uedocs/cmsUpload/st15708.en03.pdf> [4 Feb. 2005].

European Foundation (European Foundation for the Improvement of Living and Working Conditions) (2001), *Employment Status and Working Conditions: Summary*, <www.eurofound.eu.int/publications/files/EF0283EN.pdf> [2 Dec. 2004].

European Foundation (2003), 'The future of IT – now it's getting personal', *Sector Futures*, <www.eurofound.eu.int> [24 Aug. 2003].

European Foundation (2003a), 'Time and work: duration of work', <www. eurofound.eu.int/publications/files/EF0211EN.pdf> [2 Dec. 2004].

European Parliament (2004), 'Biotechnology industry', *European Parliament Fact Sheets* 4.7.9, <www.europarl.eu.int/facts/4_7_9_en.htm> [14 Dec. 2004].

Europol (2003), *2003 European Union Organised Crime Report*, <www.europol.eu.int/ index.asp?page=publications&language=> [8 Dec. 2005].

Europol (2004a), 'Trafficking in human beings 2004', <www.europol.eu.int/index.asp? page=publications&language=> [11 Oct. 2004].

Europol (2004b), 'Motor vehicle crime 2004', <www.europol.eu.int/index.asp? page=publications&language=> [11 Oct. 2004].

Europol (2004c), 'Illegal immigration 2004', <www.europol.eu.int/index.asp?page= publications&language=> [11 Oct. 2004].

Europol (2004d), 'Financial and property crime 2004', <www.europol.eu.int/ index.asp? page=publications&language=> [11 Oct. 2004].

Eurostat (2002), *Eurostat Yearbook 2002*, Luxembourg: Office for Official Publications of the European Communities.

Eurostat (2002a), *European Union Foreign Direct Investment Yearbook 2001*, <epp. eurostat.cec.eu.int/cache/ITY_OFFPUB/KS-BK-02-001/EN/KS-BK-02-001-EN.PDF> [14 Apr. 2005].

Eurostat (2002b), *The Social Situation in the European Union 2002*, <europa.eu.int/ comm/employment_social/social_situation/docs/SSR2002_en.pdf> [8 May 2004].

Eurostat (2003), 'Inequality of income distribution', <europa.eu.int/comm/eurostat/ Public/datashop/print-catalogue/EN?catalogue=Eurostat> [8 July 2003].

Eurostat (2003a), *Statistics on the Information Society in Europe 2003*, <europa.eu. int/comm/enterprise/ict/studies/is-stat-96-02.pdf> [30 Nov. 2004].

Eurostat (2003b), *Cinema, TV and Radio in the EU: Statistics on Audiovisual Services*, <epp.eurostat.cec.eu.int/cache/ITY_OFFPUB/KS-BT-03-001/EN/KS-BT-03-001-EN.PDF> [6 June 2005].

Eurostat (2003c), *The Social Situation in the European Union 2003*, <europa.eu.int/ comm/employment_social/social_situation/docs/SSR2002_en.pdf> [8 May 2004].

Eurostat (2003d), 'Trends in households in the European Union: 1995–2025', *Statistics in Focus: Population and Social Conditions*, Theme 3 – 24/2003, <europa.eu.int/comm/ eurostat/Public/datashop/print-product/EN?catalogue=Eurostat&product=KS-NK-03-024-__-N-EN&mode=download> [8 May 2004].

Eurostat (2004), 'Passenger cars per 1 000 inhabitants', <europa.eu.int/comm/euro-stat/newcronos/queen/display.do?screen=detail&language=en&product=LT&root= LT_copy_1031680375681/yearlies_copy_221546607827/e_copy_304025285327/eb_ copy_517735779954/eba_copy_712411889444/eba12048_copy_1043059021750> [6 Mar. 2004].

Eurostat (2004a), 'Sea transport of goods', <europa.eu.int/comm/eurostat/ newcronos/queen/display.do?screen=detail&language=en&product=LT&root= LT_copy_1031680375681/yearlies_copy_221546607827/e_copy_304025285327/eb_co py_517735779954/eba_copy_712411889444/eba14608_copy_621687650883> [6 Mar. 2004].

Eurostat (2004b), 'Bed places in hotels and similar establishments', <europa.eu.int/ comm/eurostat/newcronos/queen/display.do?screen = detail&language= en&product=LT&root=LT_copy_1031680375681/yearlies_copy_221546607827/e_ copy_304025285327/eb_copy_517735779954/ebb_copy_809497647438/ebb11024_ copy_ 212175605469> [6 Mar. 2004].

Eurostat (2004c), *External and Intra-European Union Trade*, <europa.eu.int/comm/ eurostat/Public/datashop/print-product/EN?catalogue=Eurostat&product=KS-AR-04-006-__-N-EN&mode=download> [20 Aug. 2004].

Eurostat (2005), 'Population and social conditions/labour market/employment and unemployment/total employment – LFS series/employment by sex, age groups and economic activity (1000)', NewCronos database, <europa.eu.int/comm/eurostat/> [11 Mar. 2005].

Eurostat (2005a), 'Population and social conditions/labour market/employment and unemployment/total employment – LFS series/employment by sex, age groups and occupation (1000)', NewCronos database, <europa.eu.int/comm/eurostat> [16 Mar. 2005].

Eurostat (2005b), 'Extra EU-15 trade by main trading partners', NewCronos database, pre-defined tables, <epp.eurostat.cec.eu.int> [14 Apr. 2005].

Eurostat (2005c), 'Population projections 2004–2050', *Eurostat News Release* 48/2005, <epp.eurostat.cec.eu.int/pls/portal/docs/PAGE/PGP_PRD_CAT_PREREL/PGE_CAT_ PREREL_YEAR_2005/PGE_CAT_PREREL_YEAR_2005_MONTH_04/3-08042005-EN-AP.PDF> [18 July 2005].

Eurostat (2005d), 'Tables/key indicators/long-term indicators/population and social conditions/population', <epp.eurostat.cec.eu.int/portal/page?_pageid=1996,45323 734&_dad=portal&_schema=PORTAL&screen=welcomeref&open=/basic/ YEARLIES_NEW/C/C1&language=en&product=EU_MAIN_TREE&root=EU_MAIN _TREE&scrollto=116> [18 July 2005].

Eurostat (2005e), 'Tables/key indicators/sustainable development indicators/ageing society', <epp.eurostat.cec.eu.int/portal/page?_pageid=1996,45323734&_dad= portal&_schema=PORTAL&screen=welcomeref&open=/&product=sdi_as&depth=2> [18 July 2005].

Eurostat (2005f), 'Youth education attainment level – total', NewCronos database, pre-defined tables, <europa.eu.int/comm/eurostat> [2 Aug. 2005].

Eurostat (2005g), 'Participation/enrolment in education by sex', NewCronos database, <europa.eu.int/comm/eurostat> [2 Aug. 2005].

Eurostat (2005h), 'Life-long learning – total', NewCronos database, pre-defined tables, <europa.eu.int/comm/eurostat> [2 Aug. 2005].

Eurostat (2005i), 'Tertiary education graduates', NewCronos database, <europa.eu.int/ comm/eurostat> [2 Aug. 2005].

Eurostat (2005j), 'Distribution of pupils/students by level', NewCronos database, <europa.eu.int/comm/eurostat> [2 Aug. 2005].

Eurostat (2005k), 'Share of women among tertiary students', NewCronos database, pre-defined tables, <europa.eu.int/comm/eurostat> [2 Aug. 2005].

Eurostat (2005l), 'Total employment rate, by highest level of education', NewCronos database, pre-defined tables, <europa.eu.int/comm/eurostat> [30 July 2005].

Eurostat (2005m), 'Live births outside marriage', <epp.eurostat.cec.eu.int/portal/page?_ pageid=1073,1135280&_dad=portal&_schema=PORTAL&p_product_code=CAB1 3584> [19 Aug. 2005].

Eurostat (2005o), 'Divorces', <epp.eurostat.cec.eu.int/portal/page?_pageid=1996, 39140985&_dad=portal&_schema=PORTAL&screen=detailref&language=en&pro duct=Yearlies_new_population&root=Yearlies_new_population/C/C1/C13/cab105 12> [23 Sept. 2005].

Eurostat (2005p), 'Real GDP growth rate', <epp.eurostat.cec.eu.int/portal/ page?_pageid=1996,39140985&_dad=portal&_schema=PORTAL&screen= detailref&language=en&product=Yearlies_new_economy&root=Yearlies_new_ economy/B/B1/B11/eb012> [27 Oct. 2005].

Eurostat (2005q), 'Average population by sex and five-year age groups', <epp. eurostat.cec.eu.int/portal/page?_pageid=1090,30070682,1090_33076576&_dad= portal&_schema=PORTAL> [25 Nov. 2005].

Eurostat (2005r), 'EU direct investment positions, breakdown by country and economic activity', NewCronos database, <epp.eurostat.cec.eu.int> [28 Apr. 2005].

Evans, G. (1999), 'Class voting: from premature obituary to reasoned appraisal', in *The End of Class Politics?* ed. G. Evans, Oxford: Oxford University Press.

EVS (European Values Study) (2003), 'European Values Study 1980–1990–2000: some results', <www.europeanvalues.nl/index2.htm> [14 Feb. 2005].

Ewald, François (1999), 'Genetics, insurance and risk', in *Genetics and Insurance*, eds T. McGleenan, U. Wiesing and F. Ewald, Oxford: BIOS.

Fahlman, Robert C. (undated), 'Intelligence led policing and the key role of criminal intelligence analysis: preparing for the 21st century', <www.interpol.int/ Public/cia/ fahlman.asp> [17 July 2003].

Falkner, Robert (2000), 'International trade conflicts over agricultural biotechnology', in *The International Politics of Biotechnology*, eds Alan Russell and John Vogler, Manchester: Manchester University Press.

FAO (Food and Agriculture Organization of the United Nations) (2000), 'FAO Statement on Biotechnology', <www.fao.org/biotech/stat.asp> [23 Oct. 2003].

FATF (Financial Action Task Force on Money Laundering) (2003a), 'Basic facts about money laundering', <www1.oecd.org/fatf/MLaundering_en.htm> [20 Oct. 2004].

FATF (2003b), *The Forty Recommendations*, <www1.oecd.org/fatf/pdf/40Recs-2003_en.pdf> [20 Oct. 2004].

Fenney, Ron (2000), *Essential Central Government 2000*, London: LGC Information.

Ferguson, Martin (2004), 'Information society', in Compston, *Handbook of Public Policy in Europe*.

Flockton, C.H., P.A. Grout and M.J. Yong (2004), 'Financial regulation', in Compston, *Handbook of Public Policy in Europe*.

Fontagné, Lionel, Michel Fouquin, Guillaume Gaulier, Colette Herzog and Soledad Zignago (2004), *European Industry's Place in the International Division of Labour: Situation and Prospects*, report prepared for the European Commission, <trade-info.cec.eu.int/doclib/docs/2004/july/tradoc_118034.pdf> [6 Oct. 2004].

Food Standards Agency (2003), 'GM food debate', <www.food.gov.uk/gmdebate/ aboutgm> [28 Feb. 2004].

Förster, Michael, with Michele Pellizzari (2000), *Trends in Income Distribution and Poverty in the OECD Area*, Occasional Paper, <www.olis.oecd.org/OLIS/2000DOC. NSF/LINKTO/DEELSA-ELSA-WD(2000)3> [6 Dec. 2003].

Förster, Michael and Mark Pearson (2002), 'Income distribution and poverty in the OECD area: trends and driving forces', *OECD Economic Studies* 34, <www.oecd.org/ dataoecd/16/33/2968109.pdf> [6 Dec. 2003].

Foster, John S. and Larry D. Welch (2000), 'The evolving battlefield', *Physics Today*, Dec.

Fox Harding, Lorraine (1996), *Family, State and Social Policy*, Basingstoke: Macmillan.

Francoeur, Robert T. (1997–2001), *The International Encyclopedia of Sexuality* Vols 1–4, <www2.hu-berlin.de/sexology/IES/> [22 Sept. 2005].

Francoeur, Robert T. (ed.) (2004), *The International Encyclopedia of Sexuality*, New York: Continuum.

Franklin, M. (1985), *The Decline of Class Voting in Britain*, Oxford: Clarendon.

Freeman, Richard (2000), *The Politics of Health in Europe*, Manchester: Manchester University Press.

Freeman, Chris, Luc Soete and Umit Efendioglu (1995), 'Diffusion and the employment effects of information and communication technology', *International Labour Review* 134(4–5): 587–603.

Freeman, Richard (2002), 'The health care state in the information age', *Public Administration* 80(4): 751–67.

Freeman, Richard and Michael Moran (2000), 'Reforming health care in Europe', *West European Politics* 23(2).

Fukuyama, F. (2003), *Our Posthuman Future*, London: Basic Books.

G10 (Group of Ten) (2001), *Consolidation in the Financial Sector*, <www.bis.org> [26 Sept. 2004].

Gaisford, James D., Jill E. Hobbs, William A. Kerr, Nicholas Perdikis and Marni D. Plunkett (2001), *The Economics of Biotechnology*, Cheltenham: Edward Elgar.

Gallaire, Hervé (1998), 'Faster, connected, smarter', in OECD, *21st Century Technologies*, Paris: OECD.

Garden, Timothy (2002), 'Air power: theory and practice', in Baylis *et al.*, *Strategy in the Contemporary World*.

Garrett, Geoffrey (1998), *Partisan Politics in the Global Economy*, Cambridge: Cambridge University Press.

Garrett, Geoffrey and Deborah Mitchell (2001), 'Globalisation, government spending and taxation in the OECD', *European Journal of Political Research* 39: 145–77.

Garrett, Laurie (2001), 'The nightmare of bioterrorism', *Foreign Affairs* 80(1).

GeneTests (2004), 'About genetic services', <www.genetests.org/servlet/access?id= 8888891&key=F-e7-QLjDBceQ&fcn=y&fw=v5rh&filename=/concepts/primer/ primerservices.html> [29 Jan. 2005].

Genetics and Insurance Committee (2004), *Second Report from September 2002 to December 2003*, Department of Health, <www.advisorybodies.doh.gov.uk/genetics/ gaic/gaicsecondreport.pdf> [27 Jan. 2005].

Genewatch UK (2003), 'UK and European regulation of environmental safety of genetically modified organisms – deliberate release', <www.genewatch.org/CropsAnd Food/Basics/releases_regs.htm> [29 February 2004].

Genewatch UK (2003a), 'What are the food safety and labelling regulations for GM food?', <www.genewatch.org/CropsAndFood/Basics/food_regs.htm> [29 Feb. 2004].

Genewatch UK (2003b), 'The GM dispute at the WTO: forcing GM foods on Europe?', *Briefing* 25, <www.genewatch.org/Publications/Briefs/brief25.pdf> [29 Feb. 2004].

Genewatch UK (2003c), 'Genetic testing in the workplace', *Briefing* 24, <www. genewatch.org/publications/Briefs/brief24.pdf> [29 Feb. 2004].

Genewatch UK (2005), 'Police DNA database needs strong safeguards for privacy and human rights', <www.genewatch.org/Press%20Releases/pr70.htm> [28 Jan. 2005].

Gershuny, Jonathan (1978), *After Industrial Society?: The Emerging Self-Service Economy*, Macmillan, cited in Frank Webster (2002), *Theories of the Information Society*, 2nd edn, London: Routledge: 50.

GGDC (Groningen Growth and Development Centre) (2003), *Total Economy Database: Hours*, <www.eco.rug.nl/ggdc/dseries/hours.shtml> [23 May 2003].

Gilpin, Robert (2000), *The Challenge of Global Capitalism*, Princeton: Princeton University Press.

Global Commons Institute (2005), 'GCI Briefing: "Contraction & Convergence"', <www.gci.org.uk/> [4 July 2005].

Global Lawyers and Physicians (2004), *Database of Global Policies on Human Cloning and Germ-line Engineering*, <www.glphr.org/genetic/genetic.htm> [27 Jan. 2005].

GM Science Review Panel (2003), *Report*, <www.gmsciencedebate.org.uk/> [25 Oct. 2003].

Goodstein, David (2004), 'The end of the age of oil', <www.odac-info.org/> [2 Nov. 2005].

Gorman, L. and D. McLean (2003), *Media and Society in the Twentieth Century*, Oxford: Blackwell.

Goure, Dan (1993), 'Is there a military–technical revolution in America's future?', *The Washington Quarterly* 16(4).

Grabosky, P.N. and Russell G. Smith (1998), *Crime in the Digital Age*, NJ: Transaction.

Grant, Wyn (2000), *Pressure Groups and British Politics*, London: Macmillan.

Graugaard, Christian, with 8 collaborators (2004), 'Denmark', in Francoeur, *The International Encyclopedia of Sexuality*.

Green, Duncan and Matthew Griffith (2002), 'Globalization and its discontents', *International Affairs* 78(1): 49–68.

Greenaway, David and Douglas R. Nelson (2001), *Globalisation and Labour Markets*, Vols 1 and 2, Cheltenham: Edward Elgar.

Greenpeace (undated), 'Genetic engineering', <www.greenpeace.org/ international_en/campaigns/intro?campaign_id=3942> [28 Feb. 2004].

Greenspan, Alan (2003), 'Global finance: is it slowing?', <www.federalreserve.gov/boarddocs/speeches/2003/20030307/default,htm> [6 Sept. 2004].

Greenwood, Justin (1997), *Representing Interests in the European Union*, Macmillan.

Grubb, Michael, with Christiaan Vrolijk and Duncan Brack (1999), *The Kyoto Protocol: A Guide and Assessment*, London: Royal Institute of International Affairs.

Ham, Christopher (2004), *Health Policy in Britain*, 5th edn, Basingstoke: Palgrave Macmillan.

Hamilton, Malcolm (2001), *The Sociology of Religion*, 2nd edn, London: Routledge.

Hansson, P. (2000), 'Relative demand for skills in Swedish manufacturing: technology or trade?', abstract, *Review of International Economics* 8(3): 533–55.

Harrison, Anthony and Jennifer Dixon (2000), *The NHS: Facing the Future*, London: King's Fund.

Hartley, Keith (2003), 'The future of European defence policy: an economic perspective', *Defence and Peace Economics* 14(2): 107–15.

Healy, Geraldine and Gill Kirton (2000), 'Women, power and trade union government in Britain', *British Journal of Industrial Relations* 38(3): 343–60.

Heath, A., R. Jowell, J. Curtice, J. Field and C. Levine (1985), *How Britain Votes*, Oxford: Pergamon Press.

Heath, A., R. Jowell, J. Curtice, G. Evans, J. Field and S. Witherspoon (1991), *Understanding Political Change*, Oxford: Pergamon Press.

Heery, Edmund, John Kelly and Jeremy Waddington (2003), 'Union revitalization in Britain', *European Journal of Industrial Relations* 9(1): 79–97.

Held, David, Anthony McGrew, David Goldblatt and Jonathan Perraton (1999), *Global Transformations*, Cambridge: Polity Press.

Henig, Ruth and Simon Henig (2001), *Women and Political Power: Europe Since 1945*, London: Routledge.

Herman, E.S. and R.W. McChesney (1997), *The Global Media*, London and New York: Continuum.

Herzog, Howard J. (2001), 'What future for carbon capture and sequestration?', *Environmental Science and Technology* 35(7): 148 A–153 A.

Hildreth, Steven A. (2001), 'Cyberwarfare', *CRS Report for Congress*, 19 June, <www.fas.org/irp/crs/RL30735.pdf> [8 Dec. 2005].

Hirsch, Robert L., Roger Bezdek and Robert Wendling (2005), 'Peaking of world oil production: impacts, mitigation and risk management', <www.odac-info.org/> [2 Nov. 2005].

Hirst, Paul and Graham Thompson (1999), *Globalisation in Question*, 2nd edn, Cambridge: Polity.

Hobson, John M. (2003), 'Disappearing taxes or "the race to the middle"?: Fiscal policy in the OECD', in *States in the Global Economy*, ed. Linda Weiss, Cambridge: Cambridge University Press.

Holm, Søren (2002), 'Going to the roots of the stem cell controversy', *Bioethics* 16(6): 493–507.

Houghton, John (2004), *Global Warming: The Complete Briefing*, Cambridge: Cambridge University Press.

Huber, E. and J.J. Stephens (2002), 'Globalisation, competitiveness and the social democratic model', abstract, *Social Policy and Society* 1(1): 47–57.

Hudson, John (2002), 'Digitising the structures of government; the UK's information age government agenda', *Policy and Politics* 30(4): 515–31.

Hummels, David, Jun Ishii and Kei-Mu Yi (2001), 'The nature and growth of vertical specialization in world trade', *Journal of International Economics* 54: 75–96.

Hundley, Richard O., Robert H. Anderson, Tora K. Bikson and C. Richard Neu (2003), *The Global Course of the Information Revolution*, <www.rand.org/pubs/monograph_reports/MR1680> [23 Mar. 2006].

IEA (International Energy Agency) (2002), *World Energy Outlook 2002*, <www.worldenergyoutlook.org/> [22 Feb. 2004].

IEA (2003), *Energy Policies of IEA Countries: 2003 Review*, <www.iea.org/textbase/nppdf/free/2000/compendium_2003.pdf> [21 Feb. 2004].

IEA (2003a), *World Energy Investment Outlook*, <www.iea.org/textbase/npsum/weiosum.pdf> [21 Feb. 2005].

IEA (2004), 'Analysis of the impact of high oil prices on the global economy', <www.odac-info.org/> [2 Nov. 2005].

Illum, Klaus (2005), 'IEA oil projections revisited', ECO Consult, Denmark, <www.odac-info.org/> [2 Nov. 2005].

ILO (International Labour Organization) (2003), 'Key indicators of the labour market', <www.ilo.org/public/english/employment/strat/kilm/> [22 July 2003].

ILO (2005), 'About the ILO', <www.ilo.org/public/english/about/index.htm> [5 May 2005].

IMF (International Monetary Fund) (2001), *International Capital Markets 2001*, <www.imf.org/external/pubs/ft/icm/2001/01/eng/pdf/chap2.pdf> [28 Sept. 2004].

IMF (2002), *International Investment Position: A Guide to Data Sources*, <www.imf.org/external/np/sta/iip/guide/> [5 Dec. 2005].

IMF (2004), *Global Financial Stability Report*, Sept., <www.imf.org/External/Pubs/FT/GFSR/2004/02/index.htm> [5 Dec. 2005].

IMF (2005), *International Financial Statistics*, <esds.mcc.ac.uk/wds_ifs/ReportFolders/ReportFolders.aspx?CS_referer=&CS_ChosenLang=en> [18 May 2005].

Inglehart, Ronald (1997), *Modernization and Postmodernization*, Princeton: Princeton University Press.

Interpol (2000), 'Frequently asked questions about DNA profiling', <www.interpol.com/Public/Forensic/dna/dnafaq> [28 Jan. 2005].

IPCC (Intergovernmental Panel on Climate Change) (2001), *Climate Change 2001: Impacts, Adaptation and Vulnerability*, Working Group 2, <www.ipcc.ch/> [20 Mar. 2003].

IPCC (2001a), *Climate Change 2001: Working Group III: Mitigation*, <www.grida.no/climate/ipcc_tar/wg3/226.htm> [24 Feb. 2005].

IPCC (2001b), *Summary for Policymakers: Climate Change 2001: Mitigation*, Report of Working Group III, <arch.rivm.nl/env/int/ipcc/images/wgIII_spm.pdf> [3 July 2005].

Jagger, Gill and Caroline Wright (1999), 'Introduction: changing family values', in *Changing Family Values*, eds Gill Jagger and Caroline Wright, London: Routledge.

James, Clive (2003), 'Global area of transgenic crops, 1996–2003: by country', International Service for the Acquisition of Agri-Biotech Applications, <www.isaaa.org/kc/> [17 Dec. 2004].

Jewkes, Yvonne (2003), 'Policing the Net: crime, regulation and surveillance in cyberspace', in *Dot.cons: Crime, Deviance and Identity on the Internet*, ed. Yvonne Jewkes, Cullompton: Willan.

Johnson, Anne M. and 11 collaborators (2001), 'Sexual behavior in Britain: partnerships, practices, and HIV risk behaviors', *The Lancet* 358: 1835–42.

Jordan, A.G. and J.J. Richardson (1987), *Government and Pressure Groups in Britain*, Oxford: Clarendon Press.

Kaivo-oja, Jari and Jyrki Luukkanen (2004), 'The European Union balancing between CO_2 reduction commitments and growth policies: decomposition analyses', *Energy Policy* 32: 1511–30.

Keep, Ewart and Ken Mayhew (2004), 'The economic and distributional implications of current policies on higher education', *Oxford Review of Economic Policy* 20(2): 298–314.

Kelly, Thomas Phelim (2001), 'Ireland', in Francoeur, *The International Encyclopedia of Sexuality*.

Kilkey, Majella (2004), 'Women', in Compston, *Handbook of Public Policy in Europe*.

Kiras, James D. (2002), 'Terrorism and irregular warfare', in Baylis *et al.*, *Strategy in the Contemporary World*.

Kirkpatrick, David L.I. (2004), 'Trends in the costs of weapon systems and their consequences', *Defence and Peace Economics* 15(3): 259–73.

Klingeman, Hans-Dieter, Richard Hofferbert and Ian Budge (1994), *Parties, Policies and Democracy*, Boulder: Westview Press.

Knox, Noelle (2005), 'Religion takes a back seat in Western Europe', *USA Today* 11 Aug., <www.usatoday.com/> [1 Sept. 2005].

Knutsen, Oddbjørn (2004), 'Religious denomination and party choice in Western Europe: a comparative longitudinal study from eight countries, 1970–97', *International Political Science Review* 25(1): 97–128.

Kok, Wim (2004), *Facing the Challenge: The Lisbon Strategy for Growth and Employment*, Report from the High Level Group chaired by Wim Kok, <europa.eu.int/growthandjobs/pdf/kok_report_en.pdf> [8 Aug. 2005].

Kontula, Osmo and Elina Haavio-Mannila (2001), 'Finland', in Francoeur, *The International Encyclopedia of Sexuality*.

Kozul-Wright, Richard (1995), 'Transnational corporations and the nation state', in *Managing the Global Economy*, eds Jonathan Michie and John Grieve-Smith, Oxford: Oxford University Press.

Krugman, Paul (1995), 'Growing world trade: causes and consequences', *Brookings Papers on Economic Activity* 1: 327–77.

Kudrle, Robert T. (2000), 'Does globalisation sap the fiscal power of the state?', in *Coping with Globalisation*, eds Aseem Prakash and Jeffrey A. Hart, London: Routledge.

Kumar, Krishan (2005), *From Post-Industrial to Post-Modern Society*, Oxford: Blackwell.

Kyoto Protocol to the United Nations Framework Convention on Climate Change (1997), <unfccc.int/resource/docs/convkp/kpeng.html> [24 Feb. 2005].

Landesmann, M., R. Stehrer and S. Leitner (2002), 'Trade liberalisation and labour markets: perspectives from OECD economies', *Employment Paper 2002/41*, ILO, <www.ilo.org/public/english/employment/strat/download/ep41.pdf> [8 Dec. 2005].

Lane, Jan-Erik, David McKay and Kenneth Newton (1997), *Political Data Handbook: OECD Countries*, 2nd edn, Oxford: Oxford University Press, cited in Norris and Inglehart, *Sacred and Secular*: 210.

Lash, Scott and John Urry (1987), *The End of Organized Capitalism*, Cambridge: Polity Press.

Latham, Andrew (1999), 'Re-imagining warfare: the "revolution in military affairs"', in *Contemporary Security and Strategy*, ed. Craig A. Snyder, Macmillan.

Launis, Veikko (1999), 'Genetic discrimination', in *Genetics and Insurance*, eds T. McGleenan, U. Wiesing and F. Ewald, Oxford: BIOS.

Lautmann, R. and K. Starke (2001), 'Germany', in Francoeur, *The International Encyclopedia of Sexuality*.

Lewis, Graham and John Abraham (2001), 'The creation of neo-liberal corporate bias in transnational medicines control: the industrial shaping and interest dynamics of the European regulatory state', *European Journal of Political Research* 39: 53–80.

Lewis, Jeffrey (2004), *What If Space Were Weaponized?*, Washington: Centre for Defense Information.

Libicki, Martin (1995), 'What is information warfare?', *ACIS Paper 3*, Institute for National Strategic Studies, <www.iwar.org.uk/iwar/resources/nud/infowar/a003cont.html> [4 July 2004].

LIS (Luxembourg Income Study) (2003), 'Income inequality measures', <www.lisproject.org/keyfigures/ineqtable.htm> [22 Nov. 2003].

Lisbon European Council (2003), *Presidency Conclusions*, <www.bologna_ berlin2003.de/pdf/PRESIDENCY_CONCLUSIONS_Lissabon.pdf> [24 Nov. 2004].

Lovenduski, Joni and Pippa Norris (2003), 'Westminster women: the politics of presence', *Political Studies* 51: 84–102.

Lyon, David (2003), *Surveillance After September 11*, Oxford: Polity.

MacKerron, Gordon (2004), 'Nuclear power and the characteristics of "ordinariness" – the case of UK energy policy', *Energy Policy* 32: 1957–65.

Madeley, John and Benjamin-Hugo LeBlanc (2004), 'Religion', in Compston, *Handbook of Public Policy in Europe*.

Manning, Francis C.R. (2000), 'Biotechnology: a scientific perspective', in *The International Politics of Biotechnology*, eds Alan Russell and John Vogler, Manchester: Manchester University Press.

Martin, Paul and Robert Frost (2003), 'Regulating the commercial development of genetic testing in the UK: problems, possibilities and policy', *Critical Social Policy* 23(2): 186–207.

MAS (Manufacturing Advisory Service) (2003), *Fact Sheets*, Department of Trade and Industry, <www.manufacturingadvice.org.uk/browse.jsp?classification=fact> [11 Nov. 2003].

Masson, Paul (2001), 'Globalization: facts and figures', *IMF Policy Discussion Paper* PDP/01/4, <www.imf.org/external/pubs/ft/pdp/2001/pdp04.pdf> [6 Dec. 2005].

May, Christopher (2002), *The Information Society: A Sceptical View*, Oxford: Polity.

Mazur, Amy (2002), *Theorizing Feminist Policy*, Oxford: Oxford University Press.

McCarthy, John (2003), 'What is artificial intelligence?', <www-formal.stanford.edu/jmc/whatisai/whatisai.html> [3 Nov. 2004].

McGleenan, Tony and Urban Wiesing (1999), 'Policy options for health and life insurance in the era of genetic testing' in *Genetics and Insurance*, eds T. McGleenan, U. Wiesing and F. Ewald, Oxford: BIOS.

McQuail, Denis (1998), 'Commercialization and beyond', in *Media Policy*, eds D. McQuail and K. Siune, London: Sage.

McQuail, Denis (2000), *McQuail's Mass Communication Theory*, 4th edn, Sage: London and New York.

McQuail, Denis (2005), *McQuail's Mass Communication Theory*, 5th edn, Sage: London and New York.

Meier, W.A. and J. Trappel (1998), 'Media concentration and the public interest', in *Media Policy*, eds D. McQuail and K. Siune, London: Sage.

Meignant, Michel, with 7 collaborators (2004), 'France', in Francoeur, *The International Encyclopedia of Sexuality*.

Michalski, Wolfgang (1999), '21st century technologies: a future of promise', *OECD Observer*, September, <www1.oecd.org/publications/observer/217/e-toc.htm> [18 Nov. 2004].

Microsoft (2004), 'Introduction to viruses, worms, and Trojan Horses', 9 Mar., <www.microsoft.com/security/articles/virus101.asp> [5 July 2004].

Millar, Jane (2003), 'Social policy and family policy', in *The Student's Companion to Social Policy*, eds Pete Alcock, Angus Erskine and Margaret May, 2nd edn, Oxford: Blackwell.

Miller, Riel, Wolfgang Michalski and Barrie Stevens (1998), 'The promises and perils of 21st century technology: an overview of the issues', in *21st Century Technologies*, OECD, Paris: OECD.

Miller, William L. and Richard G. Niemi (2002), 'Voting: choice, conditioning and constraint', in *Comparing Democracies 2*, eds Lawrence LeDuc, Richard G. Niemi and Pippa Norris, London: Sage.

Minkenburg, Michael (2002), 'Religion and public policy: institutional, cultural and political impact on the shaping of abortion policies in Western democracies', *Comparative Political Studies* 35(2): 221–47.

Mintz, Morton (2002), 'Hair-raising hair triggers', *The American Prospect* 13(23), 30 Dec.

MOD (Ministry of Defence) (1999), 'Defending against the threat of biological and chemical weapons', <www.mod.uk/issues/cbw/> [15 June 2004].

MOD (2001), 'Nanotechnology', <www.mod.uk/issues/nanotech/impact.htm> [19 May 2004].

Molander, Roger C., Andrew S. Riddile and Peter A. Wilson (1996), 'Strategic information warfare: a new face of war', <www.rand.org/publications/MR/MR661/> [4 July 2004].

Monsanto (2003), *Biotech Primer* <www.monsanto.co.uk/primer/primer.html> [23 Oct. 2003].

Moore, Nick (1997), 'Neo-liberal or dirigiste? Policies for an Information Society', *Political Quarterly*: 276–83.

Moran, M. (1999), *Governing the Health Care State*, Manchester: Manchester University Press.

MORI (2003), 'GM food opposition continues', <www.mori.com/polls/2003/gmfood. shtml> [28 Feb. 2004].

Mosley, Layna (2003), *Global Capital and National Governments*, Cambridge: Cambridge University Press.

MRIC (Media Reform Information Centre) (2004), 'Number of corporations that control nearly all U.S. media', <www.corporations.org/media/media-ownership-titled.gif> [4 Apr. 2004].

Müller-Rommel, Ferdinand (1997), 'Federal Republic of Germany: a system of Chancellor Government', in *Cabinets in Western Europe*, eds Jean Blondel and Ferdinand Müller-Rommel, London: Macmillan.

Murdock, G. and P. Golding (1995), 'For a political economy of mass communications', in *Approaches to Media: A Reader*, London: Arnold, reprinted from *The Socialist Register*, eds R. Miliband and J. Saville, London: Merlin Press, 1973.

National Institutes of Health (2002), 'Stem cell information', <stemcells.nih.gov/ infoCenter/stemCellBasics.asp> [30 Oct. 2003].

Navaretti, Paul, J. Haaland and A. Venables (undated), 'Multinational corporations and global production networks: the implications for trade policy', report prepared for the European Commission, <www.cepr.org/pubs/fdi_report.pdf> [14 Apr. 2005].

Navarro, Vicente, John Schmitt and Javier Astudillo (2004), 'Is globalisation undermining the welfare state?', *Cambridge Journal of Economics* 28: 133–52.

NCIS (National Criminal Intelligence Service) (2003), *United Kingdom Threat Assessment of Serious and Organised Crime 2003*, <www.ncis.co.uk/ukta.asp> [18 Oct. 2004].

NES Contributions to Scholarship: A Review (undated), <www.umich.edu/~nes/resources/papers/sapiro.pdf> [26 Mar. 2004].

Newhouse, John (2002), 'Assessing the threats', in *Assessing the Threats*, ed. John Newhouse, Washington, DC: Center for Defense Information.

NHGRI (National Human Genomic Research Institute) (undated), 'Issues in genetics and health', <www.genome.gov/> [30 Oct. 2003].

NHGRI (2004), 'Cloning/embryonic stem cells', prepared by K. Hanna, <www. genome. gov/10004765> [27 Jan. 2005].

NHGRI (2004a), 'Germline gene transfer', prepared by K. Hanna, <www.genome.gov/10004764> [27 Jan. 2005].

NHTCU (National Hi-Tech Crime Unit) (2004), *Hi-Tech Crime: The Impact on UK Business*, <www.nhtcu.org/NOP%20Survey.pdf> [14 Oct. 2004].

Nieto, J.A. and 9 collaborators (2001), 'Spain (Reino de España)', in Francoeur, *The International Encyclopedia of Sexuality*.

Nieuwbeerta, Paul and Nan Dirk De Graaf (1999), 'Traditional class voting in twenty postwar societies', in *The End of Class Politics?* ed. Geoffrey Evans, Oxford: Oxford University Press.

Nodin, Nuno, with Sara Moreira and Margarida Ourô (2001), 'Portugal', in Francoeur, *The International Encyclopedia of Sexuality*.

Nordström, Håkan and Scott Vaughan (1999), 'Trade and environment', *Special Studies 4*, World Trade Organization, <www.wto.org/english/tratop_e/envir_e/stud99_e.htm> [26 Aug. 2004].

Norris, Pippa and Ronald Inglehart (2004), *Sacred and Secular*, Cambridge: Cambridge University Press.

Nottingham, S. (2003), *Eat Your Genes*, London: Zed Books.

NSTC (National Science and Technology Council) (1999), *Nanotechnology: Shaping the World Atom by Atom*, <www.ostp.gov/NSTC/html/iwgn/IWGN.Public.Brochure/welcome.htm> [6 Nov. 2003].

Nuffield Council on Bioethics (2004), 'Animal-to-human transplants: the ethics of xeno-transplantation', <www.nuffieldbioetchis.org/go/ourwork/xenotransplantations/introduction.html> [27 Jan. 2005].

Nuffield Trust (2000), *Policy Futures for UK Health 2000 Report*, <www.archive.official-documents.co.uk/nuffield/policyf/r2k-p1.htm> [7 June 2003].

OECD (Organisation for Economic Co-operation and Development) (1996), *Revenue Statistics*, Paris: OECD.

OECD (1998), *Cryptography Policy: The Guidelines and Issues*, <miranda.sourceoecd.org/> [12 Mar. 2005].

OECD (1998a), *OECD Employment Outlook 1998*, <miranda.sourceoecd.org/> [12 Mar. 2005].

OECD (1998b), 'The MAI negotiating text (as of 24 May 1998)', <www.oecd.org/dataoecd/46/40/1895712.pdf> [10 May 2005].

OECD (1999), 'Biotechnology and industry: a union of promise', *OECD Observer 1*, <www.oecdobserver.org/news/> [25 Oct. 2003].

OECD (2000), *Revenue Statistics 1965–1999*, <miranda.sourceoecd.org/> [12 Mar. 2005].

OECD (2000a), *OECD Employment Outlook 2000*, <thesius.sourceoecd.org/vl=4347947/cl=66/nw=1/rpsv/~6682/v2000n9/s1/p1> [11 Mar. 2005].

OECD (2000b), *The Service Economy*, <miranda.sourceoecd.org/> [12 Mar. 2005].

OECD (2001a), *STI Scoreboard 2001*, <miranda.sourceoecd.org/> [12 Mar. 2005].

OECD (2001b), *OECD Communications Outlook 2001*, <miranda.sourceoecd.org/> [12 Mar. 2005].

OECD (2001c), *The Application of Biotechnology to Industrial Sustainability*, <miranda.sourceoecd.org/> [12 Mar. 2005].

OECD (2001d), *Health at a Glance*, <miranda.sourceoecd.org/> [12 Mar. 2005].

OECD (2001e), *Historical Statistics 1970–2000*, <miranda.sourceoecd.org/> [12 Mar. 2005].

OECD (2001f), *Indicators of Industry and Services*, <miranda.sourceoecd.org/> [12 Mar. 2005].

OECD (2001g), *OECD Environmental Outlook 2001*, <miranda.sourceoecd.org/> [12 Mar. 2005].

OECD (2001h), *The European Union Labour Force Survey: Methods and Definitions – 2001*, <miranda.sourceoecd.org/> [12 Mar. 2005].

OECD (2001i), *OECD Employment Outlook 2001*, <miranda.sourceoecd.org/> [12 Mar. 2005].

OECD (2001j), *New Patterns of Industrial Globalisation*, <miranda.sourceoecd.org/> [12 Mar. 2005].

OECD (2001k), *Measuring Globalisation* Vol. 1, <miranda.sourceoecd.org/> [12 Mar. 2005].

OECD (2001l), *OECD Environmental Indicators 2001*, <miranda.sourceoecd.org/> [12 Mar. 2005].

OECD (2002), *OECD Information Technology Outlook 2002*, <miranda.sourceoecd.org/> [12 Mar. 2005].

OECD (2002a), *OECD Employment Outlook 2002*, <miranda.sourceoecd.org/> [12 Mar. 2005].

OECD (2002b), *Genetic Inventions, Intellectual Property Rights and Licensing Practices: Evidence and Policies*, <miranda.sourceoecd.org/> [12 Mar. 2005].

OECD (2002c), *Towards Sustainable Household Consumption?: Trends and Policies in OECD Countries*, <hermia.sourceoecd.org/vl=1423619/cl=50/nw=1/rpsv/~6674/v2002n9/s1/p1l> [4 Mar. 2005].

OECD (2002d), *OECD Economic Outlook 71*, <miranda.sourceoecd.org/> [12 Mar. 2005].

OECD (2002e), *OECD Science, Technology and Industry Outlook 2002*, <miranda.sourceoecd.org/> [12 Mar. 2005].

OECD (2002f), *Forty Years' Experience with the OECD Code of Liberalisation of Capital Movements*, <miranda.sourceoecd.org/> [26 May 2005].

OECD (2003), *STI Scoreboard 2003*, <miranda.sourceoecd.org/> [12 Mar. 2005].

OECD (2003a), *The e-Government Imperative*, <miranda.sourceoecd.org/> [12 Mar. 2005].

OECD (2003b), *ICT and Economic Growth: Evidence from OECD Countries*, <miranda.sourceoecd.org/> [12 Mar. 2005].

OECD (2003c), 'Scientific, industrial and health applications of biotechnology', <www.oecd.org> [24 Oct. 2003].

OECD (2003d), 'An overview of biotechnology statistics in selected countries', *STI Working Paper 2003/13*, <www.olis.oecd.org/olis/2003doc.nsf/linkto/dsti-doc(2003)13> [17 Dec. 2004].

OECD (2003e), 'Household final consumption expenditure per head at price levels and PPPs of 1995 (US dollars)', *National Accounts of OECD Countries, Volume 1 1990–2001*, <www.oecd.org/document/28/0,2340,en_2649_201185_2750044_1_1_1_1,00.html> [6 Dec. 2003].

OECD (2003f), *OECD Economic Outlook 74*, Dec., <miranda.sourceoecd.org/> [9 Feb. 2005].

OECD (2003g), *OECD Economic Outlook 73*, <miranda.sourceoecd.org/> [12 Mar. 2005].

OECD (2003h), *Education at a Glance 2003*, <miranda.sourceoecd.org/> [19 Apr. 2005].

OECD (2003i), *OECD Employment Outlook 2003*, <miranda.sourceoecd.org/> [19 Apr. 2005].

OECD (2003j), 'Policies for an ageing society: recent measures and areas for further reform', *Economics Department Working Paper* 369, <miranda.sourceoecd.org/> [18 July 2005].

OECD (2003k), 'Social policies, family types and child outcomes in selected OECD countries', *OECD Social, Employment and Migration Working Papers* 6, <miranda.sourceoecd.org/> [15 Aug. 2005].

OECD (2004), *Labour Force Statistics 1983–2003*, <juno.sourceoecd.org/vl=4746971/cl=42/nw=1/rpsv/~6682/v2004n16/s1/p1l> [11 Mar. 2005].

OECD (2004a), *OECD Employment Outlook 2004*, <miranda.sourceoecd.org/> [22 Mar. 2005].

OECD (2004b), *Revenue Statistics 1956–2003*, <miranda.sourceoecd.org/> [20 Apr. 2005].

OECD (2005), *National Accounts of OECD Countries*, Vol. 1, Main Aggregates, <miranda.sourceoecd.org/> [10 Feb. 2005].

OECD (2005a), *The OECD STAN Database for Industrial Analysis*, <miranda.source-oecd.org/> [14 Mar. 2005].

OECD (2005b), 'Harmful tax practices', <www.oecd.org> [5 May 2005].

OECD (2005c), *Long-term Care for Older People*, <miranda.sourceoecd.org/> [18 July 2005].

OECD (2005d), *Employment Outlook 2005*, <www.oecd.org/dataoecd/36/30/35024561.pdf> [8 Nov. 2005].

Office of Naval Intelligence (2000), report cited in 'Navy names nations posing cyber threats', *Defense Week*, 5 Sept. 2000: 1, cited in Hildreth, 'Cyberwarfare': 2.

Office of the Press Secretary (2003), 'National Policy on Ballistic Missile Defence', 20 May, <www.state.gov/t/np/rls/fs/20902.htm> [28 June 2004].

Office of the Press Secretary (2004), 'President Bush signs Biodefense for the 21st Century', 28 Apr., <www.state.gov/t/np/rls/fs/32000.htm> [28 June 2004].

OPFS (One Parent Families Scotland) (2001), 'Children in one parent families', <www.opfs.org.uk/factfile/children.html> [13 Aug. 2005].

Osborne, Andrew (2004), 'GM maize "to please US"', *Guardian International*, <www.guardian.co.uk/international/story/0,3604,1133519,00.html> [29 Feb. 2004].

OTA (US Congress Office of Technology Assessment) (1993), *Proliferation of Weapons of Mass Destruction: Assessing the Risks*, Washington, DC: Government Printing Office, cited in Betts, 'The new threat of mass destruction'.

Pape, Robert A. (2004), 'The true worth of air power', *Foreign Affairs* 83(2), Mar.–Apr.

Park, A. (2000), 'The generation game', in *British Social Attitudes 17th Report*, London: Sage, cited in David Metz (2002), 'The politics of population ageing', *Political Quarterly* 73(3): 326.

Parrinder, Geoffrey (1996), *Sexual Morality in the World's Religions*, 2nd edn, Oxford: Oneworld.

Parsons, D.W. (1995), *Public Policy*, Cheltenham: Edward Elgar.

Pass, C., B. Lowes and A. Robinson (1995), *Business and Macroeconomics*, London: Routledge.

Patterson, Lee (2000), 'Biotechnology policy: regulating risks and risking regulation', in *Policy-Making in the European Union*, 4th edn, eds Helen Wallace and William Wallace, Oxford: Oxford University Press.

Pearce, D., G. Cantisani and A. Laihonen (1999), 'Changes in fertility and family sizes in Europe', *Population Trends* 95, Spring.

Perner, Rotraud A. (2001), 'Austria', in Francoeur, *The International Encyclopedia of Sexuality*.

Pierson, Paul (1996), 'The new politics of the welfare state', *World Politics* 48: 143–79.

Pillar, Paul R. (2001), *Terrorism and US Foreign Policy*, Washington, DC: Brookings, cited in Malise Ruthven (2004), *A Fury for God*, London: Granta: 30.

Porter, Tony (2005), *Globalization and Finance*, Cambridge: Polity.

Prakash, Aseem and Kelly L. Kollman (2003), 'Biopolitics in the EU and the US: a race to the bottom or convergence to the top?', *International Studies Quarterly* 47: 617–41.

Preston, Bob, Dana J. Johnson, Sean Edwards, Michael Miller and Calvin Shipbaugh (2002), *Space Weapons Earth Wars*, RAND.

Preston, John, Graeme Hayes and Dirk Lehmkuhl (2004), 'Transport', in Compston, *Handbook of Public Policy in Europe*.

Purdue, Derrick A. (2000), *Anti-GenetiX: The Emergence of the Anti-GM Movement*, Aldershot: Ashgate.

Raines, Philip (2004), 'Investment', in Compston, *Handbook of Public Policy in Europe*.

Reich, Robert (2002), *The Future of Success*, Vintage.

Reiche, D. and M. Bechberger (2004), 'Policy differences in the promotion of renewable energies in the EU member states', *Energy Policy* 32: 843–49.

Rhodes, R.A.W. (1985), 'Power-dependence, policy communities and intergovernmental networks', *Public Administration Bulletin* 49: 4–31.

Rhodes, R.A.W. (1986), *The National World of Local Government*, London: Allen and Unwin.

Rieger, Elmar and Stephan Leibfried (1998), 'Welfare state limits to globalisation', *Politics and Society* 26(3): 363–90.

Rifkin, Jeremy (1999), *The Biotech Century*, New York: Penguin Putnam.

Rightscom and TSEBA (Rightscom Ltd and Turku School of Economics and Business Administration) (2004), *Publishing Market Watch: Final Report*, European Commission, <www.publishing-watch.org/> [7 June 2005].

Robert, G. (1999), 'Science and technology: trends and issues forward to 2015 – implications for health care', paper for *Policy Futures for UK Health*, ed. C. Dargie <www.jims.cam.ac.uk/research/health/polfutures/polfutures_f.html> [30 Oct. 2003].

Roberts, Geoffrey K. (2000), *German Politics Today*, Manchester: Manchester University Press.

Roberts, Geoffrey K. (2000a), 'The ever-shallower cleavage: religion and electoral politics in Germany', in *Religion and Mass Electoral Behaviour in Europe*, eds David Broughton and Hans-Martien ten Napel, London: Routledge.

Robertson, David (2001), 'Modern technology and the future of the soldier', in *Europe's New Security Challenges*, eds H. Gärtner, A. Hyde-Price and E. Reiter, London: Lynne Riener.

Robinson, Colin (2002), 'The military and cyber-defense: reactions to the threat', Center for Defense Information, 8 Nov., <www.cdi.org/friendlyversion/printversion.cfm?documentid=349> [4 July 2004].

Rodrik, Dani (1997), *Has Globalisation Gone Too Far?* Washington: Institute for International Economics.

Rose, Richard and Ian McAllister (1986), *Voters Begin to Choose*, London: Sage.

Rubery, Jill, Mark Smith and Collette Fagan (1999), *Womens' Employment in Europe: Trends and Prospects*, London: Routledge.

Sabatier, Paul A. and Hank Jenkins-Smith (1999), 'The Advocacy Coalition Framework: an assessment', in *Theories of the Policy Process*, ed. Paul A. Sabatier, Westview Press: 117–66.

Saunders, Peter (2000), 'Afterword: family research and family policy since 1992', in *Families Without Fatherhood*, by Norman Dennis and George Erdos, London: Institute for the Study of Civil Society.

Scase, Richard (2000), *Britain in 2010*, Oxford: Capstone.

Scharpf, F. (1997), *Games Real Actors Play*, Westview Press.

Scheve, Kenneth and Matthew J. Slaughter (2004), 'Economic insecurity and the globalization of production', abstract, *American Journal of Political Science* 48(4).

Schiller, Dan (2000), *Digital Capitalism*, MIT Press.

Schuman, Robert (1950), *Declaration of 9 May 1950*, <europa.eu.int/abc/symbols/9-may/decl_en.htm> [25 Apr. 2005].

Schurman, Rachel (2004), 'Fighting "Frankenfoods": industry opportunity structures and the efficacy of the anti-biotech movement in Western Europe', *Social Problems* 51(2): 243–58.

Schwartz, Stephen I. (ed.) (1998), *Atomic Audit – The Costs and Consequences of US Nuclear Weapons since 1940*, Washington, DC: Brookings Institution, cited in Davis and Gray, 'Weapons of mass destruction': 259.

Semetko, Holli (2004), 'Media, public opinion and political action', in *The Sage Handbook of Media Studies*, eds John D.H. Dunning, Denis McQuail, Philip Schlesinger and Ellen Wartella, London: Sage.

Seoane, José, and Emilio Taddei (2002), 'From Seattle to Porto Alegre: the anti-neoliberal globalization movement', *Current Sociology* 50(1): 99–122.

Shubik, Martin (1997) 'Terrorism, technology and the socioeconomics of death', *Comparative Strategy* 16.

Sica, Vincent (2000), 'Cleaning the laundry: states and the monitoring of the financial system', *Millennium: Journal of International Studies* 29(1): 47–72, cited in May, *The Information Society*: 133.

Sidell, F. and W. Patrick (1998), *Jane's Chem-Bio Handbook*, Alexandra: Jane's Information Group, cited in Davis and Gray, 'Weapons of mass destruction': 279–80.

Sigelman, Lee (1977), 'Review of the polls: multinational surveys of religious beliefs', *Journal for the Scientific Study of Religion* 16(3): 289–94, cited in Norris and Inglehart, *Sacred and Secular*: 90.

Sigg, Roland (2002), 'Pensions at risk? The ageing of the population, the labour market and the cost of pensions', in *Labour Market and Social Protection Reforms in International Perspective*, ed. Hedva Sarfati and Giuliano Bonoli, London: Ashgate.

Silcock, Rachel (2001), 'What is e-government?', *Parliamentary Affairs* 54: 88–101.

SIPRI (Stockholm International Peace Research Institute) (2004), *SIPRI Yearbook 2004*, chapter summaries, <editors.sipri.se/pubs/yb04/aboutyb.html> [3 Feb. 2005].

Sircelj, Milivoja (2002), 'The European Population Committee's recent demographic studies and their relevance for social cohesion', *European Population Papers Series* 2, Strasbourg: Council of Europe.

Sleebos, Joëlle E. (2003), 'Low fertility rates in OECD countries: facts and policy responses', *OECD Social, Employment and Migration Working Papers* 15, <www.oecd.org/dataoecd/13/38/16587241.pdf> [18 July 2005].

Smart, John (2003), 'Privacy...in the right measure', in Zolli, *Catalog of Tomorrow*.

Smith, John E. (2004), *Biotechnology*, 4th edn, Cambridge: Cambridge University Press.

Soper, J. Christopher and Joel Fetzer (2002), 'Religion and politics in a secular Europe: cutting against the grain', in *Religion and Politics in Comparative Perspective*, eds Ted Gerard Jelen and Clyde Wilcox, Cambridge: Cambridge University Press.

Stephens, John D. (1996), 'The Scandinavian welfare states: achievements, crisis and prospects', in *Welfare States in Transition*, ed. Gøsta Esping-Andersen, London: Sage.

Stix, Gary (1995), 'Fighting future wars', *Scientific American*, Dec.

Street, A. and C. Bambra (2004), 'Health', in Compston, *Handbook of Public Policy in Europe*.

Street, John (2001), *Mass Media, Politics and Democracy*, Basingstoke: Palgrave.

Sullivan, General Gordon R. and Colonel James M. Dubik (1995), 'Land warfare in the 21st century', in *Envisioning Future Warfare*, eds General Gordon R. Sullivan and Colonel James M. Dubik, Fort Leavenworth: US Army Command and General Staff College Press.

Summers, Rita C. (1997), *Secure Computing Threats and Safeguards*, McGraw-Hill.

Swank, Duane (2003), 'Withering welfare?: Globalisation, political economic institutions and contemporary welfare states', in *States in the Global Economy*, ed. Linda Weiss, Cambridge: Cambridge University Press.

T&E (European Federation for Transport and Environment) (2001), *T&E Response to the EC White Paper on the Common Transport Policy*, <www.t-e.nu/docs/Publications/2001%20pubs/T&E01-5-CTPresponse.pdf> [8 Mar. 2004].

Tanks, David (2000), *Assessing the Cruise Missile Puzzle: How Great a Defense Challenge?* Washington, DC: Institute for Foreign Policy Analysis.

Taylor-Gooby, P. (2002), 'The silver age of the welfare state: perspectives on resilience', abstract, *Journal of Social Policy* 31(4): 597–621.

TechSector Trends (2002), <www.techsectortrends.com/document_1.html> [8 Nov. 2003].

Temple, Jonathan (2001), 'Growth effects of education and social capital in the OECD countries', *OECD Economic Studies* 33, <miranda.sourceoecd.org/> [4 Aug. 2005].

The Wellcome Trust and the Strategy Unit, Cabinet Office (2003), 'Biosciences: challenges and opportunities for government', Seminar Discussion Paper, <www.number-10.gov.uk/su/bio_seminar/downloads/issues.pdf> [23 May 2003].

Thiébault, Jean Louis (1997), 'France: Cabinet decision-making under the Fifth Republic', in *Cabinets in Western Europe*, 2nd edn, eds Jean Blondel and Ferdinand Müller-Rommel, London: Macmillan.

Thomas, Steve (2003), 'The Seven Brothers', *Energy Policy* 31: 393–403.

Trost, J.E., with M.-B. Bergstrom-Walan (2001), 'Sweden', in Francoeur, *The International Encyclopedia of Sexuality*.

Turnbull, Wayne and Praveen Abhayaratne (2003), '2002 terrorism chronology', <cns.miis.edu> [28 June 2004].

UCS (Union of Concerned Scientists) (2003), *Food and Environment*, <www.ucsusa.org/food_and_environment/> [25 Oct. 2003].

UN (United Nations) (1992), *Convention on Biological Diversity*, Article 2, <www.biodiv.org/convention/articles.asp> [26 Oct. 2003].

UN (1999), 'United Nations population ageing 1999', <www.un.org/esa/population/publications/aging99/> [7 Apr. 2003].

UN (2000), 'Transnational computer crime: the crimes of tomorrow are on our doorstep', *United Nations Convention Against Organised Crime*, <www.unodc.org/palermo/cybercrime.htm> [6 Dec. 2005].

UN (2002), 'Total recorded crime per 100,000 inhabitants', *United Nations Surveys on Crime Trends and the Operations of Criminal Justice Systems*, <www.unodc.org/unodc/en/crime_cicp_surveys.html?print=yes> [11 Oct. 2004].

UN (2003), 'World population prospects: the 2002 revision – highlights', ESA/P/WP. 180, 26 Feb., <www.un.org/esa/population/publications/wpp2002/WPP2002-HIGHLIGHTSrev1.PDF> [8 May 2004].

UN (2004), 'ISIC Rev.3: detailed structure and explanatory notes', Statistics Division, <unstats.un.org/unsd/cr/registry/regcst.asp?Cl=2> [14 Mar. 2005].

UNCTAD (United Nations Commission for Trade and Development) (2001), *World Investment Report 2001: Promoting Linkages*, New York: United Nations.

UNCTAD (2003), *World Investment Report 2003*, <www.unctad.org/en/docs//wir2003_en.pdf> [3 Sept. 2004].

UNCTAD (2004), *Globalization and Development: Facts and Figures*, <www.unctad.org/Templates/webflyer.asp?docid=4848&intItemID=1397&lang=1&mode=toc> [20 Aug. 2004].

UNCTAD (2004a), *World Investment Report 2004*, <www.unctad.org/en/docs//wir2004_en.pdf> [26 Apr. 2005].

UNICE (Union of Industrial and Employers' Confederations of Europe) (2002), *European Transport Policy 2010: Decision Time, White Paper – UNICE Opinion*, <212.3.246.118/1/PCJNMCPDIJKLPCOGFLBNKGPDPDBY9DAGP39LTE4Q/UNICE/docs/DLS/2002-03927-E.pdf> [8 Mar. 2004].

UNODC (United Nations Office on Drugs and Crime), 'World Drug Report 2000 Executive Summary', <www.unodc.org/unodc/end/wdr_executive-summary_2000.html> [17 July 2003].

US EIA (United States Energy Information Administration) (2005), *International Energy Outlook*, <www.eia.doe.gov/oiaf/ieo/pdf/0484(2005).pdf> [4 Nov. 2005].

US Department of Defense (2001), *Nuclear Posture Review*, excerpts, <www.globalsecurity.org/wmd/library/policy/dod/npr.htm> [28 June 2004].

US Department of State (undated), *Treaty on the Non-Proliferation of Nuclear Weapons*, <www.state.gov/t/np/trty/16281.htm> [3 July 2004].

US Department of State (2003), 'World military expenditures and arms transfers 1999–2000', <www.state.gov/t/vc/rls/rpt/wmeat/1999_2000/> [3 Feb. 2005].

US Department of State (2004), 'G-8 Action Plan on Nonproliferation', <www.state.gov/e/eb/rls/fs/3378.htm> [28 June 2004].

US Geological Survey (1997), *Bioremediation: Nature's Way to a Cleaner Environment*, <water.usgs.gov/wid/html/bioremed.html> [26 Oct. 2003].

Van Biezen, Ingrid and Richard S. Katz (2004), 'Political data in 2003', *European Journal of Political Research* 43: 919–26.

Van de Werfhorst, Herman G. and Nan Dirk de Graaf (2004), 'The sources of political orientation in post-industrial society: social class and education revisited', *British Journal of Sociology* 55(2): 211–35.

Van Kesteren, J.N., P. Mayhew and P. Nieuwbeerta (2000), 'Criminal victimization in seventeen industrialized countries: key findings from the 2000 International Crime Victims Survey', *Onderzoek en beleid* 187, Ministry of Justice, WODC, The Hague.

Van Liemt, Gijsbert (1992), 'Economic globalisation: labour options and business strategies in high labour cost countries', *International Labour Review* 131(4–5): 453–70.

Vatis, Michael A. (2001), 'Cyber attacks during the war on terrorism: a predictive analysis', Institute for Security Technology Studies at Dartmouth College, <www.ists.dartmouth.edu/ISTS/counterterrorism/cyber_a1.pdf> [5 July 2004].

Vigar, Geoff (2002), *The Politics of Mobility*, London: Spon Press.

Vogler, John and Alan Russell (2000), 'Introduction', in *The International Politics of Biotechnology*, eds Alan Russell and John Vogler, Manchester: Manchester University Press.

Vogler, John and Désirée McGraw (2000), 'An international environmental regime for biotechnology', in *The International Politics of Biotechnology*, eds Alan Russell and John Vogler, Manchester: Manchester University Press.

Voronin, Yuriy A. (2000), 'Measures to control transnational organised crime: summary', report prepared for the US Department of Justice, <www.ncjrs.org/pdffiles1/nij/grants/184773.pdf> [20 Oct. 2004].

Walker, Alan (1998), 'Speaking for themselves: the new politics of old age in Europe', *Education and Ageing* 13(1): 13–36.

Walker, Alan and Tony Maltby (1997), *Ageing Europe*, Buckingham: Open University Press.

Walter, Ingo and Roy C. Smith (2000), *High Finance in the Eurozone*, Edinburgh and London: Pearson.

WAN (World Association of Newspapers) (2002), *World Press Trends 2002 Edition*, Paris: WAN.

Wängnerud, Lena (2000), 'Testing the politics of presence: women's representation in the Swedish Riksdag', *Scandinavian Political Studies* 23(1): 67–91.

Wanrooij, Bruno P.F. (2001), 'Italy', in Francoeur, *The International Encyclopedia of Sexuality*.

Ward, Stephen and Wainer Lusoli (2003), 'Dinosaurs in cyberspace? British trade unions and the Internet', *European Journal of Communication* 18(2): 147–79.

Wasoff, Fran and Ian Dey (2000), *Family Policy*, London: Gildredge.

Watts, D. (1997), *Political Communication Today,* Manchester: Manchester University Press.

Webster, Frank (2002), *Theories of the Information Society*, 2nd edn, London: Routledge.

Wellings, K., J. Field, A.M. Johnson and J. Wadsworth (1994), *Sexual Behaviour in Britain: The National Survey of Attitudes and Lifestyles*, Harmondsworth: Penguin.

White House (2002), *National Strategy to Combat Weapons of Mass Destruction*, <www.whitehouse.gov/news/releases/2002/12/WMDStrategy.pdf> [29 June 2004].

White House (2003), *The National Strategy to Secure Cyberspace*, <www.us-cert.gov/reading_room/cyberspace_strategy.pdf> [7 July 2004].

Whitelegg, John and Gary Haq (2003), 'New directions in world transport policy and practice', in *The Earthscan Reader on World Transport Policy and Practice*, eds John Whitelegg and Gary Haq, Earthscan Publications.

Whittaker, Peter and Nicos C. Alivizatos (2003), 'Ethical aspects of genetic testing in the workplace', *Opinion of the European Group on Ethics in Science and New Technologies to the European Commission* 18, 28 July.

Wiesing, Urban (1999), 'Genetic discrimination and insurance in practice', in *Genetics and Insurance*, eds T. McGleenan, U. Wiesing and F. Ewald, Oxford: BIOS.

Williams, Fiona (2004), *Rethinking Families*, London: Calouste Gulbenkian Foundation.

Williams, G. (2003), *European Media Ownership: Threats on the Landscape*, Brussels: European Federation of Journalists.

Williams, Owain (2000), 'Life patents, TRIPS and the international political economy of biotechnology', in *The International Politics of Biotechnology*, eds Alan Russell and John Vogler, Manchester: Manchester University Press.

Wilson, B. (1966), *Religion in Secular Society*, London: Watts.

Wolf, Alison (2002), *Does Education Matter?* London: Penguin.

World Bank (1993), *World Development Report 1993*, New York: Oxford University Press.

World Tourism Organisation (2005), 'International tourist arrivals, 1950–2002', <www.world-tourism.org/facts/trends/inbound/arrivals/1950–2002.pdf> [4 Mar. 2005].

World Tourism Organisation (2005a), 'Long-term prospects: *Tourism 2020 Vision*', <www.world-tourism.org/facts/2020.html> [4 Mar. 2005].

World Values Study (2004), <www.worldvaluessurvey.org/services/index.html> [19 Feb. 2004, 7 Sept. 2005].

Worthington, Bryony (2003), 'Facing the new dawn', *New Economy* 10(3): 176–80.

Wortmann, Michael (2000), 'What is new about "global" corporations? Interpreting statistical data on corporate internationalisation', *WZB Discussion Paper* FS100-102, <skylla.wz-berlin.de/pdf/2000/i00-102.pdf> [8 Dec. 2005].

WTO (World Trade Organization) (2001), *WTO Policy Issues for Parliamentarians*, <www.wto.org/english/res_e/booksp_e/parliamentarians_e.pdf> [21 Aug. 2005].

WTO (2003), 'Selected long-term trends', *International Trade Statistics 2003*, <www.wto. org/english/res_e/statis_e/its2001_e/chp_2_e.pdf> [20 Aug. 2004].

WTO (2003a), *10 Benefits of the WTO Trading System*, <www.wto.org/english/res_e/ doload_e/10b_e.pdf> [21 Aug. 2004].

WTO (2004), *Understanding the WTO – Services: rules for growth and investment*, <www.wto.org/english/thewto_e/whatis_e/tif_e/agrm6_e.htm> [20 Aug. 2004].

WTO (2004a), 'Intellectual property: protection and enforcement', <www.wto.org/ english/thewto_e/whatis_e/tif_e/agrm7_e.htm> [3 Dec. 2004].

WTO (2004b), 'Overview: the TRIPS Agreement', <www.wto.org/english/tratop_e/ trips_e/intel2_e.htm> [3 Dec. 2004].

WTO (2005), *Agreement on Trade Related Aspects of Investment Measures*, <www.wto.org> [3 May 2005].

Wylie, K.R. and 23 collaborators (2004), 'The United Kingdom of Great Britain and Northern Ireland', in Francoeur, *The International Encyclopedia of Sexuality*.

Zolli, Andrew (ed.) (2003), *Catalog of Tomorrow*, Indianapolis: QUE.

Index